Integrating Blockchain Technology Into the Circular Economy

Syed Abdul Rehman Khan
Xuzhou University of Technology, China

A volume in the Advances in Industrial Ecology (AIE) Book Series

IGI Global
PUBLISHER of TIMELY KNOWLEDGE

Published in the United States of America by
IGI Global
Business Science Reference (an imprint of IGI Global)
701 E. Chocolate Avenue
Hershey PA, USA 17033
Tel: 717-533-8845
Fax: 717-533-8661
E-mail: cust@igi-global.com
Web site: http://www.igi-global.com

Library of Congress Cataloging-in-Publication Data

Names: Khan, Syed Abdul Rehman, 1987- editor.
Title: Integrating blockchain technology into the circular economy / Syed Abdul Rehman Khan, editor.
Description: Hershey, PA : Business Science Reference, [2022] | Includes bibliographical references and index. | Summary: "This book of contributed chapters focuses on the potential role of industry in reducing environmental burdens throughout the product life cycle from the extraction of raw materials, to the production of goods, to the use of those goods and to the management of the resulting wastes discussing how the integration of blockchain technology in the idea of sustainability and waste management techniques improve the field of Industrial ecology"-- Provided by publisher.
Identifiers: LCCN 2021059220 (print) | LCCN 2021059221 (ebook) | ISBN 9781799876427 (hardcover) | ISBN 9781799876434 (paperback) | ISBN 9781799876441 (ebook)
Subjects: LCSH: Recycling industry. | Refuse and refuse disposal--Technological innovations. | Industries--Environmental aspects. | Blockchains (Databases)
Classification: LCC HD9975 .I67 2022 (print) | LCC HD9975 (ebook) | DDC 363.72/82--dc23/eng/20220125
LC record available at https://lccn.loc.gov/2021059220
LC ebook record available at https://lccn.loc.gov/2021059221

This book is published in the IGI Global book series Advances in Finance, Accounting, and Economics (AFAE) (ISSN: 2327-5677; eISSN: 2327-5685)

British Cataloguing in Publication Data
A Cataloguing in Publication record for this book is available from the British Library.

For electronic access to this publication, please contact: eresources@igi-global.com.

Advances in Industrial Ecology (AIE) Book Series

MISSION

The **Advances in Industrial Ecology (AIE) Book Series** examines current, state-of-the-art studies in the areas of Industrial ecology and Circular economy. Industrial ecology is a rapidly growing field that systematically examines local, regional, and global materials along with energy uses and flows in products, processes, industrial sectors and economies. It focuses on the potential role of industry in reducing environmental burdens throughout the product life cycle from the extraction of raw materials, to the production of goods, to the use of those goods and to the management of the resulting wastes. Industrial ecology is ecological in that it (1) places human activity -- industry in the very broadest sense -- in the larger context of the biophysical environment from which we obtain resources and into which we place our wastes, and (2) looks to the natural world for models of highly efficient use of resources, energy, and byproducts. By selectively applying these models, the environmental performance of industry can be improved. Industrial ecology sees corporate entities as key players in the protection of the environment, particularly where technological innovation is an avenue for environmental improvement. As repositories of technological expertise in our society, corporations provide crucial leverage in attacking environmental problems through product and process design.

The **Advances in Industrial Ecology (AIE) Book Series** encompasses empirical, analytical, theoretical, reviews, communications, and conceptual research, and comprehensive reviews of relevant research case studies of effective applications in the areas of Industrial ecology and circular economy. It provides a practical and comprehensive forum for exchanging scientific knowledge and ideas which bridge the technological advancement and sustainable practices with industrial ecological management. The goal of this series is to bring together the expertise of professionals who are working in the field of industrial ecology and sustainability across the globe.

COVERAGE

- Blockchain and Circular Economy Practices
- Environmental Science
- Green Practices
- Environmental Input-Output Analysis (EEIOA)
- Sustainability
- Urban Metabolism
- Material Flow Analysis (MFA)
- Life Cycle Assessment (LCA)
- Industrial Symbiosis
- Pollution

The Advances in Industrial Ecology (AIE) Book Series (ISSN pending) is published by IGI Global, 701 E. Chocolate Avenue, Hershey, PA 17033-1240, USA, www.igi-global.com. This series is composed of titles available for purchase individually; each title is edited to be contextually exclusive from any other title within the series. For pricing and ordering information please visit http://www.igi-global.com/book-series/advances-industrial-ecology/270446. Postmaster: Send all address changes to above address.

Table of Contents

Preface xiii

Acknowledgment xvii

Chapter 1
Industry 4.0, Internal Green Supply Chain Practices, and the Firm's Sustainable Performance: Evidence From Emerging Economies.......................... 1
Muhammad Umar, Universiti Malaysia Terengganu, Malaysia
Khalid Farooq, Universiti Malaysia Terengganu, Malaysia
Mohd Yusoff Yusliza, Universiti Malaysia Terengganu, Malaysia
Hafiz Muhammad Zia-ul Haq, Universiti Malaysia Terengganu, Malaysia

Chapter 2
How to Improve Organizational Performance Using Big Data in the Hotels 15
Subhodeep Mukherjee, GITAM University (Deemed), India
Manish Mohan Baral, GITAM University (Deemed), India
Venkataiah Chittipaka, Indira Gandhi National Open University (IGNOU), Delhi, India

Chapter 3
Financial Market Infrastructure and Implementation of Blockchain Technology: A Critical Review for Managing Operational Risk......................... 44
Kiran Jameel, Institute of Business and Management, Pakistan
Asim Rafiq, Hamdard University, Pakistan

Chapter 4
A Study on Blockchain Technology Implementation in the Logistics Sector of Pakistan..63
Fahim Ul Amin, Chang'an University, China
Dong Qianli, Chang'an University, China
Wasim Ul Amin, North China Electric Power University, China
Iram Zulfiqar, North China Electric Power University, China
Shamsa Kanwal, North China Electric Power University, China

Chapter 5
Industrial Revolution 4.0 and Supply Chain Management 82
Adeel Shah, University of Kuala Lumpur, Malaysia
Aisha Ismail, Business School, Karachi University, Pakistan

Chapter 6
Outsourcing Transportation Management: A Case Study of an Online Shopping Company..93
Fahim Ul Amin, Chang'an University, China
Dong Qianli, Chang'an University, China
Wasim Ul Amin, North China Electric Power University, China
Iram Zulfiqar, North China Electric Power University, China
Shamsa Kanwal, North China Electric Power University, China

Chapter 7
Pitfalls and Challenges of Blockchain in Supply Chain and Logistics 108
Asad Ullah, Middle East College, Oman
Asad Ullah, Middle East College, Oman
Shahid Imran, Middle East College, Oman

Chapter 8
Supply Chain and Logistics Operations Management Under the Era of Advanced Technology..126
Muhammad Tanveer, Prince Sultan University, Saudi Arabia

Chapter 9
Blockchain Technology as Enablement of Industry 4.0 137
Fredrick Ishengoma, The University of Dodoma, Tanzania

Chapter 10
Supply Chain Management Professional Use Technologies (SM) During the Pandemic to Accomplish Tasks 165
Muhammad Tanveer, Prince Sultan University, Saudi Arabia
Abdul-Rahim Ahmad, Karachi School of Business and Leadership, Pakistan

Chapter 11
Big Data Analytics: Applications and Barriers in Supply Chain........ 184
Arsalan Zahid Piprani, Federal Urdu University of Arts, Science, and Technology, Pakistan
Amjad Ali, Hamdard University, Pakistan
Adeel Shah, University of Kuala Lumpur, Malaysia

Glossary 203

Compilation of References 204

Related Readings 234

About the Contributors 301

Index 306

Detailed Table of Contents

Preface xiii

Acknowledgment xvii

Chapter 1
Industry 4.0, Internal Green Supply Chain Practices, and the Firm's Sustainable Performance: Evidence From Emerging Economies............ 1
Muhammad Umar, Universiti Malaysia Terengganu, Malaysia
Khalid Farooq, Universiti Malaysia Terengganu, Malaysia
Mohd Yusoff Yusliza, Universiti Malaysia Terengganu, Malaysia
Hafiz Muhammad Zia-ul Haq, Universiti Malaysia Terengganu, Malaysia

The aim of the current study is to investigathe the effect of Industry 4.0 on internal green supply chain management practices (IGSCP) in the context of emerging economies. The cross-sectional data were collected from 185 manufacturing firms of Pakistan using a questionnaire, which was analyzed through structural equation modelling. In the current era, with the advent of Industry 4.0 technologies, there is emphasis on technology in every field. Organizations must acknowledge Industry 4.0 innovative contributions towards IGSCP and broaden their understanding as the literature on Industry 4.0 is still lacking and needs empirical investigation. The results indicated that Industry 4.0 has a positive and significant effect on IGSCPs. Moreover, the results also demonstrated that IGSCP practices have a positive nexus with economic and environmental performance. This research presents valuable insight for policymakers, manufacturers, and managers interested in promoting GSCM practices for improved economic and environmental sustainability.

Chapter 2
How to Improve Organizational Performance Using Big Data in the Hotels...... 15
Subhodeep Mukherjee, GITAM University (Deemed), India
Manish Mohan Baral, GITAM University (Deemed), India
Venkataiah Chittipaka, Indira Gandhi National Open University (IGNOU), Delhi, India

Big data is a collection of huge amounts of data for extracting information from data. This helps the firms know the hidden knowledge in the data. This research aims to study the adoption of big data in the hotels of India, and it is helping in improving performance. For this study, a technological-organizational-environmental (TOE) framework is used. The factors are identified from the literature review. A questionnaire is prepared for survey-based research in the hotel industry. Exploratory factor analysis and structural equation modeling are used for analysis. Three models are developed for the study. The entire proposed hypothesis for the study was accepted.

Chapter 3
Financial Market Infrastructure and Implementation of Blockchain Technology: A Critical Review for Managing Operational Risk......................... 44
Kiran Jameel, Institute of Business and Management, Pakistan
Asim Rafiq, Hamdard University, Pakistan

Blockchain is very crucial for paving new ways for how economies will function in the future, as it helps in eliminating intermediaries and thus saving time and cost. Various important uses of this new blockchain technology have been highlighted, but research and practice are still in their formative phases. The core objective of this study is to describe the impact of blockchain on existing and novel business prototypes while managing operational risk. Consequently, the authors pinpoint five similarities that improve the understanding of how blockchain technology affects current financial structure and creates new business models. This research suggested using these findings to ascertain further designs initiated by blockchain and how firms can use it to revolutionize its business model. Though there are many favorable uses of this new technology, inquiry and established procedures are still in their embryonic stages, which means it will take some time before blockchain's impact is felt on a larger scale.

Chapter 4
A Study on Blockchain Technology Implementation in the Logistics Sector of Pakistan.. 63
Fahim Ul Amin, Chang'an University, China
Dong Qianli, Chang'an University, China
Wasim Ul Amin, North China Electric Power University, China
Iram Zulfiqar, North China Electric Power University, China
Shamsa Kanwal, North China Electric Power University, China

Blockchain technology provides a number of technological features, including high transparency, traceability, and trustiness. Its use in the logistics business increases technical support and ensures the logistics industry's effectiveness, as well as records, stores, and logistics information. The transmission ensures security, prevents logistics information from being distorted, and ensures the authenticity of logistics information. The use of blockchain technology in the logistics business has a positive impact on the industry's competitiveness and technical advantages. Blockchain has emerged as a key technology advancement with the ability to solve logistics problems. It's time for Pakistan to take advantage of this new technology. Blockchain has the potential to transform Pakistan's logistics sector.

Chapter 5
Industrial Revolution 4.0 and Supply Chain Management 82
Adeel Shah, University of Kuala Lumpur, Malaysia
Aisha Ismail, Business School, Karachi University, Pakistan

Innovation is taking place rapidly, which is changing the demand level. Diversifying the supply chain with changing demand patterns is another challenge to meet. Industrial Revolution (IR) 4.0 is the new way to effectively manage the supply chain process with the updated conventional business model. The technology enhances the traditional business model and improves distance relations among companies and customers through well managed distribution channels, creates high-level customer satisfaction, and provides timely information in each stage of the supply chain process. Innovative technology allows companies to make more profit by saving time and making an additional product to meet specific demands cost-effectively. It is also reducing human efforts, which will be taking place by robotics soon. The industrial revolution is the new beginning of an environment where the supply chain will be managed by intelligent technology, improving the overall process of value chains.

Chapter 6
Outsourcing Transportation Management: A Case Study of an Online Shopping Company 93
Fahim Ul Amin, Chang'an University, China
Dong Qianli, Chang'an University, China
Wasim Ul Amin, North China Electric Power University, China
Iram Zulfiqar, North China Electric Power University, China
Shamsa Kanwal, North China Electric Power University, China

Transport management has significant importance in every organization. This chapter aims to evaluate the outsourcing decision of transportation management of an online shopping company. Recently, the company has witnessed significant growth in its operations, and it became inevitable to decide whether it continues outsourcing transportation management or go for insourcing as various problems are experienced due to outsourcing. The company has many logistics operations that include inbound receiving, warehousing, and outbound distribution. All the operations are considered and studied to understand the problem and objectives of outsourcing. In this chapter, a literature review regarding outsourcing transportation management is provided. Afterward, a research methodology is proposed and adopted, and then cost analysis is performed to check the feasibility concerning financial resources. Based on the cost analysis, it is decided to discontinue outsourcing transportation management. Some recommendations are also proposed for insourcing transportation management.

Chapter 7
Pitfalls and Challenges of Blockchain in Supply Chain and Logistics 108
Asad Ullah, Middle East College, Oman
Asad Ullah, Middle East College, Oman
Shahid Imran, Middle East College, Oman

The potential impact of block chain on supply chain management has been explored by many authors, and indeed, many articles in the popular press extol the benefits of blockchain in supply chain management. In simple terms, blockchain is a distributed ledger system, or a record book, except that it is not maintained by a single person but by anyone who is interested in keeping the records. Since blockchain is a new and revolutionary concept in technology, more techies are interested in it. However, it also has certain disadvantages. The purpose of this study is to explain the challenges and pitfalls of blockchain in supply chain and logistics. Using a systematic literature review method, this chapter identifies 31 publications that discuss the challenges and pitfalls associated with blockchain in supply chain and logistics.

Chapter 8
Supply Chain and Logistics Operations Management Under the Era of Advanced Technology 126
Muhammad Tanveer, Prince Sultan University, Saudi Arabia

Implementation and adoption of new technologies are gaining the result of smooth supply chain and logistics operations. Internet of things (IoT) artificial intelligence, including data mining, intensified in all fields of life, particularly in supply chain management and operations. Blockchain technology has the capability to reform the supply chain and logistics operations management. Blockchain provides digital database solutions for all transactions across supply chain and operations management. Radio frequency identification device (RFID) is also helping technology transmit electromagnetic waves to radio-compatible integrated circuits to look after and manage the entire supply chain and logistics operations management. The Fourth Industry Revolution 4.0 refers to the automation, interconnectivity, machine learning, and real-time data that help supply chain and logistics operations management in the 21st century.

Chapter 9
Blockchain Technology as Enablement of Industry 4.0 137
Fredrick Ishengoma, The University of Dodoma, Tanzania

Industry 4.0 (also known as smart manufacturing or industrial internet of things [IIoT]) refers to a major change in the way products are manufactured and delivered, with a focus on industrial automation and the flexible factory backed with several technologies that include the internet of things (IoT), cyber-physical systems, and artificial intelligence. Industry 4.0 gave birth to a new age of smart manufacturing, automated supply chain, and personalized goods and services. Meanwhile, the rise in the application of blockchain technology (BCT) in different sectors propels the Industry 4.0 model to extend its scope. This chapter discusses the impact of BCT as the enablement of Industry 4.0. The modified e-Delphi methodology aimed at gathering the opinions of recognized experts was used. The findings present the potential that BCT brings using a case along with emerging issues. Emerging issues such as BCT security, interoperability, smart contract issues, digital twin issues, and ethical issues are discussed, and solutions are proposed.

Chapter 10
Supply Chain Management Professional Use Technologies (SM) During the Pandemic to Accomplish Tasks 165
Muhammad Tanveer, Prince Sultan University, Saudi Arabia
Abdul-Rahim Ahmad, Karachi School of Business and Leadership, Pakistan

Syndrome-coronavirus-2 (SARS-CoV-2), commonly referred to as the COVID-19 pandemic, has caused people to spend more time online. The pandemic has spurred growth in the use of social media technologies. Organizations now train employees to use digital media to coordinate work and connect to fulfill the requirement of supply chain management (SCM). The study aims to produce effective discussion regarding the importance of SCM and technologies and how it can assist in the recent times of COVID-19 regarding job performance. Research predicts the new ways of business conducted and how communication and coordination, knowledge exchange, training, and development are helpful in carrying out effective job productivity at the workplace of SCM. The authors analyzed responses of more than 294 SCM employee who reported on "go-to" technologies and social media tools to remote office practices. The research employed quantitative methodology (i.e., emailed questionnaires) and found that social media has become an important tool for conducting business operations due to social distancing and isolation.

Chapter 11
Big Data Analytics: Applications and Barriers in Supply Chain....................... 184
Arsalan Zahid Piprani, Federal Urdu University of Arts, Science, and Technology, Pakistan
Amjad Ali, Hamdard University, Pakistan
Adeel Shah, University of Kuala Lumpur, Malaysia

As the magnitude of accessible data grows, a multitude of business intelligence (BI) tools have emerged, all of which may be together referred to as big data analytics (BDA). BDA in supply chain management-related activities is essential because it can manage global, complex, tempestuous, and dynamic value chains. The powerful influence of big data (BD) capabilities on supply chain (SC) and overall company performance is attracting operations management researchers, who see them as having a significant impact on supply chain and company performance. This chapter discussed the importance of big data analytics and connected it with its significance in the supply chain context. The authors demonstrated how big data analytics (BDA) is a critical success element for an organization in the global and dynamic market. This chapter also highlights some of the barriers and challenges in implementing big data analytics in the supply chain.

Glossary 203

Compilation of References 204

Related Readings 234

About the Contributors 301

Index 306

Preface

Writing this book provides up-to-date text at a reasonable cost. The scope of Blockchain Technology (BCT) has continued to grow in business operations with a rapid speed, which is reflected in the content of this book. The book has included core aspects of BCT and the application of BCT in business operations.

ORGANIZATION OF THE BOOK

There are 11 chapters in the book. A brief description of each of the chapters follows:

Chapter 1 investigates the effect of Industry 4.0 on internal GSCM practices in the context of emerging economies. The cross-sectional data were collected from 185 manufacturing firms of Pakistan using a questionnaire analyzed through structural equation modeling. With the advent of industry 4.0 technologies in the current era, there is an emphasis on technology in every field. Organizations must acknowledge Industry 4.0 innovative contribution towards Internal GSCP (IGSCP) and broaden their understanding of the literature on Industry 4.0 still lacks empirical investigation.

Chapter 2 studies the adoption of Big Data in the hotels of India, and it is helping in improving its performance. For this study, a technological-organizational-environmental (TOE) framework is being used. The factors are being identified from the literature review. A questionnaire is being prepared for survey-based research in the hotel industry. Exploratory factor analysis and structural equation modeling is being used for analysis. Three models are being developed for the study.

Chapter 3 describes the impact of blockchain on existing and novel business prototypes while managing operational risk. Consequently, researchers pinpoint five similarities that improve our understanding of how Blockchain technology affects the current financial structure and creates new business models. This research suggested using these findings to ascertain different designs initiated by blockchain and how firms can revolutionize their business model. Though there are many favorable uses of this new technology, inquiry and established procedures are still embryonic, and this means it will take some time before blockchain impacts are felt on a larger scale.

Chapter 4 describes the usage of Blockchain Technology in logistical operations and supply chain management. Blockchain technology provides several technological features, including high transparency, traceability, and trustiness. Its use in the logistics business increases technical support and ensures the logistics industry's effectiveness and records, stores, and logistics information. The transmission ensures security, prevents logistics information from being distorted, and ensures the authenticity of logistics information. The use of blockchain technology in the logistics business positively impacts the industry's competitiveness and technical advantages. Blockchain has emerged as a key technology advancement to solve logistics problems.

Chapter 5 discusses the applications of Industry Revolution 4.0. This technology is the new way to effectively manage the supply chain process with the updated conventional business model. The technology enhances the traditional business model and improves distance relations among companies and customers through well-managed distribution channels: it creates high-level customer satisfaction and provides timely information in each stage of the supply chain process. Innovative technology allows companies to profit by saving time and making an additional product to meet specific demands cost-effectively. It also reduces human efforts, which will be taking place by robotics soon. The industrial revolution is the new beginning of an environment where the supply chain will be managed by intelligent technology, improving the overall process of value chains.

Chapter 6 aims to evaluate the outsourcing decision of transportation management of an online shopping company. Recently, the company has witnessed significant growth in its operations, and it became inevitable to decide whether it continues outsourcing transportation management or go for insourcing as various problems are experienced due to outsourcing. The company has many logistics operations that include inbound receiving, warehousing, and outbound distribution. All the operations are considered and studied to understand the problem and objectives of outsourcing.

Chapter 7 explains the design, advantages, and challenges of the employment of blockchain in Supply chain and logistics. This paper identifies relevant publications that discuss the design, advantages, and challenges associated with blockchain in Supply chain and Logistics. According to the study's conclusions, blockchain adoption in the supply chain and logistics is a challenge envisaged in international trading groups, although some organizations have tried to implement successful pilot programs.

Chapter 8 discusses the involvement of the Internet of Things (IoT), artificial intelligence (AI), and technological innovation. Internet of thing (IoT) artificial intelligence, including data mining, intensified in all fields of life, particularly in supply chain management and operations. Blockchain technology is capable of reforming the supply chain and logistics operations management rehearses. Blockchain provides a digital database solution for all transactions across supply chain and operations management. Radio Frequency Identification Device (RFID) is also helping technology transmit electromagnetic waves to radio-compatible integrated circuits to look after and manage and look after the entire supply chain and logistics operations management. The fourth industry revolution 4.0 refers towards the automation, interconnectivity, machine learning, and real-time data that s also helping in supply chain and logistics operations management under the era of the 21st century of advanced technology.

Chapter 9 refers to a major change in the way products are manufactured and delivered, focusing on industrial automation and the flexible factory-backed with several technologies that include the Internet of things (IoT), cyber-physical systems, and artificial intelligence. Industry 4.0 gave birth to a new age of smart manufacturing, automated supply chain, and personalized goods and services. Meanwhile, the rise in the application of blockchain technology (BCT) in different sectors propels the industry 4.0 model to extend its scope. This chapter discusses the impact of BCT as the enablement of Industry 4.0. The modified e-Delphi methodology aimed at gathering the opinions of recognized experts was used. The findings present the potential BCT brings, uses case, and emerging issues. Emerging issues such as BCT security, interoperability, smart contract issues, digital twin issues, and ethical issues are discussed and solutions are proposed.

Chapter 10 aims of this study to produce effective discussion regarding the importance of SCM and technologies and how it can assist in the recent times of Covid-19 regarding job performance. Research predicts the new ways of business conducted and how communication and coordination, knowledge exchange, training, and development are helpful in carryout effective job productivity at the workplace of SCM. Researchers analyzed responses of more than 294 SCM employees who reported on “go-to” technologies and social media tools to remote office practices. The research employed quantitative methodology (i.e., emailed questionnaires) and found that social media has become an important tool for business operations due to social distancing and isolation. As per the results, it is clear that social media allows Pakistan’s management to improve the training and development communication and coordination among the employees while also being perceived as a handy tool.

Chapter 11 discusses Big Data Analytics (BDA) in supply chain management. BDA in supply chain management-related activities is essential because it can manage global, complex, tempestuous, and dynamic value chains. This chapter explained the importance of big data analytics and connected it with its significance in the supply chain context. Researchers demonstrated how big data analytics (BDA) is a critical success element for an organization’s global and dynamic market. This chapter also highlights some barriers and challenges in implementing big data analytics in the supply chain.

Syed Abdul Rehman Khan
Xuzhou University of Technology, China

Acknowledgment

This book is partially supported by the Beijing Key Laboratory of Urban Spatial Information Engineering (NO. 20210218).

Chapter 1
Industry 4.0, Internal Green Supply Chain Practices, and the Firm's Sustainable Performance:
Evidence From Emerging Economies

Muhammad Umar
Universiti Malaysia Terengganu, Malaysia

Mohd Yusoff Yusliza
Universiti Malaysia Terengganu, Malaysia

Khalid Farooq
Universiti Malaysia Terengganu, Malaysia

Hafiz Muhammad Zia-ul Haq
Universiti Malaysia Terengganu, Malaysia

ABSTRACT

The aim of the current study is to investigathe the effect of Industry 4.0 on internal green supply chain management practices (IGSCP) in the context of emerging economies. The cross-sectional data were collected from 185 manufacturing firms of Pakistan using a questionnaire, which was analyzed through structural equation modelling. In the current era, with the advent of Industry 4.0 technologies, there is emphasis on technology in every field. Organizations must acknowledge Industry 4.0 innovative contributions towards IGSCP and broaden their understanding as the literature on Industry 4.0 is still lacking and needs empirical investigation. The results indicated that Industry 4.0 has a positive and significant effect on IGSCPs. Moreover, the results also demonstrated that IGSCP practices have a positive nexus with economic and environmental performance. This research presents valuable insight for policymakers, manufacturers, and managers interested in promoting GSCM practices for improved economic and environmental sustainability.

DOI: 10.4018/978-1-7998-7642-7.ch001

INTRODUCTION

The creation and implementation of emerging technologies have emerged as one of the most widely discussed subjects in both scholarly and professional circles in the modern age of Industry 4.0 (I4.0) (Li et al., 2020). The word "digital technology" denotes the number of paradigm and various smart and creative technologies that enable networking, collaboration, and automation in I4.0 era (Ivanov et al., 2019). I4.0 consists of big data analytics, internet of things (IOT), as well as emerging platforms such as blockchain technology and cloud computing (Khan et al., 2021; Umar et al., 2021; Khan et al., 2021a). These advanced technologies set businesses toward data-based techniques for gathering data through the product development cycle, encompassing everything from material to production in a digitally-driven manufacturing environment (Tao et al., 2018) and enhancing the vertical and horizontal integration (Frank et al., 2019).

Digital technologies present a combination of threats and opportunities for the long-term development of manufacturing sectors. Through the profound mixing of intelligent technologies in the automotive industry, a well-organized and digital system for product development has emerged which helped out to increase customer services and manufacturing efficiency (Neuhofer et al., 2015), and allows successful energy redistribution and leverage total capacity (Dubey et al., 2019). In addition, emerging technologies can broaden the competitive complexities of corporate economies while also putting economic and ecological strains on manufacturers (Kiel et al., 2020). Researchers have stated that the effect of emerging technology on sustainable efficiency in terms of financial and ecological performance require more attention (Li et al., 2020).

I4.0 is changing the business model rapidly (Bai *et al.*, 2020). Due to crucial environmental sustainability aspects in organization performance, scholars focus on elaborating sustainability with I4.0 (Li *et al.*, 2020). I4.0 can encourage green initatives in supply chain operations and ensure transparency in product flow, including the product's extraction source, whether an environmentally sound resource or a renewable green resource, and the quality of the material used (Umar et al., 2021). Research on I4.0 with environmental sustainability is still in its early stages. Few recent studies have shed light on the intersection of I4.0 technologies along with eco-friendly performance. For instance, Jabbour et al. (2017) also discourse the role of big data analytics and explained that this technology facilitates the implementation of circular economy practices. The processes through which I4.0 and environmental sustainability in manufacturing firms coexist are still unknown.

Moreover, the evaluation of I4.0 in the SC is an essential aspect for scholars (Dalenogare et al., 2018). The insufficient ecological balances of traditional production systems are well-known. Conventional manufacturing processes and technologies are responsible for inefficient utilization of resources, global warming, environmental damage, and pollution (Bai et al., 2020). I4.0 is altering the business models of manufacturing companies. Various emergent communication, and intelligence technologies can support manufacturing flexibility, efficiency, and productivity (Umar et al., 2021). Overall, accurate rigorous assessment techniques and decision support frameworks may aid manufacturing companies in successfully implementing and comprehending I4.0 technologies, particularly when making the broad economic and environmental implications. These vast implications include raising the competitiveness advantage for corporations and countries, along with ecological performance (Bai et al., 2020).

Green supply chain practices (GSCP) aims to help companies in eliminating polluted waste and to conserve biodiversity (Khan & Yu 2020; Umar et al., 2021a). Businesses can save resources and reduce their environmental footprint by improving their energy consumption (Abbasi and Nilsson 2016). According to Badi & Murtagh (2019) and Khan et al. (2020c), production organizations integrate environment friendly practices in the SC because these practices help firms in sustaining the environmental performance and enable firms to achieve competitiveness, and improve profit margins in today's economic climate. Martel & Klibi (2016) stated Internal Environmental Management (IEM) as a critical aspect of GSCM practices, which instills organizations toward sustainability dimensions. IEM reflects senior management's appreciation of environmental issues and their approach to green policy implementation (Chin et al., 2015). Prior research has discussed the vital role of Iot (Ben-Daya et al., 2019; Awan et al., 2021), blockchain (Khan et al., 2021; Khan et al., 2021a); big data analytics (Liu et al., 2020) in SC. However, few studies have empirically explored how I4.0 influences IGSCP. Keeping in view the above discussion following are the key objectives of this study.

- To analyze the impact of industry 4.0 on internal green supply chain practices in manufacturing firms of Pakistan.
- To determine the effect of internal green supply chain practices on economic and environmental performance.

The study is organized as follows: Section 2 covers the literature review and develops the research hypotheses. Section 3 explains the research methodology. Section 4 provides results and discussion in the light of existing body of knowledge. In contrast, the last section provides valuable insights for managers and practitioners, which could help them strengthen their strategies.

LITERATURE REVIEW AND HYPOTHESES DEVELOPMENT

Industry 4.0 and Internal GSCM Practices

I4.0 reflects technological revolution that relies on recent mobile technologies and service-oriented approaches (Jabbour et al., 2018). I4.0 concepts involve horizontal and vertical process convergence enabled by real-time data exchange, as well as through agile production process to facilitate customization (Jabbour et al., 2018; Thoben et al., 2017). Fundamental elements of I4.0 are the internet of things, additive manufacturing, cloud computing (Kang et al., 2016), cyber-physical architectures (Drath & Horch, 2014), and blockchain (Khan et al., 2021; Khan et al., 2021a).

I4.0 have the potential to influence the manufacturing process, for instance, items could be designed with a unique electronic identity that allows the product's life cycle to be traced (Jabbour et al., 2018). This facilitates the gathering of user data, which can help businesses better identify consumer trends, increase product customization, and optimize product support aspects such as repair and update services (Sharma et al., 2021). Additionally, by using real-time information, interactions between machinery, computers, and supply chain tiers allow rapid adjustment of output and purchasing order targets (in response to consumer needs or maintenance requirements), the monitoring and management of production lines, the tracking of deliveries, and the optimization of logistics paths (Ikram & Siddiqui, 2019).

GSCP is described as removing or minimizing total externalities from forward and reverse operations of supply chain (Rao & Holt, 2005; Zhu et al., 2008). GSCM entails incorporating sustainability standards into the supply chain (SC) process, intending to mitigate or remove solid waste, lower emissions, conserve resources during the product's life cycle (Chin et al., 2015). The GSCP integrates internal and external sustainable activities, including eco-design, green sourcing, internal environmental protection, reverse logistics, collaboration with supply chain partners, and investment recovery (Zhu et al., 2008). Several scholars asserted that the effective introduction of GSCP involves an initial commitment to green supply chain activities within the organization (Feng et al., 2018; Rao & Holt, 2005). This study uses eco-friendly auditing techniques, green manufacturing, green design, and internal environmental management to evaluate IGSCP. I4.0 enables real-time monitoring and optimization of all company activities. Real-time production status monitoring avoids duplication, conserve resources, and improves efficiency. Thus I4.0 technologies are affecting IGSCP by real-time forecasting and self-optimization. Based on the above discussion, we develop the following hypothesis:

H1: Industry 4.0 has a positive impact on IGSCP.

Internal GSCM Practices and Environmental Performance

Through implementation of GSCM activities, the detrimental effect of company processes on the ecosystem can be mitigated (Song et al., 2018). Geffen & Rothenberg (2000) discovered that adopting ecological design is a critical first move toward greening an organization's whole SC processes. It has been analyzed in Chinese companies that a positive correlation exists between green practices and environmental success (Hartmann et al., 2015). IGSCP is critical for any organization as it improves and enhances ecological performance (Melnyk et al., 2003) by promoting a green culture that values resource management and emissions reduction. Businesses incorporate sustainability policies into their practices to reduce the environmental footprint of their activities. Organizations can hostilely pursue IGSCP initiatives such as green labeling, auditing and environmental compliance, internal environmental evaluations, and ISO 14001 certification to gain a competitive edge, improve brand value, maximize customer satisfaction, and increase management effectiveness (Yu et al., 2019; Zhu & Sarkis, 2004).
H2: IGSCP has a positive effect on environmental performance.

Internal GSCM Practices and Economic Performance

IGSCP allow the elimination of waste from SC processes, resulting in improved profitability (Sinha & Anand, 2017). According to Khan et al. (2017), there is a connection between long-term business plans and operating efficiency. Their findings indicated that environment friendly policies positively correlate with a company's economic well-being. Businesses are incorporating environmentally sustainable activities into their processes to increase their profitability (Khan and Yu 2020). Lin et al. (2013) stated that eco-friendly products can draw consumers willingness to pay an extra amount. Zailani et al. (2012) emphasized on adopting GSCM practices for socioeconomic and environmental protection and explained a positive relationship between GSCM practices and firm performance.

Previous research also indicated a favourable association between GSCM practices and profitability (Correia et al., 2017; Danese et al., 2019; Khan et al., 2017; Umar et al., 2021). Nonetheless, we discovered several contradictory findings in many studies. Furthermore, Khan and Yu (2020) conducted a survey on Pakistani's manufacturing firms to assess the effects of green practices on economic efficiency. Their results indicated that green practices have a beneficial influence on firm financial performance. Thus, on the basis of above discussion, we postulate the hypothesis as:
H2: IGSCP have a positive effect on firm economic performance

Research methodology

The study selected manufacturing firms that operate in the most polluting industries and have adopted green initiatives. To accomplish the study's goals, it was essential to focus exclusively on manufacturers that follow GSCP. Each organization's supply chain manager was consulted by telephone to determine if and to what degree green standards were being applied.

The survey provoked responses from production, operational and supply chain managers working in manufacturing companies of Pakistan. The data was gathered during winter of 2020 through a questionnaire. In the first round, only 123 questionnaires were returned out of 140. In the second round, only 76 questionnaires were returned out of 100. A total of 199 completed questionnaires were received, 14 forms were eliminated because of not properly filled, while 185 forms were used in CB-SEM to test the hypotheses.

We developed survey questionnaires to evaluate our study model. All measurements are derived from existing literature and adapted for use in the sense of GSCP activities. Following the creation of the survey products, we interviewed different managers from manufacturing companies to solicit input on these items. To ensure the validity, we performed a pilot study with 6 supply chain and 8 producion and plant managers in the manufacturing sector, utilizing an updated sample. We completed the survey after considering all of the respondents' suggestions and input. The questions were designed to elicit a range of responses ranging from 1 strongly disagree to 7 strongly agree.

Figure 1. Theoretical framework

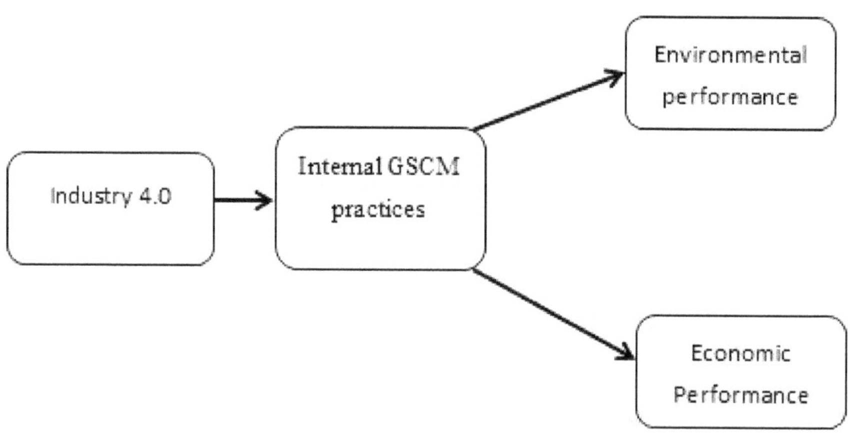

RESULTS AND DISCUSSION

The findings indicate that I4.0 has a beneficial influence on the IGSCP. 1% increase in I4.0 resulting in a 0.436 percent improvement in IGSCP. Khan & Qianli (2017) have explained that developing countries are still a long way from reaping the benefits of GSCM. The commitment of top management to environmental concerns stifles companies' efforts to implement green practices. I4.0 effectively manage the IGSCP through real-time data capabilities, integration, and automation and makes the environmental audits system more transparent for administrative authority. According to Sony (2019), industry 4.0 enables the circulation and distribution of content and facilitates the more effective implementation of GSCM activities. Moreover, the researcher also suggested companies to utilize I4.0 technologies in producing and designing activities. As, it aids in greening all SC activities, especially green manufacturing, and green product design. Chiarini et al. (2020) conducted a study to analyze the effect of I4.0 on manufacturing strategies in Italian manufacturing firms and found that I4.0 enables IGSCP (i-e., green manufacturing). Additionally, the researchers also addressed the effect of I4.0 on different GSCM activities, using various technologies such as cloud infrastructure (Talatappeh & Lakzi, 2019), large data analytics (Yu et al., 2020), and blockchain technology (Kouhizadeh & Sarkis, 2020; Khan et al. 2021; khan e al., 2021a). These researchers have affirmed that I4.0 facilitates various GSCM practices.

Table 1. Standardized parameter estimates for structural model

Hypothesis	Paths	Standardized estimate	P-value	Results
H1	I4.0 → IGSCP	0.436**	0.000	Supported
H2	IGSCP→ En. P	0.215*	0.021	Supported
H3	IGSCP→ Ec. P	0.643*	0.047	Supported

Note: ** and * indicate significance at 1% and 5% respectively.
industry 4.0 (I4.0), internal green supply chain practices (IGSCP), environmental performance (En. P) performance, economic performance (Ec.P)

Whereas the IGSCP has a positive and significant relation with the Ec.P and En.P of the organization. Adopting IGSCP improves financial efficiency by 0.643 percent and En.P by 0.215 percent. The results of this study is inline with the research work of Scur & Barbosa (2017) in which the researcher analyzed the relationship between GSCM and firm success in Brazilian home appliance industry and asserted that green supply chain practices have a beneficial effect on Ec.P. Moreover, Khan and Yu (2020) conducted a study to analyze the impact of GSCM practices on sustainability performances in Pakistani's manufacturing firms and affirmed that GSCM practices have a positive and significant effect on Ec.P and En.P. The researchers also discussed that green buying, value source mapping, sustainable architecture, biofuel usage in logistics activities, and recycling both contribute to improving commodity consistency and lowering costs. IGSCP assists firms in improving their Ec.P and En.P and process consistency (Baines et al., 2012; Govindan et al., 2015).

CONCLUSION AND PRACTICAL IMPLICATIONS

The contribution of this study is to explore the role of I4.0 in fostering IGSCP to boost operational productivity. The cross-sectional data of 185 respondents were gathered using a closed-ended questionnaire survey from manufacturing firms in Pakistan. CB-SEM technique is used to evaluate the proposed paradigm of I4.0, IGSCP, and the organization's Ec.P and En.P. The model satisfies both internal consistency and convergent and discriminant validity. The results show that I4.0 has a sizable effect on IGSCP. Moreover, IGSCP have a significant impact on organization's En.P and Ec.P.

The current research provides the following implications. For instance, the findings implicate that the adoption of I4.0 could strengthen the IGSCP, and playing a pivotal role in achieving sustainable development goals. Particularly, blockchain technology facilitates green supply chain activities such as recycling, green design, and green manufacturing. Through implementing I4.0 technologies, businesses can maintain an open and safe transaction mechanism. It can also assist them in increasing their productivity, lower their costs by resource regeneration, contribute to societal, fiscal, and environmental sustainability. Supply chain operations are susceptible to a lack of reliability, stability, and accuracy, the use of I4.0 will resolve these vulnerability. Thus, it is recommended to firms and authorities to promote I4.0 technologies in implementing IGSCP to achieve sustainability.

Finally, following are the limitation of this study: Firstly, the current study only focused on IGSCP. Future researchers can test their model by including both internal and external GSCM practices. Second, this study is limited to manufacturing firms in Pakistan. It is recommended to test the same model in other sectors and economies to provide more in depth understanding regarding this model. Third, CB-SEM is employed in the current study. Future researchers can employ mathematical modeling. Moreover, future resarchers can also test the mediating role of IGSCP between I4.0 and economic and environmental performance. Lastly, future studies can also check the effect of advanced digital technologies on different HR aspects. As the adoption of digital technologies help in making HR processes paperless, subsequently having less effect on the environment.

REFERENCES

Abbasi, M., & Nilsson, F. (2016). Developing environmentally sustainable logistics: Exploring themes and challenges from a logistics service providers' perspective. *Transportation Research Part D, Transport and Environment*, *46*, 273–283. doi:10.1016/j.trd.2016.04.004

Badi, S., & Murtagh, N. (2019). Green supply chain management in construction: A systematic literature review and future research agenda. *Journal of Cleaner Production*, *223*, 312–322. doi:10.1016/j.jclepro.2019.03.132

Bai, C., Dallasega, P., Orzes, G., & Sarkis, J. (2020). Industry 4.0 technologies assessment: A sustainability perspective. *International Journal of Production Economics*, *229*, 107776. doi:10.1016/j.ijpe.2020.107776

Baines, T., Brown, S., Benedettini, O., & Ball, P. (2012). Examining green production and its role within the competitive strategy of manufacturers. *Journal of Industrial Engineering and Management*, *5*(1), 53–87. doi:10.3926/jiem.405

Ben-Daya, M., Hassini, E., & Bahroun, Z. (2019). Internet of things and supply chain management: A literature review. *International Journal of Production Research*, *57*(15–16), 4719–4742. doi:10.1080/00207543.2017.1402140

Chin, T. A., Tat, H. H., & Sulaiman, Z. (2015). Green supply chain management, environmental collaboration and sustainability performance. *Procedia CIRP*, *26*, 695–699. doi:10.1016/j.procir.2014.07.035

Correia, E., Carvalho, H., Azevedo, S. G., & Govindan, K. (2017). Maturity Models in Supply Chain Sustainability: A Systematic Literature Review. In Sustainability (Vol. 9, Issue 1). doi:10.3390u9010064

Dalenogare, L. S., Benitez, G. B., Ayala, N. F., & Frank, A. G. (2018). The expected contribution of Industry 4.0 technologies for industrial performance. *International Journal of Production Economics*, *204*, 383–394. doi:10.1016/j.ijpe.2018.08.019

Danese, P., Lion, A., & Vinelli, A. (2019). Drivers and enablers of supplier sustainability practices: A survey-based analysis. *International Journal of Production Research*, *57*(7), 2034–2056. doi:10.1080/00207543.2018.1519265

de Sousa Jabbour, A. B. L., Jabbour, C. J. C., Foropon, C., & Godinho Filho, M. (2018). When titans meet–Can industry 4.0 revolutionise the environmentally-sustainable manufacturing wave? The role of critical success factors. *Technological Forecasting and Social Change*, *132*, 18–25. doi:10.1016/j.techfore.2018.01.017

Drath, R., & Horch, A. (2014). Industrie 4.0: Hit or hype? *IEEE Industrial Electronics Magazine*, *8*(2), 56–58. doi:10.1109/MIE.2014.2312079

Dubey, R., Gunasekaran, A., Childe, S. J., Papadopoulos, T., Luo, Z., Wamba, S. F., & Roubaud, D. (2019). Can big data and predictive analytics improve social and environmental sustainability? *Technological Forecasting and Social Change*, *144*, 534–545. doi:10.1016/j.techfore.2017.06.020

Feng, M., Yu, W., Wang, X., Wong, C. Y., Xu, M., & Xiao, Z. (2018). Green supply chain management and financial performance: The mediating roles of operational and environmental performance. *Business Strategy and the Environment*, *27*(7), 811–824. doi:10.1002/bse.2033

Frank, A. G., Dalenogare, L. S., & Ayala, N. F. (2019). Industry 4.0 technologies: Implementation patterns in manufacturing companies. *International Journal of Production Economics*, *210*, 15–26. doi:10.1016/j.ijpe.2019.01.004

Geffen, C. A., & Rothenberg, S. (2000). Suppliers and environmental innovation: The automotive paint process. *International Journal of Operations & Production Management*, *20*(2), 166–186. doi:10.1108/01443570010304242

Govindan, K., Cheng, T. C. E., Mishra, N., & Shukla, N. (2018). *Big data analytics and application for logistics and supply chain management*. Elsevier. doi:10.1016/j.tre.2018.03.011

Govindan, K., Diabat, A., & Shankar, K. M. (2015). Analyzing the drivers of green manufacturing with fuzzy approach. *Journal of Cleaner Production*, *96*, 182–193. doi:10.1016/j.jclepro.2014.02.054

Hartmann, C., Shi, J., Giusto, A., & Siegrist, M. (2015). The psychology of eating insects: A cross-cultural comparison between Germany and China. *Food Quality and Preference*, *44*, 148–156. doi:10.1016/j.foodqual.2015.04.013

Ikram, M. N., & Siddiqui, D. A. (2019). Effect of Green Supply Chain Management on Environmental Performance and Export Performance: A Case Study of Textile Industries in Pakistan. *Social Science and Humanities Journal SSHJ*, *03*(04), 1006–1019.

Ivanov, D., Dolgui, A., & Sokolov, B. (2019). The impact of digital technology and Industry 4.0 on the ripple effect and supply chain risk analytics. *International Journal of Production Research*, *57*(3), 829–846. doi:10.1080/00207543.2018.1488086

Jabbour, C. J. C., Mauricio, A. L., & Lopes, A. B. (2017). The Management of Operations Critical success factors and green supply chain management proactivity : Shedding light on the human aspects of this relationship based on cases from the Brazilian industry. *Production Planning and Control*, *7287*(May), 1–13. doi:10.1080/09537287.2017.1309705

Kang, H. S., Lee, J. Y., Choi, S., Kim, H., Park, J. H., Son, J. Y., Kim, B. H., & Do Noh, S. (2016). Smart manufacturing: Past research, present findings, and future directions. *International Journal of Precision Engineering and Manufacturing-Green Technology*, *3*(1), 111–128. doi:10.100740684-016-0015-5

Khan, S. A. R., Dong, Q., Zhang, Y., & Khan, S. S. (2017). The impact of green supply chain on enterprise performance: In the perspective of China. *Journal of Advanced Manufacturing Systems*, *16*(03), 263–273. doi:10.1142/S0219686717500160

Khan, S. A. R., & Qianli, D. (2017). Impact of green supply chain management practices on firms' performance: An empirical study from the perspective of Pakistan. *Environmental Science and Pollution Research International*, *24*(20), 16829–16844. doi:10.100711356-017-9172-5 PMID:28573559

Khan, S. A. R., Yu, Z., Umar, M., Lopes de Sousa Jabbour, A. B., & Mor, R. S. (2021). Tackling post-pandemic challenges with digital technologies: An empirical study. *Journal of Enterprise Information Management*, (20210218). Advance online publication. doi:10.1108/JEIM-01-2021-0040

Khan, S. A. R., Zia-ul-haq, H. M., Umar, M., & Yu, Z., (2021a). Digital technology and circular economy practices: An strategy to improve organizational performance. *Business Strategy & Development*.

Khan, S. A. R., Yu, Z., & Umar, M. (2021c). How environmental awareness and corporate social responsibility practices benefit the enterprise? An empirical study in the context of emerging economy. *Management of Environmental Quality*.

Kiel, D., Müller, J. M., Arnold, C., & Voigt, K.-I. (2020). Sustainable industrial value creation: Benefits and challenges of industry 4.0. In *Digital Disruptive Innovation* (pp. 231–270). World Scientific.

Kouhizadeh, M., & Sarkis, J. (2020). Blockchain characteristics and green supply chain advancement. In *Global Perspectives on Green Business Administration and Sustainable Supply Chain Management* (pp. 93–109). IGI Global. doi:10.4018/978-1-7998-2173-1.ch005

Li, G., Hou, Y., & Wu, A. (2017). Fourth Industrial Revolution: Technological drivers, impacts and coping methods. *Chinese Geographical Science, 27*(4), 626–637. doi:10.100711769-017-0890-x

Li, Y., Dai, J., & Cui, L. (2020). The impact of digital technologies on economic and environmental performance in the context of industry 4.0: A moderated mediation model. *International Journal of Production Economics, 229*(May), 107777. doi:10.1016/j.ijpe.2020.107777

Lin, R.-J., Tan, K.-H., & Geng, Y. (2013). Market demand, green product innovation, and firm performance: Evidence from Vietnam motorcycle industry. *Journal of Cleaner Production, 40*, 101–107. doi:10.1016/j.jclepro.2012.01.001

Martel, A., & Klibi, W. (2016). *Designing value-creating supply chain networks*. Springer. doi:10.1007/978-3-319-28146-9

Melnyk, S. A., Sroufe, R. P., & Calantone, R. (2003). Assessing the impact of environmental management systems on corporate and environmental performance. *Journal of Operations Management, 21*(3), 329–351. doi:10.1016/S0272-6963(02)00109-2

Neuhofer, B., Buhalis, D., & Ladkin, A. (2015). Smart technologies for personalized experiences: A case study in the hospitality domain. *Electronic Markets, 25*(3), 243–254. doi:10.100712525-015-0182-1

Rao, P., & Holt, D. (2005). Do green supply chains lead to competitiveness and economic performance? *International Journal of Operations & Production Management, 25*(9), 898–916. doi:10.1108/01443570510613956

Rehman Khan, S. A., & Yu, Z. (2020). Assessing the eco-environmental performance: An PLS-SEM approach with practice-based view. *International Journal of Logistics Research and Applications, 0*(0), 1–19. doi:10.1080/13675567.2020.1754773

Scur, G., & Barbosa, M. E. (2017). Green supply chain management practices: Multiple case studies in the Brazilian home appliance industry. *Journal of Cleaner Production, 141*, 1293–1302. doi:10.1016/j.jclepro.2016.09.158

Sharma, M., Kamble, S., Mani, V., Sehrawat, R., Belhadi, A., & Sharma, V. (2021). Industry 4.0 adoption for sustainability in multi-tier manufacturing supply chain in emerging economies. *Journal of Cleaner Production, 281*, 125013. doi:10.1016/j.jclepro.2020.125013

Sinha, A. K., & Anand, A. (2017). Towards fuzzy preference relationship based on decision making approach to access the performance of suppliers in environmental conscious manufacturing domain. *Computers & Industrial Engineering*, *105*, 39–54. doi:10.1016/j.cie.2016.12.033

Song, W., Chen, Z., Liu, A., Zhu, Q., Zhao, W., Tsai, S.-B., & Lu, H. (2018). A study on green supplier selection in dynamic environment. *Sustainability*, *10*(4), 1226. doi:10.3390u10041226

Sony, M. (2019). Green supply chain management practices and digital technology: A qualitative study. In *Technology optimization and change management for successful digital supply chains* (pp. 233–254). IGI Global. doi:10.4018/978-1-5225-7700-3.ch012

Talatappeh, S. S., & Lakzi, A. (2019). Developing a model for investigating the impact of cloud-based systems on green supply chain management. *Journal of Engineering, Design and Technology*.

Tao, F., Qi, Q., Liu, A., & Kusiak, A. (2018). Data-driven smart manufacturing. *Journal of Manufacturing Systems*, *48*, 157–169. doi:10.1016/j.jmsy.2018.01.006

Thoben, K.-D., Wiesner, S., & Wuest, T. (2017). "Industrie 4.0" and smart manufacturing-a review of research issues and application examples. *International Journal of Automotive Technology*, *11*(1), 4–16.

Umar, M., Khan, S. A. R., Yusoff Yusliza, M., Ali, S., & Yu, Z. (2021). Industry 4.0 and green supply chain practices: An empirical study. *International Journal of Productivity and Performance Management*. Advance online publication. doi:10.1108/IJPPM-12-2020-0633

Umar, M., & Khan, S. A. R., Muhammad Zia-ul-haq, H., Yusliza, M. Y., & Farooq, K. (2021). The role of emerging technologies in implementing green practices to achieve sustainable operations. *The TQM Journal*.

Yu, Y., Zhang, M., & Huo, B. (2019). The impact of supply chain quality integration on green supply chain management and environmental performance. *Total Quality Management & Business Excellence*, *30*(9–10), 1110–1125. doi:10.1080/14783363.2017.1356684

Yu, Z., Khan, S. A. R., & Liu, Y. (2020). Exploring the Role of Corporate Social Responsibility Practices in Enterprises. *Journal of Advanced Manufacturing Systems*, *19*(03), 449–461. doi:10.1142/S0219686720500225

Zailani, S. H. M., Eltayeb, T. K., Hsu, C., & Tan, K. C. (2012). The impact of external institutional drivers and internal strategy on environmental performance. *International Journal of Operations & Production Management.*

Zhou, L., Chong, A. Y. L., & Ngai, W. T. (2015). Supply chain management in the era of the internet of things. *International Journal of Production Economics, 159,* 1–3. doi:10.1016/j.ijpe.2014.11.014

Zhu, Q., & Sarkis, J. (2004). Relationships between operational practices and performance among early adopters of green supply chain management practices in Chinese manufacturing enterprises. *Journal of Operations Management, 22*(3), 265–289. doi:10.1016/j.jom.2004.01.005

Zhu, Q., Sarkis, J., & Lai, K. (2008). Confirmation of a measurement model for green supply chain management practices implementation. *International Journal of Production Economics, 111*(2), 261–273. doi:10.1016/j.ijpe.2006.11.029

Rehman Khan, S. A., Yu, Z., Sarwat, S., Godil, D. I., Amin, S., & Shujaat, S. (2021). The role of block chain technology in circular economy practices to improve organisational performance. *International Journal of Logistics Research and Applications*, 1-18.

Chapter 2
How to Improve Organizational Performance Using Big Data in the Hotels

Subhodeep Mukherjee
https://orcid.org/0000-0002-6863-4881
GITAM University (Deemed), India

Manish Mohan Baral
https://orcid.org/0000-0002-9620-1872
GITAM University (Deemed), India

Venkataiah Chittipaka
https://orcid.org/0000-0002-7804-0796
Indira Gandhi National Open University (IGNOU), Delhi, India

ABSTRACT

Big data is a collection of huge amounts of data for extracting information from data. This helps the firms know the hidden knowledge in the data. This research aims to study the adoption of big data in the hotels of India, and it is helping in improving performance. For this study, a technological-organizational-environmental (TOE) framework is used. The factors are identified from the literature review. A questionnaire is prepared for survey-based research in the hotel industry. Exploratory factor analysis and structural equation modeling are used for analysis. Three models are developed for the study. The entire proposed hypothesis for the study was accepted.

DOI: 10.4018/978-1-7998-7642-7.ch002

INTRODUCTION

The word "Big Data" (BD) was coined as a result of this data explosion. Volume, Variety, and Velocity, or the 3Vs, are three distinct characteristics of data often associated with the concept (Costa et al., 2021). Information being produced over the globe right now is staggering. The ever-changing nature of data generation and storage has piqued the interest of businesses across industries to use BD to solve specific business problems. However, as with the implementation of any new technology in an organization, BD. could pose security risks and challenges (Jin et al., 2015). Organizations that use BD can collect and process vast data, including confidential consumer and employee information, trade secrets, and intellectual property. Due to the centralization of data storage, cybercriminals try to hack (Jagadish, 2015). It demonstrates the importance of BD being adequately secured with the highest degree of protection mechanisms. Otherwise, BD has become "riskier than the Internet" due to evolving features of data treated by companies and boom in IT, saving, and re-utilizing of personal data in business analysis processes (Mukherjee et al., 2022a). As a result, there should be a shift in the way businesses handle and monitor their data (Galetsi et al., 2020; Shahbaz et al., 2019).

Security should be seen from an operational and environmental standpoint, in addition to its technical and infrastructure requirements (Brunswicker et al., 2015). As per prior studies, more study is needed to comprehend the exchange of firm and ecological effects on data security issues (Brunswicker et al., 2015; de Camargo Fiorini et al., 2018; A. Gupta et al., 2018). Even though BD became a mainstream technological choice for industrial segments in 2014, major businesses are still undecided about its acceptance (Yadegaridehkordi et al., 2020). The circumstances reinforce need for further determination of factors that impact extremely difficult adoption process in the BD context (Acharya et al., 2018; S. Gupta et al., 2018). BD has gotten a lot of consideration from researchers so far (Ranjan & Foropon, 2021). Nonetheless, only a few studies have looked into the key factors influencing an organization's decision to implement this advancement (Ghasemaghaei, 2021). BD adoption (BDA) is influenced by technical, organizational, and environmental perspectives, positively impacting firm results.

LITERATURE REVIEW

Researchers and practitioners have always been concerned with implementing and using technologies (Chen et al., 2020). As a result, numerous technology adoption studies have been performed in various settings, including healthcare, industry, economics and education (Alkhater et al., 2018; Alsetoohy et al., 2019; Cruz-Jesus et al., 2019; Kamble et al., 2019; Kumar & Krishnamoorthy, 2020; K. Nam et al., 2020; Pateli et al., 2020; Priyadarshinee, Raut, Jha, & Gardas, 2017; Priyadarshinee, Raut, Jha, & Kamble, 2017; Senyo et al., 2016; Skafi et al., 2020; Tashkandi & Al-Jabri, 2015; Wamba & Queiroz, 2020; Wong et al., 2020). To name a few industries, BD now supports analytic processes in "mobile services, retail, engineering, financial services, life sciences, and physical sciences". Initial adopters of BD. solutions realize the potential for new market opportunities and a greater awareness of their trade environment. However, a significant issue in technology adoption research is "What defines an organization's tendency to implement a specific innovation". As a result, various hypotheses have been suggested and investigated to understand better the factors that affect its adoption behavior of latest advancements in a company from both firm and single standpoint (Verma & Bhattacharyya, 2017). Also, researchers such as (Ainin et al., 2016; Garrison et al., 2015; Voola et al., 2012) have thoroughly investigated impacts of such execution of new innovation and practice on generally speaking authoritative execution improvement. By conducting interviews, (Diniz et al., 2018) investigated the BDA in banks of Brazil. The significance of supervisors in setting up the vital conditions for successful BD selection and execution were uncovered in this report. The impact of BD adoption in manufacturing companies was investigated by (Yadegaridehkordi et al., 2018). According to this research, the most critical drivers of BD. adoption are technological capabilities, perceived advantages, BD. efficiency, integration, and complexity. The effect of organizational perspective on (Mukherjee et al., 2022b) BDA in service organizations was investigated. In this analysis, firm size, data sets, and engagement were influencers of BDA. (Verma, 2017) looked into the intentions of Indian manufacturing firms to follow BD. They discovered that the efficiency and benefits of BD can have a positive impact on its adoption. (Park et al., 2015) used the TOE system and the Analytic Hierarchy Process (AHP) approach to identify and rank the factors influencing BD. adoption in Korean businesses. According to the findings, the essential background is technology, and perceived advantages are the most important influencing factor. As per (Verma et al., 2018), TOE perspective (Mukherjee & Chittipaka, 2021a) had been proposed and interviews had been conducted with Indian firm managers to better understand the factors affecting BDA. They realized that strategic importance was the driving force behind the decision to implement BD in businesses. To better understand the organizational acceptance of BD, Sun et al. 2018 combined DOI, institutional theory, and TOE. They looked at similar articles and came up with a list of contributing factors (Roy, 2021) as well as conclusions. Brock & Khan, 2017 identified perceived utility, perceived ease of use, managerial engagement, system perspectives, and transparency and examination are components of BD use from the perspective of UK students, extending TAM with the "Organizational Learning Capabilities (OLC)" context. Kwon et al., 2014; D. W. Nam et al., 2015; Shin, 2016 investigated BD.

acquisition and intention in Korea using Resource-based view (RBV), UTAUT, and TOE, respectively (Pal et al., 2021a).

According to a study of related research, the most studies on BDA has been performed in developed countries such as the United Kingdom (Brock & Khan, 2017), Korea (D. W. Nam et al., 2015; Park et al., 2015), and India (Verma, 2017; Verma et al., 2018; Verma & Bhattacharyya, 2017). There is yet to be a comprehensive theoretical framework that explores the technical, organizational, environmental, and human perspectives which can have a significant effect on BDA and firm results.

Development of hypothesis

Technological, Organizational, and Environmental (TOE) was at first presented by Tornatzky et al. (1990) to comprehend huge elements affecting latest innovation reception in associations. Any technological innovation's adoption can be expected from three different perspectives: technology, environmental, and organization, according to this structure (Pal et al., 2021b). TOE is a well-known theory that has been extensively applied in various firm-level advanced innovation adoption (Baker, 2011). TOE framework had been used in many earlier studies of technology adoption (Abed, 2020; Alsetoohy et al., 2019; Clohessy et al., 2019; Cruz-Jesus et al., 2019; Ergado et al., 2021; Fosso Wamba et al., 2020; Hiran & Henten, 2020; Mahakittikun et al., 2020; Narmetta & Krishnan, 2020; Ngah et al., 2017; Priyadarshinee, Raut, Jha, & Gardas, 2017; Priyadarshinee, Raut, Jha, & Kamble, 2017; Ramaswamy, 2015; Senyo et al., 2016; Skafi et al., 2020; Wong et al., 2020). As described by the TOE, technological factors are a company's on-site and off-site technologies involving equipment and processes (Mukherjee et al., 2021b). The characteristics, resources, and attributes of an organization are contained in the organizational standpoint, while the operational domain and structure are included in the environmental perspective (Tornatzky et al., 1990).

Technological Factors (TF)

Complexity (COMP): It means a technology is viewed as quite hard to access and utilize is referred to as complexity (Rogers, 2003). It is thought that the higher the degree of complexity, the more difficult it is to use any given advancement (Verma, 2017). The element looks at how difficult it is to use BD and its related techniques. When users decide to implement a technology, they will be worried about how difficult it will be to use (Shin, 2016). Since BD is heavily reliant on technology for analyzing huge amount of information, it is anticipated that its high intricacy will hamper its adoption (Mukherjee & Chittipaka, 2021b).

H1: COMP will have an impact on the adoption of BD.

Compatibility (COMPA): "The degree to which an idea is viewed as compatible with the current principles, past experiences, and needs of potential adopters" is how compatibility is described (Rogers, 2003). As a result, BD. adoption must be well-aligned with current IT tools and specifications. According to Shin, 2016, inventions compatible with existing technology and norms are adopted faster than those that are not. The importance of usability in innovation adoption has been recorded in numerous studies (Cruz-Jesus et al., 2019; Haryanto et al., 2020; Mahakittikun et al., 2020; Ngah et al., 2017; Pateli et al., 2020).

H2: COMPA will have an impact on the adoption of BD.

Relative Advantage (RA): "The degree to which an invention is considered as better than the concept it supersedes" is how comparative advantage is described (Sun et al., 2018). It is evaluated based on increased marketing opportunities, increased competition, and additional services offered to clients (Yadegaridehkordi et al., 2020). As per Park et al., 2015, there is no requirement for associations to execute and utilize BD without first deciding its advantages and relative benefits.

H3: RA will have an impact on the adoption BD.

Cost (C): The cost of BD. adoption is described as "the cost incurred by a company to maintain BD use and future scalability" (Sun et al., 2018). Organizations who want to use BD. technology must make a significant investment in both hardware and software. Other challenges of BD. adoption include the expense of assigning new workers and educating current employees (Verma, 2017).

H4: C will have an impact on the adoption BD.

Organizational Factors (OF)

Support of the management (SM): "The degree to which top management recognizes the value of BD technology and the extent to which it is engaged in relevant initiatives" is how management support is described (Park et al., 2015). Authority support can make it easier for organizations to deal with the challenges and complexities that come with new technologies, resulting in a faster adoption rate (Yadegaridehkordi et al., 2018).

H5: SM will have an impact on the adoption of BD.

Organizational Resources (ORE): "The degree to which a firm's technology, human, and business capital are sufficient to facilitate adoption," according to the definition of organizational resource. As per Verma et al., 2018, appropriate innovation foundations, information bases, structures, and design norms ought to be ready for a decent execution of advancement. Truth be told, quite possibly the most basic components influencing the selection of BD in associations is specialized availability (Park et al., 2015). Also, another requirement that should be stressed in the BD the adoption process is the suitability of staffs with sufficient advancement skills (Sun et al., 2016).

H6: OR will put an impact on the adoption BD.

Organizational Size (OS): "The firm's annual revenue and several employees that could help the implementation of BD" is how size is described (Tien et al., 2020). The importance of organization size in technology adoption has been demonstrated in the literature (Brock & Khan, 2017; Sun et al., 2018). Larger companies are the first to embrace innovation because they have more capital and can take more significant risks. On the other hand, small businesses are resource-poor and have difficulty administering the substantial investment needed for its adoption (Tien et al., 2020).

H7: OS will have an impact on the adoption BD.

Environmental Factors (EF.)

External Pressure (EP): The term "external pressure" refers to "influences from the outside world" (Behl et al., 2019). External pressure comes from two sources: business rivals and associates (Park et al., 2015). Sun et al., 2018, on other hand, claimed that pressures from business partners, peers and governing body could have a substantial effect on business adoption of BD. Because of pressure from competitors and partners, a company may implement an innovation. Demand or recommendations from trade partners, business managers may feel pressured to implement an innovation (Verma et al., 2018).

H8: EP will have an impact on the adoption BD.

External Support (ES): "Availability of support for implementing and using an information system" is how external support is described. As per Park et al., 2015, authority policy and funding will make BDA in organizations much more accessible. Meanwhile, vendors help fosters a constructive attitude toward technology and serves as a motivator for adoption of innovation (Baker, 2011). ES has been identified as an important component of adoption of technology in the literature (Behl et al., 2019; Park et al., 2015; Verma, 2017).

H9: ES will have an impact on the adoption BD.

Security and privacy (SP): Concerns about security and privacy are extensively stated in prior literature and cited as barriers for BDA (Shin, 2016). According to Salleh & Janczewski, 2016, B.D. the design causes various security issues, forcing organizations to implement new and improved security technologies and techniques. Organizations involved in BD, on the other hand, are continuously pressured to adhere to related laws when concentrating on their operational missions.

H10: SP will have an impact on the adoption BD.

Organizational Performance (OP): Firms can adopt new technologies in various ways, which can affect their competitive advantage and performance (Brock & Khan,

2017). As a result, efficiency and technology adoption are usually measured together. According to existing research, there is a strong link betwixt adoption of innovation and firm results (Brock & Khan, 2017; Salleh & Janczewski, 2016; Sun et al., 2018). Sun et al., 2018 agree that BD is a significant determinant for competitive advantage of firm, which includes more flexibility, cost savings, creativity, and development (Brock & Khan, 2017). BD increases firm efficiency in a variety of financial and non-financial dimensions.

H11: BDA in the context of TF will have a positive on OP.

H12: BDA in the context of OF will have a positive on OP.

H13: BDA the context of EF will have a positive on OP.

RESEARCH METHODOLOGY

Secondary and primary sources collected data. Secondary sources include a literature review and other reports, and the primary source has a collection of data through a structured questionnaire. The reliability test of the questionnaire was also done. The target populations are employees working in the hotels of India. As SEM has been utilized in this analysis, 200 and above sample size is considered adequate (Hair et al., 2010; Kline, 2011). Hence, the questionnaires are sent to 650 respondents individually, but we only got 326 filled responses. The simple random sampling method has been generalized more appropriately and allows the presence of various Indian hotels (Hair et al., 2010).

To avoid common method bias, the research team has taken few basic precautions during the pre-data collection stage. At the beginning of the questionnaire, a note was mentioned that indicated the survey is intended for academic research and confidentiality of data will be maintained (Mukherjee et al., 2021c). In the gathered dataset, the first cleansing was finished by case screening, trailed by factor screening so clarification can be given for variations in the information. Information cleaning measure it had been reasoned that missing information had been extremely sparse, and in this way, they were not viewed as a principal supporter of any predisposition (Baral et al., 2021). No cases were therefore removed. However, after the data is collected, the research team applied Harman's single factor test. EFA was performed, and the results show that first factor explains maximum variance 31.108% for TF, 20.944% for OF, and 29.985% for EF, all are below the recommended value of 50% (Podsakoff et al., 2003).

SEM and EFA method were utilized for data analysis (Baral & Verma, 2021). The data analysis was done in four stages: analysis of demographics, validity and reliability test, exploratory factor analysis (EFA), and confirmatory factor analysis (CFA) (Roy & Giduturi, 2019). EFA was done to check total variance explained to identify and group the variables using a rotated component matrix table. SPSS 20.0 was utilized for reliability tests and EFA on data collected. After that, CFA was performed for testing the proposed models underlying. AMOS 22.0 was being used for CFA on gathered data for estimating model results as CFA chooses whether a validity test on an expected model be imitated (Hair et al., 2010; Byrne, 2010). At last the model fit was determined by SEM for testing of hypothesis.

Table 1 shows the distribution of respondents based on gender and respondents current positions. 76% of the respondents who have participated in the survey are male and 24% of the respondents were female. 51% of the respondents are hotel manager, while 29% of the respondents are IT manager. Around 20% of the respondents are marketing managers.

Table 1. Respondents' Demographics

Item	Percentage
Gender	
Male	76
Female	24
Respondents Current Position	
Hotel manager	51
IT manager	29
Marketing Manager	20

DATA ANLYSIS

Reliability and validity

Cronbach's alpha

The reliability test was performed for each factor based on cronbach's alpha (α) value introduces cronbach's alpha for the constructs. The values of all variable scales should be above the recommended value of 0.70 (Nunnally and Bernstein, 1994). Utilization of 7 points Likert scale was done in preparing the structured questionnaire.

For analyzing the information collected, SPSS 20.0 and Amos 22.0 was used. For the construct TF, the latent variables along with the indicators and α value are as follows: COMP has COMP1, COMP2, COMP3, and COMP4 is 0.822; COMPA has COMPA1, COMPA2, COMPA3, and COMPA4 is 0.837; RA has RA1, RA2, and RA3 is 0.704; C has C1, C2, and C3 is 0.830; BD. has BD1, BD2, BD3, and BD4 is 0.824. For the construct OF, the latent variables along with the indicators and α value are as follows: SM has SM1, SM2, and SM3 is 0.741; ORE has ORE1, ORE2, and ORE3 is 0.746; OS has OS1, OS2, and OS3 is 0.755. For the construct EF, the latent variables along with the indicators and α value are as follows: EP has EP1, EP2, EP3, and EP4 is 0.819; ES has ES1, ES2, ES3, and ES4 is 0.831; SP has SP1, SP2, and SP3 is 0.766. Hence, all the values are within the threshold.

Composite reliability

Composite reliability (CR) was also measured for all the components. It is estimated to for inside consistency reliability due to its capacity to give better outcomes (Henseler et al., 2009). TF has four latent variables and its CR values are: COMPA is 0.889; COMP is 0.879; C is 0.791; RA is 0.835. The second context is OF and the latent variables along CR values are OS is 0.855; SM is 0.853; ORE is 0.843. The last context is GP and the latent variables along CR values are: BOR is 0.911; GOV is 0.901; FIY is 0.911; L is 0.868. Hence, all the values are within the threshold (Hair et. al. 2010).

Exploratory Factor Analysis

The first step of EFA was to evaluate the appropriateness of the sample size. SPSS 20.0 was utilized for EFA. The correlations between its items had been checked utilizing the Bartlett's test of sphericity (Hair et al. 2010). Principal axis factoring was performed to identify meaningful bias and express the same qualities. Promax rotation has been used, as it had been assumed (based on the relevant literature) that its factors have been correlated (Tabachnick & Fiddell 2007). With this test, the statistic generated should have been significant ($p < 0.05$) for an EFA to be considered as an appropriate technique (Hair et al. 2010).

Finally, the Kaiser-Meyer-Olkin (KMO) measure had been used to quantify whether that items correlated sufficiently so that the order to determine whether a factor analysis could have been performed. The KMO value for the construct TF is 0.808; OF is 0.692 and; EF is 0.793. The minimum level set for this statistic is 0.60 (Hair et al. 2010). The significance value for all the constructs is 0.000, which is less than 0.05, i.e., the probability value level acceptable (Tabachnick & Fidell

2007; Hair, et. al., 2010). Meyers et al. (2013) indicate that a variance that has been accounted for by its factors needs in meeting the lower limit by 50%.

The extraction method used was principal axis factoring. Only the eigenvalues which have values greater than one are extracted as it explains maximum variance. For the construct TF, the percentage of total variance explained by component 1 (34.229%), component 2 (13.474%), component 3 (11.012%), and component 4 (9.216%). The cumulative percentage of total variance explained by all four components is 67.931%. For the construct OF, the percentage of total variance explained by component 1 (28.467%), component 2 (22.553%), and component 3 (17.015%). The cumulative percentage of total variance explained by all three components is 68.036%. For the construct EF, the percentage of total variance explained by component 1 (35.309%), component 2 (18.806%), and component 3 (12.929%). The cumulative percentage of total variance explained by all three components is 67.044%.

The Rotated Component Matrix is important for interpreting the results of the analysis. Rotation helps in grouping the items, and each group contains more than one item at-least, which simplifies the structure. Hence, this is the aim of rotation. In this research, we have achieved this aim. This helps to identify the cross-loadings on more than one group, and then it can be corrected by removing those items which are cross-loaded. In this research, the loadings having less than |.40| are suppressed because loadings more than |.40| are typically considered high. So, in the end, we achieve a simple structure. For the TF construct there are 14 total variables which were grouped under four different components. The rotation method used was varimax rotation. All the 14 variables listed were grouped under four different components. COMPA1, COMPA2, COMPA3, and COMPA4 are grouped under the first component with values of 0.763, 0.862, 0.891, and 0.7742. COMP1, COMP2, COMP3, and COMP4 are grouped under the second component having values 0.870, 0.762, 0.766, and 0.842. C1, C2, and C3 are grouped under the third component with values of 0.849, 0.930, and 0.805. RA1, RA2, and RA3 are grouped under the fourth component with values of 0.853, 0.845, and 0.672.

For the OF construct there are 9 total variables which were grouped under three different components. The rotation method used was varimax rotation. All the 9 variables listed were grouped under three different components. OS1, OS2, and OS3 are grouped under the first component with values of 0.725, 0.867, and 0.844. SM1, SM2, and SM3 are grouped under the second component with values of 0.843, 0.775, and 0.816. ORE1, ORE2, and ORE3 are grouped under the third component with values of 0.825, 0.865, and 0.708.

For the EF construct there are 11 total variables which were grouped under three different components. The rotation method used was varimax rotation. All the 11 variables listed were grouped under three different components. ES1, ES2, ES3, and ES4 are grouped under the first component with values of 0.787, 0.866, 0.885, and 0.711. EP1, EP2, EP3, and EP4 are grouped under the second component with values of 0.868, 0.763, 0.740, and 0.824. SP1, SP2, and SP3 are grouped under the third component with values of 0.803, 0.854, and 0.831.

Confirmatory factor analysis (CFA) was performed in the next stage, for the constructs identified from the literature survey can be tested and how well the variables represent the constructs. Structural equation modeling (SEM) was used for testing the model fit of the proposed research model (Byrne, 2010). An extra thorough trial of build legitimacy is the purported factorial legitimacy, which depends on the aftereffects of the factor investigation, within the basic role of its characterizing their basic structures among its factors remembered for the examination (Hair et al. 2010). At that point when their instrument shows the normal structures inside, this could have been demonstrative to Construct Validity (CV) (Moerdyk, 2009) and, explicitly, factorial validity.

Construct validity

A significant logical idea to assess the validity of a measure to develop a CV. CV is the degree to which a test quantifies the idea or develop that it is expected to quantify. CV is generally tried by estimating the relationship in appraisals got from a few scales. There is no cut-off that characterizes CV (DeVellis, 2003).

The primary goal of the current study is to analyze structural components, CV which includes investigation of interior connections among things or subscales speaking to a specific measure, utilizing such factual examinations as correlation, exploratory and confirmatory factor analysis, and reliability analysis.

Convergent validity

It is measured by using average variance extracted (AVE). As per Fornell and Larcker (1981), AVE should be greater than 0.5 for the convergent validity. Hence, table 2 represents AVE values for the TF constructs, table 3 represents AVE values for the OF constructs and table 4 represents AVE values for the EF constructs. All the values are greater than 0.5 which satisfies convergent validity for all the constructs.

Divergent or Discriminant Validity

To evaluate this validity, Fornell and Larcker (1981) suggested that AVE of the construct should be more than the square of the correlation between that construct and the other constructs. Table II represents the values for construct correlation and AVE for TF construct. The variance extracted and squared correlation for COMPA and COMP is 0.653 and 0.121; COMPA and C is 0.703 and 0.112; COMPA and

RA is 0.644 and 0.092; COMP and C is 0.693 and 0.087; COMP and RA is 0.634 and 0.030; C and RA is 0.681 and 0.081. Hence, the value of variance extracted is more than squared correlation value. As a result, divergent or discriminant validity condition is also satisfied.

Table 2. Construct correlation and AVE for TF construct

	AVE	Variance extracted between factors			
		COMPA	COMP	C	RA
COMPA	0.815	1			
COMP	0.802	0.653	1		
C	0.861	0.703	0.693	1	
RA	0.79	0.644	0.634	0.683	1

Table 3 represents the values for construct correlation and AVE for OF construct. The variance extracted and squared correlation for OS and SM is 0.659 and 0.037; OS and ORE is 0.649 and 0.03; SM and ORE is 0.649 and 0.00001. Hence, the value of variance extracted is more than squared correlation value. As a result, divergent or discriminant validity is satisfied.

Table 3. Construct correlation and AVE for OF construct

	AVE	Variance extracted between factors		
		OS	SM	ORE
OS	0.812	1		
SM	0.811	0.659	1	
ORE	0.799	0.649	0.649	1

Table 4 represents the values for construct correlation and AVE for EF construct. The variance extracted and squared correlation for ES and EP is 0.649 and 0.208; ES and SP is 0.674 and 0.005; ES and SP is 0.663 and 0.003. Hence, the value of variance extracted is more than squared correlation value. As a result, divergent or discriminant validity is satisfied.

Table 4. Construct correlation and AVE for EF construct

	AVE	Variance extracted between factors		
		ES	EP	SP
ES	0.812	1		
EP	0.799	0.649	1	
SP	0.829	0.674	0.663	1

Structural Equation Modeling

To test the hypothesis, SEM was used (Byrne, 2010). AMOS 22.0 was utilized for this study because of its powerful graphic representations and user-friendly interfaces. The results of the model are shown here. Figure 1 represent the final model and the latent variables and their indicators and dependent variable for TF construct.

Table 5. Final Goodness of Fit Indices for the Structural Model for TF construct

Goodness-of-fit Indices	Default Model	Benchmark
Absolute goodness-of-fit measure		
CMIN/Df	2.451	⩽3
Absolute badness of fit measure		
RMSEA	0.067	⩽0.08
Incremental fit measure		
CFI	0.915	⩾0.90
IFI	0.916	⩾0.90
TLI	0.901	⩾0.90
Parsimony fit measure		
PCFI	0.784	⩾0.50
PNFI	0.742	⩾0.50

Table 5 shows model fit values and fit indices. The value of chi-square is 485.272, and the degree of freedom is 198. The estimations of absolute fit indices are: CMIN/ Df 2.451, CMIN represents the chi-square value, and Df represents the degree of freedom, and the value is less than 3, which is the accepted threshold value (McIver & Carmines, 1981). Root mean square error of approximation (RMSEA) value is 0.067 which is within the threshold value of 0.08. The comparative fit index (CFI) is 0.915; incremental fit index (IFI) is 0.916; Tucker-Lewis's coefficient (TLI) is 0.901;

Parsimony comparative of fit index (PCFI) is 0.784 and; Parsimony normed of fit index (PNFI) is 0.742 are having values in the threshold level and is acceptable (Byrne 2010). Figure 1 below shows SEM output generated after analysis in AMOS 22.0.

Figure 1. Final measurement model for the construct TF

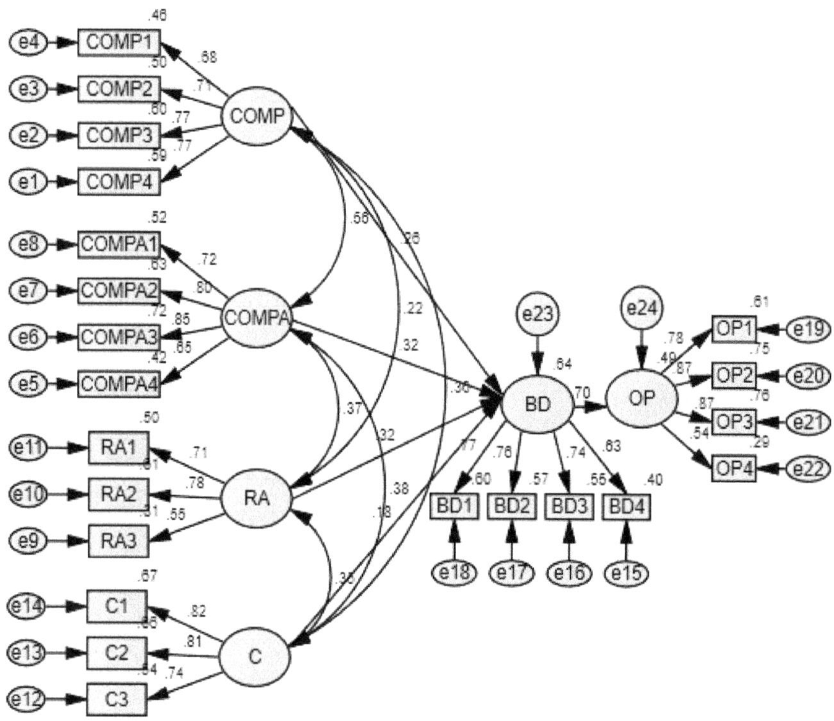

Table 6 shows the path estimate analysis results.

Table 6. Structural model results for TF construct

	Estimate	SE.	CR.	P	Hypothesis
BD<---COMP	0.258	0.058	4.448	0.000	Supported
BD<---COMP	0.325	0.078	4.167	0.000	Supported
BD<---COMP	0.321	0.072	4.458	0.000	Supported
BD<---COMP	0.183	0.044	4.159	0.002	Supported
OP<---BD	0.702	0.135	5.20	0.000	Supported

Figure 2 represent the final model and the latent variables and their indicators and dependent variable for OF construct.

Table 7. Final Goodness of Fit Indices for the Structural Model for OF construct

Goodness-of-fit Indices	Default Model	Benchmark
Absolute goodness-of-fit measure		
CMIN/Df	2.403	⩽3
Absolute badness of fit measure		
RMSEA	0.066	⩽0.08
Incremental fit measure		
CFI	0.923	⩾0.90
IFI	0.924	⩾0.90
TLI	0.906	⩾0.90
Parsimony fit measure		
PCFI	0.760	⩾0.50
PNFI	0.722	⩾0.50

Table 7 shows the model fit values and fit indices. The value of chi-square is 269.139, and the degree of freedom is 112. The estimations of absolute fit indices are: CMIN/Df 2.403, CMIN represents the chi-square value, and Df represents the degree of freedom, and the value is less than 3, which is the accepted threshold value (Kline, 2015). RMSEA value is 0.066 which is within the threshold value of 0.08. CFI is 0.923; IFI is 0.924; TLI is 0.906; PCFI is 0.760 and; PNFI is 0.722 are having values in the threshold level and is acceptable (Byrne, 2010). Figure 1 below shows SEM output generated after analysis in AMOS 22.0.

Figure 2. Final measurement model for the construct OF

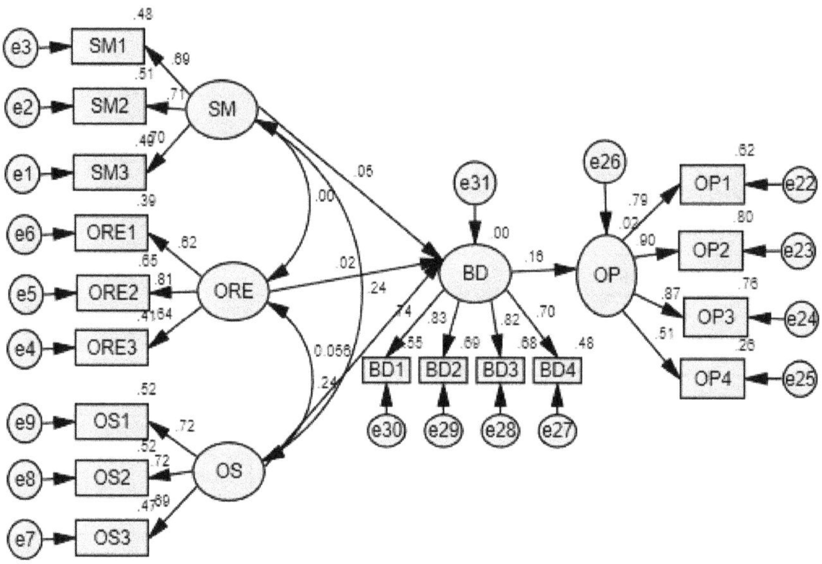

Table 8 shows the path estimate analysis results.

Table 8. Structural model results for TF construct

	Estimate	SE.	CR.	P	Hypothesis
BD<---SM	0.050	0.079	0.633	0.000	Supported
BD<---ORE	0.023	0.073	0.315	0.000	Supported
BD<---OS	0.056	0.100	0.56	0.000	Supported
OP<---BD	0.157	0.102	1.54	0.000	Supported

Figure 3 represent the final model and the latent variables and their indicators and dependent variable for EF construct.

Table 9. Final Goodness of Fit Indices for the Structural Model for OF construct

Goodness-of-fit Indices	Default Model	Benchmark
Absolute goodness-of-fit measure		
CMIN/Df	2.647	⩽3
Absolute badness of fit measure		
RMSEA	0.071	⩽0.08
Incremental fit measure		
CFI	0.912	⩾0.90
IFI	0.913	⩾0.90
TLI	0.915	⩾0.90
Parsimony fit measure		
PCFI	0.774	⩾0.50
PNFI	0.736	⩾0.50

Table 9 shows the model fit values and fit indices. The value of chi-square is 383.767, and the degree of freedom is 145. The estimations of absolute fit indices are: CMIN/Df 2.647, and the value is less than 3, which is the accepted threshold value. RMSEA value is 0.071 which is within the threshold value of 0.08. CFI is 0.912; IFI is 0.913; TLI is 0.915; PCFI is 0.774 and; PNFI is 0.736 are having values in the threshold level and is acceptable (Byrne 2010). Figure 1 below shows SEM output generated after analysis in AMOS 22.0.

Figure 3. Final measurement model for the construct EF

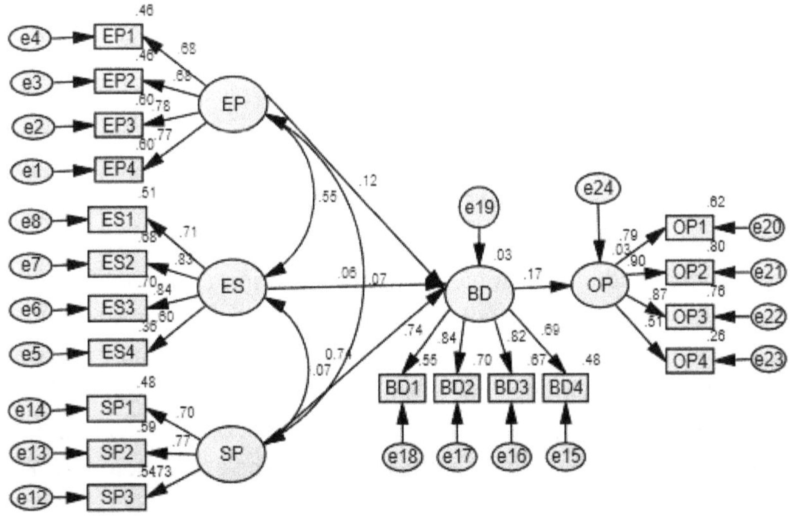

Table 10 shows the path estimate analysis results.

Table 10. Structural model results for EF construct

	Estimate	SE.	CR.	P	Hypothesis
BD<---ES	0.056	0.106	0.528	0.000	Supported
BD<---SP	0.74	0.081	9.136	0.000	Supported
BD<---EP	0.122	0.081	1.506	0.000	Supported
OP<---BD	0.169	0.102	1.657	0.000	Supported

DISCUSSION

The proposed model is based on TOE frameworks, consisting of three technological, organizational, and environmental constructs. The aftereffects of this investigation are partially upheld by related writing (Park et al., 2015; Verma et al., 2017). BD had been adopted in many industries to improve the firm performance and to achieve organizational excellence (Al-Dmour et al., 2021; Aversa et al., 2021; Diniz et al., 2018; Ghasemaghaei, 2021; Nasrollahi et al., 2020; Park et al., 2015b; Shahbaz et al., 2019; Verma, 2017; Verma et al., 2018; Yadegaridehkordi et al., 2018, 2020).

Technological Factors (TF): TF helps identify the technological factors that can impact the adoption of any technological innovations. The Cronbach's alpha and composite reliability values for the construct TF were above 0.7, which is the recommended level (Nunnally 1978; Hair et al. 2010) for the four factors. The KMO value of the construct is 0.808, which is also above the recommended level of 0.6 (Hair et al. 2010), which allows the data for factor analysis. The total variance explained was 67.931%, and in the rotated component matrix, the variables were grouped under four groups. Only the loadings which are above |.40| are considered in this research because those are considered to be typically high and hence are more significant (Hair et al. 2010).

For further analysis in this research, four components were utilized, having 14 indicators. The component is COMPA: Compatibility. COMPA showed positive influence in the study, and the proposed hypothesis is accepted. As per Rogers (2003), both organizational and technical harmony of innovation is essential components impacting BDA. Clearly benefits all around coordinated with current innovations and stages are embraced more quickly than those which are most certainly not (Shin, 2016). It comprises four COMPA1, COMPA2, COMPA3, and COMPA4 are grouped under the first component with values of 0.763, 0.862, 0.891, and 0.7742, which shows that it has very high loadings (>|.40|). The component RA: Relative advantage. BD offers critical benefits to trades and firms, like expense decrease, risk management, income creation, and improvement of decision-making (D. W. Nam et al., 2015). It comprises three indicators RA1, RA2, and RA3 are grouped under the fourth component with values of 0.853, 0.845, and 0.672, which shows that it has very high loadings (>|.40|). The component COMP: Complexity. COMP showed a positive influence on the firm performance of hotels after using BD, and the proposed hypothesis got accepted. It comprises four indicators COMP1, COMP2, COMP3, and COMP4 are grouped under the second component having values 0.870, 0.762, 0.766, and 0.842, which shows that it has very high loadings (>|.40|). Component C: Cost. Cost plays an essential role in adopting the latest technology innovation as all the firms do not have the same budgets and incomes. C showed a positive influence on the firm performance of hotels after using BD, and the proposed hypothesis got accepted. It comprises three indicators C1, C2, and C3 are grouped under the third component with values of 0.849, 0.930, and 0.805, which shows that it has very high loadings (>|.40|).

Based on EFA, the SEM was performed in AMOS 22.0. The value of chi-square is 485.272, and the degree of freedom is 198. The estimations of absolute fit indices are: CMIN/Df 2.451, CMIN represents the chi-square value, and Df represents the degree of freedom, and the value is less than 3, which is the accepted threshold value (McIver & Carmines, 1981). The root means square error of approximation (RMSEA) value is 0.067 within the threshold value of 0.08. The comparative fit index (CFI) is 0.915; incremental fit index (IFI) is 0.916; Tucker-Lewis coefficient (TLI) is 0.901; Parsimony comparative of fit index (PCFI) is 0.784 and; Parsimony normed of fit index (PNFI) is 0.742 are having values in the threshold level and is acceptable (Byrne 2010). Hence, the hypotheses H1, H2, H3, and H4 could not be rejected. In this research, the components are explained and valid with the help of the SEM approach, which is the most appropriate method to prove the validity. This technique has not been used until a date in any prior research it a unique study.

Organizational Factors (OF): The Cronbach's alpha and composite reliability values for the construct OF were above 0.7, which is the recommended level (Nunnally 1978; Hair et al. 2010) for the three factors. The KMO value of the construct is 0.692, which is within recommended level of 0.6 (Hair et al. 2010), which allows the data for factor analysis. The total variance explained was 68.036%, and in the rotated component matrix, the variables were grouped under three groups. Only the loadings which are above |.40| are considered in this research because those are considered to be typically high and hence are more significant (Hair et al. 2010).

For further analysis in this research, three components were utilized, having nine indicators. All the 9 variables listed were grouped under three different components. OS1, OS2, and OS3 are grouped under the first component with values of 0.725, 0.867, and 0.844. SM1, SM2, and SM3 are grouped under the second component with values of 0.843, 0.775, and 0.816. ORE1, ORE2, and ORE3 are grouped under the third component with values of 0.825, 0.865, and 0.708. All the values showed that it has very high loadings (>|.40|). The only research that supported the importance of organization size in the sense of BDA (Sun et al., 2018). The accessibility of sufficient human, financial, and technical assets, as per literature, can significantly speed up advancement adoption process (Hameed et al., 2012). Business with more capital can deploy new technology more quickly (Kwon et al., 2014). Diniz et al., 2018 consider firm scale to be a significant organizational factor in technology adoption. Larger companies, on the whole, have more capital and are willing to take more risks. As a result, they should make new IT easier to start and adopt.

Based on EFA, the SEM was performed in AMOS 22.0. The value of chi-square is 269.139, and the degree of freedom is 112. The estimations of absolute fit indices are: CMIN/Df 2.403, CMIN represents the chi-square value, and Df represents the degree of freedom, and the value is less than 3, which is the accepted threshold value (McIver & Carmines, 1981). The root means the square error of approximation (RMSEA) value is 0.066 within the threshold value of 0.08. The comparative fit index (CFI) is 0.923; incremental fit index (IFI) is 0.924; Tucker-Lewis coefficient (TLI) is 0.906; Parsimony comparative of fit index (PCFI) is 0.760 and; Parsimony normed of fit index (PNFI) is 0.722 are having values in the threshold level and is acceptable (Byrne 2010). Hence, the hypotheses H5, H6, and H7 could not be rejected. In this research, the components are explained and valid with the SEM approach, which is the most appropriate method to prove the validity, and this technique has not been used until a date in any prior research.

Environmental Factors (EF): The Cronbach's alpha and composite reliability values for the construct EP were above 0.7, which is the recommended level (Nunnally 1978; Hair et al. 2010) for the three factors. The KMO value of the construct is 0.793, which is also above the recommended level of 0.6 (Hair et al. 2010), which allows the data for factor analysis. The total variance explained was 67.044%, and in the rotated component matrix, the variables were grouped under three groups. Only the loadings which are above |.40| are considered in this research because those are considered to be typically high and hence are more significant (Hair et al. 2010).

For further analysis in this research, three components were utilized, having 11 indicators. ES1, ES2, ES3, and ES4 are grouped under the first component with values of 0.787, 0.866, 0.885, and 0.711. EP1, EP2, EP3, and EP4 are grouped under the second component with values of 0.868, 0.763, 0.740, and 0.824. SP1, SP2, and SP3 are grouped under the third component with values of 0.803, 0.854, and 0.831. All the values showed that it has very high loadings (>|.40|). EP has been confirmed to significantly affect an organization's decision to implement IT (Cao et al., 2014). Park et al., 2015 determined peers and collaborators as the primary environmental sources that make adoption easier in businesses and organizations.

As a result, once rivals and partners begin to use BD to bend their advantages, organization's higher authority may feel pressured to maintain a cut-throat edge. Data security and privacy mechanisms, and quality of data are still top interests in the BD world (Voola et al., 2012). In reality, the advantages of big data will help to improve the quality of life. Despite its ability to enhance the efficiency of organizations and individuals, protection and privacy concerns continue to stymie its adoption (Salleh & Janczewski, 2016). As a result, data management privacy and security monitoring techniques are essential. In the endorsement and use of BD in firms, security and storage should be considered (Verma, 2017). External support was also regarded as significant, according to Park et al., 2015, consider the dimensions of the atmosphere. It is generally agreed that an external source of information is beneficial. A favorable regulatory climate with government-issued regulatory orders encourages businesses to embrace big data (Baig et al., 2019). Costa et al., 2021, on the other hand, claimed that vendor support and marketing practices could have a significant effect on advancement technology adoption. Sun et al., 2018 backed up this claim, claiming that a firm's preparation and support for new technology will encourage it to use it to maintain internal equilibrium and meet external cooperation needs.

Based on EFA, the SEM was performed in AMOS 22.0. The value of chi-square is 383.767, and the degree of freedom is 145. The estimations of absolute fit indices are: CMIN/Df 2.647, CMIN represents the chi-square value, and Df represents the degree of freedom, and the value is less than 3, which is the accepted threshold value (McIver & Carmines, 1981). The root means the square error of approximation (RMSEA) value is 0.071 within the threshold value of 0.08. The comparative fit index (CFI) is 0.912; incremental fit index (IFI) is 0.913; Tucker-Lewis's coefficient (TLI) is 0.915; Parsimony comparative of fit index (PCFI) is 0.774 and; Parsimony normed of fit index (PNFI) is 0.736 are having values in the threshold level and is acceptable (Byrne 2010). Hence, the hypotheses H8, H9, and H10 could not be rejected. In this research, the components are explained and valid with the help of the SEM approach, which is the most appropriate method to prove the validity, and this technique has not been used to date in any prior research.

CONCLUSION

The current study aims to determine the effect of BD on the organizational performance of hotels. For this study, a structured literature review is being performed to identify the factors. TOE framework was recognized for this study, which comprises technological factors, organizational factors, and environmental factors. A questionnaire was being prepared for survey-based research in the hotel industry. The target population was mainly the employees working in the hotels. After the collection of the data, exploratory factor analysis and structural equation modeling were being performed. All the proposed hypotheses were accepted for the study.

REFERENCES

Abed, S. S. (2020). Social commerce adoption using TOE framework: An empirical investigation of Saudi Arabian SMEs. *International Journal of Information Management*, *53*, 102118. doi:10.1016/j.ijinfomgt.2020.102118

Acharya, A., Singh, S. K., Pereira, V., & Singh, P. (2018). Big data, knowledge co-creation and decision making in fashion industry. *International Journal of Information Management*, *42*, 90–101. doi:10.1016/j.ijinfomgt.2018.06.008

Ainin, S., Naqshbandi, M. M., & Dezdar, S. (2016). Impact of adoption of Green IT practices on organizational performance. *Quality & Quantity*, *50*(5), 1929–1948. doi:10.100711135-015-0244-7

Al-Dmour, H., Saad, N., Basheer Amin, E., Al-Dmour, R., & Al-Dmour, A. (2021). The influence of the practices of big data analytics applications on bank performance: filed study. *VINE Journal of Information and Knowledge Management Systems*. doi:10.1108/VJIKMS-08-2020-0151

Alkhater, N., Walters, R., & Wills, G. (2018). An empirical study of factors influencing cloud adoption among private sector organisations. *Telematics and Informatics*, *35*(1), 38–54. doi:10.1016/j.tele.2017.09.017

Alsetoohy, O., Ayoun, B., Arous, S., Megahed, F., & Nabil, G. (2019). Intelligent agent technology: What affects its adoption in hotel food supply chain management? *Journal of Hospitality and Tourism Technology*, *10*(3), 317–341. doi:10.1108/JHTT-01-2018-0005

Aversa, J., Hernandez, T., & Doherty, S. (2021). Incorporating big data within retail organizations: A case study approach. *Journal of Retailing and Consumer Services*, *60*, 102447. Advance online publication. doi:10.1016/j.jretconser.2021.102447

Baig, M. I., Shuib, L., & Yadegaridehkordi, E. (2019). Big data adoption: State of the art and research challenges. *Information Processing & Management*, *56*(6), 102095. doi:10.1016/j.ipm.2019.102095

Baker, J. (2011). *The Technology-Organization-Environment Framework Strategic Managment View project.* Springer. doi:10.1007/978-1-4419-6108-2_12

Behl, A., Dutta, P., Lessmann, S., Dwivedi, Y. K., & Kar, S. (2019). A conceptual framework for the adoption of big data analytics by e-commerce startups: A case-based approach. *Information Systems and e-Business Management, 17*(2–4), 285–318. doi:10.100710257-019-00452-5

Brock, V., & Khan, H. U. (2017). Big data analytics: Does organizational factor matters impact technology acceptance? *Journal of Big Data, 4*(1), 21. doi:10.118640537-017-0081-8

Brunswicker, S., Bertino, E., & Matei, S. (2015). Big Data for Open Digital Innovation - A Research Roadmap. *Big Data Research, 2*(2), 53–58. doi:10.1016/j.bdr.2015.01.008

Byrne, B. M. (2010). *Structural Equation Modelling with AMOS: Basic Concepts, Applications, and Programming* (2nd ed.). Taylor and Francis Group.

Chen, P. T., Lin, C. L., & Wu, W. N. (2020). Big data management in healthcare: Adoption challenges and implications. *International Journal of Information Management, 53*, 102078. doi:10.1016/j.ijinfomgt.2020.102078

Clohessy, T., Acton, T., & Rogers, N. (2019). Blockchain Adoption: Technological, Organisational and Environmental Considerations. *Business Transformation through Blockchain*, 47–76. doi:10.1007/978-3-319-98911-2_2

Costa, R. L. de C., Moreira, J., Pintor, P., dos Santos, V., & Lifschitz, S. (2021). A Survey on Data-driven Performance Tuning for Big Data Analytics Platforms. *Big Data Research, 25*, 100206. Advance online publication. doi:10.1016/j.bdr.2021.100206

Cruz-Jesus, F., Pinheiro, A., & Oliveira, T. (2019). Understanding CRM adoption stages: Empirical analysis building on the TOE framework. *Computers in Industry, 109*, 1–13. doi:10.1016/j.compind.2019.03.007

de Camargo Fiorini, P., Roman Pais Seles, B. M., Chiappetta Jabbour, C. J., Barberio Mariano, E., & de Sousa Jabbour, A. B. L. (2018). Management theory and big data literature: From a review to a research agenda. In *International Journal of Information Management* (Vol. 43, pp. 112–129). Elsevier Ltd. doi:10.1016/j.ijinfomgt.2018.07.005

Diniz, E. H., Luvizan, S. S., Hino, M. C., & Ferreira, P. C. (2018). Unveiling the big data adoption in banks: Strategizing the implementation of a new technology. *Lecture Notes in Information Systems and Organisation, 23*, 149–162. doi:10.1007/978-3-319-62051-0_13

DeVellis, R. F., Lewis, M. A., & Sterba, K. R. (2003). Interpersonal emotional processes in adjustment to chronic illness. *Social Psychological Foundations of Health and Illness*, 256-287.

Ergado, A. A., Desta, A., & Mehta, H. (2021). Determining the barriers contributing to ICT implementation by using technology-organization-environment framework in Ethiopian higher educational institutions. *Education and Information Technologies, 26*(3), 1–19. doi:10.100710639-020-10397-9

Fosso Wamba, S., Queiroz, M. M., & Trinchera, L. (2020). Dynamics between blockchain adoption determinants and supply chain performance: An empirical investigation. *International Journal of Production Economics, 229*, 107791. doi:10.1016/j.ijpe.2020.107791

Fornell, C., & Larcker, D. F. (1981). Evaluating structural equation models with unobservable variables and measurement error. *JMR, Journal of Marketing Research, 18*(1), 39–50. doi:10.1177/002224378101800104

Galetsi, P., Katsaliaki, K., & Kumar, S. (2020). Big data analytics in health sector: Theoretical framework, techniques and prospects. In *International Journal of Information Management* (Vol. 50, pp. 206–216). Elsevier Ltd. doi:10.1016/j.ijinfomgt.2019.05.003

Garrison, G., Wakefield, R. L., & Kim, S. (2015). The effects of IT capabilities and delivery model on cloud computing success and firm performance for cloud supported processes and operations. *International Journal of Information Management, 35*(4), 377–393. doi:10.1016/j.ijinfomgt.2015.03.001

Ghasemaghaei, M. (2021). Understanding the impact of big data on firm performance: The necessity of conceptually differentiating among big data characteristics. *International Journal of Information Management, 57*, 102055. doi:10.1016/j.ijinfomgt.2019.102055

Gupta, A., Deokar, A., Iyer, L., Sharda, R., & Schrader, D. (2018). Big Data & Analytics for Societal Impact: Recent Research and Trends. In Information Systems Frontiers (Vol. 20, Issue 2, pp. 185–194). Springer New York LLC. doi:10.100710796-018-9846-7

Gupta, S., Kar, A. K., Baabdullah, A., & Al-Khowaiter, W. A. A. (2018). Big data with cognitive computing: A review for the future. *International Journal of Information Management, 42*, 78–89. doi:10.1016/j.ijinfomgt.2018.06.005

Hair, J. F., Black, W. C., Babin, B. J., & Anderson, R. E. (2010). *Multivariate Data Analysis* (7th ed.). Prentice Hall.

Hair, J., Black, W., Babin, B. Y. A., Anderson, R., & Tatham, R. (2014). *Multivariate Data Analysis. A Global Perspective*. Pearson Prentice Hall.

Haryanto, B., Gandhi, A., & Giri Sucahyo, Y. (2020, November 3). The Determinant Factors in Utilizing Electronic Signature Using the TAM and TOE Framework. *2020 5th International Conference on Informatics and Computing, ICIC 2020*. 10.1109/ICIC50835.2020.9288623

Henseler, J., Ringle, C. M., & Sinkovics, R. R. (2009). The use of partial least squares path modeling in international marketing. *Advances in International Marketing*, *20*(1), 277–319. doi:10.1108/S1474-7979(2009)0000020014

Hiran, K. K., & Henten, A. (2020). An Integrated TOE-DoI Framework for Cloud Computing Adoption in Higher Education: The Case of Sub-Saharan Africa, Ethiopia. *Advances in Intelligent Systems and Computing*, *1053*, 1281–1290. doi:10.1007/978-981-15-0751-9_117

Jagadish, H. V. (2015). Big Data and Science: Myths and Reality. In Big Data Research (Vol. 2, Issue 2, pp. 49–52). Elsevier Inc. doi:10.1016/j.bdr.2015.01.005

Jin, X., Wah, B. W., Cheng, X., & Wang, Y. (2015). Significance and Challenges of Big Data Research. *Big Data Research*, *2*(2), 59–64. doi:10.1016/j.bdr.2015.01.006

Kamble, S., Gunasekaran, A., & Arha, H. (2019). Understanding the Blockchain technology adoption in supply chains-Indian context. *International Journal of Production Research*, *57*(7), 2009–2033. doi:10.1080/00207543.2018.1518610

Kline, R. B. (2015). *Principles and practice of structural equation modeling*. Guilford publications.

Kline, R. B. (2011). *Principles and practice of structural equation modeling* (3rd ed.). Guilford Press.

Kumar, A., & Krishnamoorthy, B. (2020). Business Analytics Adoption in Firms: A Qualitative Study Elaborating TOE Framework in India. *International Journal of Global Business and Competitiveness*, *15*(2), 80–93. doi:10.100742943-020-00013-5

Kwon, O., Lee, N., & Shin, B. (2014). Data quality management, data usage experience and acquisition intention of big data analytics. *International Journal of Information Management*, *34*(3), 387–394. doi:10.1016/j.ijinfomgt.2014.02.002

Mahakittikun, T., Suntrayuth, S., & Bhatiasevi, V. (2020). The impact of technological-organizational-environmental (TOE) factors on firm performance: Merchant's perspective of mobile payment from Thailand's retail and service firms. *Journal of Asia Business Studies*. Advance online publication. doi:10.1108/JABS-01-2020-0012

Mukherjee, S., & Chittipaka, V. (2021). Analysing the adoption of intelligent agent technology in food supply chain management: an empirical evidence. FIIB Business Review, 23197145211059243.

Mukherjee, S., Chittipaka, V., & Baral, M. M. (2022). Addressing and Modeling the Challenges Faced in the Implementation of Blockchain Technology in the Food and Agriculture Supply Chain: A Study Using TOE Framework. In Blockchain Technologies and Applications for Digital Governance (pp. 151-179). IGI Global.

Moerdyk, A. (2009). *The principles and practice of psychological assessment*. Van Schaik.

Nam, D. W., Kang, D., & Kim, S. H. (2015). Process of big data analysis adoption: Defining big data as a new IS innovation and examining factors affecting the process. *Proceedings of the Annual Hawaii International Conference on System Sciences, 2015-March*, 4792–4801. 10.1109/HICSS.2015.569

Nam, K., Dutt, C. S., Chathoth, P., Daghfous, A., & Khan, M. S. (2020). The adoption of artificial intelligence and robotics in the hotel industry: Prospects and challenges. *Electronic Markets*. Advance online publication. doi:10.100712525-020-00442-3

Narmetta, M., & Krishnan, S. (2020). Competitiveness, Change Readiness, and ICT Development: An Empirical Investigation of TOE Framework for Poverty Alleviation. *IFIP Advances in Information and Communication Technology, 618*, 638–649. doi:10.1007/978-3-030-64861-9_55

Nasrollahi, M., Ramezani, J., Sadraei, M., & Research, S. (2020). The Impact of Big Data Adoption on SMEs Performance. *Elsevier*, 1–12. doi:10.21203/rs.3.rs-66047/v1

Ngah, A. H., Zainuddin, Y., & Thurasamy, R. (2017). Applying the TOE framework in the Halal warehouse adoption study. *Journal of Islamic Accounting and Business Research, 8*(2), 161–181. doi:10.1108/JIABR-04-2014-0014

Nunnally, J. C., & Bernstein, I. H. (1994). *Psychometric theory* (3rd ed.). McGraw-Hill.

Pal, S. K., Mukherjee, S., Baral, M. M., & Aggarwal, S. (2021). Problems of Big Data Adoption in the Healthcare Industries. *Asia Pacific Journal of Health Management, 16*(4), 282–287.

Park, J.-H., Kim, M.-K., & Paik, J.-H. (2015). The Factors of Technology, Organization and Environment Influencing the Adoption and Usage of Big Data in Korean Firms. *26th European Regional Conference of the International Telecommunications Society (ITS): "What Next for European Telecommunications?* www.econstor.eu

Pateli, A., Mylonas, N., & Spyrou, A. (2020). Organizational Adoption of Social Media in the Hospitality Industry: An Integrated Approach Based on DIT and TOE Frameworks. *Sustainability, 12*(17), 7132. doi:10.3390u12177132

Podsakoff, P. M., MacKenzie, S. B., Lee, J. Y., & Podsakoff, N. P. (2003). Common method biases in behavioral research: A critical review of the literature and recommended remedies. *The Journal of Applied Psychology, 88*(5), 879–903. doi:10.1037/0021-9010.88.5.879 PMID:14516251

Predicting User's Web Navigation behaviour using AMD and HMM Approaches. In IOP Conference Series: Materials Science and Engineering (Vol. 1074, No. 1, p. 012031). IOP Publishing.

Priyadarshinee, P., Raut, R. D., Jha, M. K., & Gardas, B. B. (2017). Understanding and predicting the determinants of cloud computing adoption: A two staged hybrid SEM - Neural networks approach. *Computers in Human Behavior, 76*, 341–362. doi:10.1016/j.chb.2017.07.027

Priyadarshinee, P., Raut, R. D., Jha, M. K., & Kamble, S. S. (2017). A cloud computing adoption in Indian SMEs: Scale development and validation approach. *The Journal of High Technology Management Research, 28*(2), 221–245. doi:10.1016/j.hitech.2017.10.010

Ramaswamy, H. G. H. D. R. (2015). Journal of Enterprise Information Management Understanding determinants of cloud computing adoption using an integrated TAM-TOE model. *Journal of Enterprise Information Management, 28*(1), 107–130. doi:10.1108/JEIM-08-2013-0065

Ranjan, J., & Foropon, C. (2021). Big Data Analytics in Building the Competitive Intelligence of Organizations. *International Journal of Information Management, 56*, 102231. doi:10.1016/j.ijinfomgt.2020.102231

Rogers, E. M. (2010). *Diffusion of innovations*. Simon and Schuster.

Salleh, K. A., & Janczewski, L. (2016). Technological, Organizational and Environmental Security and Privacy Issues of Big Data: A Literature Review. *Procedia Computer Science, 100*, 19–28. doi:10.1016/j.procs.2016.09.119

Senyo, P. K., Effah, J., & Addae, E. (2016). Preliminary insight into cloud computing adoption in a developing country. *Journal of Enterprise Information Management, 29*(4), 505–524. doi:10.1108/JEIM-09-2014-0094

Shahbaz, M., Gao, C., Zhai, L. L., Shahzad, F., & Hu, Y. (2019). Investigating the adoption of big data analytics in healthcare: The moderating role of resistance to change. *Journal of Big Data*, *6*(1), 6. doi:10.118640537-019-0170-y

Shin, D. H. (2016). Demystifying big data: Anatomy of big data developmental process. *Telecommunications Policy*, *40*(9), 837–854. doi:10.1016/j.telpol.2015.03.007

Skafi, M., Yunis, M. M., & Zekri, A. (2020). Factors influencing SMEs' adoption of cloud computing services in Lebanon: An empirical analysis using TOE and contextual theory. *IEEE Access: Practical Innovations, Open Solutions*, *8*, 79169–79181. doi:10.1109/ACCESS.2020.2987331

Sun, S., Cegielski, C. G., Jia, L., & Hall, D. J. (2018). Understanding the Factors Affecting the Organizational Adoption of Big Data. In Journal of Computer Information Systems (Vol. 58, Issue 3, pp. 193–203). Taylor and Francis Inc. doi: 10.1080/08874417.2016.1222891

Tashkandi, A. A., & Al-Jabri, I. (2015). Cloud Computing Adoption by Higher Education Institutions in Saudi Arabia: Analysis Based on TOE. *2015 International Conference on Cloud Computing, ICCC 2015*, 1–8. 10.1109/CLOUDCOMP.2015.7149634

Tien, E. L., Ali, N. M., Miskon, S., Ahmad, N., & Abdullah, N. S. (2020). Big data analytics adoption model for malaysian smes. *Advances in Intelligent Systems and Computing*, *1073*, 45–53. doi:10.1007/978-3-030-33582-3_5

Verma, S. (2017). The adoption of big data services by manufacturing firms: An empirical investigation in India. *Journal of Information Systems and Technology Management*, *14*(1), 39–68. doi:10.4301/S1807-17752017000100003

Verma, S., & Bhattacharyya, S. S. (2017). Perceived strategic value-based adoption of Big Data Analytics in emerging economy: A qualitative approach for Indian firms. *Journal of Enterprise Information Management*, *30*(3), 354–382. doi:10.1108/JEIM-10-2015-0099

Verma, S., Bhattacharyya, S. S., & Kumar, S. (2018). An extension of the technology acceptance model in the big data analytics system implementation environment. *Information Processing & Management*, *54*(5), 791–806. doi:10.1016/j.ipm.2018.01.004

Voola, R., Casimir, G., Carlson, J., & Anushree Agnihotri, M. (2012). The effects of market orientation, technological opportunism, and e-business adoption on performance: A moderated mediation analysis. *Australasian Marketing Journal*, *20*(2), 136–146. doi:10.1016/j.ausmj.2011.10.001

Wamba, S. F., & Queiroz, M. M. (2020). Blockchain in the operations and supply chain management: Benefits, challenges and future research opportunities. In *International Journal of Information Management* (Vol. 52, p. 102064). Elsevier Ltd. doi:10.1016/j.ijinfomgt.2019.102064

Wong, L.-W., Tan, G. W.-H., Lee, V.-H., Ooi, K.-B., & Sohal, A. (2020). Unearthing the determinants of Blockchain adoption in supply chain management. *International Journal of Production Research, 58*(7), 2100–2123. doi:10.1080/00207543.2020.1730463

Yadegaridehkordi, E., Hourmand, M., Nilashi, M., Shuib, L., Ahani, A., & Ibrahim, O. (2018). Influence of big data adoption on manufacturing companies' performance: An integrated DEMATEL-ANFIS approach. *Technological Forecasting and Social Change, 137*, 199–210. doi:10.1016/j.techfore.2018.07.043

Yadegaridehkordi, E., Nilashi, M., Shuib, L., Hairul Nizam Bin Md Nasir, M., Asadi, S., Samad, S., & Fatimah Awang, N. (2020). The impact of big data on firm performance in hotel industry. *Electronic Commerce Research and Applications, 40*, 100921. Advance online publication. doi:10.1016/j.elerap.2019.100921

Chapter 3
Financial Market Infrastructure and Implementation of Blockchain Technology:
A Critical Review for Managing Operational Risk

Kiran Jameel
https://orcid.org/0000-0002-6206-8997
Institute of Business and Management, Pakistan

Asim Rafiq
Hamdard University, Pakistan

ABSTRACT

Blockchain is very crucial for paving new ways for how economies will function in the future, as it helps in eliminating intermediaries and thus saving time and cost. Various important uses of this new blockchain technology have been highlighted, but research and practice are still in their formative phases. The core objective of this study is to describe the impact of blockchain on existing and novel business prototypes while managing operational risk. Consequently, the authors pinpoint five similarities that improve the understanding of how blockchain technology affects current financial structure and creates new business models. This research suggested using these findings to ascertain further designs initiated by blockchain and how firms can use it to revolutionize its business model. Though there are many favorable uses of this new technology, inquiry and established procedures are still in their embryonic stages, which means it will take some time before blockchain's impact is felt on a larger scale.

DOI: 10.4018/978-1-7998-7642-7.ch003

1. INTRODUCTION

The curiosity with Block chain in the financial industry has resulted in an endless number of meetings among Block chain and fintech pioneers. Everyone is investigating into several alternatives for this technology. In his key Manor House lecture in June 2016, Imprint Carney, the Bank of Britain's Lead Representative, acknowledged the concept. (Carney, 2016), and In June 2016, the Central Bank introduced block chain innovation defenders to agents from 90 national banks. (Blade, 2016). Currently, block chain innovation seems to have a strong trend. In this section, we discuss the financial world's method can lead in Block chain innovation, the attributes of the technology that are being acclaimed as ground-breaking, and the benefits that the financial sector seeks to attain by implementing it.

Since 2015, the financial industry has been captivated with Block chain, resulting in the development of RE3CV, a consortium of 70 financial banks. The Linux Foundation, in collaboration with IBM and Digital Asset Holding, has recently launched program called Hyper Ledger to develop standard Block Chain technologies. Block chain technologies are also being explored by the Bank of England in partnership with the Big Four (Accounting Firms). All of the world's largest financial and technology institutions (public and private) have collaborated to recognize the potential benefits of block chain in the future. Numerous books promoting the transformational implications of block chain have emerged from the anticipation but also prospect of this technology. The majority of stakeholders are strong believers in block chain gains, with only a small number of detractors.

1.1 Block chain technology

The block chain seems to have a set of characteristics which thus make it essential for modern financial institutions. The following are the main features that are deemed building blocks of modern finance;

1. Immutability
2. Trustlessness
3. Transparency
4. Resilience

All of the aforementioned characteristics get one commonality: reliability. In this section, the scholars explore all these attributes thoroughly to see how it might assist in the development of cost - effective global financial framework.

1.1.1 Immutability

Nothing can be changed once it has been recorded because block chain functionality is irreversible. Financial transactions are executed immediately even without the possibility of human error. However, in conventional financial practices, the immutability component loses its attractiveness since there are faults and malfunctions that must be rectified. Accenture (Financial Consulting Firm) has intended to trademark "Editable Block chain" while keeping practical restrictions in mind, which has caused controversy from defenders of Public Block chain.

1.1.2 Trustlessness

Block chain technology reduces need for a third party to authorize financial transactions, making the system self-sufficient and entirely autonomous of external factors. Consequently, the peer-to-peer process eliminates intermediaries, making the ledger self-sufficient. This concept appeals the researchers because trustworthiness should be at the core of all financial systems. The block chain technology would be seen as a solution to the contemporary financial difficulties since it eliminates the uncertainties of counterparty. But don't forget that it's the component of 'Trust' that will ultimately lead developers and users to switch from a third party to a block chain.

1.1.3 Transparency

Traditional Block chains, such as Ethereum and Bitcoin, make the ledger accessible to all network users, making it entirely transparent. It allows multiple parties to monitor the ledger in real time, placed strategically to make better decisions. Simultaneous access lends credibility to this system. Uncertainty is fully eliminated when transactions are settled instantly. Some promoters of block chains argue that if they had been in place at the time of the financial crisis in 2007, it could have been mitigated. Regulators would have been notified of the current situation in real time and may have taken appropriate action, halting the tide of solvency and financial disaster.

1.1.4 Resilience

Following the financial crisis of 2009, there was an immediate need for a financial system overhaul. Slight glitches in a system can lead in a worldwide financial collapse. In recent years, the financial system's cyber security has been hacked, placing multinational corporations, countries, and even SWIFT in threat (Society for

Worldwide Interbank Financial Telecommunication). This is where the 'resilience' of Block chain comes into the equation, attracting all global financial regulators.

Reliability is the essential to block chain success. More trustworthiness leads to an increased reliance, culminating in a more speedy and efficient financial system. The risk for settlement will be eliminated, and instant clearing will strengthen the financial structure. All of these measures will lead to significant cost reductions for all parties involved in a financial cycle. However, in global financial institutions, Block chain is anticipated to be used in a variety of financial instruments, including stocks, bonds and derivatives instruments.

1.2 Operational Risk and FMIs

Before assessing the operational risk associated with open source block chains, it's essential to first comprehend what a financial system is and how critical block chains are to future financial stability. Monetary market frameworks are "multilateral frameworks are utilized for the reason for clearing, settling, or recording installments, protections, subordinates or other monetary exchanges" which "incorporates installment frameworks, focal protection stores, focal counter parties, and exchange vaults." (Central bank, 2016, p. 3)

Regulators are working together to mitigate the significant risks posed by financial system operations. Although the government and regulators are striving to eliminate various risks such as liquidity risk, credit risk, and custody risk, they also must focus on operational risk if the block chain would be established itself with a legitimate medium for future finance. Operating risk, according to the Federal Reserve, is the risk of anomalies in information systems or internal processes resulting in the erosion or failure of financial market infrastructure. The commonly accepted guidelines for mitigating the operational risk of FMIs are mostly incompatible with block chain technology. Because human involvement carries the risk of inaccuracy, it can jeopardize the entire assumption of block chains' impenetrable reliability. If financial markets rely on existing block chain technologies, they will be exposed to a new type of operational risk. Regardless of the numerous benefits of block chain in basic innovation of FMIs, it can open the path for this type of operational risk.

1.3 Open-Source Operational Risks of Public Block Chains

Block chain is essential for building new infrastructure for how economies will perform in the future. Since it seeks to eliminate intermediaries and time and cost effective. Several potential advantages of this new block chain technology have been recognized, but research and application are still in their initial stages. In this section, the authors studied the influence of block chain on existing and innovative business models. Beside, recognized five parallels that help and better comprehend how block chain technology affects existing financial institutions and generates new business models. However, organizations can be encouraged to use these observations and discover more about block chain process and how they can be used to transform their company strategies. Despite the numerous positive aspects of this new technology, research and established procedures are still in their infancy. As a consequently, it would be some period even before effects of block chain are realized on a greater scale. The fundamental goal of the monetary world is substantial, definite, and robust frameworks, and many consider that block chain innovation meets the need for a tool for record safeguarding frameworks that hold a lot of account information (Kaminska, 2016). Whatever the case may be, it is still unclear whether this expedition has come to an abrupt end. As block chain development accelerates, a critical decision must be taken about whether public or private block chains will be used to alter the universe of accounts. In late 2016, SEC Chair Mary Jo White stated that the SEC is closely monitoring whether block chain technology used in the financial sector would be permitted (White, 2016), indicating that the argument between distributed and regulated block chains is still ongoing.

This study contributes to the public-versus-private block chain argument by explaining how open block chain' use of traditional open-source technology would expose any monetary market frameworks if they moved to a new block chain system. Potentially growing operational risks in exchange for the attractive benefits they claim. All of the enhancements we make come with trade-offs, and the additional operational risks look to be substantial in this circumstance.

The authors look into a number of operational risks involved with using typical open-source programming in the formation and implementation of decentralized block chains. The following are some of the risks and techniques that are investigated;

1) The risk of impeded vibrant modifications to product code as a result of adopting the conventional informal grassroots open-source software design approach.
2) Since inadequate or risk management, there seems to be a possibility that the product will be inadequately managed.
3) Funding for the initial stages of development and management, as with many other public block chain ventures, is anticipated.
4) Risk: Because of the standard act of forking open source programming to roll out desirable modifications to it, that product (and the block chain and many designs based on it) forks, resulting in broken block chain networks.

There is no doubt that public block chains have considerable operational risks, since they've been analyzed by a number of researchers (Kiran and Stannett, 2014;

Peters et al., 2014; Walch, 2015). This investigation extended the operational risks posed by Bitcoin as public block chain programming (Walch, 2015).

Prior to bouncing into the examination, a concise introduction on open-source programming is altogether. It is programming for which the basic unit of block chain (i.e., the piece of the code that is discernible by people) is prepared openly accessible to everyone. Recognized from exclusive programming, on behalf of which the proprietor of the cryptograph doesn't create the source code accessible, and the proprietor places restrictions thus limiting its accessibility of the code network. Open-source programming accompanies a bunch of meaningful opportunities: "the rights to get to the source code, alter the program, and reallocate it, either in its unique or on the other hand altered structure."

Different practices from the public block chain programming will be clarified as we dissect them in the subsections underneath. Nonetheless, one significant qualification underlies the whole investigation: regardless of whether an decentralized project is (a) started and run by a free arrangement of programming engineers (now and then called an "self-governing" decentralized public block chain project(West and O'Mahoney, 2008), There is an array of block chain systems on which diverse distributed public block chain projects lie, conventional open source project are on the one side of the range (where command and force are shunned), while commercial public block chain is at the opposite end (where control and force are unequivocal).

1.3.1 Vulnerable Decision-Making and Grassroots Open-Source Software Development Practices

It has already been mentioned that solid administration arrangements are seen as fundamental for FMIs. This bodes well for anything viewed as basic to worldwide monetary security. On the off chance that something turns out badly with a FMI, a reasonable levels of leadership is alluring to decide rapidly, and with responsibility. This is a fundamental precept of the common understanding – that administration organizations arise, and that with important and critical matters, clearness on duty is critical. It is the reason why there is a long, clear line of progression for the workplace of Leader of the US, and why we demand a reasonable hierarchy of leadership and distinct conventions in the armed forces, law enforcement agencies and local groups of fire-fighters, clinics, atomic reactors and force plants.

Public block chains utilize a totally different administration model: the product improvement measure usually used to create and keep up basic distributed programming. It will be discussed here as to how this product improvement (administration) model obstructs the consensus building regarding alterations to the block chain's product design. Initially, a short outline regarding product advancement cycle of basic decentralized block chain programming is important.

1.3.2 Decentralized software governance

Block chain is considered revolutionary as it is not controlled by few; instead everyone connected to the block chain network has his stake in the system. There is no single custodian that controls the Block chain system. Decentralized block chains are divided in two tiers. In the first place, the organization of exchange developers and mangers that keeps up the record is decentralized, and anybody on the planet may unreservedly access this organization of PCs without requiring authorization. Secondly, and more significantly, the administration of the product code that involves public block chains is additionally decentralized and open to all. With public block chains, these code changes happen through the endeavors of a group of programming engineers indistinctly coordinated under a design specifically utilized for public block chain programming. Public block chains are for the most part worked with open-source programming. The administration cycle of open-source programming is broadly casual, with the coders who really settle on choices about changes to the code (known as center designers) bit by bit ascending to the highest point of the administration pyramid dependent on their standing and execution. The coders of decentralized public block chain projects don't work for a solitary association, also, the gathering of coders dealing with an open-source task might be very liquid. What's more, selections regarding the programming desgin are made dependent on "arbitrary consensus" as opposed to official voting process. Further, with decentralized projects, coders for the most part work voluntarily, to a great extent on the grounds that there is no business or organization there to pay them.

This has been the overall programming advancement model utilized with public block chains, especially with Bitcoin. It merits thoroughly considering the ramifications of this administration model, especially with regards to a public block chain supporting monetary market framework (or on the other hand some other basic public framework, truly). To begin with, in this model, nobody has the authority obligation regarding keeping the product operational (Walch, 2015).

Moreover, under the decentralized administration system, nobody is responsible for making choices for the organization. It has been contended already: "As there is no characterized force or responsibility structure, nobody needs to pay attention to any other person's thoughts regarding how to determine an emergency. This implies that anybody with a recommended goal to an emergency may only propose an arrangement, yet it might take too long to even think about accomplishing purchase in from different individuals from the local area to effectively carry out the arrangement in a crisis circumstance. We see this kind of contention generally made in banters over the constraints of the chief force of the Leader of the US, who may have to act rapidly in emergency without hanging tight for explicit authority from Congress." (Walch, 2015, p. 871)

Lastly, this shapeless administration system can prompt unrecognized monopolization of force, bringing about unapproachable or unchecked force. The center engineers of public block chains are more impressive than the typical engineers on these tasks. In Bitcoin, for example, few center engineers are the solitary individuals who have all time access to really alter the basic code. Additionally, they are considered as the voice of the block chain through their associations with the media, controllers, and others in the block chain biological system, as their proposals and experiences are viewed as pertinent and significant to the fate of the material block chain. With exactly assigned force, it is clear what activities one can and can't take, however with shapeless forces, the restrictions of force are haphazard (The unapproachable force that can emerge in these structures is, unexpectedly, precisely what these open frameworks were intended to battle against, as they are responses to the shut programming advancement measure for exclusive programming.) These situations depicted in this paper can either deaden or defer basic choices about the product code, imperiling all constructions based on top of it. Without a doubt, a banter is continuous in the public block chain world over which programming changes ought to be thought of simply specialized against those considered more philosophical, and these discussions make the potential for programming forks, as explained in detail in the following section .Besides, in the event that somebody goes about as though her or she has authority (like Vitalik Buterin of Ethereum), there is a possibility that the choice won't get purchase in from the block chain local area, again conceivably prompting forks in the code and block chain. Likewise with law, change is important to all products with the goal for it to keep on being valuable. On the off chance that a programming administration measure creates loss of motion, the product can't improve or conform to strike, however the standard grassroots open-source programming improvement measure shows up excessively far along the range of (ostensibly) circulated ability to administer basic frameworks like monetary market foundations. Ethereum, another public block chain, has too changed administration, depending intensely on organizer Vitalik Buterin to manage the direction of the project. Given that the worldwide principles for monetary market frameworks express that "FMIs ought to have administration plans that are clear and straightforward, advance the wellbeing and productivity of the FMI, and backing the strength of the more extensive monetary framework, other significant public interest contemplations, and the goals of applicable partners." (PFMI, 2012, p. 1)

1.3.3 Inadequate Software Maintenance and Problematic Open-Source Funding Model

It is commonly recognized that financing basic public block chain programming improvement is troublesome, as it depends on developers to add to the code without recompense, or then again to discover alternate source of financing that may bring up irreconcilable issues. It will be investigated how depending on the customary decentralized programming improvement model to store decentralized block chains opens them to the operational danger of lacking thoughtfulness regarding programming upkeep and advancement, or to specific interests molding the direction of these public designs. As cited earlier, one of the commended traits of decentralized programming is that those who foster the product code for the most part do as such without remuneration. This is essential for the philosophy of the open-source programming development, and it has been fruitful with numerous kinds of programming after the 2014 revelation of the calamitous Heart bleed virus in Open SSL (a decentralized programming). A gathering of innovation organizations framed the Center Foundation Drive to well support the advancement of basic decentralized programming projects. Many decentralized programming ventures are equipped with couple of dynamic engineers, when a significantly more considerable devoted group of coders is expected to enough keep up the product (Wheeler and Khakimov, 2015). Poor consideration regarding the code over the long run improves the probability that viruses to be detected almost negligible, so no repairs are made. The Center Framework Drive is raising finances from its individuals to pay engineers on different open-source projects that are considered to have a basic need. Mozilla, a noticeable organization that keeps up certain decentralized programming like the Firefox internet browser, as of late shaped the Protected Open Source ('SOS') task to give financial support to increment the safety of chose open-source projects. This drive expanded a 2015 Mozilla research project, that elaborates studying of network safety specialists about key dangers to online protection.

Viruses keep on being set up in basic open-source projects, including the basic weakness named "Filthy Cow" found in the Linux piece in October 2016. Bitcoin was prepared as free decentralized programming by the unknown "Satoshi Nakamoto" as early as 2008/2009, but initially it was of no importance to the general population. Starting with a local area of one (the maker), it bit by bit and it acquired boundless consideration around 2013. Furthermore, the cryptographic money traded on the Bitcoin block chain had little incentive for a foreseeable future, just progressively moving from a couple of pennies for every bitcoin to a couple of dollars, to its blast in appreciation in 2013. The programming needed to run as expected every minute of every day, and coders needed to react to emergencies on a crisis in this strategic framework. Obviously, it got outlandish for key designers to run a consistently on crucial framework as a neglected side interest. Seeing the requirement for devoted thoughtfulness regarding the code, organizations inside the Bitcoin environment (e.g., BitPay, Blockstream) started paying some center engineers. A few non-benefits (Bitcoin Establishment, MIT) additionally ventured up to support the engineers. The various ways to deal with the issue of financing open-source programming improvement are imaginative, yet more investigation into the ramifications of the financing strategies, just as their strength over the long haul, is required. If designers are attached to a specific source of funding, quite possibly the engineers will be affected by individuals who are paying them, instead of interests of individuals dependent on the block chain. This is tricky in a public design like a public block chain, especially on the off chance that it comes to lie beneath the monetary market foundations or other basic frameworks. As examined in this subsection, the utilization of decentralized public block chain programming subsidizing techniques makes operational dangers for public block chains, which contrarily sway their appropriateness to support monetary market foundations. Public block chains that have been presented, since Bitcoin acquired standard acknowledgment, trying not to have similar opportunity to commit unseen errors in their infancy. This implies that anticipating that developers should run these frameworks free of charge in their extra time is a critical danger. Acknowledgment of this issue has brought forth imaginative ways to finance the product designers for Bitcoin and other public block chains. This proposed prototype has drawn attention of protections lawyers, who fear that the launching of crypto currencies without regulation may disregard the protections laws (Byrne, 2016).

1.3.4 Fractured Networks Caused and Open-Source Software Forking Practices

Finally, I will shed some light on the concept of "Forking" related to block chain. Anyone familiar with block chain knows the fact that block chain can "Fork" into two separate networks. For instance Ethereum forked into two separate codes in 2016.According to Nyman forking is, 'it is duplicating of a current program and propagating a parallel version of it'. (Nyman, 2015, p. 1). Public accessibility of source code means it can be altered by anybody who is connect to the public block chain, which implies open source code can be "Forked" anytime by anyone. This is entirely different from the regulated codes which are very difficult to alter or reprogram by anyone. Only the proprietor has the right to do so. There is no mechanism to safeguard open source codes from Forking. (Nyman, 2015, p. 1, original emphasis.)

According to Nyman forking has both pros and cons for the block chain system. Forking of some prominent ventures like GNU/Linux or MySQL, are almost negligible, but the resulting impacts are significant in appraising the functioning risk of open Block chains. With block chain forking not only code changes but it affects the entire network so forking can have a significant impact on overall functioning of Block chain.

Block chain in fact," Distributed Ledger Technology (DLT)" has transformed the way of economic activity. Block chains can used to ensure transparency and traceability. Eventually saving time and cost related mediators. DLT also makes the mediators almost redundant. Most popular example of Block chain technology is crypto currency, such as Bitcoin. It took some time for the businesses to embrace Bitcoin and to realize that it will prove disruptive for the existing business practices.

It is established that Block chain technology has many other uses and functions other than just currencies. When we look at a broader uses of block chain as a facilitator of business connectivity meaning virtually markets that are collectively owned by everybody integrated to the system, implemented as "Distributed Autonomous Organizations (DAO)" (Diedrich 2016). This development will redefine the roles of player related to finance, making them almost redundant if not extinct.

Block chains will lead to many financial and economic changes, for instance collective economy and the cyclical economy. It is time that scientist should shift their focus from block chain frenzy to its core utilization. Help people realize block chain's enormous potential, including the potential to unsettle the conventional business structures, but there is a dire need to focus on operational side challenges ahead. It is important to meet these challenges so that scalable, reliable and secure public block chain is maintained. (Roger w.h bons, 2020)

1.3.5 March 2013 Bitcoin Hard Fork

Bitcoin had its first hard fork in March 2013 resulting in tow disparate code networks. Meaning two parallel yet perfect systems were running for the coding of block chain for Bitcoin. This resulted due to different programs used by coders.

It was hard to differentiate if tokens on the network were Bitcoins or something else. The threat was detected at earliest and engineers and coders successfully maneuvered everybody back onto a similar chain. It was done by requesting the "Big Fish" (large holder of Bitcoins) to surrender their rights and claims relinquishing their claims helped programmers to bring everybody back to single block chain.

"Threat of Hard forks needs to be eliminated in order to maintain smooth and efficient functioning of crypto currencies in daily transaction usage," says trump. He thinks that are Hard fork are main hurdles of crypto currencies development Few more changes to the coding platform and advancement of technology it is possible to reduce the recurrence of Hard Forks. (Heidelberg, a reliable crypto currency needs good governance, 2018)

1.3.6 Bitcoin Block Size Discussion

All the stakeholders related to Bitcoin have had a very hard experience of March 2013 hard fork. It has raised many red flags, making investors, coders and programmers all worried. It is believed that events like "Forking" are essential for the scalability of the crypto currency. At the same time making it more prone to operational and systematic risks, making the system more complex and fragile. Size of the Block chain must be determined purely on technical basis keeping in mind all the specifications of Block chain. But it seems that its size is determined by political reasons rather than technical. The Bitcoin was designed and developed keeping in mind the all-inclusive principal, making it as much decentralized as much possible. Decentralization is the basic principal on which entire Bitcoin structure was programmed and developed. On the other hand there are many whole believe that over all block chain system must be fluid and dynamic. It means it should evolve with time, keeping in mind the technical considerations. This dichotomy of views has led to heated debate between the two factions. Many famous coders and engineers have surrendered the Bitcoin in pursuit of reaching an agreement. But majority of the efforts have gone in vain and no consensus has been reached. Situation is similar to a societal friction where one group advocates ideological immutability while the other group consider change is the only way forward. Bitcoin stakeholders seems to be struck between its founding principles and future prospects. Revamping of existing system is inevitable yet it seems next to impossible. Changes to the system will result in fragmentation of the entire block chain resulting in deterioration of the system. System might weaken to point where it is rendered useless.

1.3.7 July 2016 Ethereum Hard Fork

Same hard fork event was repeated throughout the Mid of 2016. This time it was Ethereum not Bitcoin which was under attack. DAO (Decentralized autonomous Organization) was launched in 2016 and raised its capital through crowd funding. But soon after its launch it was hacked and almost one third of the funds amounting $ 60 million were siphoned off from the system Since DAO existed as set of contracts on Ethereum Block chain it had no formal management structure. The Ethereum developers had to face two important predicaments. Firstly, the vulnerability of existing system was exposed by the hack attack which was to be corrected immediately in order to make sure system runs smoothly and the users do not lose their trust on DAO. Second was to design and launch second version of Ethereum Block Chain. In this way developers will be able to retrieve the hacked coins (Ethers) and bring them back on the chain. This step lead to undesired change on Ethereum Block chain which founders of Ethereum had never imagined. So, eventually it lead to the bifurcation of Ethereum into two separate Block chains. First one was the new version running on newly developed Block chain tagged as Ethereum while the second which was running on the original block chain was branded as Ethereum Classic.

At last, the splitting of block chain vulnerability is confounded more in open block chains through the 51% Attack hazard. Block chains, as of now organized, are helpless against the danger that members in the exchange handling (mining) organization could hoard choices about the way of the organization, including possibly receiving new types of programming, amending past passages on the block chain. This is on the grounds that whatever 51% of the exchange preparing network chooses to perform, is executed, as the organizations faces greater part rule where majority of coders can dictate and execute accordingly. The weakness of an organization to a majority rule assault can increment quickly following a split, as the executing and controlling power previously dedicated to the single block chain network gets parted between the two disparate block chains.

1.3.8 Lessons learned

The issues of HARD FORK uncovers various significant realities about open block chains, and in this subsection, I think about what these scenes can instruct us. In the first place, the 2013 fork in the Bitcoin block chain exhibits that new programming discharges can prompt cracked organizations. A fork into isolated block chains can happen when another delivery is contradictory with prior discharges, and, on the grounds that there are no constrained programming refreshes in a public organization, it is highly unlikely to ensure that all individuals from the organization will move to the new form of the product in a convenient way.

Bitcoin fork in 2013 likewise uncovers that returning of forked block chains to initial block chain may need human synchronization (among the designers and the excavators), just as a readiness on the some portion of specific excavators to forfeit their profit on one block chain as a component of rejoining the other block chain.

Thirdly, hard fork of Bitcoin in 2013 and hacking of DAOs system of Ethereum in 2016 proves that the center designers of public block chains employ huge force in distinguishing and curing a block chain split. Stakeholders need to organize correspondences inside the mining organization, and impact which chain endures (albeit the presence of Ethereum Classic shows they can't really kill a contending chain).

Fourth, the size of the bitcoin block chain exhibits how the danger of a split organization can deaden a public block chain. Many miners in the Bitcoin system have come forward with different recommendations, showing that it is so hard to coerce an agreement on a dubious programming change.

Fifth, the hard fork of Ethereum in mid-2016 identified that with some amendments based on top of public block chains can impact choices about variations made to the basic block chain programming itself. In the case of DAO, different applications based on the Ethereum block chain were influenced by Ethereum's hard fork, despite the fact that the fork was driven by occasions related exclusively with the DAO.

Sixth, with the hack of DAO and the subsequent Ethereum hard fork clearly indicates that our human flaws can compromise the infallibility of product code that we compose. This brings up numerous issues, including commons ones like which of the fragmented chains to perceive and treat as authentic, and how legitimate rights and liabilities attached to measures based on top of the parent chain play out when the parent chain split into two chains. For example, which arrangement of exchanging accounts is real, when there are, out of nowhere, two parallel groups functioning simultaneously? The splitting of a block chain network is similar to a side project of an organization, which is an immensely intricate interaction requiring cautious regard for subtleties to guarantee that rights and commitments are suitably characterized and isolated. In this way, any frameworks working on open block chains, including monetary market frameworks, may have these complexities attached to them whenever they go through hard forks. As a consequence, diminishing any control these frameworks have over their danger openings.

For the framework to keep on having its credibility, everybody should stay on similar page. Running the product and taking an interest in the organization implies that one is focusing on remaining in total agreement as other organization members. (Thomas (2016) comparably investigates the issues raised by keeping a common state in block chains.) Splitting of block chain is inherent in public block chain technology. A public block chain's network unification (and whole incentive) is compromised each time a non-backwards compatible programming discharge is proposed by the organization. Every proposition for a hard fork is practically equivalent to requiring a limiting submission on withdrawal from the block chain. Albeit the public block chain programming model has been profoundly effective in numerous events, the forking plausibility may make it inadmissible for public block chains. At the point when we imply to install genuine worth or records of gathering occasions in block chain innovation, it becomes subjectively not quite the same as other programming

1.4 Reflections

In the end we would like to discuss certain problems lined with open source soft wares build for public block chains. Highlighting the importance of uninterrupted operations for global financial stability. Even with some changes mentioned in this paper, public block chains functions very differently from our expectations and as outlined before the open source software practices linked with public block chains are completely opposite to the more regulated practices prevalent in High stake areas.

We need to rethink the usage of open source soft wares as it performs many functions in our societies. We might be in a process of discovering why these systems have not been used for critical public practices.

To open source software advocates, these findings may be viewed as fighting words. As it is as much as an ideology as it is a technical practice. In the end we must realize that unless we are able to question we cannot fully evaluate the benefits and functions of public block chains. Constant questioning and criticism will help us in using the underline block chain technology more responsibly and efficiently.

CONCLUSION

Since Block chain functioning is unchangeable, so nothing can be altered once recorded. Financial transactions are carried out instantly, free of human error. But in prevalent financial practices immutability aspect loses its charm as there are errors and malfunction that needs to be corrected. Keeping practical limitations in mind, the issues of HARD FORK uncovered various significant realities about open block chains. A fork into isolated block chains can happen when another delivery is contradictory with prior discharges and on the grounds that there are no constrained programming refreshes in a public organization, it is highly unlikely to ensure that all individuals from the organization will move to the new form of the product in a convenient way. Block chain is considered revolutionary as it is not controlled by few; instead everyone connected to the block chain network has his stake in the system. There is no single custodian that controls the Block chain system. This study further concluded that decentralized block chains are divided in two tiers. In the first place, the organization of exchange developers and mangers that keeps up the record is decentralized, and anybody on the planet may unreservedly access this organization of PCs without requiring authorization. Secondly, and more significantly, the administration of the product code that involves public block chains is additionally decentralized and open to all. This research suggested that using these findings to ascertain further designs initiated by block chain and how firms can use it to revolutionize its business model. Though there are many favorable uses of this new technology, inquiry and established procedures are still in its embryonic stage. Which means it will take some time before block chain impacts are felt on a larger scale.

REFERENCES

Angelis, S. D., Aniello, L., Baldoni, R., Lombardi, F., Margheri, A., & Sassone, V. (2018). PBFTvs proof-of-authority: applying the CAP theorem to permissioned blockchain. *Italian Conference on Cyber Security*, 1–11.

Ante, L. (2020). A place next to Satoshi: Foundations of blockchain and cryptocurrency research in business and economics. *Scientometrics*, *124*(2), 1305–1333. doi:10.100711192-020-03492-8

Bitcoin.org. (2016). *Bitcoin Developer Guide*. Available from: https://bitcoin.org/en/developer-guide

Bons, R. W., Versendaal, J., Zavolokina, L., & Shi, W. L. (2020). Potential and limits of Blockchain technology for networked businesses. *Electronic Markets*, *30*(2), 189–194. doi:10.100712525-020-00421-8

Burton, B., & Willis, D. (2016). *Gartner's 2016 Hype Cycles Highlight Digital Business Ecosystems*. www.gartner.com

Byrne, P. J. (2016). Against Tokens (and Token Crowdsales). *The Back of the Envelope*. Available from: https://prestonbyrne.com/2016/08/12/against-crowdsales/

Carney, M. (2016). *Enabling the FinTech Transformation: Revolution, Restoration, or Reformation?* [Speech that was to have been given by Mark Carney, Governor of the Bank of England at the Lord Mayor's Banquet for Bankers and Merchants of the City of London at the Mansion House, London]. Available from: http://www.bankofengland.co.uk/publications/Documents/speeches/2016/speech914.pdf

DTCC. (2016). *Embracing Disruption: Tapping the Potential of Distributed Ledgers to Improve the Post-Trade Landscape*. Available from: https://www.dtcc.com/news/2016/january/25/blockchain-white-paper

Eha, B. P. (2016). *MUFG Aims to use bitcoin to improve cross-border payments*. American Banker.

Federal Reserve. (2016). *Policy on Payment System Risk*. Available from: https://www.federalreserve.gov/ paymentsystems/files/psr_policy.pdf

Francois, C. (2015). *The Mozilla Cybersecurity Delphi 1.0: Towards a User-Centric Policy Framework*. Available from: https://blog.mozilla.org/netpolicy/files/2015/07/Mozilla-Cybersecurity-Delphi-1.0.pdf

Giancarlo, J. C. (2016). *Regulators and the Blockchain: First, Do No Harm*. Special Address of CFTC Commissioner J. Christopher Giancarlo Before the Depository Trust & Clearing Corporation 2016 Blockchain Symposium. Available from: https://www.cftc.gov/PressRoom/SpeechesTestimony/

Grassman, R., Bracamonte, V., Davis, M., & Sato, M. (2021). Attitudes to Cryptocurrencies: A Comparative Study Between Sweden and Japan. *Rev Socionetwork Strat, 15*(1), 169–194. doi:10.100712626-021-00069-6

Kaminska, I. (2016). Blockchain and the holy real-time settlement grail. *Financial Times*. Available from: https://ftalphaville.ft.com/2016/02/26/2154510/blockchain-and-the-holy-real-time-settlement-grail/

Kiran, M., & Stannett, M. (2014). *Bitcoin risk analysis*. NEMODE. Available from: http://www.nemode.ac.uk/ wp-content/uploads/2015/02/2015-Bit-Coin-risk-analysis.pdf

Liebi, L. J. (2021). Antony Lewis: The basics of bitcoins and blockchains. *Financial Markets and Portfolio Management, 35*(1), 145–147. doi:10.100711408-020-00374-0

Nofer, M., Gomber, P., Hinz, O., & Schiereck, D. (2017). Blockchain. *Business & Information Systems Engineering, 59*(3), 183–187. doi:10.100712599-017-0467-3

Nyman, L. (2015). *Understanding Code Forking in Open Source Software: An Examination of Code Forking, Its Effect on Open Source Software, and How It is Viewed and Practiced by Developers* [Ph.D. Thesis]. Hanken School of Economics.

Perlroth, N., & Corkery, M. (2016). Details emerge on global bank heists by hackers. *The New York Times*. Available from: http://www.nytimes.com/2016/05/14/business/dealbook/details-emerge-on-global-bank-heists-byhackers. html?_r=0

Peters, G. W. (2014). *Opening discussion on banking sector risk exposures and vulnerabilities from virtual currencies: An operational risk perspective*. Available from: https://arxiv.org/ftp/arxiv/papers/1409/ 1409.1451.pdf

PWC. (2016). *Bank of England FinTech Accelerator partners with PWC on distributed ledger Proof of Concept*. Available from: https://pwc.blogs.com/press_room/2016/06/bank-of-england-fintech-accelerator-partners-withpwc-on-distributed-ledger-proof-of-concept-.html

Quentson, A. (2016). *Miners to attack ethereum classic after poloniex's listing*. Cryptocoins News. Available from: https://www.cryptocoinsnews.com/miners-attack-ethereum-classic-polonixs-listing/

Rapier, G. (2016). *Yellen reportedly urges central banks to study blockchain, bitcoin*. American Banker.

Rejeb, A., Treiblmaier, H., Rejeb, K., & Zailani, S. (2021). Blockchain research in healthcare: A bibliometric review and current research trends. *J. of Data Information & Management, 3*(2), 109–124. Advance online publication. doi:10.100742488-021-00046-2

Rizzo, P. (2016). *Linux, IBM share bold vision for hyperledger project, a blockchain fabric for business*. CoinDesk. Available from: https://www.coindesk.com/linux-ibm-hyperledger-blockchain-business/

Sedlmeir, J., Buhl, H.U., & Fridgen, G. (2020). The Energy Consumption of Blockchain Technology: Beyond Myth. *Bus Inf Syst Eng, 62*, 599–608. doi:10.1007/s12599-020-00656-x

Sharma, A., Bahl, S., Bagha, A. K., Javaid, M., Shukla, D. K., & Haleem, A. (2020). Blockchain technology and its applications to combat COVID-19 pandemic. *Research on Biomedical Engineering*. Advance online publication. doi:10.100742600-020-00106-3

Spurr, A., & Ausloos, M. (2020). Challenging practical features of Bitcoin by the main altcoins. *Quality & Quantity*. Advance online publication. doi:10.100711135-020-01062-x

Thomas, S. (2016). *The Subtle Tyranny of Blockchain*. Available from: https://medium.com/@justmoon/the-subtletyranny-of-blockchain-91d98b8a3a65#.l4jt4z2ze

Trump, B. D., Wells, E., Trump, J., & Linkov, I. (2018). Cryptocurrency: Governance for what was meant to be ungovernable. *Environment Systems & Decisions, 38*(3), 426–430. Advance online publication. doi:10.100710669-018-9703-8

Waking, J., Mandalenakis, M., & Hein, A. (2020). The impact of block chain technology on business models – a taxonomy and archetypal patterns. *Electronic Markets, 30*(2), 285–305. doi:10.100712525-019-00386-3

Walch, A. (2015). The bitcoin blockchain as financial market infrastructure: A consideration of operational risk. *NYU Journal of Legislation & Public Policy, 18*(4), 837–893.

West, J., & O'Mahony, S. (2008). The role of participation architecture in growing open sponsored open source communities. *Industry and Innovation, 15*(2), 145–168. doi:10.1080/13662710801970142

Wheeler, D. A., & Khakimov, S. (2015). *Open Source Software Projects Needing Security Investments.* White Paper of the Institute for Defense Analysis and the Linux Foundation. Available from: https://www. coreinfrastructure.org/sites/cii/files/pages/files/pub_ida_lf_cii_070915.pdf

Yano, M. (2020). *Economics, Law, and Institutions in Asia Pacific*. doi:10.1007/978-981-15-3376-1

Chapter 4
A Study on Blockchain Technology Implementation in the Logistics Sector of Pakistan

Fahim Ul Amin
Chang'an University, China

Dong Qianli
Chang'an University, China

Wasim Ul Amin
North China Electric Power University, China

Iram Zulfiqar
North China Electric Power University, China

Shamsa Kanwal
North China Electric Power University, China

ABSTRACT

Blockchain technology provides a number of technological features, including high transparency, traceability, and trustiness. Its use in the logistics business increases technical support and ensures the logistics industry's effectiveness, as well as records, stores, and logistics information. The transmission ensures security, prevents logistics information from being distorted, and ensures the authenticity of logistics information. The use of blockchain technology in the logistics business has a positive impact on the industry's competitiveness and technical advantages. Blockchain has emerged as a key technology advancement with the ability to solve logistics problems. It's time for Pakistan to take advantage of this new technology. Blockchain has the potential to transform Pakistan's logistics sector.

DOI: 10.4018/978-1-7998-7642-7.ch004

1 INTRODUCTION

The distribution of information has proliferated in the age of network technology. The communication problem has been dramatically improved in the Internet application. However, the communication's genuineness is a concern. There are still no reliable guarantees regarding the accuracy of information transmission. Information security is provided by blockchain technology and a combination of the Internet (Kersten et al., 2017). The logistics industry is extensive. This industry successfully incorporates Internet technology into the logistics industry's innovation. Simultaneously, creating logistics and supply chain information assurance has become a crucial concern (Sun et al., 2021). The use of blockchain technology in logistics and the supply chain provides information assurance. The logistics sector ensures information security, logistics security, and capital flow security through various agreements in creating logistics ecological infrastructure, consequently boosting the logistics industry's competitiveness. This is the logistics sector in the 21st century, as well as modern Internet technologies. (Li et al., 2020) The successful integration of technology has completely fulfilled the development needs of the logistics industry. It may be used to improve the existing management condition of the logistics industry, increase logistics efficiency, and assure logistics safety. In the logistics industry, it is a strong basis of trust. (Park, 2020)

Blockchain originated at the end of the subprime mortgage crisis in 2008; Blockchain technology first appeared in the foundational paper "Bitcoin: A Peer-to-Peer Electronic Cash System" published by a scholar with the pseudonym "Satoshi Naka-moto" (Satoshi Naka-moto, 2008) in the cryptography mailing group. Satoshi Tanaka-moto proposed the concepts of "block" and "chain," which later developed into "blockchain."(Viriyasitavat & Hoonsopon, 2019) Blockchain technology itself is an application of data structure technology in simple transactions. The completion of each transaction records the information of the trader's block and point and records the trader's integrity and anti-counterfeiting marks. (Yang et al., 2021) The integrity records on the entire chain can be queried and traced, and there is no so-called central node with privileges. An encryption algorithm ensures the information of each block and points to ensure its safety and no leakage. Because there is no so-called central node, even if a particular block on the chain is lost, it will still not affect the blockchain's overall information security and integrity. (Bhambhwani et al., 2020)The blockchain technology has progressed through three stages: Blockchain 1.0 focuses on cryptocurrency transactions, and the functions of digital currency transfer, remittance, and payment form a new ecosystem known as the "Internet of Money"; Blockchain 2.0 uses a similar transaction mechanism but includes a broader range of financial applications; and Blockchain 3.0 introduces a new type of application known as "smart contracts," which expands transactions from a single transaction to a series of transactions.(Bhambhwani et al., 2020) A blockchain-based smart contract is a computational software that runs on the blockchain and automatically verifies and executes the contract's provisions.(Zheng et al., 2017).This chapter first introduces the overview and development of blockchain technology, Principle and Characteristics of Blockchain Technology, secondly the feasibility and value of blockchain technology in the Logistics industry; thirdly, it summarizes the Importance of Blockchain in Pakistan and Technology Status and Existing Problems of the Logistics Industry, afterward Advantages of Blockchain Technology in the Logistics Industry will be explained categorically. Finally, it points out Blockchain Technology Framework for Logistics Industry.

2 THE PRINCIPLE AND CHARACTERISTICS OF BLOCKCHAIN TECHNOLOGY

Blockchain technology is essentially Internet database technology used to construct Internet databases and is based on the Internet. Defined, the database functions as a ledger, and accounting behavior refers to the process of saving and reporting data in the database. (Bhambhwani et al., 2020) The goal of blockchain technology is to find accounting objects and keep the ones that are most efficient in terms of accounting. Also, convey the data from the ledger to other system objects. As a result, blockchain technology can also be referred to as a distributed ledger because it is a technical means of publishing data in a database to every node of the entire network. Blockchain technology is based on the Internet and allows for the creation of particular computer-based applications. (Zhao et al., 2016) Distributed data storage, peer-to-peer transmission, consensus mechanisms, and encryption algorithms, among other things, are all included in the blockchain technology application—data storage and transfer, as well as data exchange and security. As a result, decentralization, openness and transparency, and joint involvement are technological properties of blockchain technology. (Viriyasitavat & Hoonsopon, 2019) This method of database maintenance is a distributed system that is tough to adapt from a data standpoint. The database also comprises a distributed record of data, in addition to the distributed storage of data. As a result, blockchain is not a single technology. It combines several technical tools and provides some technological benefits and features in technical applications. (Sultana et al., 2020)

2.1 Principles of Blockchain Technology

2.1.1 Block structure

The database structure has been transformed by blockchain technology. Data is divided into different blocks using this technology, and each block is linked to the preceding block's back using specific information supplied in a sequential order. Data in its entirety. These data are preserved in electronic records indefinitely, and the files that store them are known as blocks. During the block creation phase, the block will keep track of transaction data, and the block's primary body will be a collection of transaction data. The blockchain's structure is separated into two sections: the header and the body. The block header's purpose is to provide a connection to the previous block. This section is responsible for ensuring the blockchain database's integrity. The block body stores all of the confirmed records of value exchanges that took place during the block's construction. The block structure has two key features: the first ensures the database's integrity, and the second ensures that the data cannot be tampered with. (McBee & Wilcox, 2020)

2.1.2 Distributed structure

The next step is to consider recording and storage after you've solved the data problem with blocks and chains. Data is stored in one single location in most systems nowadays. Blockchain technology, on the other hand, allows each node involved in a data transaction to capture and save all of the information.(Sultana et al., 2020) The main idea is to create a comprehensive set of protocol mechanisms that will allow all nodes in the network to check the data's validity while recording it.Only when all nodes in the network agree that the data is correct are data records written to the block.In terms of data storage, the blockchain creates a distributed network in which all data in the database is saved and updated in real-time by all nodes participating in the record. As a result, even if certain nodes are broken or hacked, the data records and information updates in the database as a whole will not be affected. Accounting duties are dispersed with distributed accounting, and they are documented by all network participants. It also spreads every transaction throughout all nodes in the network, giving data information a high fault tolerance rate as long as it isn't distributed throughout the entire network. The database system can keep running even if all of the nodes crash at the same time. (McBee & Wilcox, 2020)

2.1.3 Asymmetric encryption

An asymmetric encryption technique is used in the blockchain encryption system's principle. In the encryption and decryption procedure, this algorithm often uses public and private keys, which are asymmetric passwords. Both of these forms of encryption are available. Only the other comparable key can be decrypted after one of the keys has been encrypted. If the public key is used to encrypt data information, the data information must be decrypted using the corresponding private key, and if the private key is used to encrypt data information, the data information must be decrypted using just the corresponding public key. (Sultana et al., 2020) The public key can be made public, whereas the private key belongs to a single person and is not accessible to others. As a result, when utilising the blockchain to process data, users must maintain the private key secret in order to avoid data leakage owing to the private key's publication. Multi-private key encryption technology has been derived from actual application requirements in the present blockchain system to satisfy more flexible and sophisticated scenarios such as multi-signature. (McBee & Wilcox, 2020)

2.2 Characteristics of Blockchain Technology

Blockchain technology has only been around for a few years. However, its exceptional characteristics are the cause for its quick development of influence: a high level of openness and sharing, decentralised high security, transparent transactions with privacy protection, anti-tampering, dishonesty, and traceability (Bhambhwani et al., 2020) (1) A high level of transparency and sharing Anyone who wants to join the blockchain system can set up a participating node on their device and become a block on the blockchain. You can receive the complete chain Copy of the information as long as you follow the chain's integrity contract and related rules. You can enjoy the information of the complete chain that fits your identity as long as you become a block on the chain. Because of its high level of openness and sharing, blockchain technology has a wide range of applications. (Viriyasitavat & Hoonsopon, 2019) (2) Decentralization's strong security. A network or system structure is used to put up a node with the highest authority (also known as an administrator), producing a privileged central location. This phenomenon has been completely bypassed thanks to blockchain technology. Special restrictions ensure that nodes and digital signatures created on the chain are secure. Nodes that do not adhere to the chain's rules cannot participate in it or finish transactions. The blockchain eliminates possible node privileges and ensures the security of transactions between nodes based on fairness by removing the central node. (Bhambhwani et al., 2020) (3) Transparent transactions protected by privacy. The functioning rules of the blockchain are apparent across the chain due to the high level of transparency and sharing. Transactions between blocks are visible transactions that must follow the blockchain's rules, and information about the transaction process is available to everyone on the network. Traders might choose to remain anonymous during the transaction if they do not want to reveal their personal information. This ensures that personal privacy is protected while transactions remain transparent. (Viriyasitavat & Hoonsopon, 2019) (4) Anti-tampering and dishonesty have a long history. Once your transaction data is incorporated in a certain block of the blockchain, it becomes publicly accessible data across the whole network. It is impossible to erase the records on the entire chain by tampering with the information on a block because each block has the right to duplicate the full blockchain transaction information. This also demonstrates that if there is a problem of dishonesty in a block's transaction process, it will almost certainly be traced back because the records of all blocks on the chain cannot be destroyed.

Figure 1. Characteristics of Blockchain Technology
(Atlam & Wills, 2019)

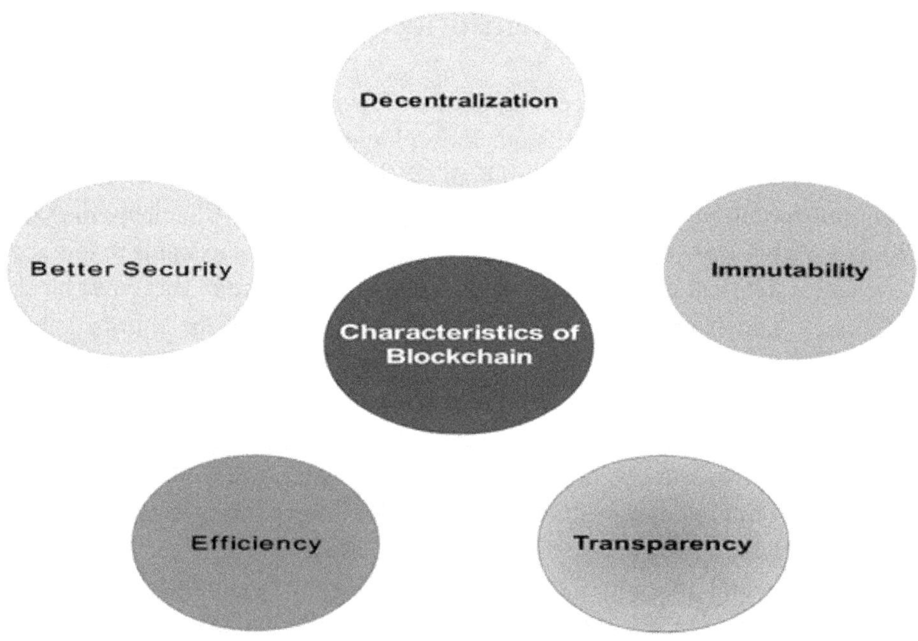

The blockchain, in general, is a technology for storing data and information. The application of blockchain technology is impossible to tamper with, deny, traceable, and extremely transparent due to the collaborative maintenance of numerous technologies; each data transaction node records and stores data information. It is difficult to tamper with or manipulate data information. Simultaneously, the data is encrypted using blockchain technology's encryption algorithms. The data-sharing method can help establish data information protection, and the transaction process can help to improve trust and collaboration. (Petersson & Baur, 2018)

3 THE IMPORTANCE OF BLOCKCHAIN IN PAKISTAN AND TECHNOLOGY STATUS AND EXISTING PROBLEMS OF THE LOGISTICS INDUSTRY

Pakistan took a positive step forward last year by allowing blockchain technology in the country. Malaysian remittances were chosen as a source of income. Remittances increased 13% in the first quarter as a result of this. However, it is necessary to comprehend how it may affect many sectors of the country, including logistics, banking, and government. (Batada, n.d.) The utilization of blocks is at the heart of blockchain technology. These serve as information storage places, and once full, they connect to the previous block, establishing a chain as more blocks are filled. This chain ensures that the acts are permanent and cannot be modified without risking detection.There's a hash in every block. They're similar to fingerprints in that each block has its own set of them. Every block also contains the hash of the previous block. As a result, if a block is modified, the block after it will be aware of the change because the hash of the modified block will change as well.Aside from security, blockchain offers increased tracing capabilities, transparency, and efficiency. Given these considerations, it is clear that incorporating blockchain technology into a country like Pakistan can be beneficial. (Batada, n.d.)

Blockchain technology offers the ability to give government, citizen, and commercial data with safe storage. It can help the government by acting as a central repository for both public and private assets. The blockchain-powered digital identity mechanism can provide a comprehensive national database that stores personal information such as birth certificates, marriage licences, driver's licences, and passport information for each citizen. Furthermore, streamlining the data management method for public services reduces labor-intensive operations significantly. Furthermore, it not only lowers excessive prices but also establishes foolproof accountability procedures. By establishing property titles, blockchain also provides a platform for carrying out safe property transactions. (Batada, n.d.) The use of blockchain technology has the potential to improve how government entities manage their most sensitive data. The enhanced level of security ensures that the public has more faith in and collaboration with the court system. Vote-buying and intimidation, which are common outside polling precincts or booths, are also eliminated by blockchain technology. It also improves voter security by removing the need for voters to return home to vote. Furthermore, fraud and tampering are less likely to occur. Because of the restricted time allowed for each block, tampering with the data is exceedingly difficult. In India, this approach has been in existence for some time and has resulted in a substantial improvement in the country's voting process. (Batada, n.d.)

Blockchain has been used for international trade by developed countries such as the United States, China, and the United Kingdom. They do so because this technology makes the ledgers of other countries, or even firms with whom they trade, more visible and accessible, allowing countries to better understand what they are getting into. Developed countries like China, Singapore, and South Korea have already reaped significant benefits from embracing cryptocurrencies as a payment method. It has also prompted investors to investigate the possibilities of investing more money in these countries' activities.Blockchain has risen to prominence as a significant technology advancement with the ability to address global concerns. It is past time for Pakistan to take use of this new technology. Blockchain has the potential to transform the country's logistics business. Blockchain regulation should be created, and effective application should be practised. (Ahmad et al., 2021)

The logistics sector is now one of the world's largest. In simple terms, it is the act of carrying products from one location to another. Commodity trading has become an important element of people's life as the network information society evolves. Under the current social background and societal necessities, goods distribution and logistics transportation have become the focus of development, causing more people to pay attention to the development of the logistics business. With the rapid growth of the express delivery and e-commerce industries, the logistics sector must modify its activities and further adapt to the changing needs of society and industrial development through technological innovation and reform. (Kersten et al., 2017) The key challenge is adapting to the industry's development needs. A variety of new technologies have evolved as a result of the rapid development of the logistics industry and the quick improvement of the logistics industry's competitiveness, and the logistics industry's shortcomings have gradually surfaced. It's not straightforward to establish security assurances for logistics data. People's faith in the logistics business has been eroded by information distortion, information asymmetry, and various concerns such as information islands and information leakage. This type of issue reflects the industry's general development issues. Technical means with practical guarantees are required to completely tackle this type of problem in the industry. As a result, technological advancements in the logistics business are on the horizon. The following issues still exist in today's logistics technology. (Petersson & Baur, 2018)

3.1 Low transparency

The logistics industry is a complex system composed of various contents such as commerce, trade routes, freight bills, and industry laws and regulations. In the logistics system, various contents are scattered, and it is tough to realize the integration of different contents. (Tijan et al., 2019) The original computer Technology and documentation tools are challenging to achieve the integration of the logistics system, so in the logistics industry, it has multiple uncertainties, and it is even more challenging to maintain the trust of both parties in the transaction. Participating in the logistics and supply chain is affected by the trust of the transaction. Generally, they are unwilling to share the contract and contract information in detail, making it difficult to effectively use data and information such as funds, sales, and supply. The logistics companies in the supply chain The visibility is small, and it harms both parties to the transaction. In the absence of data transparency and trust mechanisms, the development of the logistics industry has gradually fallen into a trust dilemma. (Orji et al., 2020) (Ahmad et al., 2021)

3.2 Low traceability

The existing logistics industry's standards make it impossible for a single organisation to efficiently track the components in the supply chain, resulting in a lack of traceability and the retention of a vast volume of data. These data sources can be utilised to promote big data, however under existing logistics industry technical standards, it is impossible to play an effective role or accomplish the effect of cost savings. (McBee & Wilcox, 2020) Low transparency is currently affecting the problem of low traceability in the logistics business. There is distrust between the two parties in the transaction due to the inadequate transparency of data information. Data information distortion, omission, and loss are all possibilities during the transaction process. Assure the logistics industry's continued development. (Sultana et al., 2020)

3.3 Complex Technology and Weak Adaptability

In the logistics industry's technical means, a huge number of logistics organisations handle logistical information using paper and pen, then scan, copy, and file paper documents to create a database for data and information storage. As a result, the logistics industry's technical application procedure is hard, and in many situations, computer system software does not give adequate support. As a result, the implementation of old technical approaches is low, and it has been difficult to adapt to the background and needs of modern society. (Li et al., 2020) The logistics technology methods are difficult, the operations are slow, and there are many unknowns. Errors in operation are caused. This necessitates technical maintenance in order to maintain the feasibility of technical application, and maintenance expenditures far exceed the budgeted amount. As a result, there are still issues with the logistics industry's current technical procedures, such as limited technical flexibility, technical complexity, error-proneness, and high cost. In the logistics industry, technological innovation has become an unavoidable tendency. (McBee & Wilcox, 2020)

3.4 Data information confusion

The logistics industry's existing technology application lacks transparency and information traceability, and it is reliant on outmoded technologies. This immediately leads to a lack of knowledge needed for strategic decision-making in the logistics industry's development. A lot of data and information is available at the same time. Different chain entities are recorded in different ways, causing data and information to become muddled and imposing substantial limits on information management in the logistics industry. (Sun et al., 2021) Although the cost of information management increased, it had a significant impact on the growth of logistics businesses and the sector as a whole. There are many constraints. It can be said that in the current logistics industry, the overlapping of multiple contents, the difficulty of technical application to form a sufficient guarantee, and the chaotic arrangement of data and information have hampered the logistics industry's stable development and imposed limitations on its growth. (Sultana et al., 2020)

3.5 Low information authenticity

In the long run, the logistics business has gained significant competitive advantages, while the economic benefits of the industry have also improved. This has given the logistics business a boost, but it has also highlighted the industry's flaws. The information has a poor level of veracity. Criminals may employ logistics to conduct unlawful operations, such as the quick delivery of contraband parts like weapons. It is difficult to accomplish practical outcomes in logistics monitoring since the accuracy of logistics information is difficult to ensure. (Li et al., 2020) The consequences of this lack of authenticity in logistics data on the logistics sector and even society must be addressed as soon as possible. It's tough for relevant supervisory units to thoroughly check the data given by logistics companies, and it's even more difficult to verify the accuracy of logistical data. At the same time, it has created insecurity in the industry's development order, making it difficult to provide a strong assurance for the logistics sector. (Sun et al., 2021)

4 ADVANTAGES OF BLOCKCHAIN TECHNOLOGY IN THE LOGISTICS INDUSTRY

The flexibility of logistics technology is still relatively low among the existing technical approaches in the logistics sector, making it difficult for the logistics industry to fulfil the different needs of today's society. Meeting the complicated and massive logistics system's own criteria is likewise difficult. As a result, it is vital to develop the logistics industry's technical methods, utilising the technological advantages of the Internet era, as well as the coupling of blockchain technology and the logistics industry, which is beneficial to logistics industry technical innovation.(Patel, 2018) The use of blockchain technology in the logistics business ensures the validity, security, privacy, transparency, and traceability of logistics information records, as well as other data recording benefits. It can also verify that both parties to the transaction are trustworthy and accountable. The system is critical for the logistics industry's continued expansion and technological advancement. The following are some of the most significant blockchain application benefits in the logistics business. (Wu & Duan, 2019)

4.1 Provide services

The storing and recording of logistics data has been made easier thanks to blockchain technology. In addition to these benefits, blockchain-based intelligent contracts may be used to verify end-to-end manufacturing processes, which is the same as verification work. It serves as a source of information and can also offer basic contract assurances. (Patel, 2018)

4.2 Increase industry competitiveness

The logistics industry offers strong growth possibilities, as well as demonstrable economic and development benefits. However, while analysing contemporary industry rivalry and industry influence on logistics enterprises, the logistics market is divided into various dominant circumstances. (Wu & Duan, 2019) The development of the logistics market and industry has been stifled by power and monopoly capabilities. This is not good for the logistics industry's growth. It is difficult to give better development space for new logistics enterprises, resulting in a self-circulation of the logistics industry. Outward development options are severely limited, making it difficult for small and medium-sized logistics firms to stand apart. As a result, applying blockchain technology to the logistics industry can help the industry improve its current state, provide small and medium-sized logistics companies and new logistics companies with good corporate development advantages, and expand operations by lowering corporate operating costs and increasing operational benefits. Simultaneously, the application of blockchain technology can provide logistic companies with cooperative advantages, promote the development of small and medium-sized logistics companies, and promote the long-term development of the logistics industry and the logistics market in a healthy competitive environment. (Patel, 2018)

4.3 Improve Data Transparency and Provide a Good Sense of Trust

The technological characteristics of blockchain technology include extreme transparency and trustlessness. This offers the advantage of boosting the authenticity and trustworthiness of information for the logistics business, and it may be able to alleviate the problem that the industry is now facing. Many companies and logistics industry transactions require that all links in the supply chain protect the company's privacy, which means that privacy protection of logistics information and corporate information resources is required, and information transparency is harmed, but this is due to low information transparency. The resulting information blockade has had a greater influence on the information's legitimacy. The legitimacy of information cannot be guaranteed due to a lack of trust between the participants to a transaction, but blockchain technology can help solve this problem. (Ahmad et al., 2021) The private blockchain application allows objects in the logistics supply chain to have a clear concept of the information resources required and to use that information in the form of information access. At the same time, using blockchain technology to manage information means that the data is no longer owned. Tampering, which safeguards the information in each data block, allows internal information to be communicated when it is accurate and cannot be tampered with, and it increases information transparency with an access mechanism. (Pournader et al., 2020)

4.4 Smart Contract Innovation Agreement Model

The blockchain-based intelligent contract ensures the security of the logistics industry's automated legal agreements. The smart contract may monitor all links and operations in the logistics system and evaluate the accuracy and scientificity of the coding regulations, ensuring that each contract's requirements are met. The degree of confidence among the parties to the transaction is unaffected by the contract provisions, which can improve the transaction's quality. Smart contracts give both parties in a logistical transaction with assurances of trustworthiness. For some small and medium-sized logistics organisations, or start-up logistics companies, blockchain technology can meet the development needs of entering the supply chain due to a lack of corporate reputation and value protection. With smart contracts, you may create a contract guarantee. (Patel, 2018)

4.5 Information protection

In the past, the security of the ledger system in the logistics business rested solely on the system's upkeep. It is difficult to properly prevent external access to steal information or tamper with supply chain data information when the outside world intentionally targets it. It provides a decentralised information platform for data information, ensures the security and accuracy of the information platform, and uses encryption tools to check and verify the access objects in the information platform in an all-around manner using blockchain technology. To make certain that data and information are entered or changed in a practical and secure manner. With the continual advancement of Internet technology and information technology, public interest in digital information security has grown. As the blockchain system takes shape, information security protection for the logistics industry should be further researched and updated. (Wu & Duan, 2019)

4.6 Improve Asset Management Clarity

Information resources can be monetized via blockchain technology. Assets can be tracked using the blockchain's digital ledger technology, which improves asset management clarity and eliminates asset information confusion. It also has a permanent follow-up in asset transfer and verification, which increases the logistics information management efficiency. It can help numerous stakeholders create effective asset management and increase asset management clarity. (Wang & Xie, 2020)

Figure 2. Advantages of Blockchain Technology in the Logistics Industry

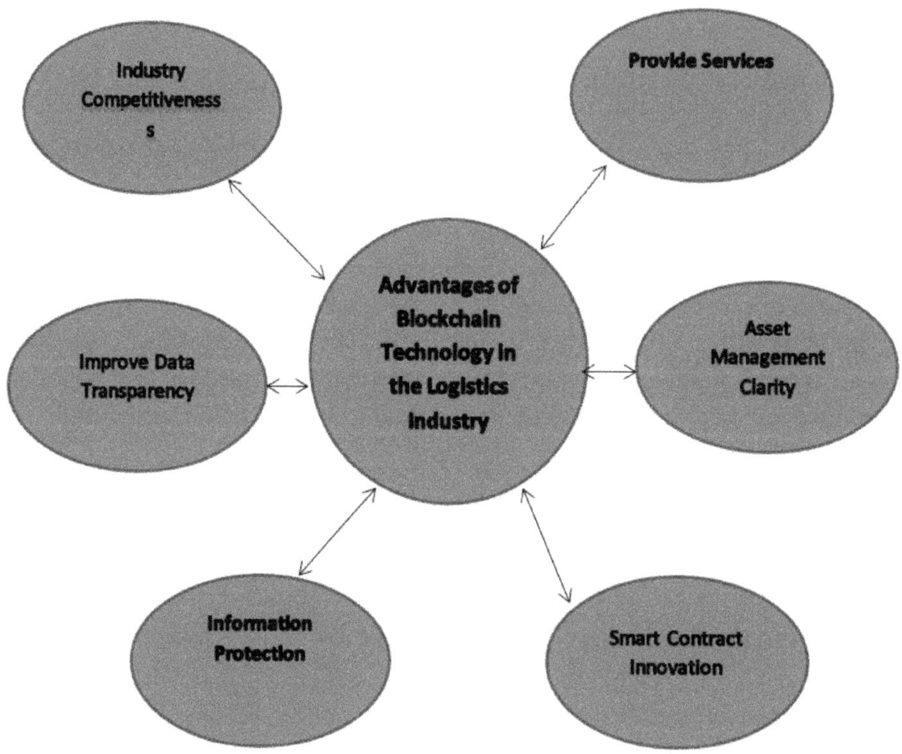

5 BLOCKCHAIN TECHNOLOGY FRAMEWORK FOR LOGISTICS INDUSTRY

The advantages and technical qualities of blockchain technology can be used to examine how blockchain technology is being used in the logistics business. Its use in the logistics industry can help the industry not just with information, but also with stability. Enhance and expand the logistics order guarantee. (Tijan et al., 2019)

5.1 Application of Blockchain Technology to Logistics Information Recording

The use of blockchain technology in the logistics industry has helped to enhance the system's complex structure. A blockchain system is created by connecting multiple nodes. Each node is linked to the others, but they do not interact. The record of logistics data has been reinforced thanks to this blockchain system. Each node associated with data information can store its relevant information content, ensuring that all supply chain links are flexible and that information traceability is easier to complete. Each link and procedure, from the purchase of the transaction object to logistics transportation and delivery, creates information and data that is recorded and kept in the district. The flow of information in the blockchain is likewise flexible, and data can be extracted at any point along the way. (Yi, 2021)

5.2 Blockchain Technology Applied to Logistics Information Protection

Instead of creating paper information in the traditional paper-and-pen mode, blockchain technology is used in the logistics business to apply Internet information technology and computer technology to the logistics system. They may, however, record and flow data in the form of digital data. The use of blockchain technology in the logistics system uses information encryption technology to form the security protection of digital information resources, which not only improves the authenticity of the information but also increases mutual trust between the two parties in the transaction while also lowering the logistics enterprise's capital costs to provide even better societal advantages.(Yi, 2021)(Petersson & Baur, 2018) The blockchain technology is used to secure the integrity of data. Security protection technology is integrated with logistics information to produce technical protection for logistics information flow, thanks to the storage of information in blockchain technology. Because every link in the blockchain can be assured to be in a single state, it increases the traceability of logistics data and the security of data usage. The construction of data copies support for both parties in the private blockchain makes it hard for outsiders and other transaction parties to view and modify the copies when blockchain technology is used to safeguard logistics information. As a result, logistics data can provide not just authenticity guarantees but also long-term tracking. (Jabbar et al., 2021)

5.3 Application of Blockchain Technology in Logistics Commodities

The use of blockchain technology in the logistics business has a direct impact on the creation and security of logistics data. At the same time, blockchain technology may directly capitalise and value informationized commodities in the logistics system, allowing the logistics business to have more information and better quality assurance. (Kummer et al., 2020) Logistics data cannot be altered with when blockchain technology is used. As a result, the sole ownership of logistics products and goods has been established, and the traceability of logistics information has also generated an asset transformation for logistics goods. As a result of the use of blockchain technology in logistics products, logistics products now have the qualities of commodities under logistics information and provide capitalization attributes. Through the node control of intelligent contracts, blockchain technology is used to directly screen logistical products. Illegal products in the logistics industry are filtered out in this way, and transit is prohibited. At the same time, it gives consumers more privacy protection, which is a great method to boost consumer confidence in logistics companies and encourage the logistics industry's orderly growth. (DHL Trend Research, 2019)

5.4 Application of Blockchain Technology in Logistics Credit Investigation

The logistics business is using blockchain technology to store and transmit data. As a result of the logistics industry's generally low credit system integrity, both parties to the transaction frequently present insufficient information transparency, resulting in information distortion. As a result, to steer the logistics sector's healthy development, an industry self-discipline management organization must be established. In a connected model that involves multi-party cooperation, blockchain technology can function directly in the logistics credit reporting system, providing credit reporting guarantees for the logistics business. (Li et al., 2020) Data information will not be disclosed thanks to the security guarantees of blockchain technology. Data and information can also be assured not to be tampered with, lost, or distorted, allowing data and information to be shared. This has a positive impact on the logistics industry's credit system Supportive of the logistics industry's orderly expansion. (Aslam et al., 2021)

6 CONCLUSION

In this chapter, we proposed research on the implementation of blockchain technology in logistics sector of Pakistan. In the logistics industry, blockchain has a lot of potential benefits. It allows businesses to improve efficiency, transparency, and traceability while also enhancing supply chain security by ensuring that the origin and authenticity of items are known, verified, and shared. However, underdeveloped countries are still cautious of blockchain technology, and logistics firms are waiting for a game-changing answer for logistics. In terms of technology and its uses, there is a lack of confidence and comprehension. Blockchain technology is applied in all walks of life as an emerging technology, although it is still in its early stages in the logistics industry, with numerous technical issues to be resolved. This chapter proposes some suggestions for using blockchain in the logistics business by investigating blockchain technology and its use in various scenarios. It outlines the issues that arise from the application of technology. How to overcome these problems in the future of blockchain and Pakistan's development will be challenges and possibilities.

REFERENCES

Ahmad, R. W., Hasan, H., Jayaraman, R., Salah, K., & Omar, M. (2021). Blockchain applications and architectures for port operations and logistics management. *Research in Transportation Business & Management*, *41*, 100620. Advance online publication. doi:10.1016/j.rtbm.2021.100620

Aslam, J., Saleem, A., Khan, N. T., & Kim, Y. B. (2021). Factors influencing blockchain adoption in supply chain management practices: A study based on the oil industry. *Journal of Innovation and Knowledge*, *6*(2), 124–134. Advance online publication. doi:10.1016/j.jik.2021.01.002

Atlam, H. F., & Wills, G. B. (2019). Technical aspects of blockchain and IoT. In Advances in Computers (Vol. 115). doi:10.1016/bs.adcom.2018.10.006

Batada, D. I. (n.d.). *Blockchain for Pakistan*. https://www.thenews.com.pk/print/752179-blockchain-for-pakistan

BhambhwaniS. M.DelikourasS.KorniotisG. M. (2020). Blockchain Characteristics and the Cross-Section of Cryptocurrency Returns. SSRN *Journal*.

DHL Trend Research. (2019). Blockchain in Logistics: Perspectives on the upcoming impact of blockchain technology and use cases for the logistics industry. DHL Customer Solutions & Innovation.

Jabbar, S., Lloyd, H., Hammoudeh, M., Adebisi, B., & Raza, U. (2021). Blockchain-enabled supply chain: Analysis, challenges, and future directions. *Multimedia Systems*, *27*(4), 787–806. Advance online publication. doi:10.100700530-020-00687-0

Kersten, W., Blecker, T., Ringle, C. M., Hackius, N., & Petersen, M. (2017). Digitalization in Supply Chain Management and Logistics Blockchain in Logistics and Supply Chain: Trick or Treat? Blockchain in Logistics and Supply Chain: Trick or Treat? *Proceedings of the Hamburg International Conference of Logistics (HICL)*.

Kummer, S., Herold, D. M., Dobrovnik, M., Mikl, J., & Schäfer, N. (2020). A systematic review of blockchain literature in logistics and supply chain management: Identifying research questions and future directions. *Future Internet*, *12*(3), 60. Advance online publication. doi:10.3390/fi12030060

Li, X., Lv, F., Xiang, F., Sun, Z., & Sun, Z. (2020). Research on Key Technologies of Logistics Information Traceability Model Based on Consortium Chain. *IEEE Access: Practical Innovations, Open Solutions*, *8*, 69754–69762. Advance online publication. doi:10.1109/ACCESS.2020.2986220

McBee, M. P., & Wilcox, C. (2020). Blockchain Technology: Principles and Applications in Medical Imaging. In Journal of Digital Imaging (Vol. 33, Issue 3). doi:10.100710278-019-00310-3

Orji, I. J., Kusi-Sarpong, S., Huang, S., & Vazquez-Brust, D. (2020). Evaluating the factors that influence blockchain adoption in the freight logistics industry. *Transportation Research Part E, Logistics and Transportation Review*, *141*, 102025. Advance online publication. doi:10.1016/j.tre.2020.102025

Park, K. O. (2020). A study on sustainable usage intention of blockchain in the big data era: Logistics and supply chain management companies. *Sustainability (Switzerland)*, *12*(24), 10670. Advance online publication. doi:10.3390u122410670

Patel, A. (2018). *The Top Advantages of Blockchain For Businesses*. Smartdatacollective.Com.

Petersson, E., & Baur, K. (2018). *Impacts of Blockchain Technology on Supply Chain Collaboration-A study on the use of blockchain technology in supply chains and how it influences supply chain collaboration* [Master Thesis]. Jönköping University.

Pournader, M., Shi, Y., Seuring, S., & Koh, S. C. L. (2020). Blockchain applications in supply chains, transport and logistics: A systematic review of the literature. *International Journal of Production Research*, *58*(7), 2063–2081. Advance online publication. doi:10.1080/00207543.2019.1650976

Sultana, M., Hossain, A., Laila, F., Taher, K. A., & Islam, M. N. (2020). Towards developing a secure medical image sharing system based on zero trust principles and blockchain technology. *BMC Medical Informatics and Decision Making*, *20*(1), 256. Advance online publication. doi:10.118612911-020-01275-y PMID:33028318

Sun, Y., Li, X., Lv, F., & Hu, B. (2021). Research on Logistics Information Blockchain Data Query Algorithm Based on Searchable Encryption. *IEEE Access: Practical Innovations, Open Solutions*, *9*, 20968–20976. Advance online publication. doi:10.1109/ACCESS.2021.3054557

Tijan, E., Aksentijević, S., Ivanić, K., & Jardas, M. (2019). Blockchain technology implementation in logistics. *Sustainability (Switzerland)*, *11*(4), 1185. Advance online publication. doi:10.3390u11041185

Viriyasitavat, W., & Hoonsopon, D. (2019). Blockchain characteristics and consensus in modern business processes. *Journal of Industrial Information Integration, 13*, 32–39. Advance online publication. doi:10.1016/j.jii.2018.07.004

Wang, X., & Xie, Z. (2020). *Research on the Application of Blockchain Technology in Logistics Industry*. doi:10.2991/aebmr.k.200402.032

Wu, B., & Duan, T. (2019). The advantages of blockchain technology in commercial bank operation and management. *ACM International Conference Proceeding Series*. 10.1145/3340997.3341009

Yang, J., Ma, X., Crespo, R. G., & Martínez, O. S. (2021). Blockchain for supply chain performance and logistics management. *Applied Stochastic Models in Business and Industry, 37*(3), 429–441. Advance online publication. doi:10.1002/asmb.2577

Yi, H. (2021). A secure logistics model based on blockchain. *Enterprise Information Systems, 15*(7), 1002–1018. Advance online publication. doi:10.1080/17517575.2019.1696988

Zhao, J. L., Fan, S., & Yan, J. (2016). Overview of business innovations and research opportunities in blockchain and introduction to the special issue. In Financial Innovation (Vol. 2, Issue 1). doi:10.118640854-016-0049-2

Zheng, Z., Xie, S., Dai, H., Chen, X., & Wang, H. (2017). An Overview of Blockchain Technology: Architecture, Consensus, and Future Trends. *Proceedings - 2017 IEEE 6th International Congress on Big Data, BigData Congress 2017*. 10.1109/BigDataCongress.2017.85

Chapter 5
Industrial Revolution 4.0 and Supply Chain Management

Adeel Shah
https://orcid.org/0000-0001-8477-5310
University of Kuala Lumpur, Malaysia

Aisha Ismail
Business School, Karachi University, Pakistan

ABSTRACT

Innovation is taking place rapidly, which is changing the demand level. Diversifying the supply chain with changing demand patterns is another challenge to meet. Industrial Revolution (IR) 4.0 is the new way to effectively manage the supply chain process with the updated conventional business model. The technology enhances the traditional business model and improves distance relations among companies and customers through well managed distribution channels, creates high-level customer satisfaction, and provides timely information in each stage of the supply chain process. Innovative technology allows companies to make more profit by saving time and making an additional product to meet specific demands cost-effectively. It is also reducing human efforts, which will be taking place by robotics soon. The industrial revolution is the new beginning of an environment where the supply chain will be managed by intelligent technology, improving the overall process of value chains.

1. INTRODUCTION TO INDUSTRIAL REVOLUTION 4.0

The IR 4.0 is the "Fourth Industrial Revolution," an ongoing process where we deal with complex hardware systems, software mechanisms, and big data centers in one

DOI: 10.4018/978-1-7998-7642-7.ch005

particular product (Brettel, 2014). The advanced stage in the IR emphasizes different modes of interconnectivity, machine learning, meantime data, and automation in the supply chain process. It is called IR 4.0 because it consists of four industrial revolution stages, where each stage defines the changing technologies. The first stage is production methods to machines; the second stage represents the technology revolution; the thirst stage explains the digital revolution. At the same time, the fourth stage defines IR 4.0 strategy computerizing the manufacturing process real-time production improving the efficiency of the supply chain process overall.

IR 4.0 is also an intelligent engineering process connecting physical production & operation lines through new digital technology. Big-scale M2M (machine-to-machine) communication and the Internet of things (IoT) integrates for incremented automation, amended communication, and self-monitoring machines that can analyze and diagnose issues without human involvement.

Industry 4.0, sometimes referred to as IIoT or digital manufacturing, encompasses physical integration and operations with new digital technology, machine learning, and extensive data to create a more holistic and well-connected ecosystem for companies that fixate manufacturing and supply chain management. While every company and organization operating today is different, they all face a prevalent challenge—the desideratum for connectedness and access to authentic-time insights across processes, partners, products, and people.

New developments in extensive data and analytics platforms denote that systems can scan through big data sets that can be acted upon expeditiously. We are witnessing profound shifts across all industries, marked by the emergence of advanced business models, the disruption 1 of incumbents, and the reshaping of integration, consumption, conveyance, and distribution systems (World Economic Forum, 2016). IR 4.0 optically discerning factories become increasingly automated, and self-monitoring as the machines within are given the faculty to analyze and communicate with each other. This then free ups their human co-workers, granting companies much smoother processes that leave employees open for different tasks.

Investing in advanced technology (IR 4.0) will improve overall business performance and ameliorate manufacturing efficacy in the supply chain process while revolutionizing business operations. Industry 4.0 principles have been applying by companies; they have sometimes been rebranding. For example, the aerospace components manufacturer Meggitt PLC has branded its research project on IR 4.0. The digitization of industry 4.0 will affect the labor market, which is being in the discussion under labor 4.0.

1.1 Design principles

The design principles of IR 4.0 consist of the below components.

1. Interconnection

It is the ability of machines and people to connect and communicate better through the Internet of things (IoT).

2. Information Transparency

The information transparency availed by IR 4.0 gives operators complete information to make vital decisions.

3. Technical Assistance

The technology provides a system facility to help humans in problem-solving and decision-making while having the skill to do the unsafe task.

4. Decentralized Decisions

Internet of things can decide on their own and perform some tasks as independently as possible.

1.2 IR 4.0 model

The IR 4.0 revives the whole product life cycle and supply chain process (product design, sales, inventory management, product scheduling, product quality, engineering, and customer service. All information is shared relevant and up-to-date with real-time analytics. Adopting a 4.0 to a company can be beneficial as it makes the entire supply chain process run smoothly.

- **Market competitive** against giant companies like Alibaba and Amazon. It helps companies to optimize the overall supply chain management process. Investing in technology is an advantage for big companies while providing better customer services.
- **Innovative,** it helps you to attract a young workforce. Companies that are positioned well retain new workers.
- **Increase Efficiency,** IR 4.0 increases the businesses' efficiency, helping departments collaborate well, enables predictive analytics, and leverages meantime data to make vital decisions.
- **Solving issues,** automation, analytics, and real-time data can solve a company's potential supply chain-related issues in the meantime.

- **Increase Profit** IR 4.0 helps cut the manufacturing cost and provides insight into making intelligent decisions for your business that can increase profit.

2. SUPPLY CHAIN MANAGEMENT

IR plays a vital role in supply chain management, as it is the core of the business processes. The supply chain is the key through which a product moves onto a different channel. The revolution of industry 4.0 is a significant need for the future, where everything will be the IoT, and every traditional manufacturing process has to be redefined to ease the overall supply chain process. IR is bringing a change in the manufacturing industry by redefining manufacturing processes, including digitalization, automation, and efficiency in operations such as supply chain networks (see figure 1). A supply chain network is a heterogeneous ecosystem linking product development, manufacturing, and supply process.

Figure 1. Characteristic Features of supply chain management in IR 4.0

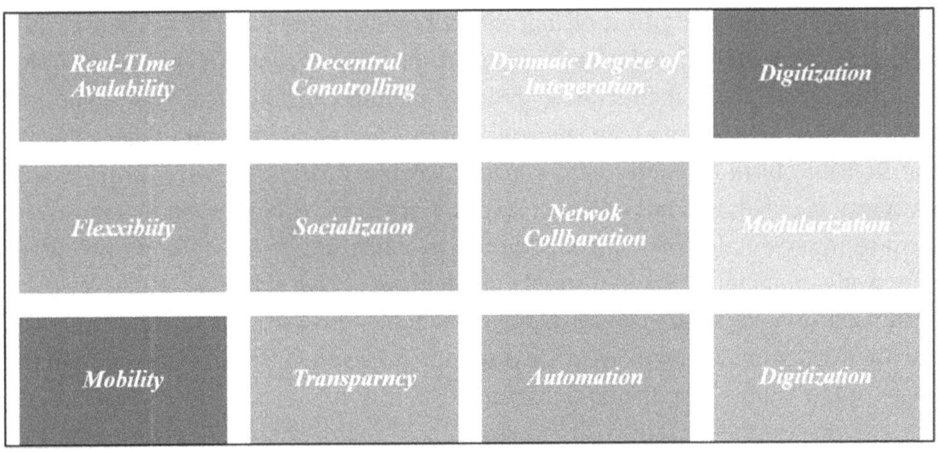

Digitalization help companies retain internal processes and improvise communication channels. Atomization allows making solid decisions based on algorithms. Industry 4.0 value chain transparency of the whole supply chain process. Mobility will enable organizations to communicate well and share instant data by completely changing interaction between stakeholders: IR 4.0 empowering value chains and product modularization through adjusting product facilities. Like business networks, there are social networks that monitor all activities and processes through network collaboration. Machines interact and communicate with other intelligent devices or with any other human in a much-socialized manner.

3. INVENTORY MANAGEMENT

IR 4.0 is an essential part of inventory management, where everything is digitalized on the intelligent system. Products are getting smart, and customers are demanding a product that gives them great satisfaction. Manufacturing and services are parallel, thus managing the visible supply chain process that is decentralized during inventory management. Digitalization is the essence of industry 4.0, with fast progress concerning technology, product optimization, and inventory management to a new level. It has transformed inventory systems and optimized them to a new level that benefits the industry.

IR has transformed industries into digitalization, a blend of the physical and digital realm. IR 4.0 is a technology fusion that helps to integrate cyber, machines, and humans domains. It includes the Internet of things (IoT), artificial intelligence, autonomous vehicles, robotics, quantum computing, and material science. It is enabled by intelligent digitization that connects and integrates the new digital world. Inventory is directly related to cash flow and appears to be indifferent from visible/invisible form. The manufacturing process includes visual form (raw material, work-in-process inventory management, and finished good inventory management) and invisible form (memory card capacity, memory, and bandwidth). In IR 4.0, inventory management has different stages. Each stage is conducted in a digitized form to improve customer satisfaction while managing inventory and operations effectively, reducing costs in a supply chain process (see figure 2). However, it is promising to hold stock in some stages. It contains product depreciation and cash retention to optimize inventory at the downstream level while upholding minimum inventory to maintain supply and demand.

Figure 2. The four aspects of inventory system in IR 4.0

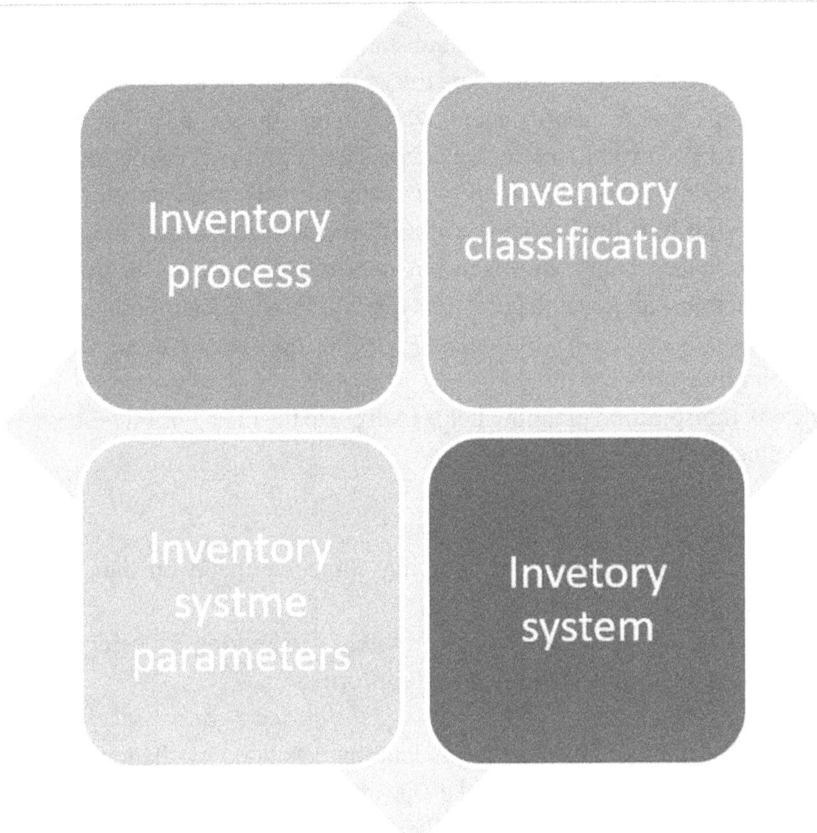

According to figure 2, below are an explanation of each factor illustrated.

1. Inventory process: In IR 4.0, it empowers the process of purchase and fulfillment digitized.
2. Inventory classification: In this aspect, IR 4.0 provides product ranking concerning dollar value available in real-time.
3. Inventory system parameters: The digitized system inventory system has different parameters, including ordering cost and meantime supply: current problems like maintaining MOQ (minimum order quantity) and the active price challenge inventory intelligent system management.
4. Inventory system review: In IR 4.0, the periodic review helps determine the level of inventory and fresh orders placed during this time. It systematically provides meantime information.

4. TRANSPORTATION

In transportation and logistics, IR 4.0 is substantial to increase the quality of data and its availability as technology is changing the world rapidly, determined by disruption of software impacting the supply chain, which in turn creates a shift in processes in the upward and downward stream. Businesses are adopting IT solutions that have more visibility to their supply chain processes and help them develop intelligent factories to bring E2E (end-to-end) visibility inside companies, linking to unlike points on the value chains. Digitized business models help to do transportation planning with transparency and good data quality. It increases mobilization among different channels in the transportation system and creates more value in the distribution process.

In IR 4.0, transpiration planning helps to digitize the distribution process, which allows evaluating the key points:

- Exact demand and shipping forecasts
- Identify flexible routing and shipping choices depend on data restriction, real-time traffic, and weather.
- Respond in a more agile way to possible disruptions by using up-to-date warehouse usage and freight capacity information.

Before industrial 4.0, transportation planning was done by shadow IT and data silos which were not enough to make optimum decisions in the meantime. IR helps retain more updated data and timely available information, preventing failed transportation planning in certain conditions. It improvises communication between key stakeholders and transport planners likely to meet the overall business goal. Innovative logistic technology like sensors placed on transport goods or lorries sends timely information about status and position through a telecommunication network. IoT gives real-time information to companies about their goods flow and resources used for Transportation (Uckelmann, 2008). Traceability helps to increase the quality of service in business-to-business and business-to-consumer deliveries. The transportation and logistics chain is more foreseeable, meaning more value can be drawn upstream and downstream in the supply chain process. Following are the applications for transport management systems in IR 4.0

1. Resource Planning: It helps increase productivity, agility, and flexibility to the fluctuations that might have arisen in the supply chain process due to complexities. It is increasing the level of transparency and visibility to ensure the effectiveness of the transportation system.

2. Warehouse management system: The flow of goods warehouse plays a vital role in the supply chain. It is a competitive advantage for logistic providers that serve as a critical source to increase reach efficiency. IR 4.0 model has embarked on innovative change in keeping (WMS) warehouse management system up-to-date by providing minute information with every warehouse activity to meet inbound logistic requirements in the 4.0 paradigm.
3. Transportation management systems: A TMS (transportation management system) is centered on transportation logistics as part of supply chain management. It allows interaction between the distribution center and the order management system or warehouse. A GPS in TMS helps companies to locate and monitor freight movement during deliveries.
4. Intelligent transportation system: In transportation systems, ITS (intelligent transportation system) is an innovative field that interoperates in diverse areas. IR4.0, the emergence of creative technology, helps in large operations being an essential factor of transportation. It increases the reliability of the transport system and reduces the risk of any incident during transportation.
5. Information security: A rise in the internet-based application have promoted the development of cloud-based systems, big data analytics, IoT, bring your device and choose your device technology has changed the business approach that organization conducts.

5. WAREHOUSING

In IR 4.0, essential warehouse and logistic operations processes use innovative technology like stock and loading management. It is about robots who undertake repetitive tasks, but it is about using intelligent computers to collect massive data, disclose processes, and improve further. However, using smart features in warehousing helps measure stock levels more accurately and automate order processes. Devices and human operators' actions can be tracked easily via an intelligent technology system implemented in the warehouse. It helps monitor key points' error and inefficacy and poor interactions and processes while keeping stock management.

WMS is used in many warehouses operations under industrial 4.0 to run smooth deliveries and store buffer stock effectively by utilizing timely available information. WMS is a nerve center of massive digital operations, data collection, and send out orders to a crowd of autonomous and mobile platforms. Each task is controlled and classified by the independent system, with having only one or two human involvement. Businesses are taking plentiful benefits from innovative technology for warehouse systems. IR 4.0 provides accurate inventory management to reduce waste and the potential for stocking, while robotics doing repetitive tasks benefits health and safety. Processes optimized to ensure environmental-friendly include the usage of rechargeable batteries. Intelligent devices, such as glasses with heads-up displays, improve the worker's action, letting them pick out and receive instructions more rapidly than traditional ones. The combined effect of all makes warehouse and logistics operations more efficient, which ultimately improving delivery times.

Design changes in warehouses accommodating new workers and workflows. Some areas of a warehouse will be altered to be entirely run by robots, resulting in high-density racking and storage accessible by people. Industry 4.0 and other automation are aligned technologies that are reliable for significant operations such as Amazon. Continuous growth in this area indicates that it is wise to explore more possibilities of an upgrade, to make sure smooth transition as much as possible. Tracking the warehouse's goods throughout the supply process results in good delivery quality for placed orders by companies. Below are the popular technologies for IR 4.0 are:

- GPS (Global Positioning System)
- RFID (Radio Frequency Identification)
- WSN (Wireless sensor networks)
- NFC (Near Field Communication)
- NB IoT (NarrowBand-Internet of Things)

The intelligent technology IoT provides us better insight into the flow of goods, like upstream between warehouse and factory, and downstream between store and warehouse through a sensor placed on containers, send meantime information about the current status or position of the delivery.

6. INDUSTRIAL REVOLUTION IN PORT MANAGEMENT

Implementing IR 4.0 and digitalizing the port will be beneficial in enhancing the communication and interaction of sea, rail, and road carriers. This digitalization at port comes with optimizing traffic situations and reducing the waiting hours, which will further direct towards an enhanced flow of traffic at the seaport and the area around it (Port & Magazine, 2020).

A vast and considerable amount of information and data will be produced, which will be helpful in many ways in the various procedures followed by the port. Transparency in the operations will be improved to optimize the processes (Port & Magazine, 2020). Visibility will be high, but the security will not be compromised. Smart contracts with the help of blockchain and IoT can be made, reducing the lead times and the cost.

Digitalization of the port will lead to efficient and effective utilization of the available capacity at the port (Port & Magazine, 2020); this will contribute to the optimization of the operations and the increase of revenue generation and cost benefits, eventually leading towards a better economy of the country.

The innovation design of seaports is directly correlated with digital infrastructure. And such a structure can be brought through three divisions, self-communicating portals for paperless transactions, developing digital methods & manuals, and an adaptive user port interface for ease of implementation. Nowadays, sports networks have been recreated by the applications and framework of information technology and competitive information systems. These services and designs evident a concrete roadmap for internal and external communication systems, database dashboard creations, production optimizations, and safe-work methods at both sea and dry port.

7. CONCLUSION

The computers were introduced to reduce the human workload and provide ease in performing the mathematical and different operations. Initially, it was a machine operated by humans. Now that technology has been evolved, massive disruptions in the technology industry have been made. In today's era, computers have been transformed into intelligent robots that can perform various and multiple actions or operations independently without any human intervention, more efficiently and effectively. Machine learning, artificial intelligence, big data analytics, additive manufacturing, augmented reality, cloud computing, and IoT are the best evidence of the technological advancement which have triggered the disruption in the other industries. Many manufacturing industries realized the changing environment, accepted the change, and adapted it to convert traditional operations into intelligent operations. Manufacturing industries are not the only ones who have been affected and attracted by this technological change, but the supply chain has also realized the importance of these technological trends emerging in the marketplaces. It has been acknowledged by various countries, which play a vital role in global trading and generating foreign income, should be transformed through implementing these technologies. The operations can be run more smoothly while enhancing the efficiency and effectiveness of the industries internally and externally. The economically stable countries and advanced manufacturing technology stand out globally. The era of this revolution with such a technological change was named the IR4.0. Whereas developed countries have transformed the supply chain using digital technologies and are now working on futuristic innovative ideas. Stakeholders in the supply chain use digital technology, different ports worldwide are using IR 4.0. The technology is helping ports to can connect to many countries and provide shorter routes for trading. The behavior of change resistance still exists in many industries that need to be catered to by governments backing the idea of industry 4.0 in the developing world. The implementation in the business operations will transform conventional industries into technically advanced industries.

REFERENCES

Brettel, M. (2014). How Virtualization, Decentralization and Network Building Change the Manufacturing Landscape: An Industry 4.0 Perspective. *International Journal ofMechanical, Aerospace, Industrial and Mechatronics Engineering, 8*(1), 37.

Porter, M. E., & Heppelmann, J. E. (2015). Wie smarte Produkte den Wettbewerb verän-dern. Harvard Business Manager, 12, 1.

Uckelmann, D. (2008). *Definition Approach to Smart Logistics*. Wireless Advanced Networking. doi:10.1007/978-3-540-85500-2_28

Chapter 6
Outsourcing Transportation Management:
A Case Study of an Online Shopping Company

Fahim Ul Amin
Chang'an University, China

Dong Qianli
Chang'an University, China

Wasim Ul Amin
North China Electric Power University, China

Iram Zulfiqar
North China Electric Power University, China

Shamsa Kanwal
North China Electric Power University, China

ABSTRACT

Transport management has significant importance in every organization. This chapter aims to evaluate the outsourcing decision of transportation management of an online shopping company. Recently, the company has witnessed significant growth in its operations, and it became inevitable to decide whether it continues outsourcing transportation management or go for insourcing as various problems are experienced due to outsourcing. The company has many logistics operations that include inbound receiving, warehousing, and outbound distribution. All the operations are considered and studied to understand the problem and objectives of outsourcing. In this chapter, a literature review regarding outsourcing transportation management is provided. Afterward, a research methodology is proposed and adopted, and then cost analysis is performed to check the feasibility concerning financial resources. Based on the cost analysis, it is decided to discontinue outsourcing transportation management. Some recommendations are also proposed for insourcing transportation management.

DOI: 10.4018/978-1-7998-7642-7.ch006

INTRODUCTION

Outsourcing is the tactical usage of external resources to carry out activities that are generally performed by in-house resources (Elmuti 2003). Outsourcing is different from collaboration or partnerships in a way that the flow of resources is unidirectional, from the provider to the user (Katsanis 2007). In the last few decades, an increasing trend has been witnessed in outsourcing among many multinational national organizations (Zachariasz 2010). It is gradually becoming common practice for organizations to outsource some of their jobs to concentrate on their core or primary professional activities. Firms are outsourcing everything from logistics management to entire functions such as human resources (Katsanis 2007).

Logistics is comprised of two discrete but joined operations; material management and product distribution. Material management includes all operations related to the parts' production and finished product, whereas product distribution refers to the steps involved in providing these parts and finished products to the consumer. The later operation involves the transportation and warehousing of products (Rodrigue 2014). Transportation management refers to the aspect of logistics, which deals with the physical distribution of goods or products to the customer. It involves the observation of the operation and the communication with carriers, which accomplish the transportation of the goods or products from the warehouses, and additionally selection of carriers according to different locations. Many organizations have started to uptake the concept of transport management outsourcing, but some organizations are in doubt after undertaking the path of outsourcing transport operations. This is because due to some market factors such as competitiveness, increased cost, and uncertainty present in Pakistan's economy.

The paper aims to evaluate the outsourcing of transportation management of an online shopping company, which we will name D-Company due to company confidentiality. The D-Company is making significant progress in the online shopping domain of the Pakistani market and provides a variety of products ranging from groceries to toys, furniture, electronics items, etc. to customers' doorstep. When the company was established, the company was not able to run its transport department; therefore transportation management is outsourced from the beginning. Later on, with an increase of customers and their demands, the company opened offices in all districts of Pakistan but the outsourcing decision remained unchanged. However, the logistic provider further assigned transportation operations to different courier companies in different cities. However, outsourced transportation management resulted in complaints increased on daily basis. Firstly, the main problem faced by the company's employees is that loads of time and effort are being made by them for jobs that should be technically handled by the logistics provider. For example, if clients have some issues with the delivery of the product, they contact to company's officials rather than the logistics provider, thus a significant time of employees is wasted in sorting out these issues for which the logistics provider is being paid. Thus, it is believed that D-company is paying a significant amount of money to the logistic provider for activities being performed in the company. Another important problem is the price standardization of the logistics providers' cost of delivery. The logistics provider is offering different prices for different sections and the tariff of various departments are not consistent such as different tariff for the grocery section as compare to the tariff of the electronics section. The lack of appropriate understandings leads to the doubts that the logistics provider is costly than when the transport is managed by the company itself.

This work aims to evaluate whether it is beneficial to outsource transportation management of the company or the operation should be insourced. Initially, theory and state of the art in outsourcing are discussed in the literature review. Afterward, research methodology is presented in which research questions are developed in the context of the company's operation. Based on the research questions, qualitative analysis and cost analysis are performed to evaluate whether it is good to insource the operation of the company should keep going with outsourcing. A concise discussion is provided in this regard. The rest of the structure of the paper is as follows: Preliminaries of the subject are presented in Section 2. The literature review is provided in Section 3. The research methodology is presented in Section 4. Research findings and cost analysis is shown in Section 5. Section 6 provides a discussion of this research. Finally, Section 7 concludes the paper.

PRELIMINARIES

Logistics service levels. Logistics services and transportation management of a company have different levels that depend on its structure and operations. (Fadile et al. 2018) has reviewed a variety of literature available on outsourcing decisions of logistics service levels. Their research has suggested three levels of logistic services:

- Level 1- Basic logistics: Basic logistic services are transportation and warehousing. Activities at this level are outsourced to a large degree in companies;
- Level 2- Value-added logistics: Value-added logistics services are re-labeling and re-packaging, or customization of the final product. For example, Olives are imported in Pakistan and packed with different labels in various packaging and then transported.
- Level 3- Advanced logistics: Advanced logistic services include inventory and transport management, or distribution network design, and road/carrier

selection. This level of logistics is often managed by companies and is not common to outsource.

Logistic service providers. The logistics service provider can be defined as "an external provider who manages, controls, and carries out logistics services on behalf of a firm" (Hertz and Alfredsson 2003).

Logistics service providers are categorized with various nomenclatures in the literature concerning the level of services they provide to companies. However, the common and popular categorization based on services provided by logistics service providers falls within six families. These are called 1PL, 2PL, 3PL, 3PL+/LLP, 4PL, and 5PL. The detail of each family is provided in brief:

- 1PL- First-party logistics is the term used for companies that have in-sourced logistics. The companies have all logistics assets and carry out all logistics operations.
- 2PL-Asset-based logistics companies, perform the traditional logistics operations such as transportation, material handling, and warehousing.
- 3PL-Third party logistics has progressed from 2PL as logistics service providers started to incorporate the traditional logistics operations that were provided separately earlier. 3PL logistics providers can also offer value-added operations such as inventory management, packaging, assembly, and labeling. In 3PL, the relationship between the company and the logistics provider is often defined as a logistics association or strategic alliance that is a close relationship between the outsourcing company and a logistics provider subjected to a long-term contract (Skjoett-Larsen 2000). 3PL performs the transportation of customer products, or outsource transport to third-party carriers.
- 3PL+, or Lead Logistics Provider (LLP), is similar to the 4PL as both families provide the same logistics services. The difference is in having assets as a 3PL+ provides services with mixed-assets i.e. it performs logistic services by using both own and other logistics providers' assets.
- 4PL or Fourth Party Logistics is developed based on 3PL. 4PL are different from aforementioned logistics providers in a way that they only provide business services and don't own any physical assets such as warehouses, trucks, etc. 4PL combines resources of various service providers, plan and operate complex operations. 4PL is more about the supervision and management of logistics services to provide an effective and efficient logistics system to the company (Alt and Schmid 2000; Delfmann et al. 2002).
- 5PL is a new notion of logistics provider established to work for the e-commerce market. The major concern of 5PL is to provide an automated

intelligent system to improve the logistics and supply chain of e-business. 5PL logistics providers handle all events of the supply chain in e-business with the help of new technologies.

LITERATURE REVIEW

A significant amount of research has been done on decision-making for outsourcing. A detailed literature review in this regard has been performed by (Perunović 2007), in which authors deduced that the outsourcing process starts with cost analysis, which is the basis of Transaction Cost Economics (TCE) and Agency Theory (Gottschalk and Solli-Sæther 2006). However, with an increase in outsourcing practice, the paradigm also shifted to the resource stage, where Resource-based view (RBV) theory is also being considered in outsourcing (El Mokrini et al. 2016). (Hsiao et al. 2010) also acknowledged TCE and RBV as the two main methodologies additionally suggested Supply Chain Management Theory. More recently, (Fadile et al. 2018) have surmised that TCE and RBV are the theories widely conferred in the literature. Most of the researchers are agreed that there are three major theories of outsourcing i.e.

(i) Transaction Cost Economics (TCE),
(ii) The resource-based view (RBV)
(iii) Agency Theory

The TCE is one of the fundamental theories in management sciences about outsourcing. Any organization's growth and sustainability highly depend on identifying the cheaper way to perform different operations either in-house or to external agents as outsourcing (Hong et al. 2010). The cost to perform these outsourcing activities is called transactional cost. The TCE theory has been greatly influenced by (Ouchi and Williamson 1977), which further elaborated three dimensions of TCE as (i) asset specificity, (ii) uncertainty, and (iii) frequency (Eccles and Williamson 1987).

Asset specificity is a significant element for TCE in logistics management (Hong et al. 2010). Asset specificity narrates the fact that the management of product distribution, at times require special handling which is normally due to unique or non-standard products or market it is aimed for. Since the company has heavily invested in its product, they face the risk of opportunistic behavior by the logistics providers in this regard (Dickmann and Tyson 2005). This situation has been stated by various researchers in the field of logistics management (Lamminmaki 2005; Spraakman and Davidson 1998; Verbeke and Kano 2010; De Vita and Tekaya 2015)

The second important element of TCE is uncertainty, which is further categorized as environmental uncertainty and behavioral uncertainty. Environmental uncertainty is associated with an exchange between a company and logistics provider and includes demand, supply, and technology uncertainty (Huo et al. 2018). Behavioral uncertainty is associated with performance verification (Heide and Rindfleisch 1997). The effect of behavioral uncertainty on transaction costs is mainly due to negotiation, monitoring, and executing arrangements (Schoenherr 2010), which eventually vary the bargaining transaction costs and enforcement transaction costs, which are two of the three main transaction cost categories.

The third element of TCE is transaction frequency. The higher the transaction frequency of a certain product, the more the company should seek a hierarchical governance form (Eccles and Williamson 1987). However, research findings of the significant effect of transaction frequency on transaction costs are rare (Heide and Rindfleisch 1997).

The RBV theory is about the consideration of resources own by the company for outsourcing decision-making. The RBV theory is concerned about the resources, proficiencies, and abilities of a company as compared to TCE theory where all focus is on the transaction. Thus RBV is rather used as an instrument to validate outsourcing decisions, which is also perceived by many researchers in decision-making theory (Duncan 1998; Espino-Rodriguez and Padrón-Robaina 2006; Goles 2003). The RBV theory negates Porter's hypotheses that product and market positions decide sustainable competitive advantages. (Espino-Rodriguez and Padrón-Robaina 2006). On the contrary, it suggests that disparity in the possession of resources and competencies between companies decides the sustainable competitive advantages, which also affects the performances over time (Wernerfelt 1984). The RBV theory supports the company to decide in using in-house resources or outsourcing thus encourages the company to explore market resources for outsourcing rather than involving the company in other domains (Silverman 1999). However, this theory works in cases when tangible or intangible resources are specific and unconventional. Unconventional resources are valuable, rare, unique, and non-substantial, which also define the company's performance (Duschek 2004).

The Agency theory is different from the aforementioned theories in a way, it applies to resolve issues of already outsources products or services. Thus, it is not used to decide to outsource, rather it is used to manage or reconsider outsourcing decisions (Geis 2007; Logan 2000). The agency theory is used to solve the various problems in Agency Relationship. The Agency Relationship is defined as the association in which a company or the principal hires another entity or an Agent to perform the work assigned to the company. This relationship is also developed in outsourcing as the outsourcing company is the principal and the contractor is the Agent. The agency relationship affects outsourcing as it improves the outsourcing by improving contracts.

RESEARCH METHODOLOGY

Research objectives. The objective of this research is to evaluate and determine the best solution regarding the outsourcing of transportation management. The research is divided into two parts. The first part is to understand the current problems and situations about transportation management. Secondly, perform the cost analysis to determine whether outsourcing is the best solution or not concerning the economic point of view. No hypotheses are formed and tested, and the findings are only relevant to outsourcing of transportation management.

Research questions. To address the research objectives, and to find the optimal usage of transportation management, it is essential to plan the research. In this regard some research questions have been formulated, which are given below:

Research question 1 (RQ1): What problems are experienced by the D-company employees due to transportation management?

Research question 2 (RQ2): What is the Cost analysis of transportation management with outsourcing and insourcing?

Research question 3 (RQ3)): Based on RQ1-RQ2, what would be the best options for the company regarding in- or outsourcing its transport management?

Research approach. This research is a mixed type and combination of qualitative and quantitative methods. The research approach is divided into two main areas. The first area focuses on existing problems faced by the D-company and employees, whereas the second area is concerned about cost analysis.

In the first part of this research, the literature study was conducted to get insights into outsourcing theories. In this part, a qualitative approach has been applied to identify the existing problems in D-company, and problems faced by the employees due to transportation management. The data was collected through interviews, company documents, communication, and complaints record, and reports regarding transportation management.

In the second part of the research, cost analysis is performed based on statistical and numerical data. The data was collected from company internal records, data transactions; logistics service providers' transaction logs, and communication records.

Data collection. The data collection was performed by interviews, observations, and the company's internal data, records, and documents. The data collected used for both qualitative and quantitative research methods.

RESEARCH FINDINGS

Qualitative Study and Findings. During the first phase of research, existing problems faced by the D-company and employees are studied. Based on the qualitative study, the following problems are identified.

1. The transportation cost is not timely provided by the logistics provider.
2. There exist discrepancies in the records and responsibilities of employees.
3. The logistics provider does not update product tracking to both the client as well as the company.

Transportation cost: The logistic provider is bounded to timely inform transportation costs to the company so that they could be included in the product invoice. However, the study shows that the lack of this practice is creating issues and double effort is being applied in client communication. In addition, sometimes double invoices are being generated. In some sections, this delay is more than a week.

Discrepancies: The study has also revealed other important issues, which are discrepancies in transaction records, communication and, knowledge of Operating Procedures (OP) between the company and logistics provider. The study also found a lack of overview of transportation management by the logistics provider.

Tracking information: The study also found that if a consignment is not sent by a standard courier (such as TCS, M&P, FedEx, etc.); the logistic provider doesn't generally provide tracking information to the company as well as the client. This issue often causes the customers to contact the company to get tracking information, which is the job of the logistics provider, for which the one is being paid. This causes the company employees to put extra effort and work double more often.

Cost analysis. The cost analysis is performed to check whether it is economically suitable to outsource transportation or not. The cost analysis is performed via important cost factors such as implementation cost, transaction cost, personnel cost and tariff cost. Each cost factor is obtained separately for insourcing and outsourcing. The option with overall high score is preferred and recommended. It is worth mentioning that cost analysis score doesn't reflect the expenses for the corresponding option. The comparatively high score shows the relatively low cost and expenses.

To determine the cost analysis, firstly important cost factors are defined. These factors are measured on a five-point Likert scale. These factors are then determined based on a survey, transaction records, and internal records for insourcing and outsourcing both options. These factors are calculated for all sections separately and then summed up to find the complete effect of that factor for the whole company. The factors and description of their Likert scale are defined below:

1. Implementation Cost (1 = very high, 5 = very low) is the cost that will be required for processes involved in adapting the new implementation and internal structuring.
2. Transaction Cost (1 = very high, 5 = very low) is the cost involved in negotiating, trading, or information gathering due to high asset specificity or behavioral uncertainty of the agent.
3. Personnel Cost (1 = very high, 5 = very low) is the increase in the hiring of new personnel cost for transportation management.
4. Tariff Cost (1 = very high, 5 = very low) is the tariff for the particular option.

The scores for all factors are set up in such a way that an option with the high score is the more feasible option.

Cost Factor Scores for Outsourcing Transportation Management: The score and discussion for each cost factor are discussed below.

1. Implementation Cost. The continuation of outsourced transportation management doesn't require major structural and procedural changes. However, a lot of effort is inevitable to improve the existing structure. The collective score received from all sections is 23.
2. Transaction Cost. The transaction costs of outsourced transportation management should be increased. In addition, the nature of the asset remains specific and outsourced, which leads to behavioral uncertainty and opportunistic behavior. The collective score is of this criterion is 15.
3. Personnel Cost. The continuation of outsourced transportation management doesn't change anything concerning personnel costs. Therefore, this criterion receives a score of 40.
4. Tariff Cost. Since the tariff cost is unfairly distributed among different sections. Therefore this criterion received different scores from different sections. The collective score of all sections is 15.

Cost Factor Scores for Insourcing Transportation Management: The score and discussion for each cost factor are discussed below.

1. Implementation Cost. The insourcing of transportation management requires a substantial amount of restructuring/re-bargaining because of new carrier negotiation and selection. The collective score of this criterion is 14.
2. Transaction Cost. The transactional costs of information gathering and enforcement will be minimum as the company retains overall control, and insourcing will offer a transparent cost overview of the different carriers available. The collective score of this section is 40.

3. Personnel Cost. However, the insourcing requires the induction of extra personnel but according to different sections, the overall cost will be reduced. The collective score of this section is 32
4. Tariff Cost. The tariff will be fairly declared and will be available to all sections transparently, so this cost will be reduced as compared to outsourcing solutions. This criterion received a score of 40 from all sections. Table 1 shows a summary of the cost analysis.

Table 1. Cost Analysis

No.	Cost Factor	Insourcing Score	Outsourcing Score
1.	Implementation Cost	14	23
2.	Transaction Cost	40	15
3.	Personnel Cost	32	40
4.	Tariff Cost	40	15
Total Score		126	93

It is clear from Table 1 that insourcing transportation management has received a higher score based on the cost analysis. An obvious reason is that the continuation of outsourcing of transportation management only offers some improvements to the current situation; however, it does not eradicate the main problems that cause errors within the framework of outsourcing.

DISCUSSIONS

Decision of outsourcing transportation operation is a critical decision for a profit making organization as it effects not only on company revenue but also its reputation. The research questions formulated for this research provided focus and direction for this research, to achieve the research goal and provide an optimization solution for regarding the selection of outsourcing or insourcing.

The first question RQ1 regarding the problems faced by the company was answered in the Research Finding section, where major problems faced by the company are outlined. The major two problems were the discrepancies in the records and responsibilities of employees and lack of product tracking update to the client and the company

The Second question RQ2 regarding cost analysis has been also answered in the Research Finding section, in which cost factors are defined and the score regarding these factors collected from all sections is used to determine the overall score for insourcing and outsourcing. It is clear that implementation cost factor receives lower score for insourcing which clearly indicates that insourcing will require more implementation cost. However, other factors' scores and overall score for the insourcing is comparatively lower for insourcing transport management. The score clearly shows that insourcing transport management is economically better for the D-company and will require less financial resources.

Keeping in view the solutions of RQ1 and RQ2, it is recommended that the D-Company should start insourcing transportation management. It means the activities of carrier selection and carrier negotiation, alongside carrier monitoring, should be insourced under the responsibility of the company's employees. Additional employees can be hired for this purpose or already available employees should commit to these responsibilities, whereas the extra hired employees can take over the responsibilities of the respective sourcing employees.

The following recommendations are also presented to run the insourcing transportation management effectively.

1. The contract with selected couriers should be outcome-based. It means the fee should be agreed on the outcome of transport and performance rather than baseline tariffs.
2. There must be an agreement about the assignment of duties and extra transportation costs. The risk analysis should be performed in this regard before the agreement.
3. The contract length should not be short-term. This will improve mutual interest and benefit.
4. The Audit should also be part of the contract to maintain control of the process and prevent opportunistic behavior.
5. There must be clear clauses regarding outcome-based rewards and incurred tariff in the contract

Furthermore, the company is recommended to streamline communication, prevent discrepancies and make a good tracking and trace department for improved customer care.

CONCLUSION

This work was about to evaluate the outsourcing of transportation management of an online shopping company. Since its inception, transportation management was outsourced. However, after business growth outsourced transportation management resulted in complaints increased daily. The work was aimed to review whether the company should continue outsourcing transportation management or should go for insourcing or in-house transportation management. In this work, initially, theory and state of the art in outsourcing have been discussed. Afterward, research questions were formulated and research methodology was presented which combined both qualitative approach and quantitative approach. The qualitative study was conducted to get insight into problems being faced by the company. Whereas quantitative study i.e. cost analysis was performed to evaluate whether it is good to insource the operation of the company should keep going with outsourcing. The qualitative study and cost analysis both resulted in favor of insourcing. Finally, a concise discussion is provided regarding the selection of insourcing transportation management.

REFERENCES

Alt, R., & Schmid, B. (2000). *Logistik und Electronic Commerce--Perspektiven durch zwei sich wechselseitig erganzende Konzepte. (With English summary).* Zeitschrift fur Betriebswirtschaft.

De Vita, G., & Tekaya, A. (2015). Hotel outsourcing under asset specificity: 'The good, the bad and the ugly.'. *Tourism Management*, *47*, 97–106. doi:10.1016/j.tourman.2014.09.012

Delfmann, W., Albers, S., & Gehring, M. (2002). The impact of electronic commerce on logistics service providers. *International Journal of Physical Distribution & Logistics Management*, *32*(3), 203–222. doi:10.1108/09600030210426539

Dickmann, M., & Tyson, S. (2005). Outsourcing payroll: Beyond transaction-cost economics. *Personnel Review*, *34*(4), 451–467. doi:10.1108/00483480510599770

Duncan, N. B. (1998). Beyond opportunism: A resource-based view of outsourcing risk. *Proceedings of the Hawaii International Conference on System Sciences*, 675–684. 10.1109/HICSS.1998.654829

Duschek, S. (2004). Inter-Firm Resources and Sustained Competitive Advantage. *Management Review*, *15*(1), 53–73.

Eccles, R. G., & Williamson, O. E. (1987). The Economic Institutions of Capitalism: Firms, Markets, Relational Contracting. *Administrative Science Quarterly*, *32*(4), 602. doi:10.2307/2392889

El Mokrini, A., Dafaoui, E. M., El Mhamedi, A., & Berrado, A. (2016). A decision framework for outsourcing logistics in the pharmaceutical supply chain. *Proceedings of 2015 International Conference on Industrial Engineering and Systems Management, IEEE IESM 2015*, 748–756.

Elmuti, D. (2003). The Perceived Impact of Outsourcing on Organizational Performance. *American Journal of Business*, *18*(2), 33–42. doi:10.1108/19355181200300010

Espino-Rodriguez, T. F., & Padrón-Robaina, V. (2006). A review of outsourcing from the resource-based view of the firm. *International Journal of Management Reviews*. Advance online publication. doi:10.1111/j.1468-2370.2006.00120.x

Fadile, L., El Oumami, M., & Beidouri, Z. (2018). Logistics outsourcing: A review of basic concepts. *International Journal of Supply Chain Management*, *7*(3), 53–69.

Geis, G. S. (2007). Business outsourcing and the agency cost problem. *The Notre Dame Law Review*.

Goles, T. (2003). Vendor capabilities and outsourcing success: A resource-based view. *Wirtschaftsinformatik*, *45*(2), 199–206. doi:10.1007/BF03250900

Gottschalk, P., & Solli-Sæther, H. (2006). Maturity model for IT outsourcing relationships. *Industrial Management & Data Systems*, *106*(2), 200–212. doi:10.1108/02635570610649853

Heide, J. B., & Rindfleisch, A. (1997). Transaction Cost Analysis : Past, Present, and Future Applications. *Journal of Marketing*.

Hertz, S., & Alfredsson, M. (2003). Strategic development of third party logistics providers. *Industrial Marketing Management*, *32*(2), 139–149. doi:10.1016/S0019-8501(02)00228-6

Hong, E., Son, B. G., & Menachof, D. (2010). Exploring the link between IT systems and the outsourcing of logistics activities: A transaction cost perspective. *International Journal of Logistics Research and Applications*, *13*(1), 41–57. doi:10.1080/13675560903233682

Hsiao, H. I., van der Vorst, J. G. A. J., Kemp, R. G. M., & Omta, S. W. F. O. (2010). Developing a decision-making framework for levels of logistics outsourcing in food supply chain networks. *International Journal of Physical Distribution & Logistics Management*, *40*(5), 395–414. doi:10.1108/09600031011052840

Huo, B., Ye, Y., Zhao, X., Wei, J., & Hua, Z. (2018). Environmental uncertainty, specific assets, and opportunism in 3PL relationships: A transaction cost economics perspective. *International Journal of Production Economics*, *203*, 154–163. doi:10.1016/j.ijpe.2018.01.031

Katsanis, C. J. (2007). Outsourcing. *Workplace Strategies and Facilities Management*, 378–394.

Lamminmaki, D. (2005). Why do hotels outsource? An investigation using asset specificity. *International Journal of Contemporary Hospitality Management*, *17*(6), 516–528. doi:10.1108/09596110510612158

Logan, M. S. (2000). Using Agency Theory to Design Successful Outsourcing Relationships. *International Journal of Logistics Management*, *11*(2), 21–32. doi:10.1108/09574090010806137

Ouchi, W., & Williamson, O. E. (1977). Markets and Hierarchies: Analysis and Antitrust Implications. *Administrative Science Quarterly*, *22*(3), 540. doi:10.2307/2392191

Perunović, Z. (2007). Outsourcing Process and Theories. *POMS 18th Annual Conference, 8*(5), 35.

Rodrigue, J.-P. (2014). *The Geography of Transport Systems: Transportation and the Urban Form*. Routledge. https://people.hofstra.edu/geotrans/eng/ch6en/conc6en/ch6c1en.html

Schoenherr, T. (2010). Outsourcing decisions in global supply chains: An exploratory multi-country survey. *International Journal of Production Research*, *48*(2), 343–378. doi:10.1080/00207540903174908

Silverman, B. S. (1999). Technological Resources and the Direction of Corporate Diversification: Toward an Integration of.... *Management Science*, *45*(8), 1109–1124. doi:10.1287/mnsc.45.8.1109

Skjoett-Larsen, T. (2000). Third party logistics - From an interorganizational point of view. *International Journal of Physical Distribution & Logistics Management*, *30*(2), 112–127. doi:10.1108/09600030010318838

Spraakman, G., & Davidson, R. (1998). Transaction cost economics as a predictor of management accounting practices at the hudson's bay company, 1860 to 1914. *Accounting History*, *3*(2), 69–101. doi:10.1177/103237329800300204

Verbeke, A., & Kano, L. (2010). Transaction Cost Economics (TCE) and the family firm. *Entrepreneurship Theory and Practice*, *34*(6), 1173–1182. doi:10.1111/j.1540-6520.2010.00419.x

Wernerfelt, B. (1984). A resource-based view of the firm. *Strategic Management Journal*, *5*(2), 171–180. doi:10.1002mj.4250050207

Zachariasz, E. (2010). The European Agency for Safety and Health at Work Informs. *Medycyna Pracy*, *61*(4), 489. PMID:20865861

Chapter 7
Pitfalls and Challenges of Blockchain in Supply Chain and Logistics

Asad Ullah
Middle East College, Oman

Asad Ullah
Middle East College, Oman

Shahid Imran
Middle East College, Oman

ABSTRACT

The potential impact of block chain on supply chain management has been explored by many authors, and indeed, many articles in the popular press extol the benefits of blockchain in supply chain management. In simple terms, blockchain is a distributed ledger system, or a record book, except that it is not maintained by a single person but by anyone who is interested in keeping the records. Since blockchain is a new and revolutionary concept in technology, more techies are interested in it. However, it also has certain disadvantages. The purpose of this study is to explain the challenges and pitfalls of blockchain in supply chain and logistics. Using a systematic literature review method, this chapter identifies 31 publications that discuss the challenges and pitfalls associated with blockchain in supply chain and logistics.

DOI: 10.4018/978-1-7998-7642-7.ch007

1.0 INTRODUCTION

Block chain is a decentralized, distributed database that maintains a continuously growing list of secure data records. It first emerged in the context of Bitcoin, where it serves as a decentralized, distributed digital ledger recording all Bitcoin transactions. Bitcoin is a currency that is controlled by the network of users instead of by centralized banks. The following quote from Jay (2017), expresses the concept of block chain in a simple description:

"Imagine a piece of paper with a name printed on it, and that name rights a person to a pot of wealth. You place it in a room with 50 doors, each of which has a lock. However, someone could break one of the locks and change the name on the sheet of paper. This is the same as a centralized database. Block chain, on the other hand, will duplicate that paper 50 times and put it in 50 different room. In this setting, if someone wants to break the system and change the name on the papers needs to break [at least 25] rooms at the same time."

Thus, the data saved in a block chain cannot be deleted or edited by unauthorized individuals given that several copies are maintained in a decentralized network, which is a key distinction as compared with a regular centralized network. In a centralized database, there is always the risk of fraud or external hacker attacks, whereas in a block chain, unless an attacker manages to take control of the majority of the network, the network will work consistently. Blockchain is visualized as a system to reduce the probability of fraudulent transactions significantly by virtue of distributed maintenance of transactions and capturing of provenance data on every transaction agent and event executing an updated or modified transaction (Khairuddin, 2019; Siddiqui *et al.*, 2020; Sigwart *et al.*, 2020). Block chain supports secured trading on the Internet by capturing the identity and provenance data during each transactional event. It facilitates backward traceability of trust mechanisms and authorizations used by certifying authorities in executing each step forward historically till the current state of a contract visible to the interested parties. Simply stated, secure trading on the Internet through controlled trust establishment and verification is feasible. This attribute facilitates removal of mediating third-parties ensuring security of a contract (Benning, 2016). Tian (2016) states: "Since the whole system is running transparently, the system is absolutely open source and there is no need for trust among every single node because a single node cannot cheat all other nodes on the block chain".

Block chain is also known as the "Internet of Value", and its proponents believe it has the potential to disrupt nearly every business (Tapscott and Tapscott, 2016). While block chain is being used in a variety of industries, such as fine art, luxury goods, pharmaceuticals, medical devices, and jewelry, for anti-counterfeiting and tracking, as well as import/export, real estate, and design and architecture for record-keeping, many recent researchers believe that block chain has the potential to revolutionize supply chain management (Esmaeilian *et al.*, 2020; Copigneaux et al., 2020). One may consider that adopting Bitcoin's block chain design can eliminate the necessity for banks in the supply chain at least in theory. This may allow anyone to trade directly through the Internet. One could trade directly with unknown persons while being anonymous via the block chain. With this view in mind, block chain is being heralded as the next big thing in supply chain circles. The $40 trillion global supply chain sector might become an intriguing future use case for block chain (Parker, 2016). The challenges of adopting block chain in supply chains are the topic of this research (which we call block chain-enabled supply chain).

1.1 Preliminaries

Several authors have looked into the possible impact of block chain on supply chain management, and numerous pieces in the popular press extol the benefits of block chain in the short term. Jeremy Wilson, vice-chairman of Barclays Corporate Banking, for example, believes that block chain can cut supply chain paper work significantly. He brings up the first ever block chain-based trade financing agreement. The time it takes from the time the letter of credit is issued to the time it is approved is normally between seven and ten days, which might be achievable in as less as four hours using block chain ledgers (Lehmacher, 2017). Import, export, and port documentation all have the potential to reduce lead times in global supply chains. According to Hofmann et al., (2018), employing block chain in supply chain finance could speed up operations and reduce total financing expenses. For example, blockchain might make payment insurance simpler by minimizing the need for letters of credit and so lowering transaction fees, enhancing speed and transparency, and so on. Some specific products are reasonably easy to identify, while certain products are very difficult to identify and reproduce. In these cases, proving provenance of things being exchanged is critical where block chain can capture and provide transparent, secure, non-editable, and non-deletable provenance data that can benefit all stakeholders in the supply chain (Khairuddin, 2019; Siddiqui *et al.*, 2020; Sigwart *et al.*, 2020).

While the potential for these impacts and applications to lower costs and speed up supply chain chores should not be overlooked, they are far from revolutionary improvements to present supply chain operations (Alkhudary, Brusset, Fenies, 2020; Allen et al., 2019; Veisi, 2019). However, much of the discussion of block chain's impact on supply chain management is more forward-looking, concentrating on hypothetical future supply chains rather than how block chain might impact supply chains today. In their book, Block chain Revolution, Tapscott and Tapscott investigate the prospects of employing block chain technology for the end-to-end supply chain (Tapscott and Tapscott, 2016). They describe how Smart Contracts will allow organizations to contract for pricing, quality, and delivery dates with a few mouse clicks, and they offer a number of other ways the block chain can affect supply chain management. Other papers have highlighted the applications in supply chain risk management (Alkhudary, Brusset, Fenies, 2020), reducing transportation, information processing, coordination and communication costs (Allen *et al.*, 2019), capturing provenance data for backward traceability (Siddiqui *et al.*, 2020; Veisi, 2019), energy and emissions management (Esmaeilian *et al.*, 2020), and special application areas involving Internet of Things (like, Vaccine supply chains, supply chain forensics, and healthcare supply chains) (Sigwart *et al.*, 2020). However, because all of these application scenarios are presented at a conceptual level, it's impossible to judge how practical they shall be going forward.

According to Alsmiller (2016), block chain can be used to trace commodities from suppliers to guarantee that they are authentic, appropriately stated, and carried safely and correctly. Williams and Gerber (2015) highlighted the advantages of supply chain transparency, concentrating on how block chain will allow us to identify where our food was grown. In theory, we could trace each ingredient in our food back to its source, allowing us to determine whether the bottle of olive oil we just purchased is 100% olive oil or if it is combined with other types of oil. According to Project Provenance Ltd, because every transaction in a block chain-enabled supply chain can be audited, smart phone applications will be able to present all necessary information to consumers in real time, and this information will be totally trustworthy. However, there are a number of roadblocks that make leveraging block chains in this fashion difficult, if not impossible—we'll go over them below. RFID has also been investigated for use in agri-food traceability by a number of academics. Tian (2016, 2018) looked into the possibilities of an agri-food supply chain that uses RFID tags and block chain technology. He brings out a crucial point that hasn't been addressed before: "whether the information given by supply chain members in traceability systems can be trusted". He also claims that RFID and block chain can improve the efficiency and reliability of the agri-food supply chain because he believes the biggest problem with traditional centralized agri-food supply chain supervision is a "monopolistic, asymmetric, and opaque information system that could result in the trust problem, such as fraud, corruption, tampering, and falsifying information". Indeed, these and similar viewpoints argue that markets will no longer require third intermediaries to maintain trust and ensure quality, resulting in lower pricing (Copigneaux *et al.*, 2020; Francisco and Swanson, 2018; Terzi *et al.*, 2019; Tian, 2018). Block chain will enable the tracking of every component of a product back to its source. Many pundits suggest that block chain-enabled supply chains provide this benefit at a fundamental level. For these aspirations to become a reality, we believe that block chain and related technologies will need to be significantly improved. In this paper, we explore the key problems associated with the use of Block Chain technology in Logistics and Supply Chain.

1.2 Methodology

This section presents a description of the research process followed in this research and how the data was collected to identify papers relevant for this study. As the first step the research questions addressed by this study are:
RQ1. What are the key concepts of blockchain technology?
RQ2. What are the possible applications of blockchain technology for Supply chain and logistics?
RQ3. What are the challenges in using blockchain technology in Supply chain and Logistics?
The followed steps were followed to define the inclusion/exclusion criteria:

1. Exclusion of papers having availability of only abstracts;
2. Considering only papers written in English language;
3. Including papers published for WTO and UN;
4. Papers published in reputed journals and master and PHD published theses on websites of global universities;

For the next step, data collection, the keywords used were defined as: Block Chain; Technology; Pitfalls; Challenges; Supply Chain and Logistics. They were used to run semantic searches in online journals databases and scholarly databases and also Google Scholar. The keywords should be found in the paper title, paper keywords and/or paper abstracts. Then the papers were read to assess their relevance and contribution to the present study, and as a final step the discussion of the findings for the future work.

2.0 LITERATURE REVIEW

2.1 What is Block chain?

Bitcoin's underlying technology, the original concept of blockchain, is a type of Distributed Ledger Technology defined as a "distributed, shared, encrypted database that acts as an irreversible and incorruptible store of information" (Wright, 2015). It is constantly growing by adding new blocks to the chain every 10 minutes. It is done by data miners to keep track of the most recent transactions. The blockchain contains all blocks in chronological sequence. When a data miner joins the Bitcoin network, a copy of the updated blockchain is automatically downloaded to each node. The blockchain contains all information about all transactions that have ever been completed (Swan, 2015). The information of transactional exchanges and bitcoin ownership once committed in the bitcoin blockchain became permanent records impossible to edit or delete. The network and database of blockchain is safe and easy to use. The bitcoin blockchain can create transactions based on mathematically specified and mechanically enforced criteria (DTCC, 2016). The important point is that because of its many elements, including technological, operational, legal, and regulatory, blockchain does not have a single definition. As blockchain can permit both instant and long-term economic transactions, and more intricate financial contracts, one way to grasp it is to compare it to the new application layer for Internet protocols. It can be used as a layer for asset, currency, and financial contract transactions. Furthermore, block chain could be used to manage a registry and inventory system for recording, tracking, monitoring, and transacting all assets. As a result, Block chain can be applied to any type of asset, including finance, economics, and money (Swan, 2015).

2.2 Technical concepts

To comprehend the implications of the various architectures in terms of regulation, security, performance, and privacy, it is necessary to explore the technical ideas of blockchain. There are several distinct blockchain-based technologies that have been developed to solve various problems. As a result, different blockchain-type technologies are more or less available for particular needs (Kakavand *et al.*, 2016). Blockchain is a tamper- and revision-proof digital platform that stores the whole history of all transactions between block users across the network. Blockchain is also a database for digital currency transactions, such as those on the Bitcoin and Ethereum networks.

Cryptographic algorithms check all transactions between users or counter-parties, which are subsequently bundled into blocks and added to the Block chain (Copigneaux *et al.*, 2020; Ganne, 2018; Kakavand *et al.*, 2016). As the information in blocks is stored on several nodes and is linked together, no one can change it. Every node in the Bitcoin network has its own copy of the Block chain, which is synchronized with other nodes using a peer-to-peer protocol. This reveals the futility of a central authority and, as a result, participants lose faith in the integrity of any one entity. Without the use of third parties, block chain allows diverse transactions to be processed and secure consensus to be reached. According to Drescher (2017), Kakavand *et al.* (2016), and Swan (2015), the following are the fundamental technical concepts of block chain technology.

(a) Node: A peer, also known as a node, is a computer that maintains the "blocks" using the standard blockchain software.

(b) Network: The blockchain network connects all nodes, allowing them to receive and send transactions. It is the system of all nodes running the common blockchain software cooperating to communicate with one another.

(c) Smart contracts: These are contracts transformed into codes maintained and stored by the parties signing the contracts. They comprise the following steps:

   i. Transaction submission: When users send transactions to the network, they are sent to the nearest accessible nodes. The transactions are then replicated to the other nodes.
   ii. Validation of transactions: The Block chain network's nodes cryptographically validate all transactions using exchange of keys. Invalid transactions are rejected.
   iii. Formation of a block: It is a collection of transactions gathered by nodes into a single bundle. Blocks must be formed according to a set of rules in order to be valid. They must not be larger than a certain number of bytes, they should include a certain number of transactions, and should relate to the most recent valid block.
   iv. Formation of the blockchain as a type of digital ledger: It is a series of blocks ordered according to a defined system. The new blocks added are connected to the most recent valid blockchain.
   v. Consensus generation: It's a consensus reached by all nodes in the blockchain. Multiple processes collaborate with one another to enable distributed system operation. Because faults can arise anywhere in such systems, consensus techniques are used.

(d) Hash function: It is a function that identifies a data block based on its unique digital fingerprint. It's a one-way function that converts a variable-size input to a fixed-size output termed hash. A cryptographic hash function has the following properties:

   i. It is easy to get the hash given the input;
   ii. It is impossible to generate the original input given the hash, and
   iii. It is practically impossible for two comparable inputs to have the same result in a so-called "collision."
   iv. Cryptographic hash SHA256 is an example of a hash function.

2.3 Permission-Driven and Permission-less Block Chains

Anyone can access a distributed ledger, like the Bitcoin, and connect with anyone else to buy or sell Bitcoins (Drescher, 2017; Swan, 2015). Further, anyone can read or write to such ledgers as long as they are entering a transactional agreement.

All agreements and Bitcoin exchanges are executed anonymously. Hence, Bitcoin block chains are essentially permission-less. Nonetheless, there are a variety of situations in which the transacting parties may like to keep all transaction details secret, such as several financial transactions, the exchange of medical records, or the conveyance of commodities (Kakavand et al., 2016). Such block chains are essentially permission-driven. Given their suitability and relevance for a wide range of business applications, permission-driven or private block chains will likely be in high demand in the future. The use of private block chains allows for the determination of any network participant's access rights and accessibility while keeping their information private (Swan, 2015). New members are invited to join the network by the existing members. There are several types of invitations driven by algorithms, such as unanimous agreement, single user invitations, and core group acceptance of a pre-determined set of parameters (Kakavand *et al.*, 2016).

2.3 Metrics

As block chain technology advances a range of new database systems and distributed protocols have emerged. All of these technologies are relevant to a wide range of sectors, necessitating standardization (Copigneaux *et al.*, 2020). The fundamental goal of standardized technology development should be to improve block chains by addressing their scalability and throughput capacity, as well as ensuring their security, performance, and durability. Various forms of distributed ledger technology with differing degrees of decentralization cover these domains (Crosby *et al.*, 2016). A block chain node keeps track of the network's present and historical status. On both a qualitative and quantitative level, the metrics described below can be used to evaluate the performance of the block chain architecture (Drescher, 2017; Kakavand *et al.*, 2016; Swan, 2015):

(a) Submission throughput: The maximum number of transaction submissions per second that each node and the entire network can handle is called submission throughput.
(b) Validation Throughput (Maximum/Average): This is the parameter that determines the network's maximum/average transaction processing speed.
(c) Validation of Transactions on the Average Latency: It is the average time taken for a transaction to be validated from the time it is submitted. This metric measures how long users have to wait for their transactions to be validated and placed in a block. It's crucial to note that each block chain's block confirmation and definition of validation may differ.
(d) Latency Volatility: It is a term used to describe how volatile a blockchain system is.

(e) Security: A threat model is needed to evaluate the security system since it may specify the types and breadth of adversaries and attacks on the system. In any Block chain application, such threat models could be distinct. The following analyses are necessary for the security evaluation:
   i. Transaction and block immutability
   ii. Resistance to transaction censorship
   iii. Resistant to Denial of Service
   iv. Users and oracles must have faith in one other.
   v. Services for protocol governance and node membership

(f) Confidentiality: It refers to a node's capacity to keep the contents of a transaction and the identity of the participants in the transaction hidden from other nodes.

(g) Fees for transactions: Users must pay a fee to the network in order to perform transactions or execute smart contracts. These fees cover the cost of maintaining the block chain as well as providing protection from malicious computational processes.

(h) Hardware:
   i. Memory/storage: It is the total amount of memory/storage required per node.
   ii. Processor: This refers to the amount of computing power needed to validate transactions and blocks.
   iii. Network utilization: This is the usage of network resources over time;
   iv. Network growth: The hardware requirements of each node will increase as the network grows enabling additional requirements for throughput, bandwidth, latency, and storage;

(i) Scalability:
   i. Number of nodes: increase in number of nodes requires auto scalability of resources;
   ii. Transaction volume: when the number of transactions submitted per second increases, the system's performance changes;
   iii. Number of users: when the number of active users making transactions grows, the system's performance changes;
   iv. Geographic dispersion: when the geographic dispersion of nodes increases, system performance changes;

(j) Validation process: This is a crucial component to consider when determining the network's performance because complex validation processes will require dedicated authority and certifying nodes or entire clouds;

(k) Complexity: It is a measure of the difficulty of developing, maintaining, and operating the blockchain infrastructure.

(l) Limitations of smart contracts: The smart contract scripting language and the underlying consensus protocols are the two main restrictions that can affect the ability of the code published on the block chain.

2.4 Applications of Blockchain for Supply Chain and Logistics

Supply chain in modern industries are complex networks interconnecting several echelons following multipath links from the raw materials suppliers at the extreme upstream end to the customers at the extreme downstream end (Christopher, 2016). Given the dynamism of supplies and demands, it is getting increasingly difficult to trace events within the supply chain networks. Further, lack of transparency within the supply chain can affect backward traceability of the products or services. Accountability of illegal activities in a supply chain, such as supplies of counterfeit products, is very difficult to establish. Blockchain solution can serve as an insurer of transparency and security for fixing the transparency and traceability problems of supply chains (Copigneaux *et al.*, 2020; Esmaeilian *et al.*, 2020). Registering products manufactured and in transit on the digital ledger of a blockchain customized for supply chain can help in ensuring provenance, traceability, and tracking.

Several efforts were made to use blockchain for improving Supply Chain Management (Dickson, 2016). Some of the successful case studies are reviewed as the following:

Walmart: Walmart is a U.S. retail giant that presented a pilot program of leverage distributed ledger technology to trace the origin of pork in China and its production within the U.S. (Ramamurthy, 2016). It was one a pilot test project of blockchain technology outside the financial sector. This technology was tested to eliminate transaction errors and missed deadlines with a goal to make the supply chain network more efficient (Prisco, 2016).

Ever ledger: Ever ledger is a startup business aiming to scale down risks and frauds for retail banks and open marketplaces. They used blockchain technology, machine vision, smart contracts and other emerging technologies (Dickson, 2016). Their platform runs on global digital ledger that provides ability to trace goods throughout all the echelons of a supply chain. Records in block chain contain defining characteristics, history, ownership, and provenance data of products registered. Ever ledger has built a hybrid technical model using private and public blockchains deployed on cloud computing.

Provenance: Provenance is a London-based company that aimed to make their supply chain more transparent by deploying block chains. They focused on product performance, product originality, and environmental impact of the products by tracing provenance data from the origin points (Allison, 2016). Further, Provenance used block chains for eliminating worker exploitation and forced labor practices (Dickson, 2016).

Maersk: Today, 90% of products in global trade are transported by the shipping industry (Lieber, 2017). However, the supply chain is slowed by the complexity and sheer volume of point-to-point communication across a loosely coupled web of land transportation providers, freight forwarders, customs brokers, governments, ports and ocean carriers. Processing documents and knowledge for a container shipment is estimated to cost quite twice the expenses from the particular physical transportation. IBM and Maersk have addressed this problem on a "distributed permission platform" accessible to the supply chain managers designed for exchanging data on events and manage document exchange workflows. Currently, it has been enabled as trade blockchains in selected trading lanes (Armonk, 2017). In a test by Maersk, one container of flowers was shipped from Kenya to the port of Rotterdam with end-to-end provenance data capturing managed through exchange of documents at every major event (Lieber, 2017).

Transparency and accountability are the main selling points of blockchain application in supply chains. Sharing information between all parties within the supply chain can improve the relationships between them and make them more efficient. These are several blockchain features influencing improvement of transparency and accountability in the logistics industry (Copigneaux *et al.*, 2020; Esmaeilian *et al.*, 2020; Ganne, 2018):

(a) Opens access to information concerning the activities within the supply chain.
(b) Provides customers with the power to gauge the merchandise, service, supplier, carrier etc. before making a choice;
(c) Provides customers with the knowledge they need concerning product origins and freight route;
(d) Reduces risk in reference to fraud or counterfeit goods;
(e) Enables monitoring, tracking and tracing transports;
(f) Simplifies exchange of products and payment systems;
(g) High security, traceability, and immutability of products' data;
(h) A transparent, distributed, decentralized, and secured architecture for multi-party trust and integrity in the supply chain;
(i) Automation of contracts execution, supply chain processes linked with the contract, and delivery and payments;
(j) Risk mitigation and compliances assurance for all the contracting parties;

In block chain system, all information concerning shipping processes are digitalised, which enables all participants to urge the relevant data at any moment (Bodkhe *et al.*, 2020; Sigwart *et al.*, 2020). Consequently, this reduces risks and increases the delivery quality. Moreover, it allows organizations to decrease the quantity of waste, spoilage and defects. Using Internet of Things with machine to machine communications allows direct monitoring and control of supply chain processes and transactions captured from the machines, equipment, and robots involved in conducting the transactions

Block chain is beneficial for logistics by enabling synchronized audit trails between partners and optimizing them during a real time. It increases trust across the supply chain, consequently simplifying the choice making process at every stage. (Lieber, 2017). Finally, the permission-driven and instantaneous access to data within the digital ledger can allow collaborative forecasting for all parties. Companies can use block chain technology to create efficient relationships with their partners, make their business more transparent for patrons and avoid numerous errors across the availability chain. These concepts appear favorable when a few organizations may attempt to collaborate forming a blockchain. In the broader spectrum of international logistics and supply chain management, there may be multiple dimensions of challenges where solutions have not yet been envisaged. The next section presents a review.

2.5 Challenges in Using Blockchain for Logistics and Supply Chain

There needs to be a right balance of cost versus benefits in using blockchain technology for supply chain management. The technology is complex and requires specialized knowledge and resources (Copigneaux *et al.*, 2020; Ganne, 2018). Further, blockchain has not yet been standardized as a system across the global trading borders. The current trading processes may require significant modifications in adopting blockchain technologies. The top challenges in using blockchain for supply chain and logistics are the following:

Trade dimensions: International trading occurs as per a defined construct globally. There are unique characteristics of trading prevailing in several trading zones agreed among the countries. The participating nations will need to discuss the changes in trading systems and processes for adopting blockchain technologies. There needs to be verification if blockchain is the only option or there are other ways possible under the evolving Industry 4.0 paradigm. The current documentation exchange for international trading is already very complex. Adding the complexity of blockchains may require establishing of feasibility and a possible roadmap.

Technical dimension: The "reliability with anonymity" feature of blockchains may appear to be a novel innovation, but will require a paradigm shift in the way authentication, authorization, and accounting systems are functioning in the current trading systems. There may be threat perceptions in operating permission-less blockchains whereby permission-driven blockchains may be perceived as too expensive to operate. Countries may end up splitting, customizing, and privatizing blockchains for meeting their specific interests, which may defeat the claimed advantages of running the blockchain.

Privacy and trust dimension: The blockchains offer transparency and trust as a significant benefit. However, the privacy laws of countries (such as general data protection regulation of the European Union) may not accept anonymity. Under privacy laws, the personal data of the contracting parties need to be protected from the possibilities of misuse. Provenance capture may not be acceptable as per the EU GDPR because the process may automate capturing of several privacy-related records in an uncontrollable manner.

Adoption of blockchain dimension: The participating countries in trading groups will need to cross several barriers to adopt blockchain as an infrastructure for trading and supply chain operations. The participating countries need to be setup digital infrastructures encompassing trading systems of multiple countries. There needs to be a willingness to replace the existing documentation system by the blockchain-driven framework in fully electronic format. Standardized electronic documentation formats needs to be established among the trading partners. Systems for interoperability for smooth and secured exchange of documents and records with traceable authorizations need to be established. Overall, a significant willingness to change is needed for adopting the digitalization technologies (Internet of Things and its framework of sensory and actuation systems) and digitization technologies (digital communications and cloud computing systems). An ecosystem of trust and integrity needs to be formed among the participating nations in a trading domain. There may be several economic, political, and social barriers in adopting digitalization and digitization technologies for adopting blockchains in logistics and supply chains. The machine to machine communications involving Internet of Things will need standardized operating protocols, device designs, hardware and software standardization, authorization and accounting, and communication protocols.

3.0 CONCLUSION

Blockchain has emerged as a novel technology framework taking the concepts of Bitcoin and Ethereum networks. The system of validation and high security record keeping has attracted significant interest of researchers in the recent past. Its ability to form and record reliable contracts in distributed ledger maintaining high accountability and transparency while maintaining anonymity has evolved new application domains. One of the application domains recognized is logistics and supply chain management. This domain has been reviewed in this research. The technology system of blockchain is perceived to be highly complex and expensive requiring collaborative partnerships and investments. Given the usage of advanced cryptography and decentralized networking, establishing controls in network management will require future studies. In logistics and supply chains, several transactional advantages of blockchain were envisaged in this paper. However, when analyzed from the perspective of multinational strategic framework for designing, implementing, and operating a blockchain for logistics and supply chains, several challenges were discovered. These challenges appear to suggest a difficult way forward for adoption of blockchain in the future trading groups. However, with rapid spread of digitalization and digitization technologies under the Industry 4.0 framework, the participating countries may be able to find ways to adopt blockchain for enabling future contracts execution and exchange of documents in international trading domains. There needs to be a multi-country strategic framework for upgrading the existing trading processes and documentation formats and systems to digital blockchain formats. The blockchains will need to be hosted as multinational networks in the form of trade specific cloud computing. For machine to machine communications, standardizations of devices, protocols, and communication formats may have to be envisaged.

This is a short theoretical positioning paper based on review of literature, published commercial reports, and few published media reports. This paper could present a limited understanding about blockchain, its design and application for supply chain and logistics, and its challenges in global trading applications. More detailed studies coupled with primary data collection and analysis may result in discovery of the finer points leading to theory formulation. The researchers suggest conducting surveys among organizations those have adopted block chains or have run pilot programs. The researchers also suggest study of advanced blockchain design in laboratory simulation environments to understand the challenges at the operations level. This research domain is wide open and has significant potential for new empirical discoveries.

REFERENCES

Ahlman, R. (2016). *Finnish City Partners with IBM to Validate Block Chain Application in Logistics.* Coin Telegraph. Available at: https://cointelegraph.com/news/

Alkhudary, R., Brusset, X., & Fenies, P. (2020). Blockchain and Risk in Supply Chain Management. In *LDIC 2020-Dynamics in Logistics* (pp. 159-165). Springer.

Allen, D. W. E., Berg, C., Davidson, S., Novak, M., & Potts, J. (2019). International policy coordination for blockchain supply chains. *Asia Pacific Policy Studies, 6*, 367-380.

Allison, I. (2016). *Provenance has a big year ahead delivering supply chain transparency with Bitcoin and Ethereum.* IBTimes. Available at: https://www.ibtimes.co.uk/

Alsmiller, C. (2016). *Block chain: The Next Big Thing in the Supply Chain.* Appterra. Available: http://appterra.com/ uncategorized/blockchain-the-next-big-thing-in-the-supply-chain/

Ammous, S. (2016). *Block chain Technology: What is it good for?* Available at: https://capitalism.columbia.edu/

ARMONK. (2017). *Maersk and IBM Unveil First Industry-Wide Cross-Border Supply Chain Solution on Block chain.* https://www-03.ibm.com/press/us/en/press release/51712.wss

Baker, J., & Steiner, J. (2015). *Blockchain: The solution for transparency in product.* Provenance. Available at: https://www.provenance.org/whitepaper

Benning, K. (2016). *Block chain Consumerism.* Shop! Association. Available: http:// www. shopassociation.org/block chain-consumerism/

Bodhke, U., Tanwar, S., Parekh, K., Khanpara, P., Tyagi, S., Kumar, N., & Alazab, M. (2020). Blockchain for Industry 4.0: A Comprehensive Review. *IEEE Access: Practical Innovations, Open Solutions*, *8*, 79764–79800.

Christopher, M. (n.d.). *Logistics and Supply Chain Management* (5th ed.). London: Pearson.

Copigneaux, B., Vlasov, N., Bani, E., Tcholtchev, N., Lämmel, P., Fuenfzig, M., Snoeijenbos, S., & Flickenschild, M. (2020). *Blockchain for supply chains and internatiional trade, European Parliamentary Research Service, Scientific Foresight Unit.* STOA.

Crosby, M. N., Pattanayak, P., Verma, S., & Kalyanaraman, V. (2016). Block chain Technology: Beyond Bitcoin. *Applied Innovation Review.* Available at:http://scet.berkeley.edu/wp-content/uploads/AIR-2016-Blockchain.pdf

Dickson, B. (2016). *Block chain has the potential to revolutionize the supply chain.* Tech Crunch. Available at: https://techcrunch.com/2016/11/24/

Drescher, D. (2017). *Blockchain basics: A Non-technical Introduction in 25 Steps.* Frankfurt, Germany: APress.

Esmaeilian, B., Sarkis, J., Lewis, K., & Behdad, S. (2020). Blockchain for the future of sustainable supply chain management in Industry 4.0. *Resources, Conservation & Recycling, 163*(105064), 1-15.

Francisco, K., & Swanson, D. (2018). The Supply Chain Has No Clothes: Technology Adoption of Blockchain for Supply Chain Transparency. *Logistics, 2*(2), 1-13.

Ganne, E. (2018). Can Blockchain Revolutionalise International Trade. World Trade Organisation.

Gilbert, D. (n.d.). *Block chain Technology Could Help Solve $75Billion Counterfeit Drug Problem.* Ibtimes. Available at: https://www.ibtimes.com/

Hancock, M., & Vaizey, E. (2016). Distributed ledger technology: beyond blockchain. Academic Press.

Hofmann, E., Strewed, U. M., & Bosia, N. (2018). *Supply Chain Finance and Blockchain Technology: The Case of Reverse Securitization.* Springer Nature. Available https://link.springer.com/10.1007/978-3-319-

Jay, M. L. (2017). Building Better Supply Chains with Block chain. *MHI Solutions*, 20–26. Available: http://www.nxtbook.com/naylor/MHIQ/MHIQ0217/index.php?startid=90#/20

Kakavand, H., Kost De Serves, N., & Chilton, B. (2016). *The Block chain Revolution: An Analysis of Regulation And Technology Related To Distributed Ledger Technologies.* Available at:http://www.fintechconnectlive.com/wp-content/uploads/2016/11/Luther-Systems-DLA-Piper-Article-on-Blockchain-Regulation-and-Technology-SK.pdf

Khairuddin, I. E. (2019). *Understanding and Designing for Trust in Bitcoin Blockchain* [PhD Thesis]. Lancester University.

Kosba, A., Miller, A., Shi, E., Wen, Z., & Papamanthou, C. (n.d.). *Hawk: The Block Chain Model of Cryptography and Privacy-Preserving Smart Contracts.* https://pdfs.semanticscholar.org/

Lehmacher, W. (2017). *Why block chain should be global trade's next port of call.* World Economic Forum. Available: https://www.weforum.org/agenda/2017/05/blockchain-ports-global-trades/

Lieber, A. (2017). *Trust in Trade: Announcing a new block chain partner.* IBM. Available at: https://www.ibm.com/blogs/blockchain/2017/03/

Parker, L. (2016). *Block chain tech companies focus on the $40 trillion Supply Chain market.* Brave New Coin. Available: https://bravenewcoin.com/news/blockchain-tech-companies-focus-on-the-40-trillion-supply-chainmarket/

Prisco, G. (2016). Walmart Testing Block chain Technology for Supply Chain Management. *Bitcoin Magazine.* Available at: https://bitcoinmagazine.com/articles/

Ramamurthy, S. (2016). *Leveraging block chain to improve foodsupply chain traceability.* IBM. Available at: https://techcrunch.com/2016/11/24/

Robinson, A. (2016). *What is Block Chain Technology, and What Is Its Potential Impact on the Supply Chain?* Cerasis. Available at: http://cerasis.com/2016/06/29/blockchain-technology/

Siddiqui, M. S., & Syed, T. A. (2020). A Lightweight Blockchain-based Provenance Message Tracking in IoT. *International Journal of Advanced Computer Science and Applications, 11*(4), 463–470.

Sigwart, M., Borkowski, M., Peise, M., Schulte, M., & Tai, S. (2020). A secure and extensible blockchain-based data provenance framework for the Internet of Things. *Personal and Ubiquitous Computing.* https://doi.org/10.1007/s00779-020-01417-z

Smart, E. (2016). *Top 5 Block chain Technology Myths the Mainstream Has Fallen For.* Bit connect. Available at:https://bitconnect.co/bitcoin-news/

Swan, M. (2015). Blockchain. O'Reilly Media.

Tapscott, D., & Tapscott, A. (2016). *How the Technology Behind Bitcoin Is Changing Money, Business, and the World.* Portfolio Penguin.

Terzi, S., Nizamas, A., Tzovaras, D., Zacharaki, A., Votis, K., Stamelos, I., & Ioannidis, D. (2019). Transforming the Supply-Chain management and Industry Logistics with Blockchain Smart Contracts. In *PCI '19.* ACM.

Tian, F. (2016). *An agri-food supply chain traceability system for China based on RFID & block chain technology. In 2016 13th International Conference on Service Systems and Service Management.* ICSSSM. Available https://ieeexplore.ieee.org/abstract/document/7538424/

Tian, F. (2018). *An information System for Food Safety Monitoring in Supply Chains based on HACCP, Blockchain and Internet of Things* [PhD Thesis]. WU Vienna University of Economics and Business.

Veisi, P. (2019). *Visualising Provenance in a supply chain using Ethereum Blockchain* [Master Thesis]. University of Saskatchewan, Saskatoon.

Williams, R. (2015). *How Bitcoin Tech Could Make Supply Chains More Transparent.* Coin Desk. Available: https://www.coindesk.com/how-bitcoins-technology-could-make-supply-chains-more-transparent/

Wright, A., & De Filippi, P. (2017). *Decentralized Block Chain Technology and the Rise of Lex Cryptographies.* Available at: https://ssrn.com/abstract=2580664

Chapter 8
Supply Chain and Logistics Operations Management Under the Era of Advanced Technology

Muhammad Tanveer
Prince Sultan University, Saudi Arabia

ABSTRACT

Implementation and adoption of new technologies are gaining the result of smooth supply chain and logistics operations. Internet of things (IoT) artificial intelligence, including data mining, intensified in all fields of life, particularly in supply chain management and operations. Blockchain technology has the capability to reform the supply chain and logistics operations management. Blockchain provides digital database solutions for all transactions across supply chain and operations management. Radiofrequency identification device (RFID) is also helping technology transmit electromagnetic waves to radio-compatible integrated circuits to look after and manage the entire supply chain and logistics operations management. The Fourth Industry Revolution 4.0 refers to the automation, interconnectivity, machine learning, and real-time data that help supply chain and logistics operations management in the 21st century.

1. INTRODUCTION

Supply Chain Management (SCM) is very important now a days and especially to improve the business-processes by using SCM technologies for more competitiveness.

DOI: 10.4018/978-1-7998-7642-7.ch008

SCM is helping companies to improve produces and services (Machowiak, 2012).

In the digital age firms are concentrating on proper monitoring and implementation of information systems to increase the performance (Khan and Qianli, 2017; Zhang et al., 2019). SCM and logistics has significantly impact on performance management through technologies (Stockhammer et al. 2021).

Radio Frequency Identification Device (RFID) is a new technology, a means of data storage and recovery by transmitting electromagnetic waves to radio-compatible integrated circuits (Ahmad 2015; Altaf et al. 2020; Astrachan et al. 2014). However, there are various devices of different applications and systems, such as electronic license plates, logistics labels, etc. Nevertheless, they have almost the same functions and principles. RFID can increase visibility and velocity in supply chain operations, ultimately reducing variability and disruption in operations management (Çankaya and Sezen, 2019; Geng et al., 2017).

As economic globalization accelerates, the requirement for the response speed to the supply chain is constantly increasing. Promote the global logistics industry to constantly explore new technologies to improve efficiency and service quality (Jabbour et al. 2010; Tanveer et al. 2020). Modern logistics makes full use of information technology to organically combine transport, storage, loading and unloading, processing, sorting, and distribution to form a complete supply chain (Hofmann and Rüsch, 2017; Jabbour, 2011).

The fundamental purpose of modern logistics is to improve logistics efficiency, reduce logistics costs and satisfy the customers' needs (Ji et al. 2012; Jia and Wang, 2019). In last couple of years, technological innovation in the logistics industry has been booming, and firms are aggressively implementing advanced technology, including Industry 4.0, Internet-of-Things, Big Data, and GPS (Kalyar et al. 2019; Kouhizadeh and Sarkis, 2020; Longoni et al. 2016; Munim and Schramm, 2018). There is no doubt that technology is the core mockery of modern logistics and will play a pivotal role in the information construction of the logistics industry (Printo, 2020; Raut et al. 2019; Silva et al. 2018).

There is currently more theoretical research on Industry 4.0 and Big Data technology, and the concept is also relatively new, hindering enterprises from adopting in their operations (Talatappeh and Lakzi, 2019; Khan et al. 2021). In terms of customs express clearance, there are many attempts at RFID technology, and there are some problems in practical application, which are the barriers for enterprises to adopt these technologies. The most common barrier is the considerable cost associated with advanced technology and the second barrier is a scarcity of IT experts (Sony, 2019).

Figure 1. IoT technology
(Cvar at al. 2020)

With the development of the Internet of Things technology, the logistics industry continues to use this technology to promote the development of this sector and socio-economic development (Tiwari and Khan, 2020). The use of Internet of things technology reduces various costs of the logistics industry and significantly improves the efficiency of the logistics industry. IoT technology has had a significant impact on all aspects of the logistics industry, promoted the development of the logistics industry, enabled the logistics industry to adapt to social development and flourish in the modern information society, thus affecting the management process of the logistics industry (Yong et al. 2020). Logistics management is a complex process because the nature of transportation packaging makes each packaging different, which makes the management more difficult. In order to work more intelligently, efficiently and avoid complex work problems, the application of Internet of things technology greatly reduces the cost of the logistics industry and improves the efficiency of the logistics industry (Zaid et al., 2018).

2. IoT USAGE OF TECHNOLOGIES

2.1 Development Level of IoT technology

In the traditional logistics management mode, the use of computer is affected by the new era. Whether it is management mode or management mode, the right of labor is dominant. Therefore, the computer Internet of things technology came into being, breaking the traditional ideas, establishing a reliable information system, using computers to highlight the characteristics of scientific standardization and optimize social and economic benefits. It helps to promote the continuous progress of enterprises and achieve the best management effect through the use of such technical measures (Ahmad 2015).

2.2 Combine IoT Technology with Logistics

The application of computer Internet of things technology in logistics can improve enterprises' efficiency to a certain extent. The application of Internet of things technology can optimize the logistics path by planning the transportation route and determining the appropriate delivery place. Adjusting solutions under the best conditions can reduce human resources and reduce operating costs to a certain extent. By using Internet of things technology in warehousing and logistics, employees can better understand the information stored in the warehouse, including quantity, time, and usage. In addition, information can be retrieved very easily, and managers can quickly track the information of goods stored in the warehouse, making information very accurate. Improving the use efficiency of inventory information can reduce the management cost related to logistics. The application of Internet of things computer technology in logistics optimizes the logistics management process (Altaf et al. 2020). Nowadays, the logistics industry is developing rapidly under the promotion of people, and its influence is increasing day by day. However, the supply chain of the logistics industry is very complex and difficult to manage logistics effectively. In addition, transportation is an important part of logistics management and an integral part of major logistics management activities. By using Internet of things technology during transportation, employees can better track and locate cargo information. Therefore, using computer Internet of things technology for transportation is very effective in reducing logistics costs, improving logistics, and improving transportation efficiency (Astrachan et al. 2014).

2.3 Means of Improving Logistics Information Management System

The integration of computer technology and the Internet of things improves the logistics information management system, wastes unnecessary human and material resources, improves the efficiency of the overall logistics management and improves the overall logistics management level. In addition, it optimizes the way information is processed. In order to avoid the loss of economic and logistics information over time, it is necessary to pay attention to the effect of logistics information management and adopt more perfect management methods to ensure more reliable and stable operations. On this basis, the appropriate use of IT technology means establishing a reliable logistics information management system to support the progress of national logistics companies.

3. ADVANTAGES OF ADVANCED TECHNOLOGY

Enterprises and customers are most concerned about transportation speed and information accuracy. RFID can just meet its concerns in the application of the express industry. Have the following advantages:

- Read and write quickly. Barcodes can only be scanned with one barcode at a time: the RFID identifier recognizes several RFID tags at once.
- Reading and writing distance is long. In covered cases, the RFID can penetrate non-metallic or non-transparent materials such as paper, wood, and plastic and conduct penetrating communication while the barcode scanner must be close and without object blocking. You can read the barcode.
- Reusable. Now barcodes can not be changed when printed, and RFID tags can be added, modified, and deleted repeatedly.
- The chip itself can store information. The 1 D barcode has 50 bytes with a maximum capacity of 2 to 3000 characters and the maximum RFID capacity. With the development of memory vectors, the data capacity will carry more and more information, and the demand for volume expansion will increase accordingly.
- Resistance to pollution and durability. The carrier of traditional barcodes is paper and therefore susceptible to contamination, but RFID is highly resistant to substances such as water, oil, and chemicals. Moreover, because the barcode is attached to a plastic bag or outer carton, it is particularly vulnerable to compromise; the RFID volume label keeps the data in the chip and can be protected from contamination.

4. TECHNOLOGY IN LOGISTICS OPERATIONS

The whole express operation process, from the collection of goods after the input of information, transportation, customs clearance, sorting, and other processes to finally customers, can play an important role in each node (Figure 2).

Enter the Information

When the express business personnel receives the Hong Kong business point of the express company, paste the electronic label to the surface of the express package (ensure the firmness of the label paste), and input the express related information with the reader and writer. The information is directly transmitted to the information system of the express company and the integrated information platform through the network. In this way, the customs declaration company can arrange the customs declaration the first time, which can speed up the customs clearance speed, reduce the time and cost of labor input, and reduce the error.

Figure 2. Advanced technology in Supply Chain
(Ross, 2015)

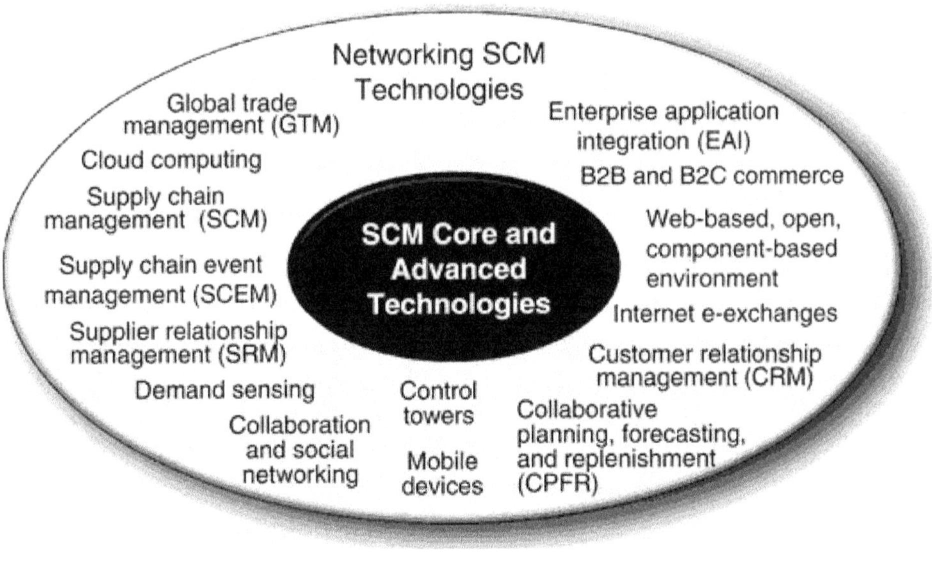

Information technology applications have caused revolution in SCM that is the reason industry concept and practice have changed to next level (Ross, 2015).

Customs clearance process

To ensure the read accuracy of the electronic labels, we will install three readers and writers at the position of the original manual scanning barcode and set up three read levels. Furthermore, install the software compatible with the customs clearance database system when the goods pass through the level. The cargo information read by the reader and writer is automatically transmitted to the system database, through which the Customs can compare with the previous customs declaration list.

Express Sorting and Other Processes

Improve the sorting efficiency. In the express sorting center, use the reader to identify the cargo information. The automatic sorting system automatically recognizes the distribution area information of goods distribution, significantly reducing the labor cost. Reduce the sorting error.

Read the information

When each cargo goes to a transport node with readers installed, the reader can read the information in the electronic label and write the information to be added. It is also transmitted to the information platform through the network. At this time, when any node on the express supply chain needs to understand the express status information, you can use the RFID reading information function to query through the information platform.

Label recycling

After the goods safely delivered to the customer, the distribution personnel is responsible for the label from the goods box and bring back to the company's business point, at the same time can be combined with the VI flow to different closed-loop deployment, considering the unbalanced quantity of goods in and out of VI, can in a direction of electronic label accumulation too much when the label to the other side of the mainland / Hong Kong, to achieve the full use of the label.

Goods tracking

In the process of cargo transportation and storage. An alarm system can be designed to automatically alarm when cargo is beyond the reading range of the reader. This keeps the goods safe during the transportation/storage process. Prevent the loss of goods.

At the same time, GPS technology can track the location of goods in real-time and reasonably arrange vehicles and goods transportation, maximizing transport efficiency.

5. CONCLUSION

The wide application of advanced technology, including Internet-of-Things, Blockchain, Big Data, and RFID technology in logistics, is the current trend. However, relevant researchers must find the existing problems, analyze, solve, and innovate them to find that computer Internet of things technology in logistics is a sustainable application. The road of development is unlimited. Through continuous exploration and research, researchers will find more innovative methods to apply Internet of things technology to all aspects of the logistics industry and provide more vitality.

REFERENCES

Ahmad, S. (2015). Green human resource management: Policies and practices. *Cogent Business & Management, 2*(1), 1030817.

Altaf, B., Ali, S. S., & Weber, G. W. (2020). Modeling the relationship between organizational performance and green supply chain practices using canonical correlation analysis. *Wireless Networks*, *26*(8), 5835–5853. doi:10.100711276-020-02313-3

Astrachan, C. B., Patel, V. K., & Wanzenried, G. (2014). A comparative study of CB-SEM and PLS-SEM for theory development in family firm research. *Journal of Family Business Strategy*, *5*(1), 116–128. doi:10.1016/j.jfbs.2013.12.002

Çankaya, S. Y., & Sezen, B. (2019). Effects of green supply chain management practices on sustainability performance. *Journal of Manufacturing Technology Management*.

Cvar, N., Trilar, J., Kos, A., Volk, M., & Stojmenova Duh, E. (2020). The Use of IoT Technology in Smart Cities and Smart Villages: Similarities, Differences, and Future Prospects. *Sensors (Basel)*, *20*(14), 3897. doi:10.339020143897 PMID:32668714

Geng, R., Mansouri, S. A., & Aktas, E. (2017). The relationship between green supply chain management and performance: A meta-analysis of empirical evidences in Asian emerging economies. *International Journal of Production Economics*, *183*, 245–258. doi:10.1016/j.ijpe.2016.10.008

Hofmann, E., & Rüsch, M. (2017). Industry 4.0 and the current status as well as future prospects on logistics. *Computers in Industry*, *89*, 23–34. doi:10.1016/j.compind.2017.04.002

Jabbour, C. J. C. (2011). How green are HRM practices, organizational culture, learning and teamwork? A Brazilian study. *Industrial and Commercial Training*, *43*(2), 98–105. doi:10.1108/00197851111108926

Jabbour, C. J. C., Santos, F. C. A., & Nagano, M. S. (2010). Contributions of HRM throughout the stages of environmental management: Methodological triangulation applied to companies in Brazil. *International Journal of Human Resource Management*, *21*(7), 1049–1089. doi:10.1080/09585191003783512

Ji, L., Huang, J., Liu, Z., Zhu, H., & Cai, Z. (2012). The effects of employee training on the relationship between environmental attitude and firms' performance in sustainable development. *International Journal of Human Resource Management*, *23*(14), 2995–3008. doi:10.1080/09585192.2011.637072

Jia, X., & Wang, M. (2019). The Impact of Green Supply Chain Management Practices on Competitive Advantages and Firm Performance. In *Environmental Sustainability in Asian Logistics and Supply Chains* (pp. 121–134). Springer. doi:10.1007/978-981-13-0451-4_7

Kalyar, M. N., Shoukat, A., & Shafique, I. (2019). *Enhancing firms' environmental performance and financial performance through green supply chain management practices and institutional pressures*. Sustainability Accounting, Management and Policy Journal. doi:10.1108/SAMPJ-02-2019-0047

Khan, S. A. R., Ponce, P., Tanveer, M., Aguirre-Padilla, N., Mahmood, H., & Shah, S. A. A. (2021). Technological Innovation and Circular Economy Practices: Business Strategies to Mitigate the Effects of COVID-19. *Sustainability*, *13*(15), 8479. doi:10.3390u13158479

Khan, S. A. R., & Qianli, D. (2017). Impact of green supply chain management practices on firms' performance: An empirical study from the perspective of Pakistan. *Environmental Science and Pollution Research International*, *24*(20), 16829–16844. doi:10.100711356-017-9172-5 PMID:28573559

Kouhizadeh, M., & Sarkis, J. (2020). Blockchain Characteristics and Green Supply Chain Advancement. In *Global Perspectives on Green Business Administration and Sustainable Supply Chain Management* (pp. 93–109). IGI Global. doi:10.4018/978-1-7998-2173-1.ch005

Longoni, A., Luzzini, D., & Guerci, M. (2016). Deploying environmental management across functions: The relationship between green human resource management and green supply chain management. *Journal of Business Ethics, 151*(4), 1081–1095. doi:10.100710551-016-3228-1

Machowiak, W. (2012). Risk management-unappreciated instrument of supply chain management strategy. *LogForum, 8*(4), 277–285.

Munim, Z. H., & Schramm, H. J. (2018). The impacts of port infrastructure and logistics performance on economic growth: The mediating role of seaborne trade. *Journal of Shipping and Trade, 3*(1), 1. doi:10.118641072-018-0027-0

Pinto, L. (2020). Green supply chain practices and company performance in Portuguese manufacturing sector. *Business Strategy and the Environment, 29*(5), 1832–1849. doi:10.1002/bse.2471

Raut, R. D., Luthra, S., Narkhede, B. E., Mangla, S. K., Gardas, B. B., & Priyadarshinee, P. (2019). Examining the performance oriented indicators for implementing green management practices in the Indian agro sector. *Journal of Cleaner Production, 215*, 926–943. doi:10.1016/j.jclepro.2019.01.139

Ross, D. F. (2015). Information Technology and Supply Chain Management. In *Distribution Planning and Control*. Springer. doi:10.1007/978-1-4899-7578-2_15

Silva, M. E., Pereira, S. C., & Gold, S. (2018). The response of the Brazilian cashew nut supply chain to natural disasters: A practice-based view. *Journal of Cleaner Production, 204*, 660–671. doi:10.1016/j.jclepro.2018.08.340

Sony, M. (2019). Green supply chain management practices and digital technology: A qualitative study. In *Technology optimization and change management for successful digital supply chains* (pp. 233–254). IGI Global. doi:10.4018/978-1-5225-7700-3.ch012

Stockhammer, V. M., Pfoser, S., Markvica, K., Zajicek, J., & Prandstetter, M. (2021). Behavioural Biases Distorting the Demand for Environmentally Friendly Freight Transport Modes: An Overview and Potential Measures. *Sustainability, 13*(21), 11783. doi:10.3390u132111783

Talatappeh, S. S., & Lakzi, A. (2019). Developing a model for investigating the impact of cloud-based systems on green supply chain management. *Journal of Engineering, Design and Technology*.

Tanveer, M., Hassan, S., & Bhaumik, A. (2020). Academic Policy Regarding Sustainability and Artificial Intelligence (AI). *Sustainability*, *12*(22), 9435. doi:10.3390u12229435

Tiwari, K., & Khan, M. S. (2020). Sustainability accounting and reporting in the Industry 4.0. *Journal of Cleaner Production*, *258*, 120783. doi:10.1016/j.jclepro.2020.120783

Yong, J. Y., Yusliza, M. Y., Ramayah, T., Chiappetta Jabbour, C. J., Sehnem, S., & Mani, V. (2020). Pathways towards sustainability in manufacturing organizations: Empirical evidence on the role of green human resource management. *Business Strategy and the Environment*, *29*(1), 212–228. doi:10.1002/bse.2359

Zaid, A. A., Jaaron, A. A., & Bon, A. T. (2018). The impact of green human resource management and green supply chain management practices on sustainable performance: An empirical study. *Journal of Cleaner Production*, *204*, 965–979. doi:10.1016/j.jclepro.2018.09.062

Zhang, Y., Khan, S. A. R., Kumar, A., Golpîra, H., & Sharif, A. (2019). Is tourism really affected by logistical operations and environmental degradation? An empirical study from the perspective of Thailand. *Journal of Cleaner Production*, *227*, 158–166. doi:10.1016/j.jclepro.2019.04.164

Chapter 9
Blockchain Technology as Enablement of Industry 4.0

Fredrick Ishengoma
https://orcid.org/0000-0002-3337-6210
The University of Dodoma, Tanzania

ABSTRACT

Industry 4.0 (also known as smart manufacturing or industrial internet of things [IIoT]) refers to a major change in the way products are manufactured and delivered, with a focus on industrial automation and the flexible factory backed with several technologies that include the internet of things (IoT), cyber-physical systems, and artificial intelligence. Industry 4.0 gave birth to a new age of smart manufacturing, automated supply chain, and personalized goods and services. Meanwhile, the rise in the application of blockchain technology (BCT) in different sectors propels the Industry 4.0 model to extend its scope. This chapter discusses the impact of BCT as the enablement of Industry 4.0. The modified e-Delphi methodology aimed at gathering the opinions of recognized experts was used. The findings present the potential that BCT brings using a case along with emerging issues. Emerging issues such as BCT security, interoperability, smart contract issues, digital twin issues, and ethical issues are discussed, and solutions are proposed.

INTRODUCTION

Industry 4.0 is transforming the way industries produce, develop, and sell their goods. Manufacturers are incorporating enabling technologies such as the Internet of Things (IoT), cloud computing and analytics, artificial intelligence (AI), cloud computing, big data analytics, smart sensors, location detection technologies, adaptive

DOI: 10.4018/978-1-7998-7642-7.ch009

robotics, and machine learning into their manufacturing operational activities (Zheng *et* al., 2018; Alcácer & Cruz-Machado, 2021; Oztelev & Gursev, 2020; Yang & Gu, 2021; Bartodziej, 2021). The real strength of Industry 4.0 lies in the integration of technologies in the network of industrial machines that generate, exchange information, and make decisions based on that information. Industry 4.0 pushes the impact of digital transformation to a whole new stage by leveraging interconnectivity via IoT, accessibility and decision making based on real-time data, and the integration of cyber-physical systems (Trunzer *et al.*, 2019; Gaiardelli *et al.*, 2021). Put, Industry 4.0 transforms traditional factories into "smart" factories.

As manufacturers embrace Industry 4.0, evolving smart factories deliver several potential opportunities. Smart factories, for example, can analyze large quantities of data collected from industrial sensors and machinery in real-time, offering real-time tracking of manufacturing properties and conducting predictive maintenance based on the data to minimize downtime.

"Block-chain" has been a common buzzword since Satoshi Nakamoto leveraged the technology as the data structure for Bitcoin in 2008 (Nakamoto, 2008). The focal point of blockchain technology (BCT) was on financial applications (Nofer *et al.*, 2017). As a result, it's unsurprising that it's fairly well-employed for handling financial operations where trust can be gained by the use of blockchains. The blockchain's role in Industry 4.0 is unleashing a slew of emerging innovations. For instance, BCT can guarantees that the Cyber-Physical Systems (CPS) that make up smart factories can order a required spare part independently and safely, streamline the manufacturing processes to reduce power usage, predict future supply chain defects before they occur, and many other benefits (Zhao *et al.*, 2016). As a result, BCT is a promising enabler in the evolution of Industry 4.0.

Because of blockchain's efficiency in handling transactions, industries are now looking for it to solve other issues, including a variety of manufacturing-related issues. A blockchain, for instance, can link ledgers across a production process to increase the accuracy and reliability of product traceability. By enhancing tracking capabilities, a cumbersome, multi-day operation can be turned into an automated process that takes just seconds. For instance, if you employ BCT between smart Enterprise Resource Planning (ERP) and parts supplier, as well as the cyber-physical infrastructure that makes up the industrial plant, machines can procure spare parts securely and fully autonomous.

Besides that, blockchain's ability to allow secure and open transactions between any range of smart devices makes it critical for the economic changes that industry 4.0 implies. In a smart factory, automated controllers exchange data from a complex network of equipment, parts, and processes. Designers, distribution firms, and equipment suppliers are among the many players in the value chain. As it transforms a series of components into a finished product, blockchain can track and record every step of the process. Risk factors such as locating defective parts may be mitigated with BCT.

In this chapter, the author provides a detailed discussion of the potential of blockchain technology for Industry 4.0. The organization of the chapter is as follows: Section 2 presents an overview of blockchain technology and industry 4.0. In this chapter, the blockchain generations and the role of CPS in industry 4.0 are presented. Section 3 describes the enablement of blockchain technology in industry 4.0 along with use cases. Section 4 introduces emerging issues that impact the deployment of blockchain technology in industry 4.0 and the chapter is concluded in section 5.

BLOCKCHAIN TECHNOLOGY AND INDUSTRY 4.0

Blockchain technology

The blockchain platform was first conceived in the financial sector in 2009 when it was referred to as a peer-to-peer electronic cash system [9]. It began as the basis for a completely distributed crypto-currency unit (bitcoin), but currently, it is spreading into other fields, including healthcare, banking, agriculture, as well as e-commerce. Although concepts for the blockchain were circulating in computer science spheres for some time, it was Satoshi Nakamoto, the anonymous founder of Bitcoin, who presented the blockchain as we recognize it in the white paper for BTC (Xu *et al.*, 2019).

The bitcoin network, also known as blockchain 1.0, launched the 1st generation of the technology in 2009. The formation of the first cryptocurrencies occurred during this generation. The concept revolved around payment and how it could be used to produce cryptocurrency (Casino *et al.*, 2019). Blockchain technology has been dubbed the "internet of money" since its ability to allow the peer-to-peer transaction without depending on the oversight or approval of an intermediary such as a state or financial regulator.

In 2010, smart contracts and financial services for different purposes were implemented as the second stage of BCT (Singh *et al.*, 2020). Smart contracts were perhaps the most significant breakthrough in the second generation brought on by Ethereum (Figure 1). This era introduced blockchain architecture using the Ethereum and Hyperledger systems. In simple terms, Ethereum suggests that BCT can be used to make digital asset management possible without demanding platform ownership. For the very first time, Ethereum offers a solution to the internet's "centralization" (which has assisted companies like Google and Facebook) by essentially incorporating BCT in their platform.

The 3rd generation is predominantly concerned with real-time services on public ledgers and distributed databases (Casino *et al.*, 2019). At this level, Industry 4.0-based technologies are seamlessly incorporated. A range of emerging technologies is integrated with machinery and BCT. In this generation, scalability is one of the most significant challenges that blockchain faces (Singh *et al.*, 2020; Pawar *et al.*, 2021; Dennis & Disso, 2019). Although many newer cryptocurrencies claim to be able to handle more transactions in a second, one of the most important features a third-generation blockchain would need to provide is a reliable scaling solution – whether that means changing the features of the blockchain itself or using a 'second-layer solution to handle more transactions.

Even though blockchain technology is still in its infancy, it has made considerable progress in the last five years (Pilkington, 2016; Gamage *et al.*, 2020). BCT makes transaction tracking and processing much more open and stable. In BCT, any time a service transaction is completed, a new block of data is recorded on the blockchain, which will remain there indefinitely and be visible to all parties. The details in the BCT are extensively encrypted to prevent tampering with the transactions.

Figure 1. Evolution of blockchain technology

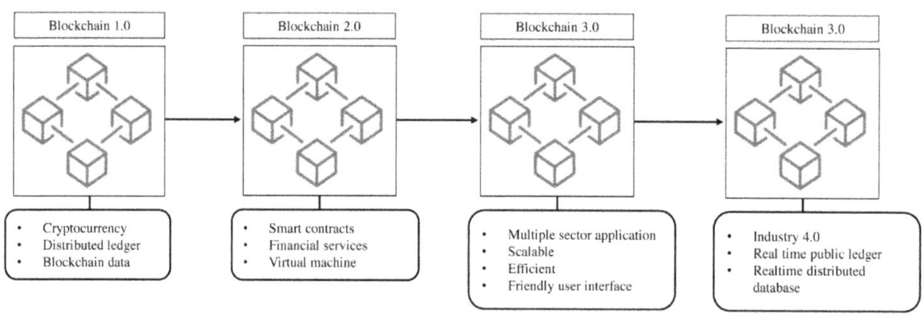

Since the ledger is permanent and distributed throughout the network in different locations, blockchain provides greater security. This means it can keep working even if a network unit fails or if one of the chain's participants exits. Moreover, there is no involvement from a third party (middlemen). Blockchain removes middlemen and removes the need for the central system, making operations quicker, effective and safe (Vogel-Heuser *et al.*, 2016). Transactions are used to send and receive digital assets such as money, financial data, personal data, health information, computer activity records, and just about any other digital asset that can be sent. The block contains transaction information which is connected to the chain using hash values, forming a blockchain with full data integrity. Each additional block is connected to the one before it. Every one of the system's actors is in charge of distributing and verifying new transactions, as well as encoding them into new blocks (Figure 2).

Figure 2. Decentralization in blockchain technology

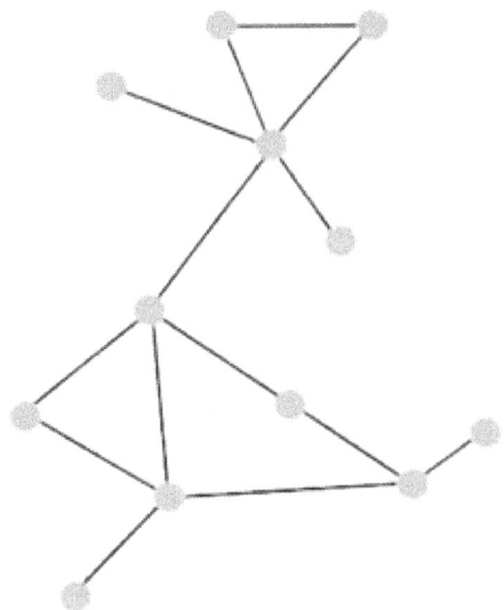

The BCT decentralization feature enables stable, open, persistent, and reliable data sharing with nodes taking on the position of the current center point. Every node possesses a copy of blockchain at about the same time. As a result, the data stored in the blockchain cannot be manipulated by a single entity since all other nodes must agree.

Industry 4.0

Industry 4.0 also known as smart manufacturing or Industrial IoT (IIoT), is the current state which encompasses the 4th industrial revolution that employs the Internet of Things (IoT) as well as other technologies to digitally boost manufacturing lines and transform them into "smart" lines (Thames *et al.*, 2017). In industry 4.0, improved performance in the manufacturing process is optimized through real-time huge data analysis which results in almost real-time autonomous decision making.

In the 3rd industrial revolution, companies started to integrate Information and Communication Technologies (ICTs) in their industry through the advancement of industrial computers, workstations, sensors, automation, and the Internet in manufacturing plants. Unlike past revolutions, the primary idea of Industry 4.0 is not fueled by a particular technology. Industry 4.0 features the interconnection of multiple technologies present in the industrial world, allowing for data collection, analysis of big industrial data, and making the right decisions based on the information collected from the industrial processes.

Cyber-Physical System (CPS)

Cyber-physical system (CPS) is a crucial component in the application of Industry 4.0. CPS refers to an Industry 4.0-enabled manufacturing system that allows real-time information collection, analysis, and visibility in all aspects of the manufacturing process. With CPS, means of production becomes networked and able to 'share information,' allowing for new production processes, value creation, and real-time adjustments (Dafflon & Moalla, 2021). CPS offers integration of various systems of diverse natures with the primary goal of controlling a physical process and adapting to new circumstances in real-time through feedback (Mosterman & Zander, 2016. Equipped with computing capability, control modules, sensors, and actuators, CPS can be IP address-assigned entity that self-monitor, generate information about its activity, and communicate with other related entities or even the outside world.

CPS allows both computational and communication technologies to be integrated into a wide range of physical structures. CPS is centered on a large computational capacity and certain characteristics that grant freedom to make decisions based on the integration of disruptive technology and acquired data from the surrounding in which it is incorporated. As a result, extreme integration between the physical and digital worlds is feasible, for example, sensors or machinery can send data to the CPS, which then takes action based on its database of information. Besides that, CPS is the potential for breaking down the industrial hierarchical levels, facilitating the so-called horizontal and vertical integration of the industrial world, allowing any computer at any industrial scale to communicate and interoperate with just another device from every other place. With this, data from different industrial processes can be integrated and used by any other party in the industrial chain.

RESEARCH METHODOLOGY

The modified e-Delphi method was used in this study (Meshkat *et al.,* 2014). The Delphi method is an iterative process that employs a series of data collection and analysis techniques in response to expert decisions at regular intervals (Donohoe *et al.*, 2012). The Delphi method is a method for gaining individual consensus on issues where there is little to no conclusive proof and where consensus is relevant. The traditional Delphi method intends to elicit group opinion through an anonymized, multi-level group interaction, with several rounds monitored by a mediator to find agreement (Zheng *et al.*, 2018). The anonymity factor prevents issues arising from influential experts, community influence, and status, which are often more noticeable in the hierarchy of professionals.

The electronic Delphi (e-Delphi) technique utilize online tools. Researchers may use this approach to develop expert consensus using the World Wide Web's tools for simplicity, ease of use, and intensity of the discussion. The internet research tools used in this analysis were Google Drive and Gmail. The number of "rounds" or iterations is generally decided upon at the start of the analysis and varies from 2 to 4. As shown in Figure 3, there were 3 rounds of information and consensus building in this study.

Figure 3. Modified e-Delphi methodology employed in the study

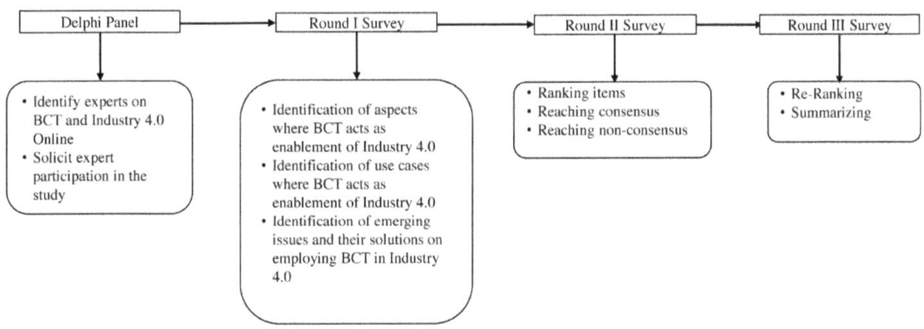

Panel selection

Potential panel participants were chosen based on a study of the literature, with top scholars who have researched in the fields of BCT and industry 4.0 in reputable international journals were considered. Potential panelists were contacted by email after the selection process to request their approval. Following approval, a follow-up letter is communicated to the experts who approved the invitation to participate, along with the necessary research forms. The method for selecting panelists in this study is tabulated in Table 1. 31 experts were approached and invited to participate in the study using the table 1 procedure (between November 2020 and January 2021). Those who wanted to take part in the study were asked to provide an email address to which all research correspondence would be used.

Table 1. Procedure for the panel selection

Phase	Process	Result
Phase I	Review the literature to assemble a list of possible panel members based on BCT and industry 4.0 publications.	Expert names compilation
Phase II	Look for evidence of BCT and industry 4.0 expertise in books and journal articles by the same researcher.	Record evidence
Phase III	Examine the total number of citations of the researcher.	Record number of citations
Phase IV	Determine the value of the experts' contributions to the academic discussion of BCT and industry 4.0.	Rate on the scale of 1-3 (1-not useful, 2- moderately useful, 3-very useful)
Phase V	Make a final list of possible expert members.	The final list of experts
Phase VI	Communicate with the final list of experts through email	Email invitation to participate in the study

e-Delphi round 1

The survey was sent via Google Drive to protect the privacy and confidentiality of the responses. The questions were developed using the Google Drive form application and then sent to the panelist via e-mail addresses. This system benefits from quick responses and immediate analysis, and it encourages the use of technological advances to reach consensus among experts who often most of them have limited time. There were three Delphi iterations in total. The degree of consensus is typically defined before the analysis and is determined by the study's goals and implications for practice (Hasson *et al.*, 2000; Keeney *et al.,* 2006). In this study, we set a threshold level of 70% consensus.

e-Delphi round 2

The Round 1 responses were emailed to the panelists in the second Delphi iteration so that they could revisit their responses and adjust or strengthen their Round 1 responses (Zheng *et al.*, 2018). In the second round, each email address received the list of responses from round one. On a scale of one to nine, each panelist was asked to rate the item's significance. On a 9-point scale, scores 1-3 suggest that panelists believe the item is not significant, 4-6 indicate equivocality and 7-9 indicate that the item is significant. If all ratings fall under one of these ranges, there is absolute consensus; if ranks fall within each of the scale categories, there is a broad concept of agreement. Points for which 70% of panelists did not score within the scale of 7-9 were omitted after analysis. The panelists were then given the results for round three.

e-Delphi round 3

In round 3, panelists used the same 9-point measure to rate the components, however this time with an awareness of the group's ratings. As a result, participants may focus on their score and make adjustments in light of the group's score while remaining anonymous to the rest of the panel. Each round had seen a decline in the number of participants, with the last round having just 16 responses. Round 3 results were evaluated in the same way as round 2 results were, and a final number of points was settled upon. This list was then divided into major themes.

FINDINGS AND DISCUSSION

This section of the chapter presents the findings of the study particularly on how blockchain acts as enablement of industry 4.0. Based on the findings of the modified e-Delphi panel, the author presents and discusses several ways on how BCT can impact industry 4.0, emerging issues. The aspects were BCT acts as enablement which was identified as of very high significance by 70% of the expert panel were: 1) Trackability with Smart Contracts, 2) End to end visibility 3) Quality 4.0, 4) Intellectual Property (IP) Protection, 5) Product safety, 6) Fraud prevention, 7) Data & Communication Security and 8) Neighborhood Microgrid.

Trackability with Smart contract

Smart contracts are simply computer code that can perform complex functions automatically and operate with a basic "if x then y" logic (Cuccuru, 2017; Lauslahti *et al.*, 2017; Brownsword, 2019). For instance, a smart contract can be coded so that when it gets the data verifying that a shipment of cargo has been delivered by the buyer, the data is checked for authenticity, and the smart contract immediately transfers payment that has been held in escrow. Compared with traditional contracts where human confirmation is required for the operation of a contract, to review the terms of service and determine the next steps by the signed agreement. With smart contracts, information is shared reliably, and safely across complex supply chains. Smart contracts offer unalterable, persistent digital records of items, components, and goods, fostering transaction openness between all participants (Hewa *et al.*, 2020). By using smart contracts, the transaction is marked with a special tag which is beneficial due to (1) lack of trust among members beneficial (2) the supply chain includes several parties with their different IT systems, or (3) new party can be inducted into the chain.

Smart contracts minimize payment delay, mitigate billing and payment inconsistencies, and connect processes to real-world physical experiences. Since smart contracts are stored on a single, distributed ledger, anybody with the proper authorization can access them. This implies that all participants in the supply chain will see all smart contracts at any time (Li, 2019). They can also see the contract's conditions, as well as how near it is to being met along with the contract's records.

It's worth remembering that smart contracts aren't just digital copies of paper contracts; they're pieces of code. They're established as "if-then" conditions in programmatic coding, thus, if one condition happened, another happens. Depending on the contract and the number of parties involved, these conditions may require one or more steps. Aside from offering a method to increase transaction performance, advocates of smart contracts promote its potential to remove non-enforced terms in conventional contracts. For example, if two parties agree to procedural code language in a contract but find that implementing one element of the contract is economically unviable or impractical, they can simply exclude the phrase in a smart contract.

Use Case: Logistics 4.0

Numerous operations in the logistics industry, such as agreement terms, fraud prevention, records management, transactions, cash flow, and more, can be simplified and secured by smart contracts (Casado-Vara *et al.*, 2019). Smart contracts can track deliveries from the start to the end of their journey — as they exit the factory and find their way to the customer (Tsiulin *et al.*, 2020). The blockchain stores all of the details about its journeys, and when the terms are met, smart contracts are executed. Trucking companies are now attempting to invest in good tracking technology, but the security of these systems is doubtful. Furthermore, since these technologies lack a secure authentication mechanism, cybercriminals or bad actors can still access the network's data. The blockchain can radically offer the solution in these situations. Blockchain can verify all of the driver records for every new carrier, much as it can validate a used vehicle. Many companies are increasingly concerned with data being tampered with, duplicated, or even full of inaccuracies on their load boards. This can contribute to a distorted portrayal of customer needs. with the BCT for logistics tracking feature, importers can directly update the blockchain with timestamps. There is no risk of mistake or replication since all of the data in the blockchain is checked.

End to End Visibility

Within complex supply chains, industries may use BCT to share data instantly, efficiently, and safely. Blockchain can provide an unchangeable, persistent digital record of items, pieces, and goods, fostering end-to-end visibility and providing all parties with a single source of reality (Jabbar *et al.*, 2020). Transactions can have a unique tag added to them in the blockchain records. These real-time activity logs can be used by manufacturers to monitor the movement of source parts and finished products. All orders, sales, and inventory can be tracked by all parties, allowing them to stay on top of things. Consider the effect that complete supply chain visibility would have on businesses. They'll be able to see where parts were sourced, who was involved in the manufacturing process, and how the product went from one end of the supply chain to the other. This provides complete accountability for industries and aids in the strengthening of corporate relationships.

Use Case: Aircraft Industry

A completely operational commercial plane needs millions of small and large parts, many of which come from different sources. As a result, knowing the history of each component of the aircraft is crucial. Despite developments in sensor technology, IoT, data analytics, and cloud computing, there is still a lack of real-time access to details such as components, settings, and service schedules. In reality, obtaining comprehensive, real-time details of an airliner, let alone an entire fleet is incredibly difficult. And there's the blockchain. By balancing openness and security on a distributed ledger, it has the potential to resolve this. Not only can blockchain trace the origin of various parts, but it also has the potential to record the setup of a plane for any flight during its long operational life by providing a snapshot of all the pieces and processes. BCT keeps the capacity of creating a digital record for each component mounted in a plane and updating it after each service or inspection. Tail numbers, part positions on planes, suppliers, part admissibility, the name of each mechanic who worked with the part, and the service location are all examples of data that could be captured

Quality control

Quality 4.0 is the extension of the fourth industrial revolution to the field of quality (Brandenburger *et al.*, 2021). The central principle of Quality 4.0 is to integrate quality management practices with evolving Industry 4.0 capabilities to help industries achieve operational excellence. The rapid, efficient aggregation of data from different sources, which enables informed and efficient decision-making, is a major aspect of Quality 4.0 (Zonnenshain *et al.*, 2020). Furthermore, automatic assessment reduces the possibility of human error in interpreting the data. Non-contact inspection automation also allows for the processing of even larger volumes of data for more in-depth research. With BCT, blockchain provides immutable records of quality checks and manufacturing process details, in addition to assisting clients in tracking and tracing shipment parts through a supply chain. Any transaction, adjustment, or quality check is automatically entered on the blockchain database, which tags each product differently. The development setup typically includes automated quality checks that produce and document measurements directly to the blockchain. The quality assurance/check ensures that industries track machines for signs of potential failures and repair them making sure high efficiency all of the time, rather than waiting for them to break down (Lee *et al.*, 2019).

Use Case I: Pharmaceutical Industry

To maintain quality management and regulatory enforcement over the transportation of medical goods, the pharmaceutical industry employs a number of complex and stringent environmental control mechanisms (e.g., temperature and humidity). Quality assurance in the supply chain is possible with blockchain, such as binding medications that need temperature regulation to a temperature sensor and incorporating it with the Internet of Things. The sensor will simply log a deviation of temperature controls if the temperature exceeds a certain level, which the supplier could not reverse. The same approach may be used to send patient health information without fear of it being intercepted. Any data sent over the blockchain is recorded permanently. Hence, when submitting a prescription, for instance, both the medical center and the patient will track the prescription's validity.

Use Case 2: Food Safety

From time-to-time people have been getting sick from infected lettuce or other products. When this happens, supermarkets and other retailers do as we would expect: they remove the product from the shelf to be safe. Walmart, on the other hand, has been at the forefront of reforming this strategy in recent years. Walmart revealed in 2018 that it will be using BCT to monitor every package of spinach and head of lettuce after a 2-year pilot scheme (Galvez *et al.*, 2018). Then, Walmart requested that more than 100 farms from which it procured enter precise information about its goods into a blockchain database. The people managing the Walmart supply chain make an entry on the blockchain at each step in the supply chain, signing when they acquire the food product and when they send it on to the next individual in the chain. Food is tracked from the farm, through cleaning and processing facilities, to the factory, and finally to the supermarket, using BCT (Orzechowski, 2019).

Treum is a BCT-based supply chain business that, in collaboration with the World Wildlife Fund, is now using the technologies to assist revolutionize the tuna industry (Larissa & Parung, 2021). To show how it functions, a tuna fish is fitted with an RFID tag as soon as it is captured, and its address is sent to the Ethereum blockchain. This demonstrates how technology can be used for product traceability and ensures that the fish was captured lawfully and sustainably. The fish can be monitored to the store, consumers can use their phone to scan a QR code to check where, when, and by whom the fish was captured.

Intellectual Property (IP) Protection

When it comes to monetizing digital assets, blockchain is one of the technologies that can help a business secure and retain ownership of its intellectual property (IP) (Ito & O'Dair, 2019). IP protection is a must for companies in all manufacturing industries. In the event of a patent dispute, a corporation may use blockchain technology to help prove the ownership of IP (Li *et* al., 2020). Bernstein Technology (Bernstein, 2021), for example, has created a web service that allows users to register IP addresses in a blockchain.

Nevertheless, since Blockchain is still in its early stages of growth, we will see many more advanced Blockchain applications for intellectual property in the coming years. Brand owners may use a ledger that shows who owns what as a point of reference for their rights and the degree to which those rights are being used in the market. This may be especially useful in jurisdictions where evidence of first or genuine use is needed, or where the scope of use is critical, such as in trademark disputes or other disputes involving well-known marks, or in defending trademarks. A ledger that shows who owns what, who is an approved licensee, and so on will allow everybody in the supply chain, including customers and customs officials, to verify a real product and tell it apart from a counterfeit.

Among the most compelling use cases of BCT in IP protection is attaching scannable blockchain-connected tags, tamper-resistant seals, to goods, which could play a vital role in combating counterfeit goods. If a brand owner tells customs officials of the security features that legitimate goods should have, then the lack of such features is an easy way to identify fakes.

Use Case: 3D Printing Industry

IP theft is a major issue in the 3D printing industry. Traditional methods of moving files with designs to vendors and their printing machines leave designers susceptible to theft. To combat this, the blockchain system can provides an automated audit trail, allowing users to monitor the proper use of the 3D model, as well as the materials used in the production. This is especially important because control mechanisms for preventing the import of counterfeits and plagiarism becomes increasingly difficult, if not impossible.

Fraud prevention

The manufacturing sector is the most susceptible to fraud. Since supply chains are complicated and typically include a large number of people and moving parts, there are many opportunities for fraud to occur and go unnoticed (Jabbar *et al.*, 2020). Goods may be counterfeited to the point that they are indistinguishable from the real thing. Inventory fraud is one illustration of a pervasive problem that undermines consumer and distributor trust in producers.

Manufacturing entrepreneurs can suffer significant financial losses as a result of ineffective regulation, improper record-keeping systems, and other weaknesses in the industry's architecture. Besides that, the manufacturing industry is vulnerable not just to inventory, vendor, and procurement fraud, but also cyber threats, shady middlemen, and billing schemes (Chhetri *et al.*, 2018). For example, with BCT, if a buyer has questions about a gold seller's credibility and origins, he or she may check the data collected, which contains information archived from the time the mineral was mined until the last supplier, ensuring its validity and the sellers' integrity. Similarly, it could be used to ensure the consistency of a product, such as in the case of a high-priced product buyer who wants to ensure not just the sellers' authenticity, but also the authenticity of every particular raw material used to produce the product.

Use Case: Anti-Money Laundering

Digital exchanges and financial institutions all over the world are currently designing mechanisms to improve enforcement and enforce higher standards of regulation in their systems to comply with know you the customer (KYC) and new AML (Anti-Money Laundering) standards, as the old ones have been criticized as inadequate (Haffke *et al.*, 2020; Frick, 2019). The global financial model is changing, partly as a result of creativity and partly as a result of necessity. The previous AML guidelines and policies are inadequate, leading to poor management and low enforcement, placing customers at risk of fraud. To conform to KYC regulations, a distributed ledger could minimize errors through automation, avoid duplication, and create a database of all checks performed for each client.

Data and Communication Security

BCT enables parties to have full control over data and privacy without depending on a single point of control, making it incredibly cost-effective and productive. This presents the potential to use blockchain to build a safe and trustworthy, management and sharing system, which will speed up the data-sharing process. For a hacker to tamper with the data in the blockchain, the hacker will have to delete the data stored on every user's device in the global network. Thousands of computers may be involved, everyone holding a copy of all or most of the data. Undamaged machines, also known as "nodes," will keep operating to check and keep track of all the data on the network unless the hacker could take the whole network down at that point (which is almost unfeasible).

Enforcing blockchain technology will also decentralize the domain name system (DNS), disseminating its contents across a vast number of nodes and making hacking nearly impossible. Domain editing privileges would be given only to those who need them (domain owners), and no other user would be allowed to make adjustments, minimizing the possibility of data being accessed or altered by unauthorized parties substantially. To prevent distributed denial-of-service (DDoS) attacks, few companies have been deploying blockchain in this region. Blockstack (Ali *et al.*, 2016), for example, offers a completely decentralized DNS option. The company's philosophy is to decentralize the entire global network by eliminating all third-party management of web servers, ID systems, and databases. IBM's Watson IoT platform, for instance, includes the ability to control IoT data in a private blockchain ledger that is incorporated into Big Blue's cloud services (Kouzinopoulos, 2018). App developers using GE's Predix PaaS platform can use Ericsson's Blockchain Data Integrity service to get completely auditable, compliant, and reliable data.

Use Case: Smart Healthcare

In smart healthcare analyzing and storing this data in a safe manner is a major challenge. Hospitals, patients, physicians, and medical supply stores should all have secure access to this information. The secure transmission of these data is crucial because it impacts important decisions such as the preparation of future hospital facilities, recommending physicians, and assessing symptoms of various diseases or health problems (Bertino *et al.,* 2015). Traditional access control policies are insufficiently secure to allow highly confidential patient information to be exchanged from one party to another. Furthermore, most people do not tell their physicians about their medical background. Patient history is required in the event of a medical emergency, but they are not accessible due to poor record management. While smart healthcare has the potential to solve many of the industry's major problems, there are some obstacles to overcome. These problems can be solved with the help of blockchain technology. Indeed, the distributed ledger between different users such as patients, physicians, medical shops, and insurance providers can transform smart healthcare. Despite ongoing academic studies (Saha *et al.*, 2019; Ellouze *et al.*, 2020; Narikimilli *et al.*, 2020; Noshina *et al.,* 2020; Tandon *et al.,* 2020) and a high level of interest from the industry, BCT-based healthcare data management systems have yet to be implemented.

Energy

To fulfill consumer energy needs, a way must be discovered to better link people with renewable energy sources. Energy blockchain start-ups are creating a new ecosystem where people can be linked in interconnected microgrids using the BCT, share their consumption data, and manage local renewable energy between them based on prices and individual interests. The majority of pilots on the energy sector are in the initial stages, especially in the field of peer-to-peer energy trading, whereby small-scale producers can sell excess generation directly to other customers. In effect, blockchain allows industries and companies to determine energy consumption and generation more effectively, as well as detect network irregularities, which can increase response time in the event of a breakdown or outage. Authentication of renewables from source of origin or keeping track of emissions are two other potential uses. Many people are thinking of using it as a grid management solution that can monitor power flow and highlight grid irregularities.

Use case: microgrid

the first "blockchain microgrids" are systems that use an integrated blockchain to exchange neighborhood power generated by rooftop solar (Lai *et al.* 2021). The use of blockchain technology allows for the purchasing and sale of renewable energy produced by neighborhood microgrids (Choudhry *et al.*, 2019). Smart contracts based on Ethereum can instantly allocate surplus power produced by solar panels. In the distributed energy space, blockchain is being used to create a slew of fresh concepts and solutions. For all types of transactions and ledgers, blockchain has certain inherent advantages. Since microgrids and smart grids would be highly transactive, providing an efficient, well-validated, and safe ledger of these transactions would be extremely beneficial. However, while blockchain may make this possible, it does not address the underlying issues of pricing, control, and decision-making. Agreements between larger facilities and utilities are now getting more complicated, and figuring out the dynamic economics of complicated systems with multiple decisions is proving to be difficult. Consensys (Consensys, 2021), is working on "Transactive Grid", a project they're collaborating on with LO3, a distributed energy firm, where Ethereum smart contracts are currently being used in a pilot project to automate the control and distribution of microgrid resources.

EMERGING ISSUES

Although the industry faces some of the issues such as supply chain management and automotive safety concerns, new challenges are evolving as the technology is advancing and to support industry 4.0. In this section, the author presents the emerging issues that arouse in employing blockchain technology in industry 4.0. This section discusses emerging issues that have been identified as a result of the research conducted for this chapter.

Issues in Smart contract

Since smart contracts and distributed ledgers are still in their early growth stage, there are several challenges to consider in addition to the benefits. First is the issue of compatibility. Industries should determine if their current technology is compatible with the technology needed to implement a smart contract. For instance, is freight forwarders' existing shipment tracking equipment capable of digitally interacting with the smart contract code without human intervention? Or does it necessitate any human involvement? Moreover, computer coding is used to create smart contracts. This is specialized expertise that few companies would have on staff. Hence, industries need to hire programmers to code and manage smart contracts compared to traditional contracts where only attorneys were hired.

Additionally, there are some restrictions on what a smart contract can do. Smart contracts are often referred to as "unalterable." That is, when the smart contract has been incorporated into the distribution ledger, what's been coded cannot be modified. As a result, if the parties change their minds at a later time, the smart contract cannot be changed to reflect the new conditions. As previously mentioned, the code operates on an "if y, then x" basis. As a consequence, if the parties' agreement allows for a price change to be resolved at a future date, this cannot be coded into the smart contract. The smart contract will be unable to carry out an instruction such as "if y, then the parties will agree on a price variation collectively."

BCT interoperability

The resurgence of interest in blockchains has sparked a slew of research and development projects. As a result, today's blockchain ecosystem is extremely diverse, with users having access to a variety of incompatible BCTs. Since interoperability between BCTs is rarely planned in current protocols and standards, functions such as transmitting tokens from one party to another or triggering and implementing smart contracts are limited to a single blockchain (Schulte *et al.*, 2019).

When developing a blockchain, developers often neglect standards to achieve more flexibility, but this often led to interoperability and communication issues. Various blockchain networks with various criteria such as consensus models, smart contract features, and transaction mechanisms are the most emerging challenge to interoperability (Ermyas *et all.*, 2019). Making two separate blockchains interoperable, that is, allowing one to send data from one blockchain to another, may be of interest. A few standardization projects are underway to resolve this issue. For instance, IBM and Microsoft are relying on an existing GS1 standard to establish an interoperable blockchain (Bajwa *et al.*, 2019). In certain cases, such as "atomic exchanges" and hash-locking, the problem of interoperability is addressed by using game theory (Dai *et al.*, 2020).

BCT-Based Digital Twin

Using their education, experience, and skills in data science, statistics and mathematics, computer algorithms, and other fields, tech experts begin creating groundbreaking BCT-based digital twins. Via actionable insights generated by digital twins, future product models are initiated, and production process is continually studied and refined. By building a digital twin on the blockchain, all details about a physical product can be stored in an immutable manner. Digital twins help industries by improving their production and productivity, but they also raise ethical, legal, and social concerns. Consider a situation in which hundreds of robots and people collaborate, each with their own digital twin. What happens if the industrial robot collapses and has to be substituted? Will the replaced digital twin be able to learn from the experience of the former robot? If human workers will quit, pass away, or simply switch careers. What would occur to the digital twin in such a situation? Will such a digital twin continue to be the industry's asset? Is it possible for the industry to train new employees using their digital twin?

Industrial robots and Connected Autonomous Vehicle (CAVs)

Since BCT enables automated industrial robots and vehicles to communicate with other parties via smart contracts, blockchain is significant in this field. As a result, blockchain-based robots and vehicles will work together and transact business with one another and with third parties in a fully autonomous manner. There have been concerns regarding the potential for connected vehicles to be hacked. This challenge could be resolved by employing BCT. BCT provides natural protection which makes it virtually impossible for malicious actors to hack because it is not easy to access or modify data in a block after it has been stored and a degree of encryption is applied to each transaction. This encryption, though, isn't without disadvantages.

Since processing time is a major bottleneck in practical uses, careful consideration is needed. To synchronize data copies that are shared by multiple AVs, the Blockchain algorithm necessitates a significant CPU processing power and resources. However, CAVs lack the computing power to manage such a challenging computing task, hence reducing throughput and increasing latency in the CAV system. Due to BCT complexity, it is still argued whether it will be effective or not in an environment where autonomous cars need to communicate with networks in microseconds.

Business transactions legally are to be performed among physical persons or legal entities such as companies or organizations. CAV are neither natural beings nor legal entities in the eyes of the law which pose a new challenge.

Ethical and Legal Issues

The ethical implications of BTC have yet to be identified, unlike other fields of tech ethics. Building the area of blockchain ethics is challenging. People, businesses, and devices are all considering using blockchain to store their digital identities. The underlying transparency and immutability of blockchain is a truly distinctive value proposition. However, when it comes to handling confidential identity data, these very strengths can be disadvantageous. There are some legal issues to consider. For instance, is it appropriate to give the general public access to classified information? What if this information leads to people being victimized? Is it possible for data miners or validators to exploit the information? Furthermore, some countries forbid the collection of confidential data outside of their borders. Blockchain is a global ecosystem of participants from all over the world. How do we guarantee that the knowledge does not cross a particular jurisdiction? People may request that businesses remove their personal information under data privacy laws. How will Blockchain-based businesses react to this request? While smart contracts automate processes, they are written by humans. When humans are involved, the mechanism is contaminated with prejudice. The challenge is, how do we infuse ethics with anti-bias characteristics and lead to an ethical blockchain?

Another thing to note is how the parties will be able to rewrite the smart contract if the law changes and made the commitments coded illegal. Smart contracts can pose issues about their lawfulness, validity, and governing law status. Besides that, smart contracts can effectively remove some legal options, such as the right to halt the execution of contract agreements or cancel the contract.

Security issues

Storing the same data through several systems protects the data from attacks. There is no single point of failure for blockchains, and they cannot be modified by a single device. However, on the other hand, hackers now have many likely targets. How do we keep these systems secure all over the world? State-of-the-art encryption techniques can be used to encrypt the data stored. To access any instance of a blockchain and modify them together at the same time, lots and lots of computational power will be needed and more than 51% hashrate. Nevertheless, post-quantum cryptography and other futuristic approaches can be used. To avoid a 51 percent attack, hashrate should be increased, and the Proof-of-Work (PoW) consensus process should be avoided.

Another security issue is Cryptojacking. Cryptojackers are people who want to take advantage of the benefits of cryptocurrency mining without having to incur the high costs of hardware or huge energy bills. Cryptojacking codes, unlike other forms of malware, do not harm machines or the data of their targets. They do, nevertheless, take computer processing power. Industries with a large number of cryptojacked systems can incur significant expenses of customer support and IT effort wasted tracing down performance problems and replacing hardware or systems in the hopes of resolving the problem.

CONCLUSION

Blockchain's implementation and usage have long outgrown its original intent as the foundation of the world's first decentralized cryptocurrency. Other industries have recognized the importance of a trustless, decentralized ledger with historical immutability, and are looking to adopt the key principles to their current business processes. Existing major technology firms are investing in this technology, and numerous attempts are being made to build publicly open-sourced platforms. These activities demonstrate the promise of blockchain technology and its convergence with Industry 4.0.

Even though both Industry 4.0 and Blockchain technology has strong prospective future, both trends are still too immature to be applied on a wide scale in a real-world setting. In a progressively commoditized and global environment, manufacturers and technology professionals must collaborate to find out how blockchain can rejuvenate factories. A new way of thinking, as well as a creative and agile approach, is needed to fully realize blockchain's potential in this domain.

This study used e-Delphi to address the BCT as enablement in Industry 4.0. The e-Delphi method and online surveys were found to be cost-effective in terms of the researcher's time and finance, as well as promoting rapid contact between experts from various fields. The decrease in response rate over the Delphi rounds is a shortcoming. This is believed to be due to respondents losing interest as they are asked to rate the very same issues several times. Despite the decrease in response rates, the final results revealed a variety of aspects where consensus was reached.

The e-Delphi technique, on the other hand, proven to be a method enriched in qualitative data and an effective way of getting experts together to examine, argue, and coordinate a body of data to develop a validated instrument, reach consensus on a topic, discover common causes, or forecast patterns.

ACKNOWLEDGMENT

This research received no specific grant from any funding agency in the public, commercial, or not-for-profit sectors.

REFERENCES

Abebe, E., Behl, D., Govindarajan, C., Hu, Y., Karunamoorthy, D., Novotny, P., Pandit, V., Ramakrishna, V., & Vecchiola, C. (2019). *Enabling Enterprise Blockchain Interoperability with Trusted Data Transfer* (Industry Track). In *Proceedings of the 20th International Middleware Conference Industrial Track (Middleware '19).* Association for Computing Machinery. 10.1145/3366626.3368129

Alcácer, V., & Cruz-Machado, V. (2019). Scanning the Industry 4.0: A Literature Review on Technologies. *International Journal for Manufacturing Systems, Engineering Science and Technology*, *22*(3), 899-919. doi:10.1016/j.jestch.2019.01.006

Ali, M., Nelson, J., Shea, R., & Freedman, M. J. (2016). Blockstack: A global naming and storage system secured by blockchains. *Proceedings of the 2016 USENIX Annual Technical Conference*, 181–194.

Bajwa, N., Prewett, K., & Shavers, C. (2019). Is your supply chain ready to embrace blockchain? *Journal of Corporate Accounting & Finance*, *31*(2), 54–64. Advance online publication. doi:10.1002/jcaf.22423

Bartodziej, C. J. (2021). The concept Industry 4.0. In *The Concept Industry 4.0.* BestMasters. Springer Gabler. doi:10.1007/978-3-658-16502-4_3

Bernstein. (2021). *How it works - Bernstein - Blockchain for intellectual property.* https://www.bernstein.io/how-it-works

Bertino, E., Deng, R. H., Huang, X., & Zhou, J. (2015). Security and privacy of electronic health information systems. *International Journal of Information Security*, *14*(6), 485–486. doi:10.100710207-015-0303-z

Brandenburger, J. (2021). Quality 4.0 - Transparent Product Quality Supervision in the Age of Industry 4.0. In V. Colla & C. Pietrosanti (Eds.), *Impact and Opportunities of Artificial Intelligence Techniques in the Steel Industry. ESTEP 2020. Advances in Intelligent Systems and Computing* (Vol. 1338). Springer. doi:10.1007/978-3-030-69367-1_5

Brownsword, R. (2019). Regulatory Fitness: Fintech, Funny Money, and Smart Contracts. *European Business Organization Law Review*, *20*(1), 5–27. doi:10.100740804-019-00134-2

Casado-Vara, R., González Briones, A., Prieto, J., & Corchado R. (2019). *Smart Contract for Monitoring and Control of Logistics Activities: Pharmaceutical Utilities Case Study*. doi:10.1007/978-3-319-94120-2_49

Casino, Dasaklis, & Patsakis. (2019). A Systematic Literature Review of Blockchain-based Applications: Current Status, classification and Open Issues. *Telematics and Informatics*, *36*, 55-81. doi:10.1016/j.tele.2018.11.006

Chhetri, S. R., Faezi, S., Rashid, N., & Al Faruque, M. A. (2018). Manufacturing Supply Chain and Product Lifecycle Security in the Era of Industry 4.0. *Journal of Hardware System Security*, *2*(1), 51–68. doi:10.100741635-017-0031-0

Choudhry, A., Dimobi, I., & Isaac Gould, Z. M. (2019). Blockchain Driven Platform for Energy Distribution in a Microgrid. In Data Privacy Management, Cryptocurrencies and Blockchain Technology. Springer. doi:10.1007/978-3-030-31500-9_18

Consensys. (2021). *Blockchain technology solutions*. https://consensys.net/

Cuccuru, P. (2017, Autumn). Beyond Bitcoin: An Early Overview On smart contracts. *International Journal of Law and Information Technology*, *25*(3), 179–195. doi:10.1093/ijlit/eax003

Dafflon, B., Moalla, N., & Ouzrout, Y. (2021). The challenges, approaches, and used techniques of CPS for manufacturing in Industry 4.0: A literature review. *International Journal of Advanced Manufacturing Technology*, *113*(7-8), 2395–2412. doi:10.100700170-020-06572-4

Dai, B., Jiang, S., Zhu, M., Lu, M., Li, D., & Li, C. (2020) Research and Implementation of Cross-Chain Transaction Model Based on Improved Hash-Locking. In Blockchain and Trustworthy Systems. Springer. doi:10.1007/978-981-15-9213-3_17

Dennis, R., & Disso, J. P. (2019). An Analysis into the Scalability of Bitcoin and Ethereum. In *Third International Congress on Information and Communication Technology*. Springer. 10.1007/978-981-13-1165-9_57

Donohoe, H., Stellefson, M., & Tennant, B. (2012). Advantages and Limitations of the e-Delphi Technique. *American Journal of Health Education, 43*(1), 38–46. doi:10.1080/19325037.2012.10599216

Ellouze, F., Fersi, G., & Jmaiel, M. (2020). Blockchain for Internet of Medical Things: A Technical Review. In M. Jmaiel, M. Mokhtari, B. Abdulrazak, H. Aloulou, & S. Kallel (Eds.), Lecture Notes in Computer Science: Vol. 12157. *The Impact of Digital Technologies on Public Health in Developed and Developing Countries. ICOST 2020*. Springer. doi:10.1007/978-3-030-51517-1_22

Frick, T. A. (2019). Virtual and cryptocurrencies—regulatory and anti-money laundering approaches in the European Union and in Switzerland. *ERA Forum, 20*, 99–112. 10.100712027-019-00561-1

Gaiardelli, P., Pezzotta, G., Rondini, A., Romero, D., Jarrahi, F., Bertoni, M., Wiesner, S., Wuest, T., Larsson, T., Zaki, M., Jussen, P., Boucher, X., Bigdeli, A. Z., & Cavalieri, S. (2021). Product-service systems evolution in the era of Industry 4.0. *Service Business, 15*(1), 177–207. doi:10.100711628-021-00438-9

Galvez, J. F., Mejuto, J. C., & Simal-Gandara, J. (2018). Future challenges on the use of blockchain for food traceability analysis. *Trends in Analytical Chemistry, 107*, 222–232. Advance online publication. doi:10.1016/j.trac.2018.08.011

Gamage, H. T. M., Weerasinghe, H. D., & Dias, N. G. J. (2020). A Survey on Blockchain Technology Concepts, Applications, and Issues. *SN. Computer Science, 1*(2), 114. doi:10.100742979-020-00123-0

Haffke, L., Fromberger, M., & Zimmermann, P. (2020). Cryptocurrencies and anti-money laundering: The shortcomings of the fifth AML Directive (EU) and how to address them. *J Bank Regul, 21*(2), 125–138. doi:10.105741261-019-00101-4

Hasson, F., Keeney, S., & McKenna, H. (2000). Research guidelines for the Delphi survey technique. *Journal of Advanced Nursery, 32*(4), 1008-15.

Hewa, T., Ylianttila, M., & Liyanage, M. (2020). Survey on Blockchain based Smart Contracts: Applications, Opportunities and Challenges. *Journal of Network and Computer Applications, 177*, 102857. Advance online publication. doi:10.1016/j.jnca.2020.102857

Ito, K., & O'Dair, M. (2019). A Critical Examination of the Application of Blockchain Technology to Intellectual Property Management. In H. Treiblmaier & R. Beck (Eds.), *Business Transformation through Blockchain*. Palgrave Macmillan. doi:10.1007/978-3-319-99058-3_12

Jabbar, S., Lloyd, H., & Hammoudeh, M. (2020). Blockchain-enabled supply chain: Analysis, challenges, and future directions. *Multimedia Systems*. Advance online publication. doi:10.100700530-020-00687-0

Keeney, S., Hasson, F., & McKenna, H. (2006). Consulting the oracle: ten lessons from using the Delphi technique in nursing research. *Journal of Advanced*, *53*(2), 205-12. doi:10.1111/j.1365-2648.2006.03716.x

Kouzinopoulos, C. S. (2018). Using Blockchains to Strengthen the Security of Internet of Things. In *Communications in Computer and Information Science* (Vol. 821). Springer. doi:10.1007/978-3-319-95189-8_9

Lai, C. S., Lai, L. L., & Lai, Q. H. (2021). Blockchain Applications in Microgrid Clusters. In *Smart Grids and Big Data Analytics for Smart Cities*. Springer. doi:10.1007/978-3-030-52155-4_3

Larissa, S., & Parung, J. (2021). Designing supply chain models with blockchain technology in the fishing industry in Indonesia. *IOP Conference Series: Materials Science and Engineering*, 1072. 10.1088/1757-899X/1072/1/012020

Lauslahti, K., Mattila, J., & Seppala, T. (2017, January). Smart Contracts – How Will Blockchain Technology Affect Contractual Practices? *ETLA Reports*, (68). Advance online publication. doi:10.2139srn.3154043

Lee, S. M., Lee, D., & Kim, Y. S. (2019). The quality management ecosystem for predictive maintenance in the Industry 4.0 era. *Int J Qual Innov*, *5*(1), 4. doi:10.118640887-019-0029-5

Li, W., Fu, C., & Cheng, D. (2020). Comments on the development of blockchain technology from the perspective of patent analysis. *Front. Eng. Manag.*, *7*(4), 615–617. doi:10.100742524-020-0101-9

Li, Y. (2019). Emerging blockchain-based applications and techniques. *SOCA*, *13*(4), 279–285. doi:10.100711761-019-00281-x

Meshkat, B., Cowman, S., Gethin, G., Ryan, K., Wiley, M., Brick, A., Clarke, E., & Mulligan, E. (2014). Using an e-Delphi technique in achieving consensus across disciplines for developing best practice in day surgery in Ireland. *Journal of Hospital Administration*, *3*(4), 1. Advance online publication. doi:10.5430/jha.v3n4p1

Mosterman, P. J., & Zander, J. (2016). Industry 4.0 as a Cyber-Physical System study. *Software & Systems Modeling*, *15*(1), 17–29. doi:10.100710270-015-0493-x

Nakamoto, S. (2008). *Bitcoin: A Peer-To-Peer Electronic Cash System*. https://bitcoin.org/bitcoin.pdf

Narikimilli, N. R. S., Kumar, A., Antu, A. D., & Xie, B. (2020). Blockchain Applications in Healthcare– A Review and Future Perspective. In Z. Chen, L. Cui, B. Palanisamy, & L. J. Zhang (Eds.), Lecture Notes in Computer Science: Vol. 12404. *Blockchain – ICBC 2020. ICBC 2020*. Springer. doi:10.1007/978-3-030-59638-5_14

Nofer, M., Gomber, P., Hinz, O., & Schiereck, D. (2017). Blockchain. *Business & Information Systems Engineering*, *59*(3), 183–187. doi:10.100712599-017-0467-3

Noshina Qamar, A., & Muhammad, A. (2020). Farrukh A. (2020). Blockchain and Smart Healthcare Security: A Survey. *Procedia Computer Science*, *175*, 615–620. doi:10.1016/j.procs.2020.07.089

Orzechowski, E. (2019). The Traceability of Bulk Food Products. In J. McEntire & A. Kennedy (Eds.), *Food Traceability. Food Microbiology and Food Safety*. Springer. doi:10.1007/978-3-030-10902-8_5

Oztemel, E., & Gursev, S. (2020). Literature Review of Industry 4.0 and Related Technologies. *Journal of Intelligent Manufacturing*, *31*(1), 127–182. doi:10.100710845-018-1433-8

Pawar, M. K., Patil, P., & Hiremath, P. S. (2021). A Study on Blockchain Scalability. In M. Tuba, S. Akashe, & A. Joshi (Eds.), *ICT Systems and Sustainability. Advances in Intelligent Systems and Computing* (Vol. 1270). Springer. doi:10.1007/978-981-15-8289-9_29

Pilkington, M. (2016). Blockchain Technology: Principles and Applications. In F. X. Olleros & M. Zhegu (Eds.), *Research Handbook on Digital Transformations* (pp. 225–253). doi:10.4337/9781784717766.00019

Saha, A., Amin, R., Kunal, S., Vollala, S., & Dwivedi, S. (2019). Review on "Blockchain technology based medical healthcare system with privacy issues". *Security and Privacy*, *2*(5). Advance online publication. doi:10.1002py2.83

Schulte, S., Sigwart, M., Frauenthaler, P., & Borkowski, M. (2019). Towards Blockchain Interoperability. In *Lecture Notes in Business Information Processing* (Vol. 361). Springer. doi:10.1007/978-3-030-30429-4_1

Singh, A., Parizi, R. M., Han, M., Dehghantanha, A., Karimipour, H., & Choo, K. K. R. (2020). Public Blockchains Scalability: An Examination of Sharding and Segregated Witness. In K. K. Choo, A. Dehghantanha, & R. Parizi (Eds.), *Blockchain Cybersecurity, Trust and Privacy. Advances in Information Security* (Vol. 79). Springer. doi:10.1007/978-3-030-38181-3_11

Tandon, A., Dhir, A., Islam, A. K. M. N., & Mäntymäki, M. (2020). Blockchain in healthcare: A systematic literature review, synthesizing framework and future research agenda. *Computers in Industry*, *122*, 103290. doi:10.1016/j.compind.2020.103290

Thames, L., & Schaefer, D. (2017). *Industry 4.0: An Overview of Key Benefits*. Technologies, and Challenges. doi:10.1007/978-3-319-50660-9_1

Trunzer, E., Calà, A., Leitão, P., Gepp, M., Kinghorst, J., Lüder, A., Schauerte, H., Reifferscheid, M., & Vogel-Heuser, B. (2019). System architectures for Industrie 4.0 applications. *Prod. Eng. Res. Devel*, *13*(3-4), 247–257. doi:10.100711740-019-00902-6

Tsiulin, S., Reinau, K. H., Hilmola, O.-P., Goryaev, N., & Karam, A. (2020). Blockchain-based applications in shipping and port management: A literature review towards defining key conceptual frameworks. *Review of International Business and Strategy*, *30*(2), 201–224. doi:10.1108/RIBS-04-2019-0051

Vogel-Heuser, B., & Hess, D. (2016). Guest Editorial Industry 4.0–Prerequisites and Visions. *IEEE Transactions on Automation Science and Engineering*, *13*(2), 411–413. doi:10.1109/TASE.2016.2523639

Xu, M., Chen, X., & Kou, G. (2019). A Systematic Review of Blockchain. *Financ Innov*, *5*(1), 27. doi:10.118640854-019-0147-z

Yang, F., & Gu, S. (2021). *Industry 4.0, A Revolution that Requires Technology and National strategies*. Complex Intell. Syst. doi:10.100740747-020-00267-9

Zhao, J. L., Fan, S., & Yan, J. (2018). Overview of Business Innovations and Research opportunities in Blockchain and Introduction to the Special Issue. *Financ Innov*, *2*(1), 28. doi:10.118640854-016-0049-2

Zheng, P., wang, H., Sang, Z., Zhong, R. Y., Liu, Y., Liu, C., Mubarok, K., Yu, S., & Xu, X. (2018). Smart Manufacturing Systems for Industry 4.0: Conceptual Framework, Scenarios, and Future Perspectives. *Frontiers of Mechanical Engineering*, *13*(2), 137–150. doi:10.100711465-018-0499-5

Zonnenshain, A., & Kenett, R. (2020). Quality 4.0—The challenging future of quality engineering. *Quality Engineering*, *32*(4), 1–13. doi:10.1080/08982112.2019.1706744

ADDITIONAL READING

Kumari, P. L. (2021). Blockchain-Autonomous Driving Systems. In A. K. Tyagi, G. Rekha, & N. Sreenath (Eds.), *Opportunities and Challenges for Blockchain Technology in Autonomous Vehicles* (pp. 87–114). IGI Global. doi:10.4018/978-1-7998-3295-9.ch006

Mason, N., Halgamuge, M. N., & Aiyar, K. (2021). Blockchain and Cryptocurrencies: Legal and Ethical Considerations. In Z. Mahmood (Ed.), *Industry Use Cases on Blockchain Technology Applications in IoT and the Financial Sector* (pp. 132–159). IGI Global. doi:10.4018/978-1-7998-6650-3.ch007

Mathur, S., & Mendiratta, S. (2020). Industry 4.0: A Practical Approach. In S. B. Buckley (Ed.), *Promoting Inclusive Growth in the Fourth Industrial Revolution* (pp. 201–219). IGI Global. doi:10.4018/978-1-7998-4882-0.ch008

Noor, M. A., Khanum, S., Anwar, T., & Ansari, M. (2021). A Holistic View on Blockchain and Its Issues. In H. Patel & G. S. Thakur (Eds.), *Blockchain Applications in IoT Security* (pp. 21–44). IGI Global. doi:10.4018/978-1-7998-2414-5.ch002

Pani, S. K., Hota, C., Qu, G., Lau, S., & Liu, X. (2021). *Blockchain and AI Technology in the Industrial Internet of Things*. IGI Global. doi:10.4018/978-1-7998-6694-7

Sever, Y., & Angin, P. (2021). Blockchain Integration into Supply Chain Operations: An Analysis With Case Studies. In Z. Mahmood (Ed.), *Industry Use Cases on Blockchain Technology Applications in IoT and the Financial Sector* (pp. 329–350). IGI Global. doi:10.4018/978-1-7998-6650-3.ch014

Show, A. K., Kumar, A., Singhal, A. N. G., & Vengatesan, K. (2021). Future Blockchain Technology for Autonomous Applications/Autonomous Vehicle. In A. K. Tyagi, G. Rekha, & N. Sreenath (Eds.), *Opportunities and Challenges for Blockchain Technology in Autonomous Vehicles* (pp. 165–177). IGI Global. doi:10.4018/978-1-7998-3295-9.ch010

Williams, I. (2020). *Cross-Industry Use of Blockchain Technology and Opportunities for the Future*. IGI Global. doi:10.4018/978-1-7998-3632-2

KEY TERMS AND DEFINITIONS

Blockchain: Blockchain is a distributed, decentralized ledger that makes tracking transactions and monitoring assets in a value chain much easier.

Cyber-Physical System: CPS monitors physical components with computer-based algorithms connected to internet, using a mixture of computers, sensory sensors, embedded cognitive computing, and multiple communications mechanisms.

Digital Twin: A digital versions of physical objects.

Industry 4.0: The use of new smart technology to advance automation of conventional manufacturing and industrial practices.

Logistics 4.0: A term coined to describe the application of Industry 4.0 technologies in logistics domain.

Microgrid: A decentralized network of electricity generating units that is usually connected to and synchronous with the conventional wide-area synchronous grid, but that can also detach to "island mode" and run independently.

Quality 4.0: Under the framework of Industry 4.0, a concept that refers to the future of quality and organization performance.

Smart Contract: A code that runs on the blockchain network and defines certain criteria that all parties must enforce.

Chapter 10
Supply Chain Management Professional Use Technologies (SM) During the Pandemic to Accomplish Tasks

Muhammad Tanveer
Prince Sultan University, Saudi Arabia

Abdul-Rahim Ahmad
Karachi School of Business and Leadership, Pakistan

ABSTRACT

Syndrome-coronavirus-2 (SARS-CoV-2), commonly referred to as the COVID-19 pandemic, has caused people to spend more time online. The pandemic has spurred growth in the use of social media technologies. Organizations now train employees to use digital media to coordinate work and connect to fulfill the requirement of supply chain management (SCM). The study aims to produce effective discussion regarding the importance of SCM and technologies and how it can assist in the recent times of COVID-19 regarding job performance. Research predicts the new ways of business conducted and how communication and coordination, knowledge exchange, training, and development are helpful in carrying out effective job productivity at the workplace of SCM. The authors analyzed responses of more than 294 SCM employee who reported on "go-to" technologies and social media tools to remote office practices. The research employed quantitative methodology (i.e., emailed questionnaires) and found that social media has become an important tool for conducting business operations due to social distancing and isolation.

DOI: 10.4018/978-1-7998-7642-7.ch010

INTRODUCTION

Our paper fills a gap in know-how and research by presenting a study of managerial practices during COVID-19 quarantine. Usually, SCM, SCM, and directors give instructions face-to-face, share expectations, and identify the path forward on workplace tasks. COVID-19 has reached out over the globe that adversely impacted the corporate sector. There are many confirmed cases for each nation, yet the pandemic is unevenly dispersed because most economies are consistent at various phases of confronting the disease. The world has engaged in the process of adjusting to the new world of digital marketing (Khan et al., 2021; Junusi, 2020). Consider Singapore and Hong Kong, which have just observed a renaissance and will undertake new endeavors in the face of COVID-19.

At the same time, Western European economies have seen variable measures of neighborhood pandemics, either on the rise or decrease. Every nation has suffered greatly during the crisis; each must consider how to restart their economy and determine the best path to recovery. The use of social media is recognized as crucial in influencing business operations globally. Moreover, the role of digital marketing (social media) that includes communication and coordination that enhances job engagement and performance is recognized as new normal for businesses around the world (Arif et al., 2009). Numerous countries have appointed advisory and health task forces and appointed well-being ambassadors who quickly develop stopgap health measures and crisis management plans through knowledge sharing and exchange. Numerous territories of the planet see a sensational ascent in COVID-19 occurrences. Economies like Russia and Turkey are seeing an acceleration in current periods. India, however, has had a tremendous spike in the number of mishaps until the start of April, and its global response has only narrowed through territorial isolation (Tanveer et al., 2021). The study aims to produce effective discussion regarding the importance of social media and how it can assist in the recent times of Covid-19 regarding job performance. Research predicts the new ways of business conducted and how communication and coordination, knowledge exchange, training, and development are helpful in carryout effective job productivity at the (Tanveer et al., 2020).

The COVID-19 outbreak and its infection fallout have become a social tragedy broadly influencing the lives of billions of individuals. No end to the crisis appears to be in sight. Loss of human lives and administration of organizations have evidenced the pandemic. Foremost, work-from-home (online) or remotely has not been (Tanveer et al., 2020). CEOs and business partners alike have adopted various job performance approaches to support their organizations through mediums like strong coordination and teamwork (Hwang et al., 2020). These new norms and values have been communicated for job performance, various indicators contribute to the development of productivity, and their significance has changed the landscape of businesses (Hwang et al., 2020). At the same time, workplaces have been transformed by physical isolation, transportation limits, goods procurement, organizational and public policies governing social distance, usage of personal protective equipment (PPE), as well as peak operation and practices of hospitals and long-term recovery and care facilities. The pandemic has stressed organizations and ruined businesses whose knowledge-exchange practices and disease prevention methods have lagged behind the steep curve of the outbreak (Kniffin et al., 2020; Tanveer et al., 2021). Self-isolation can be most difficult in busy urban areas, for example, and contact tracing in places such as Germany and the US, and touch tracking applications and automated devices used in places such as China, might not be suitable elsewhere.

The dependencies of these initiatives are another struggle for nations and organizations—for instance, considerations of their reliability and observances, such as physical distancing steps, influence whether other methods can be applied (Kniffin et al., 2020; Stanford, 2020). The study focused on the consequences that Covid-19 has impacted on the development of job performance that can be directed to shape discussion that outlines social media usage and importance that can be evaluated through perceived usefulness (Harris, 2020). Moreover, organizations and public actors have seen learning consortia and coalitions taking shape over recent months, with numerous actors—including states, retailers, educational experts, infrastructure companies, and network operators—working to leverage new channels as a potential response to the problem" [8]. Due to the spread of COVID-19, people in organizations often work from home to stay safe, increasing their productivity of employment (Kassim, 2020). Due to the lockout, SCM and SCM use social media to communicate with remote workers (Nabbout, 2020).

As stated in previous studies, the Pakistani Government has banned external visits and travel to the workplace due to the outbreak. Office closures and travel bans were motivated by the desire to keep workers safe (Haq et al., 2020). As a result, Pakistani companies required employees to work from home (Tanveer, 2020). The ICT sector is still making progress on the software and telecom side. People contact each other via different networks. However, the telecom sector is always operational. Similarly, the internet has assumed more central importance for business operations in the COVID era. Remote workers are supposed to be available on chats and assume and fulfill assignments over the phone and the internet, making it feasible to work from home (Bodewits, 2020). So, it is more important for these two sectors to share, work on the entire demand, and remain operative. By comparison, performance in the education sector may increase, in keeping with other organizations (Chaturvedi, 2020). but, due to COVID- 19, social media channels will be called upon to boost employee motivation and capacity through perceived usefulness to fulfill workplace tasks (Abueish, 2020).

However, at the same time, mass media platforms have experienced a bit of a dive with individuals all over the world observing virtual isolating, yet only in nationwide shutdown has there been a large concomitant increase in companies' investment efforts and time on social media (e.g., accessing articles, building knowledge repositories, and utilizing Facebook and Twitter). There have been multiple channels on social media helping to connect people that increase communication and coordination from the outset of the pandemic; however, the current scenario has increased the use of these social media platforms (Al-Thaqafi, 2020). As people are spending more time online, organizations that used to work in company offices have trained employees through training and development to use digital media to coordinate and connect to each other while working from home (Tanveer & Karim, 2018). The need for new and creative ideas and availability to meet virtually during office hours has further spurred growth by effective techniques and tools fostering high yield achievements in job performance [Tanveer & Hassan, 2020]. To carry out this research, we have conducted a study on four different media platforms that have primarily helped SCM conduct office tasks and coordinate with external colleagues and internal staff members (Walker et al., 2019). These tools are WhatsApp, Skype, IMO, Facebook, and some others. Social media are now in demand, and internet service providers are providing pivotal connectivity to the users.

LITERATURE REVIEW

The Pakistani government has worked rapidly to resolve the unforeseen COVID-19 impact and repercussions, informed by Pakistani Finance Minister Mohammed bin Abdullah Al-Jadaan, and in coordination with the Acting Minister of Economy and Planning (, 2020). The country has taken urgent steps to ensure the protection of its people and inhabitants and resolve political, macroeconomic effects. Foremost, the Pakistani government took preventive, rigorous steps to protect people in the Kingdom and fully ensured available financial options.

One of the most important variables that influence job performance is that of training and development. According to notable researchers (Khan et al., 2021) and scholars in the domain of human resource management and staffing, employee morale is boosted when fully trained and groomed for a task assigned to them. On the other hand, the theoretical postulations of another school of thought are that training and development practically satisfy the condition of intrinsic motivation needs of the individual employees of an organization, thereby leading them to perform effectively in order to contribute their level best towards the organizational objectives (Demircioglu and Chen, 2019; Tanveer et al., 2020).

Hypothesis 1: training and development have a significant statistical relationship between job performances.

The second important concept is that of the perceived usefulness of social media. Social media may also be considered an essential tool for consumers and conventional business organizations to market the products. However, this is the actual usefulness of social media. On the other hand, the perceived usefulness of social media refers to the usefulness of the same as perceived by the customers and the businesses alike (, 2020). The perceived usefulness of social media to enhance the job performance of individual employees has not been targeted in the previous research studies in this domain. It is because of this reason that this particular concept remains quite new and untapped (Stanger, 2017). Due to this reason, this present research study frames its second hypothesis in the following manner:

Hypothesis 2: there is a statistically significant impact of perceived usefulness of social media on job performance.

The exchange of knowledge and prevalent information symmetry between the employers and the employer is another important factor that influences the employees' job performance. Businesses operating in any industry must, and now information is dispensed at frequent intervals (Trotman, 2020). At the same time, the employees must be allowed to communicate with the business's senior SCM hip to inform them of any areas of concern for the business, including but not limited to operational bottlenecks. According to (Hang, 2020), this keeps the employees motivated and engaged, thereby affecting their job performance.

Hypothesis 3: frequent and mutual exchange of knowledge influences job performance of employees.

Communication and coordination are final variables that have been chosen as the independent variable for this study. Effective communication in the organizational context has no replacement; this is the most critical factor that can rule out all the other variables involved in this study and directly affect the organization's performance in the organization head-on (Sbeih, 2020). The employee must focus extensively on improving communication and coordination by utilizing Google Docs, Facebook Groups, WhatsApp Chat Groups, etc. An in-depth communication eventually engages the employees and helps them understand that they are a useful asset to the company.

Hypothesis 4: communication and coordination significantly impact job performance.

First, our data suggest that workers' social networking usage is strongly linked to the need for personal fulfillment and workplace morale (, 2020). Throughout the shutdown, major players reported use of social media, and participation levels of media streaming and other live sessions increased dramatically with a growing number of information and viewer-generated opinions. Even with growing internet use, advertisers and sponsors privileged digital advertising, which predicted a revolt (Tanveer et al., 2020). The COVID-19 era is frightening and unpredictable. However, one of the good aspects of the crisis has been the desire and determination of communities to work together to support each other.

Second, our data substantiated how we live distracted, greedy, and disconnected lives yet how people and companies uncharacteristically stepped up to support their neighborhoods (, 2020). At face value, working from home may interfere or blunt workers' ability to complete tasks while simultaneously honoring family members' commitments. We discovered in our research that globally shared internet forums or message boards foster remote collaboration; meantime, these online collaboration spaces allow several devices to be active simultaneously for all workplace functions. Meanwhile, globally shared forums help keep workers as versatile as possible (Verbeemen, 2020) to meet the organization's needs (Khan et al., 2021; Adams, 2020). For instance, workers can connect via laptop to a wide display for dynamic and interactive work and allow worker switches through multiform audio, messaging, project management, and coordinated use of whiteboard equipment. Khusid explains, "*Focus with your smart device—with all its low power consumption and webcam—to just get quick Slack explanations or minutes of Zoom calls unless you are on the go.*"

Survey participants also identified many blogs available to help people understand the current health and workplace standards because many organizations require workers to operate from home. For remote job tips and remaining associated with coworkers and customers, LinkedIn has published a robust collection of papers. LinkedIn produces a daily news page devoted to the coronavirus outbreak, where the site collects and disseminates current outbreak coverage (Khan & Khan, 2020;, 2020). With a plan geared to different regional areas, many organizations in Pakistan have established disaster reduction units, task groups, and commissions, including a national committee to track global updates (Femi, 2014). Such task forces work periodically to formulate strategies to offer up-to-date details about COVID-19, best practices, personal safety, infection avoidance strategies, PPE, hygiene practices for SCM, administrators, and front-line staff (Omar et al., 2020)

Moreover, our data analysis supports the finding that performance metrics are hugely different in virtual work (Isaac et al., 2016). There have been few Pakistani governmental regulations to curtail the development of a giant remote job community. Among our findings, Stanford indicated a noticeable rise in virtual workplace production, including among workers who worked just a few days a week from home. The telecommuting company reported a thermodynamic efficiency gain of 13 percent over department-based regulation during the test (Khan et al., 2021; Reshma, 2015). In reality, remote employees were reported to have earned a full day's worth of extra efficiency over the two-year study span. However, Global Workplace Analytics reports that perhaps a median workplace will save an average of $11,000 per telecommuter half time per annum [Nakrošienė & Goštautaitė, 2019). Eventually, per the results of the same report, 80 percent of remote employees are satisfied at work compared to just 55 percent of onsite workers (Iki & Tomizawa 2018). Remote employment helps organizations, in part, because it is performed on a lower cost, part-time basis.

Although devices are readily enabled to conduct remote research, this is not just a matter of plug and play. Staff ought to feel confident, connected, and encouraged to perform well away from the workplace. Of course, the joint effort is central to the success of every enterprise, but given people functioning remotely, such coordinated effort could be challenging to facilitate. When transition takes shape, SCM need to direct the staff through the transition. That requires preparation and oversight of the correct selection of devices (Cheng et al., 2020; Khan et al., 2021). Luckily, there are multiple ways for digitally forming and bringing teams together and keeping workers informed, linked, and motivated. Our research shows how combining this coordinated approach with a Learning Management System (LMS) allows the training to increase skil1l and trust (Abdullah, 2020).

RESEARCH METHODOLOGY

To carry out the research study, the SCM of businesses were contacted over the phone via Skype and WhatsApp. The research methodology used both quantitative and qualitative methods to analyze and interpret the data. Following the literature review, data collection was carried out by using social media, voice and text messages, and survey questionnaires. The survey tool was designed 1) to apprehend the use of daily apps for official collaboration; 2) to determine ways in which social media helps organizational SCM conduct business, set tasks, and "get the job done"; and 3) to calibrate the performance (i.e., ease of access, efficiency) and rate of usage of different social media applications.

The data collection instrument used for the study was a survey questionnaire. A survey questionnaire was designed in order to collect primary quantitative data from the research participants. On the other hand, the qualitative data collected for analysis in this study was secondary, so that no need for a primary data collection instrument arose. The survey questionnaire designed to collect primary quantitative data from the research participants aimed first to collect demographic information of the participants, followed by collecting data for the variables involved in this study using a Likert scale. Open-ended questions and leading/loaded questions were avoided.

Survey participants were asked certain questions to correlate to the problem statement, and the survey questionnaires were emailed to >300 participants. However, since many of the survey requests were either rejected or not responded to, and many of the filled responses could not be assured of the quality of the results, they had to be discarded. 300 was the exact size of the study/ Nonprobability sampling strategy of purposive sampling used for the sampling finalization. The rationale behind using this strategy was that it allows the researcher to use his or her judgment to identify the prospective potential candidates for the sample.

The table below highlights five sample questions that directed our research and in talk/text interviews and questionnaires. It took 28 days to distribute and compile the questionnaire results.

Sample survey questions for research on SCM' use of social media

1. What technologies (social media) tools used for the coordination?
2. What tools SCM find the most useful for the meetings?
3. Which tool is easily accessible to all team members?
4. How do you rate each tool concerning efficiency (WhatsApp, Skype, IMO, Facebook)?
5. How do you rate each tool regarding ease of access (WhatsApp, Skype, IMO, Facebook)?

Our research fills a disconnect in the literature between the creative workarounds that have arisen during COVID-19 and the emerging practices and theory now streamlining and enhancing efficiencies in business operations.

DATA ANALYSIS

Demographics

The following data was collected to call liberate the demography of the respondents.

Table 1. Demographics

Variable	Frequency	Percentage
Female	82	27.8%
Male	212	72.1%
SCM Respondents Age		
20 – 39	138	46.93%
40 years and above	156	53.06%
Grade		
Mid-Level SCM	156	53.06%
Senior SCM	112	38.09%
C-Level Executive	26	8.84%

The demographic data were collected on respondents. Of 300 participants in the survey questionnaire, 82 were female (27.8%), and 212 were male (72.1%). In terms of age brackets, 1 46.93% percent of participants were age 20-39, and age 40 or above (53.06%). In terms of job title, there were 156 mid-level SCM (53.06%), 112 senior SCM (38.09%), and 26 executives (8.84%).

Correlation analysis

The correlation technique is a common technique of statistics that is mainly utilized for evaluating the association of the variables with each other. There are a wide number of correlation techniques available for the researcher to utilize, which consist of Spearman, Kendall and Pearson's correlation [38, 39]. By utilizing the IBM SPSS for generating the results, the Pearson's correlation (PC) is utilized for measuring the association of the variable with each other. There are mainly three major aspects analyzed through Pearson's correlation which comprises significance, direction, and strength. Hence, on these three components, the correlation technique is examined.

The fundamental objective of the study is to mainly examine the influence of social media among the SCM at the time of Covid-19, where the main region was targeted in Pakistan. On this basis, the factors examined in the context of social media by the usefulness of management are training and development, perceived usefulness, knowledge exchange, communication and coordination, and job performance. Due to job performance being the major determinant in the study; therefore, its association with the other components has been assessed in social media on the Covid-19 pandemic. As shown in the correlation results, it is determined that the variables training and development, perceived usefulness, knowledge exchange, and communication and coordination have significant association with the variable job performance. This can be reflected on the Sig. (2-tailed) value representing the significance value where it is computed as 0.000 and below the threshold of 0.05. Therefore, this indicates that the variables training and development, perceived usefulness, knowledge exchange, communication, and coordination are highly connected with job performance. In addition, the coefficient value for training and development, perceived usefulness, knowledge exchange, and communication and coordination are computed as 0.970, 0.983, 0.923and 0.982, respectively. Hence, this shows that the variables have a positive and stronger connection with the job performance, which determines the direction and strength. As per the results, it can be illuminated that through social media, the organization SCM in Pakistan can enhance the training and development, perceived usefulness, knowledge exchange, and communication and coordination that overall led to the boost of job performance.

Table 2. Correlation Analysis

Correlations		TD	PU	KE	C&C	JP
Training and Development	PC	1	.986**	.912**	.964**	.970**
	Sig. (2-tailed)		0.000	0.000	0.000	0.000
Perceived usefulness	PC	.986**	1	.936**	.984**	.983**
	Sig. (2-tailed)	0.000		0.000	0.000	0.000
Knowledge exchange	PC	.912**	.936**	1	.939**	.923**
	Sig. (2-tailed)	0.000	0.000		0.000	0.000
Communication and Coordination	PC	.964**	.984**	.939**	1	.982**
	Sig. (2-tailed)	0.000	0.000	0.000		0.000
Job performance	PC	.970**	.983**	.923**	.982**	1
	Sig. (2-tailed)	0.000	0.000	0.000	0.000	

MULTIPLE REGRESSION

Other than the correlation technique, the regression analysis technique is also applied to the data collected. The purpose behind conducting the regression was to mainly determine the role of social media influencing training and development, perceived usefulness, knowledge exchange, and communication and coordination on the overall job performance. Hence, on this basis, the dependent variable is determined to be job performance. In contrast, the independent is training and development, perceived usefulness, knowledge exchange, and communication and coordination in respect to social media. By conducting the regression analysis from IBM SPSS, three major tables were provided, which comprise model summary, ANOVA, and coefficients.

Therefore, the results of these three tables are examined for evaluating the results of the regression. The equation model for the regression analysis is the following:

$$JP = \alpha + \beta_1 TD + \beta_2 PU + \beta_3 KE + \beta_4 C \,\&\, D +$$

Table 3. Regression Diagnostics

Model Summary	R	R Square	Adjusted R Square	Std. Error of the Estimate
1	.987a	0.974	0.974	0.14961

The above table represents the model summary where the main factor assessed from the model is the R-square or the coefficient of determination. The R-square mainly reflects on the model's prediction, where the high value of the R-square demonstrates a higher prediction of explanation. As per the results, the R-square is computed as 0.974 or also determined as 97.4%. The value being significant close to 1 indicates that the model has a strong prediction. In general terms, it can be stated that the variables of social media such as training and development, perceived usefulness, knowledge exchange, and communication and coordination are significantly able to predict or explain the job performance among the organizations in Pakistan.

Table 4. Regression Diagnostics

ANOVA		Sum of Squares	df	Mean Square	F	Sig.
1	Regression	660.7	4	165.171	7379.69	.000b
	Residual	17.79	795	0.022		
	Total	678.5	799			

The table above reflects on the ANOVA where the major function of the table is to evaluate the significance of the model where the major component that is assessed is the significance value. The significance value is computed as 0.000, which illuminates that the model is significant as it is below 0.05.

Table 5. Regression Analyses

Coefficients	B	Std. Error	Beta	t	Sig.
(Constant)	0.027	0.011		2.409	0.016
Training and Development	0.101	0.033	0.108	3.058	0.002
Perceived usefulness	0.419	0.053	0.42	7.904	0.000
Knowledge exchange	-0.047	0.019	-0.043	-2.483	0.013
Communication and Coordination	0.518	0.034	0.505	15.055	0.000

The above table reflects the major parts of the regression results where the influence of social media factors is assessed regarding training and development, perceived usefulness, knowledge exchange and communication, and coordination on the job performance. The results illuminate that training and development [r=0.101; p-value=0.002], perceived usefulness [r=0.419; p-value=0.000], knowledge exchange [r=-0.047; p-value=0.013] and communication and coordination [r=0.518; p-value=0.000] are determined to have significant influence on job performance as the p-value is lower than 0.05 threshold. Moreover, the values of beta indicate that training and development, perceived usefulness, and communication and coordination are found to positively influence job performance by 0.101, 0.419, and 0.518 units. In contrast, knowledge exchange has a negative impact on job performance by -0.047 units. Thus, it is clear that the utilization of social media allows Pakistan's management to improve the training and development and communication and coordination among the employees while also being perceived as a highly useful tool.

DISCUSSION

In Pakistan, like many other countries, the situation of COVID-19 is unruly and dangerous, as seen when the Pakistani Government announced a complete lockdown of major commercial and residential areas and ordered a national work-from-home policy (voluntary or involuntary). The problem statement that spurred our research study was whether business SCM' productivity would remain the same if they worked from home. It seems that the use of apps like IMO, WhatsApp, and Skype smooth the transition to working from home and facilitate business SCM' ability to assign new tasks to their team members and schedule remote meetings. In the IT and Telecom sector, digital devices are of much importance. Our study manifests how social media platforms have influenced the performance during the COVID-19 situation and work-from-home policy. Similarly, software engineers manage tasks through project management software and get ready for meetings with clients, preferably, in Skype and IMO. In addition to this, the communication and coordination has been considered pivotal for completion of assigned tasks and to get desired work quality. It has been theorized that work-from-home policy may be considered an effective from point of health issues, but it may also be the fact that telecommuting reduces the coordination and cooperation since there always remains a lack of communication due to geographical constraints.

The lack of communication, coordination and lack of training and development regarding the use of technology and social media for telecommuting are major concerns that remained for the organization. Hence, to empirically study this fact, the following study was carried out by over 294 SCM from different organizations of Pakistan. In the study sample, the majority of participant 72.01% were male, and in terms of age and grade, different SCM were included in the study. The study's survey consists of different participants with different managerial roles and belongs to different age groups; this makes the study unbiased and reliable because it considered the opinion of diversified people working in different industries. Hence, this makes the study to be generalized in the context of Pakistan from which certain implications and recommendations could be formed for the organizations that how could telecommuting be improved if further required amid Coronavirus.

In empirical results, it has been found that there is a positive interrelation of training and development, perceived usefulness, knowledge exchange and communication, and coordination positively correlated with job performance. This implies that during the pandemic, work from home has not affected the employees' job performance. Coordination and communication are free and easier today as users have access to free WhatsApp during the quarantine. Hence, employees have no issue in communication and coordination concerning work. Communication and coordination allow to continue work and ensure the exchange of knowledge between the employees. In addition, previous studies have also suggested that users of social networking during the pandemic have increased, which has affected the firms to manage their employees to ensure productivity. However, employees are also required to ensure job performance (Tanveer & Karim, 2018; Tanveer & Hassan, 2020).

Furthermore, it has been found in regression analysis that training and development, perceived usefulness, and communication and coordination have a positive and significant impact on job performance. However, knowledge exchange has been found to have a negative effect on job performance. It can be interpreted that during the pandemic, the SCM' job performance was not affected due to COVID-19 and work-from-home policy. However, the use of social media platforms has turned to be an effective means of communication between employees, subordinates, and management. Therefore, it has been suggested that the need for time to collaborate takes precedence, no matter the medium or social platform. However, it is crucial that attention should be given to the amount of time the app uses while launching and shutting off. The use of Skype takes a little bit longer time to launch than WhatsApp, which is because WhatsApp is considered to be more effective for communication and coordination. In addition, opportunities offered by Skype are unmatchable by any other app or medium. However, to the same extent, the new feature of WhatsApp to video call and group video call tends to be closer to Skype. Therefore, it is determined that social media platforms during the pandemic have helped SCM maintain their job performance.

CONCLUSION, LIMITATIONS, AND RECOMMENDATIONS

There appears to be a universal sense that everyday life seems like a thing of the past only after a short time of emotional and social distancing in the COVID-19 era. Computer-mediated activities put the outer environment inside, too, as well as supplying remote users with a glimpse of what events are like beyond their personal space. Meanwhile, Google, Skype, WhatsApp, and many other applications' usage has increased dramatically more than double in recent months. The people might joke that it took a pandemic for such mechanisms to ever really take off. For marketers, apps and web platforms have become among the most coveted aspects of homegrown content and remote work-life projects. Today's business SCM consent to function and work remotely because of the constraint of living safely in COVID-19 times while granted assurances that an individual has the right resources to execute tasks related to the position. Hence, the following study was conducted that does emergence of COVID-19 has affected job performance. Today's desktops and laptops link securely from home to the corporate network. The top apps identified for the purpose of communication and coordination include Skype, Imo, WhatsApp, and G-Suite. These tools are accessible on client machines and provide telephone and video conferencing capabilities and other features for business interaction. However, one problem that all workers might face is a lack of expertise in using some remote collaboration tools. It follows that SCM and business SCM must facilitate the training of colleagues to help them out.

This COVID-19 pandemic is over, but most business SCM must be adept at using apps and remote engagement tools. This is the age of digital appliances and electronics, but there can be no guarantees that our globe triggers only one worldwide pandemic. However, many other tools can be utilized in the industry. However, respondents seem interested in sticking to four or five platforms (WhatsApp, Skype, IMO, Facebook, and others). Meanwhile, in regards to, following study was conducted to determine how use of social media by SCM in era of COVID-19 has affected the job performance. The empirical results suggest that even during the pandemic, the coordination, communication, usefulness and training and development has positive influence on the job performance. Since workers are not in any one place, it is also possible to miss interactive moments (small personal exchanges boost morale and stay largely in the ether) that inform meetings, report planning, and core busines operations. It is imperative that organizations must have a highly interactive platforms that does not only ensure coordination among the teams but are also user-interactive as well.

RECOMMENDATIONS

As a recommendation, more measured and narrow attention in terms of app usage will ensure that everybody stays connected and focused solely on important activities. We also urge business practitioners working remotely not to forget to celebrate quality work, particularly when complete. Meanwhile, upon consideration of the peer-to-peer relationship, the top priority will be to ensure everyone's health. It becomes quick and easy to lose interest in each other's safety and welfare when we do not see each other every day. Therefore, it is recommended that SCM arrange personal five-minute video chats to link with remote workers and screen to make sure they can manage the office tasks well and not find any ambiguity or roadblocks to deliver the required results. This recommendation has brought the positive impact of digital media to the forefront, rather than just web browsing or watching videos on YouTube and TikTok.

LIMITATIONS

The importance of social media platforms cannot be denied during the COVID19 era of using social media to get the job done remotely. The scope of the following study has been limited to ho use of social media in the pandemic era has affected the SCM in terms of job performance given the reason for the work-from-home policy. We strongly recommend that researchers identify more apps and comprehensive platforms independently and holistically to explore functionality, dissemination, accessibility, and usage in organizations that could also give employees maximum efficiency even at home. Although this paper fills a gap in the research, our current findings will need to be validated in other studies. We also recommend that researchers look to apply similar methodologies in inter-organizational and cross-national settings. We expect that organizations in different business sectors and various life-stages (e.g., startup versus mature) and different scales of business and partnerships will yield new findings of the use of social media among SCM. It also seems likely that different tiers of users (e.g., front-line workers to top SCM) will also manifest different types of social media apps and usage parameters. Another direction for future research may be gender and opportunity-specific analyses. Our research study has been limited to the use of social media platforms and their effect on job performance.

REFERENCES

Aarti. (2020). *Saudi Orders All Private Sector Employees to Work from Home, Suspends Prayers at Mosques.* Gulf Business. gulfbusiness.com/saudi-orders-all-private-sector-staff-to-work-from-home-suspends-prayers-at-mosques/

Abueish, T. (2020). Coronavirus: Pakistan Issues 'Work from Home' Guideline for Private Sectors. *Al Arabiya.* english.alarabiya.net/en/News/gulf/2020/03/17/Coronavirus-Saudi-Arabia-issues-work-from-home-guideline-for-private-sectors

Adams, C. (2020). Social Media for Brands during Lockdown - How to Adapt to the New Normal. *The Drum.* www.thedrum.com/opinion/2020/04/08/social-media-brands-during-lockdown-how-adapt-the-new-normal

Akif & Chen. (2020). Public Employees' Use of Social Media: It's Impact on Need Satisfaction and Intrinsic Work Motivation. *Government Information Quarterly, 36* (1), 51-60. doi:10.1016/j.giq.2018.11.008

Al-Thaqafi. (2020). Saudi Companies Ask Employees to Work from Home. *Arab News.* www.arabnews.com/node/1639606/saudi-arabia

Algaissi, Alharbi, Hassanain, & Hashem. (2020). Preparedness and response to COVID-19 in Pakistan: Building on MERS experience. *Journal of Infection and Public Health, 13*(6), 834-838. doi:10.1016/j.jiph.2020.04.016

Arif, M., Jan, K., Marwat, Z. A., & Ullah, I. (2009). Performance enhancement through effective communication: A study of the role of external and internal communication. *Interdisciplinary Journal of Contemporary Research in Business, 1*(7), 119–148.

Bodewits, K. (2020). Working from Home Because of COVID-19? Here Are 10 Ways to Spend Your Time. *Science.* www.sciencemag.org/careers/2020/03/working-home-because-covid-19-here-are-10-ways-spend-your-time

Chaturvedi, A. (2020). 21 Day Lockdown: Social Media Platforms, Users Find Novel Ways to Stay Engaged. *The Economic Times.* economictimes.indiatimes.com/tech/internet/21-day-lockdown-social-media-platforms-users-find-novel-ways-to-stay-engaged/articleshow/74915654.cms?from=mdr

Cheng, W., Vyas, R., Gopalakrishnan, R., Clay, E. R., & Singh, M. (2020). Exploring Correlation among Different Elements of Student Evaluation of Teaching. In 2020 IEEE Frontiers in Education Conference (FIE) (pp. 1-7). IEEE. doi:10.1109/FIE44824.2020.9273999

Chu, T. (2020, March). A Meta-Analytic Review of the Relationship Between Social Media Use and Employee Outcomes. *Telematics and Informatics*, *50*, 101379. doi:10.1016/j.tele.2020.101379

El Junusi, R. (2020). Digital Marketing During the Pandemic Period; A Study of Islamic Perspective. *Journal of Digital Marketing and Halal Industry*, *2*(1), 15–28. doi:10.21580/jdmhi.2020.2.1.5717

Femi, A. F. (2014). The impact of communication on workers' performance in selected organisations in Lagos State, Nigeria. *IOSR Journal of the Humanities and Social Sciences*, *19*(8), 75–82.

Gottlieb, M. S. (2020). *Keeping Your Team Productive While They Work from Home*. ITProPortal. www.itproportal.com/features/keeping-your-team-productive-while-they-work-from-home/

Haq, I. U., & Tanveer, M. (2020). Status of Research Productivity and Higher Education in the Members of Organization of Islamic Cooperation (OIC). *Library Philosophy and Practice (ejournal), 3845*. https://digitalcommons.unl.edu/libphilprac/3845

Harris, K. (2020). *Tracking the Global Impact of the Coronavirus Outbreak*. Bain. www.bain.com/insights/tracking-the-global-impact-of-the-coronavirus-outbreak-snap-chart/

Hwang, M.-Y., Hong, J.-C., Tai, K.-H., Chen, J.-T., & Gouldthorp, T. (2020, January 1). The Relationship between the Online Social Anxiety, Perceived Information Overload and Fatigue, and Job Engagement of Civil Servant LINE Users. *Government Information Quarterly*, *37*(1), 101423. doi:10.1016/j.giq.2019.101423

Iki, K., Sato, S., & Tomizawa, S. (2018). Decomposition of Parsimonious Independence Model Using Pearson, Kendall and Spearman's Correlations for Two-Way Contingency Tables. *International Journal of Statistics and Probability*, *7*(3), 105. doi:10.5539/ijsp.v7n3p105

Isaac, O., Abdullah, Z., Ramayah, T., Mutahar, A. M., & Alrajawy, I. (2016). Perceived usefulness, perceived ease of use, perceived compatibility, and net benefits: an empirical study of internet usage among employees in Yemen. In *The 7th International Conference Postgraduate Education (ICPE7)* (pp. 899-919). Academic Press.

Kanski, A. (2020, March). Social Networks Tackle COVID-19 Challenges, Misinformation - Media News. *Medical Marketing & Media, 23*. www.mmm-online.com/home/channel/media-news/social-networks-tackle-covid-19-challenges-misinformation/

Kassim, N.H., Noor, N.M., Kasuma, J., & Saleh, J. (2020). *Impact of perceived usefulness, perceived ease of use and behavioral intention in using WhatsApp towards job performance*. Academic Press.

Khan, N. A., & Khan, A. N. (2019, July). What Followers Are Saying about Transformational SCM Fostering Employee Innovation via Organizational Learning, Knowledge Sharing and Social Media Use in Public Organizations? *Government Information Quarterly*, *36*(4), 101391. Advance online publication. doi:10.1016/j.giq.2019.07.003

Khan, S. A. R., Ponce, P., Tanveer, M., Aguirre-Padilla, N., Mahmood, H., & Shah, S. A. A. (2021). Technological Innovation and Circular Economy Practices: Business Strategies to Mitigate the Effects of COVID-19. *Sustainability, 13*(15), 8479. doi:10.3390/su13158479

Khan, S. A. R., Ponce, P., Thomas, G., Yu, Z., Al-Ahmadi, M. S., & Tanveer, M. (2021). Digital Technologies, Circular Economy Practices and Environmental Policies in the Era of COVID-19. *Sustainability, 13*(22), 12790. doi:10.3390/su132212790

Kniffin, K. M., Narayanan, J., Anseel, F., Antonakis, J., Ashford, S. J., Bakker, A. B., Bamberger, P., Bapuji, H., Bhave, D. P., Choi, V. K., & Creary, S. J. (2020). COVID-19 and the Workplace: Implications, Issues, and Insights for Future Research and Action. Academic Press.

Nabbout, M. (2020). *Employees in GCC May Soon Be Asked to Work Remotely Due to COVID-19*. StepFeed. stepfeed.com/employees-in-gcc-may-soon-be-asked-to-work-remotely-due-to-covid-19-8322.

Nakrošienė, A., Bučiūnienė, I., & Goštautaitė, B. (2019). Working from home: Characteristics and outcomes of telework. *International Journal of Manpower*.

Omar, N., Munir, Z. A., Kaizan, F. Q., Noranee, S., & Malik, S. A. (2019). The Impact of Employees Motivation, Perceived Usefulness and Perceived Ease of Use on Employee Performance among Selected Public Sector Employees. *International Journal of Academic Research in Business & Social Sciences*, *9*(6). Advance online publication. doi:10.6007/IJARBSS/v9-i6/6074

Pakistan Implements Urgent Measures to Mitigate Impact of Coronavirus on Economy. (2020). gulfnews.com/business/saudi-arabia-implements-urgent-measures-to-mitigate-impact-of-coronavirus-on-economy-1.1584723908834

Reshma, P. S., Aithal, P. S., & Acharya, S. (2015). An empirical study on Working from Home: A popular e-business model. *International Journal of Advance & Innovative Research, 2*(2).

Sbeih, M. (2020). *Gulf Employees Look to Governments for COVID-19 Guidance.* APCO Worldwide. apcoworldwide.com/blog/gulf-employees-look-to-governments-for-covid-19-guidance/

Stanger, N. (2017). *View of How Do Saudi Youth Engage with Social Media? | First Monday.* firstmonday.org/article/view/7102/6101

Tanveer, M., Bhaumik, A., Hassan, S., & Ul Haq, I. (2020). COVID-19 pandemic, outbreak educational sector and students online learning in Pakistan. *Journal of Entrepreneurship Education, 23*(3).

Tanveer, M., & Hassan, S. (2020). The role of new and creative ideas in developing industries of education, software and manufacturing in Pakistan. *Journal of Entrepreneurship Education, 23*(3).

Tanveer, M., Hassan, S., & Bhaumik, A. (2020). Covid-19 quarantine and consumer behavior that change the trends of business sustainability & development. *Academy of Strategic Management Journal, 19*(4).

Tanveer, M., & Karim, D. (2018). Higher Education Institutions and the Performance Management. *Library Philosophy and Practice (e-journal), 2183.* https://digitalcommons.unl.edu/libphilprac/2183

Tanveer, M., Kaur, H., Thomas, G., Mahmood, H., Paruthi, M., & Yu, Z. (2021). Mobile Phone Buying Decisions among Young Adults: An Empirical Study of Influencing Factors. *Sustainability, 13*(19), 10705. doi:10.3390/su131910705

Trotman, A. (2020). *Social Media's Crucial Role in COVID-19 Lockdown.* www.businesscloud.co.uk/opinion/social-medias-crucial-role-in-covid-19-lockdown

University, S. (2020). *The Productivity Pitfalls of Working from Home in the Age of COVID-19.* Stanford News. news.stanford.edu/2020/03/30/productivity-pitfalls-working-home-age-covid-19/

Verbeemen, E. (2020). *Why Remote Working Will Be the New Normal, Even after COVID-19.*http:/// www.ey.com/en_be/covid-19/why-remote-working-will-be-the-new-normal-even-after-covid-19

Walker, S. (2020). The Disinformation Landscape and the Lockdown of Social Platforms. *Information, Communication & Society, 22*(11), 1531–1543. doi:10.1080/1369118X.2019.1648536

Chapter 11
Big Data Analytics:
Applications and Barriers in Supply Chain

Arsalan Zahid Piprani
Federal Urdu University of Arts, Science, and Technology, Pakistan

Amjad Ali
https://orcid.org/0000-0003-1686-0016
Hamdard University, Pakistan

Adeel Shah
https://orcid.org/0000-0001-8477-5310
University of Kuala Lumpur, Malaysia

ABSTRACT

As the magnitude of accessible data grows, a multitude of business intelligence (BI) tools have emerged, all of which may be together referred to as big data analytics (BDA). BDA in supply chain management-related activities is essential because it can manage global, complex, tempestuous, and dynamic value chains. The powerful influence of big data (BD) capabilities on supply chain (SC) and overall company performance is attracting operations management researchers, who see them as having a significant impact on supply chain and company performance. This chapter discussed the importance of big data analytics and connected it with its significance in the supply chain context. The authors demonstrated how big data analytics (BDA) is a critical success element for an organization in the global and dynamic market. This chapter also highlights some of the barriers and challenges in implementing big data analytics in the supply chain.

DOI: 10.4018/978-1-7998-7642-7.ch011

1. INTRODUCTION

In the twenty-first century, data flowed at a breakneck speed. The rapid proliferation of data over the last two decades has led to the birth of Big Data (Addo-tenkorang and Helo, 2016). The flood of digital technology further substantiates the rise of big data. As technology becomes accessible, citizens worldwide become increasingly accustomed to the sensors, communication tools, actuators, and data processors that come with it (Raj et al., 2019; Tiwari et al., 2018). Furthermore, according to a 2011 study by the International Data Corporation, the globe has already created one zettabyte of data. Rising numbers have been accelerating; the total amount of data had increased to 7ZB in 2014 (Shayaa et al., 2018) and reached more than 50 ZB of data in 2020. Textual data accounts for at least half of that, as produced by social media platforms like Facebook, Twitter, and mobile instant messaging applications like WhatsApp and Telegram. Big data growth estimates as per the recent Statista platform project that in 2025, data will reach the colossal figure of 180 zettabytes, which is 1.3 trillion terabyte growth over 2020. This surge in data volume is attributable to the growing demand for remote learning, working, and entertainment due to the rise in popularity of telecommuting, working remotely and taking leisure time online during the COVID-19 lockdown times (Novikov, 2020). In addition to this, millions of network sensors are embedded in smartphones, smart energy meters, cars, and industrial equipment in the physical environment. Advancements in digital sensors and communication technologies have fuelled the Internet of Things (IoT) (Saleem et al., 2019). According to IDC, 127 new devices are constantly joining the internet every second throughout the world. Over the next fifteen years, the developed connected devices will have generated about five quintillion bytes of data per day, equal over 79.4 Zettabytes of data. The primary functions of IoT devices depend on the intended use of the devices and the kinds of data the devices are designed to gather. Companies use the Internet of Things (IoT) to regulate their operations better and increase their market reach by adding sensors and security systems.

As businesses increasingly demand better decision-making processes to succeed, data becomes essential to help drive such improvements. While all companies can take advantage of information system infrastructure expenditures, not all can transform those investments into better results (Chavez et al., 2017). The ability to leverage big data is regarded as one of its advantages since it may be unique and challenging to reproduce in the near to intermediate-term. Once industries have used big data to expand their market shares, some experts believe that exploiting and harnessing big data is the forthcoming "blue ocean" in terms of overall business performance (Ali et al., 2020). The literature has reported that digital transformation and technological breakthroughs continue to be the leading drivers of rising Big Data investment.

Businesses must continuously innovate to be relevant in the marketplace, especially with so much competition in every field (Shafiq et al., 2019). Industry specialists require the proper amount of data to make informed judgments, and Big Data analytics give just that. These judgments can help a company advance by properly recognizing a market trend that could increase revenue. Global expenditure on Big Data was already over $180 billion at the end of 2019, and it is expected to rise at a growth rate of 13.2 percent between 2020 and 2022 (Business Wire). According to reports, IT expenditures, hardware purchases, and business services might be the areas where the most money is spent on Big Data analytics.

2. BIG DATA COMPATABILITY

Every aspect of the global economy is infused with large volumes of data (Manyika et al., 2011). Companies utilize data to their advantage in various settings, from retail outlets to commercial airplanes. The term "five V's of data" is often used to characterize the many facets of the subject of big data (Wamba et al., 2015). Big data is described as high-volume (big scale), high-velocity (moving/ streaming), and high-variety (e.g., numerical, text, and video). Besides, big data also entails information assets that necessitate cost-effective, creative information processing for improved insight and decision making (Chae et al., 2013; Wright et al., 2019). However, with the evolution of the big data concept, two additional V's has been added to this definition of big data. One of the V's is called "value," which addresses the requirement to produce economic value. The other is 'Veracity,' which refers to the quality of information rather than the amount (Wamba et al., 2015). The usage of big data is a developing phenomenon that reflects the growing importance of data in terms of volume, variety, velocity, value, and veracity (the "5Vs"). The methodologies, algorithms, applications, and systems used to uncover, extract, store, examine, and report meaningful information helps the firm to make an optimized and calculated decision. Big data analytics has lately ascended to great attention because of the increased capacity to gather vast volumes of data and apply more sophisticated analytical tools to enormous data sets. The ability to collect large (and varied) data as well as use sophisticated analytical approaches to such data allows them to manage immensely complicated choices that were formerly reliant (primarily or exclusively) on human cognition and hunches (Chen et al., 2015).

Predictive data analytics, natural language processing, data mining, and machine learning algorithms are tools used in various scenarios, all to extract critical insights and produce meaningful conclusions (Ertemel, 2015; Rao et al., 2019). However, there is ambiguity in the definition of data analytics throughout the literature. Data analytics, big data analytics, supply chain, and predictive analytics are often used in tandem. The concept covers organizational capabilities, including data collection, storage, and processing, allowing organizations to get valuable insights that enhance their competitive position.

3. SUPPLY CHAIN ANALYTICS

In recent years, supply chains have become increasingly complicated, multi-tiered, and globally dispersed (Piprani et al., 2020). Nonetheless, the need to cut costs without jeopardizing other competitive considerations like providing excellent customer service and high-quality products and services is growing (Wilhelm et al., 2016). Additionally, ICT advancements, such as Web 2.0 and the internet of things (IoT), have vastly expanded the volume of global data (Wang et al., 2016). As a result, businesses have been looking for new and improved technology and innovative solutions to help them overcome the challenges. Data-driven information technologies that allow for collecting and analyzing large amounts of data using advanced techniques like data mining, artificial intelligence, and machine learning provide an analytical approach that can yield new intuitions for improving supply chain efficiency (Gunasekaran et al., 2017). This can lead to an analytical capacity for the company when it is implemented correctly and paired with adequately educated personnel. Supply chain analytics is a technology-based capability that creates new possibilities and opportunities by extracting critical value from massive amounts of supply chain data (Ramanathan et al., 2017). Supply chain analytics, in particular, may help a company make better and more effective decisions and increase supply chain efficiency, resulting in more excellent financial performance (Wamba et al., 2020). Supply chain performance has even been said to be revolutionized by big data. When it comes to supply chains, businesses are using big data to learn about their products, suppliers, and consumers, as well as market prospects. The objective is to build supply networks driven by data. The supply chain that is gone through data is better able to organize, analyze, and analyze data all along the supply chain, enabling them to optimize supply chain design and gain superior competitive advantage (Chavez et al., 2017).

As a result, many companies invest or plan to invest in data processing information technologies and analytics capabilities. It has been reported that international purchases of technology and analytics-related solutions by the banking and manufacturing sectors exceeded $150 billion in 2017, representing a 12.5% increase from the last year (Shirer and Goepfert, 2018). In the supply chain context, many opportunities are open to companies interested in developing BDA tools and using BDA procedures in supply chains due to the emerging tools and methods. Manufacturing supply chains, controlling and reducing risks, refining operational procedures, bringing new goods to the market, performing market assessments for specific products — all of these BDA-assisted processes may improve and contribute to a business's overall success (Moktadir et al., 2018)

4. TYPES OF BIG DATA ANALYTICS CAPABILITY

4.1 Descriptive analytics

Descriptive analytics allows information to be incorporated into helpful reporting formats and used to answer questions like "what happened?" (Mortenson et al., 2015). The descriptive analytics community focuses on finding what has happened in the past. Historical data is beneficial when it comes to identifying patterns. This data may have been collected through supply chain planning tools and other sources that offer information to companies, distributors, and consumers. With data analytics, patterns may be detected and possible causes for change speculatively proposed. Experts may then use this knowledge and data in these visualizations and reports to understand and predict changes and develop connections to improve business results (Tiwari et al., 2018). The descriptive analysis uses conventional analysis, which keeps the level of complexity manageable. The interpretation, reporting, and data management process takes time and needs competent leaders to understand the facts thoroughly before making an informed choice.

4.2 Predictive analytics

While descriptive analytics just examines current facts, predictive analytics further develops this kind of analysis and uses data mining to detect connections and correlations that had not before been seen. Predictive analytics has been offered in the supply chain, often referred to as supply chain predictive analytics. Supply chain predictive analytics uses diverse techniques to aid supply chain design and sustainability. The primary tool it uses is the combination of pre-and future coordination of business applications and associated costs and quality of service (Jeble et al., 2018). A previous analysis of historical data patterns is used to determining the variations that may happen in the future, and a prediction is made from these past trends. With this method, the causes for unknown actions and occurrences are determined with precise forecasts of the future to discover the data gaps. Even mathematical methods like regression are unable to anticipate future events correctly. In predictive analytics, businesses may identify and forecast future trends of commercial transactions, including the behaviors of customers and buyers, and devise a plan to deal with these trends (Hofmann and Rutschmann, 2018). We can anticipate customer demand, track down missing supplies, and keep track of daily company operations using these techniques. Some research studies have utilized predictive analysis to anticipate demand and inventory levels, evaluate suppliers and predict risks in supply chain management (Soleimani et al., 2014). However, a more comprehensive set of abilities is required for predictive analysis than descriptive analysis (Sanders, 2016). Approaches like predictive modeling, such as linear regression, may start with and allow for further experimentation. Although being better equipped to reduce statistical biases, Rigorous analytics have shown to be more accurate; nevertheless, greater care must be taken to avoid such prejudices (Wang et al., 2016).

4.3 Prescriptive analytics

Descriptive and predictive analysis, together with optimization models, are a part of prescriptive analysis methods. It concentrates on the process of describing and predicting, and proposing solutions utilizing optimization models (Lepenioti et al., 2020; Souza, 2014). It has been evident from the literature that prescriptive supply chain solutions are most frequently implemented at the operational and strategic levels (Hahn and Packowski, 2015). Although undoubtedly applicable to all aspects of a business, Prescriptive analytics promises optimizing distribution network operation. Companies have used predictive analytics to pursue operation manufacturing, supply chain management, and other business functions. Pre-emptive forecasting techniques have helped to reliably and pre-emptively forecast future amounts to avoid excess prediction error at the beginning of the supply chain (Hassani and Silva, 2015).

Moreover, in contemporary times, optimization techniques are more effective in ensuring complex supply chains can deliver products at a higher level of specification (Osaba et al., 2018). For instance, machine learning and operational research to improve inventory choices led to greater productivity (Priore et al., 2019). Also, using optimization tools, the transportation companies tracked the length of time and cost for last-mile delivery to calculate the optimal path.

5. APPLICATION OF BIG DATA IN OPERATIONS MANAGEMENT

Big data applications in operations and supply chain management have already demonstrated their promise in the literature (e.g., Akter et al., 2016; Dubey et al., 2019). It assumes that the availability of timely and actionable data from the supply chain will enable businesses to detect and address defects and rework, which, in turn, would contribute to lower product development time, improved customer responsiveness, and improved efficiency. The preceding and succeeding justification illustrate the necessity of a data-driven supply chain for manufacturing-related operational capability improvements.

5.1 Big Data and Strategic Sourcing

Technologists and specialists working in a supply chain setting face constant data streams used to reorganize and analyze supply chain operations and better support supply chain performance (Hazen et al., 2018). The sheer quantity of data created by manufacturing may be found via various channels, including sensing systems and industrial processes. Analytical activities like processing and mapping large volumes of data for performance analysis, or continuous monitoring of methods and devices, may be facilitated by big data. Because the market is primed for growth, an organization must have the readiness and anticipatory capability for future advances. Manufacturers must use big data and analytic methods to increase their manufacturing and operational capabilities. For instance, the firm can use this in the sourcing stage (Lamba and Singh, 2017). Even with such a wide range of selection and evaluation tools, the process of finding a qualified and appropriate supplier for the supply chain is challenging.

Furthermore, having access to data from multiple functional areas of an organization and diverse supply chain partners is crucial to finding improvements in supply chain effectiveness and efficiency (Sanders, 2016). The information must be shared across all supply chain partners to use the data to its most significant possible benefit. Both inside and outside the organization, and used to build a process perspective that brings all of the organization's supply chain partners together in a single unified process view. Within the firm, dissemination of the information across the organization would allow the functions in the internal chain to visualize discrepancies in the supply chain and track the tactical and operational performance swiftly (Chavez et al., 2017). Information may be provided outside the company along the supply chain to link partners and provide end-to-end access to supply chain data.

For instance, manufacturers in the supply chain can utilize their data combined with customers and suppliers. The data relating to raw material, delivery, promotion, and inventory enhances accuracy in demand forecasting and supply planning. This data-driven approach in the supply chain enables a company to form strategic alliances with supply chain partners and collaborate more effectively. Furthermore, it also facilitates firms in the supply chain to exploit unique and precise methods in attaining superior business and operational performance (Talwar et al., 2021). Besides, it includes joint product development initiatives based on market insight, collaborative planning, forecasting replenishment, and applying the lean methodology to achieve operational excellence (Waller and Fawcett, 2013).

5.2 Big Data Analytics and Sustainable Supply Chain

Business professionals widely accept socially and environmentally sustainable company practices (Shrivastava and Guimarães-Costa, 2017). Despite many attempts by non-governmental organizations (NGOs) to react to outside forces such as governmental policy, consumer demand, and internal pressures such as a leader's expectations, the underlying facts are still up for dispute. Supply networks are becoming more concerned about sustainability. As a result, successfully addressing the mounting social and environmental needs is a huge issue for companies. Supply chain decision-making is complex when many entities or environmental problems are at play, especially when choices are made throughout the supply chain or are reliant on ecological systems. In figuring out the environmental effect of their supply chains, companies may not have all the relevant information. As a result, most organizations are forced to use resources sparingly because of a lack of data and knowledge about the environmental challenges they confront, how ecological concerns interact, and the implications of these relationships. Scholars have argued that strengthening openness and collaboration among supply chain partners may help them join efforts to accomplish shared sustainability objectives (Bag et al., 2020).

It is believed that the massive amount of data generated by big data will have significant implications for environmental studies. For instance, Pirelli, the fifth-biggest tire manufacturing organization globally with the assistance of SAP, a German software firm, used big real-time data to address inventory problems. Real-time big data provide Pirelli with the ability to manage its inventory, ensuring tires don't end up in landfills or contributing to greenhouse emissions in the environment (Dubey et al., 2019). The literature also reported the application of big data analytics in green product development. Bag et al. (2020) that green product development operations may be planned and executed effectively using Big Data Analytics management capabilities. BDA provides many avenues for green goods to be developed and marketed to customers across the world. Green product performance in the field may be predicted using predictive analytics. Accurate forecasting will aid in establishing the appropriate marketing and operational strategies, which will also enable companies to manage their supply chain expenses better. BDA technologies would allow organizations to use a proactive approach and capitalize on opportunities before their rivals. The studies mentioned above confirmed that data analytics might help support the company's aim of advancing social and environmental sustainability.

5.3 Big Data Analytics and Supply Chain Resilience

In 2011, Japan had a catastrophe of unprecedented proportions, resulting in several international companies, such as Honda and Sony, halting production due to a shortage of critical resources (Pettit et al., 2013; Revilla et al., 2017). It has been evident from the literature that business process improvements and the implementation of supply chain resilience with the use of big data would assist in minimizing the risks of interruptions in the supply chain and therefore increase overall performance (Gunasekaran et al., 2017). It is important to note that building data analytics capabilities also necessitates supply chain visibility. According to Srinivasan and Swink (2018), organizations that can create and implement data analytics systems are better situated to cultivate and increase demand and supply chain visibility. Mubarik et al. (2021) claim that in Industry 4.0 era, supply chain visibility is a desirable skill, and supply chain disruptions may be mitigated as a result. Because visibility is essential to supporting analytics, we contend that those organizations that spend in building analytics capacity will also invest in visibility. Similar contentions were made by Srinivasan and Swink (2018) that visibility and analytical skills are both valuable and complimentary. The extant literature offers a significant amount of empirical evidence showing that increased supply network visibility capacity is likely to decrease both the likelihood and the effect of supply chain interruption. The visibility in the supply chain improves supply chain resilience as well: a supply chain risk procedure requires full awareness of all supply chain vulnerabilities. Because of this, managers will need data technology that helps them detect potential risks or causes of interruption to assist them in creating business continuity strategies. Hence, firms that consider all of these factors may end up being more resilient, competitive, and responsive.

6. BARRIERS IN IMPLEMENTING BIG DATA ANALYTICS

While it is feasible to do analyses on large amounts of data, many impediments hinder the big data project initiatives in the organization. The idea of BDA is fresh and has the potential to propel the digital business into the future. There is still a high proportion of grey literature (i.e., unpublished or obscure sources) in current research. More recently, however, contributions in academic journals have begun to emerge. Nevertheless, the body of scholarly research examining the problems, obstacles, and barriers connected with BDA and BDA's implementation seems to be lacking. The following discussion covers barriers to implementing BDA in manufacturing organizations.

6.1 Organizational barriers

In terms of organizational barriers, culture, especially organizational culture, greatly influences an organization's strategy, structure, and procedures. Design and structure are developed depending on how top management views and understands corporate values and norms. Consequently, many big data challenges may stem from company culture rather than data or technology because of these factors. An organization may be aware of the strategic potential of big data as it doesn't fully comprehend how big data might enhance its operations, and as a result, sees little value in adopting big data projects (Kache and Seuring, 2017). The literature has dramatically emphasized building a data-driven culture, identified as a significant difficulty when implementing big data strategy. A data-driven culture is one in which people make decisions using data insights (Maroufkhani et al., 2020). The absence of data-driven culture is one of the main reasons, so many big data initiatives fail. Many executives depend on intuition or previous experiences in place of facts-based and data-driven decisions. Managers' conduct may influence how everyone else in the company approaches decisions.

Furthermore, Industry 4.0 will need an abundance of data across companies and industries. For the bulk of the businesses, limitations on resources threaten their success: this occurs because top managers of companies are often reluctant to embrace technology solutions. Furthermore, implementing any technical solutions is a strategic choice. It is hard to build a digital strategy to successfully deploy such technologies if senior management is reluctant to approve them (Cubric, 2020).

However, the deployment of any technological solution demands an effective change management strategy. It has been witnessed that technology has affected change over the past decade in many significant ways. The change process was often seen as transactional and straightforward, but now, it is seen as complicated, multifaceted, open-ended, and long-term (Raj et al., 2019). In other words, it has transformed into a revolutionary concept, making it more challenging to implement effectively. Entrepreneurs, technologists, and organizational experts anticipate that open-ended systems will be more complicated than ever, and effective change management will be critical for companies to deploy any technological solutions in the organization successfully.

6.2 Data related barriers

Data-driven choices are already becoming the norm for companies, but processing data is still problematic for the most vulnerable regions. Without access to information, these sectors are losing out on making clear choices for their company (Seddon et al., 2017). Industries have many data-related challenges that interfere with their ability to make data-related choices. Difficulty in handling data arises because of the intricacy of the data. In addition to this, data privacy and security have captured industrialist's and manufacturer's attention since it is an essential issue for their businesses, and trade plans might be jeopardized if private data was compromised (Alharthi et al., 2017).

Furthermore, the emergence of colossal IoT networks has necessitated increased security and privacy concerns. Data security concerns, like those at the enterprise level, need special attention from an SC perspective, as businesses frequently rely on data from external firms. As a result, data and information security are the significant SC problem (Mohammadzadeh et al., 2018). Data security threats might make it difficult for participating organizations to implement BDA. They are hesitant to share data with chain entities because they are anxious about losing control of sensitive information. Failure to successfully satisfy these concerns puts everything on the line, which, when that happens, may potentially result in extensive damages, work stoppage, or even loss of life. At the same time, to maintain the security of the gathered data, the confidentiality of the service and the whole IoT system must be ensured. A significant challenge is the variety of IoT devices and the environment in which they operate.

6.3 Technology related barriers

A significant part of successfully implementing big data analytics involves appropriate technological infrastructure (Yasmin et al., 2020). However, a considerable investment in software and technology is required to analyze hundreds of millions of records in real-time, which is needed for big data analytics (Shafiq et al., 2019; Yu et al., 2017). It seems that most of the current solutions were not specifically developed to satisfy the data analytics needs that are rising. Integrated systems, including a wide range of computer hardware via the internet, including cloud-based solutions, are predicted to be useful for large data sets. When much data is handled, technologies often fail for technical and economic reasons (Alharthi et al., 2017). For example, it would take 750 days to process one petabyte of data if all 1,000 processing nodes were linked through a cloud (one petabyte equals one million gigabytes). If this system were built, it would cost more than $6 (Alharthi et al., 2017). Even yet, businesses may not benefit from heterogeneous and cloud computing when managing significant data processing bottlenecks because of big data. For that matter, firms located in developing countries tend to contract out third-party infrastructure and collaborate on IT services as they build their businesses. Many companies begin by implementing these technologies inside their existing IT infrastructure, and then they add more as the need and funding dictate (Raj et al., 2019; Tabesh et al., 2019).

Additionally, as 4.0 evolves, every channel member will be integrated. Digital infrastructure, therefore, is an essential element in the development of industry 4.0. As technological developments become more critical in the current age, businesses today are increasingly cooperating in infrastructure development instead of fighting for it.

6.4 Economic related barriers

In manufacturing, the use of BDA is made possible through capital investments. It has been stated that most businesses suffer financial issues when it comes to capital due to their restricted resources (Gawankar et al., 2020). Between 20% and 50% of their profits are devoted to investment (Mohanty et al., 2013). Although so far, the connection between corporate investment in BDA and effectiveness in implementing BDA has not been fully shown, it is believed that investments act as a source of fuel for deploying big data analytics in the organization (Mikalef et al., 2019). Research suggests that businesses intending to adopt big data analytics successfully would have to increase their capital expenditures by 50% in the next five years. Firms need to re-engineer their current strategy and spend substantially to accomplish those objectives. In addition, Kache and Seuring (2017) argue that considerable investment is required both at the corporate and supply chain levels to execute the strategy above. However, Breunig et al. (2016) viewed that most companies are reticent to make investments in technology, as this requires massive investment.

6.5 Workforce related barriers

To get the full benefits of BDA, a firm must first grasp the knowledge and comprehension of the concepts involved. Also, workers' expertise and competence in using the tools come into play in making the adoption successful (Tabesh et al., 2019). As for workers, it has been shown that although most of the workers are functional and successful in their regular job, they have trouble incorporating change when it comes to new technology. Employees' critical analytical skills are fundamental to determining how any manufacturing company implements BDA (Alharthi et al., 2017). In addition, companies cannot possibly reap the full benefits from using data analytics technologies unless they have appropriately qualified and highly skilled personnel to oversee data analytics technologies (Long et al., 2016). Adopting big data analytics in businesses doesn't often stem from a lack of knowledge but rather how employees perform. In some cases, workers will not alter how they operate to take advantage of big data analytics. Workers find new technology and procedures frustrating, especially if they see them disruptive to their current workflow.

7. CONCLUSION

The growing level of consumer preferences, the increasing prevalence of technological innovations, and the implementation of the digital transformation continually escalate the degree of dynamism and complexity in the supply chain. Effective decision-making in uncertain circumstances is needed to manage these dynamics. Big data analytics is a relevant issue in a variety of disciplines, including SCM. Applying appropriate analytic methods in this area provides many possibilities for growth; thus, growing information demands, many SCM applications (BDA included) offer great potential. This chapter provides a broad introduction to the fundamental ideas and modern big data analytics methods within the supply chain. There are various BDA uses at different supply chain stages and many consequences across the supply chain. BDA technology applications have contributed to many supply chain improvements. Firms increasingly use BDA tools in developed nations to increase company performance, cut manufacturing time, and avoid incurring risks.

Moreover, BDA may be effective in helping to build and enhance a reactive and reliable SC. SC's colossal complexity requires an excellent information management strategy and a system like BDA. To carry out this goal, however, companies must build skills to use BDA effectively. BDA implementation is a necessity if a company wants to get supply chain performance using technology. However, the implementation of BDA in manufacturing supply chains presents difficulties for manufacturers. One of the significant challenges for the supply chain in the modern age is having adequate analytic skills. To realize this, a multidisciplinary approach that integrates SC entities is required, along with the ability to share and retrieve essential data across the SC. The five V's of big data enable supply chain managers to make better decisions as real-time data is available for decision-making. The tools now available due to the technology are allowing companies to increase their operational and financial performance. Due to operating efficiencies, the overall cost of business operations has been reduced. Big data as a technology satisfies customer satisfaction and enhances its overall experience as companies now know their customers better.

REFERENCES

Addo-tenkorang, R., & Helo, P. T. (2016). Big data applications in operations / supply-chain management : A literature review. *Computers & Industrial Engineering, Elsevier Ltd*, *101*, 528–543. doi:10.1016/j.cie.2016.09.023

Akter, S., Wamba, S. F., Gunasekaran, A., Dubey, R., & Childe, S. J. (2016). How to improve firm performance using big data analytics capability and business strategy alignment? *International Journal of Production Economics, Elsevier, 182*, 113–131. doi:10.1016/j.ijpe.2016.08.018

Alharthi, A., Krotov, V., & Bowman, M. (2017). "Addressing barriers to big data", *Business Horizons*, "Kelley School of Business. *Indiana University, 60*(3), 285–292.

Ali, S., Poulova, P., Yasmin, F., Danish, M., Akhtar, W., & Usama Javed, H. M. (2020). How Big Data Analytics Boosts Organizational Performance: The Mediating Role of the Sustainable Product Development. *Journal of Open Innovation, 6*(4), 190. doi:10.3390/joitmc6040190

Bag, S., Wood, L.C., Xu, L., Dhamija, P., & Kayikci, Y. (2020). Big data analytics as an operational excellence approach to enhance sustainable supply chain performance. *Resources, Conservation and Recycling, 153*, 104559.

Breunig, M., Kelly, R., Mathis, R., & Wee, D. (2016). *Getting the Most out of Industry 4.0.* McKinsey Global Institute. Available at: https://scholar.google.com/scholar?hl=en&as_sdt=0%2C5&q=Breunig%2C+M.%2C+Kelly%2C+R.%2C+Mathis%2C+R.%2C+%26+Wee%2C+D.+%282016%29.+Getting+the+most+out+of+Industry+4.0&btnG=

Chae, B. K., Olson, D., & Sheu, C. (2013). Understanding big data analytics capabilities in supply chain management: Unravelling the issues, challenges and implications for. *International Journal of Production Research, 52*(16), 4695–4710. doi:10.1080/00207543.2013.861616

Chavez, R., Yu, W., Jacobs, M. A., & Feng, M. (2017). Data-driven supply chains, manufacturing capability and customer satisfaction. *Production Planning and Control, Taylor & Francis, 28*(11–12), 906–918. doi:10.1080/09537287.2017.1336788

Chen, D. Q., Preston, D. S., & Swink, M. (2015). How the use of big data analytics affects value creation in supply chain management. *Journal of Management Information Systems, Routledge, 32*(4), 4–39. doi:10.1080/07421222.2015.1138364

Cubric, M. (2020). Drivers, barriers and social considerations for AI adoption in business and management: A tertiary study. Technology in Society, 62, 101257.

Dubey, R., Gunasekaran, A., Childe, S. J., Papadopoulos, T., Luo, Z., Wamba, S. F., & Roubaud, D. (2019). Can big data and predictive analytics improve social and environmental sustainability? *Technological Forecasting and Social Change, Elsevier, 144*(April), 534–545. doi:10.1016/j.techfore.2017.06.020

Ertemel, A. (2015). Consumer insight as competitive advantage using big data and analytics. *International Journal of Commerce and Finance*, *1*(1), 45–51.

Gawankar, S. A., Gunasekaran, A., & Kamble, S. (2020). A study on investments in the big data-driven supply chain, performance measures and organisational performance in Indian retail 4.0 context. *International Journal of Production Research, Taylor & Francis*, *58*(5), 1574–1593. doi:10.1080/00207543.2019.1668070

Gunasekaran, A., Papadopoulos, T., Dubey, R., Wamba, S. F., Childe, S. J., Hazen, B., & Akter, S. (2017). Big data and predictive analytics for supply chain and organizational performance. *Journal of Business Research, Elsevier Inc.*, *70*, 308–317. doi:10.1016/j.jbusres.2016.08.004

Hahn, G., & Packowski, J. (2015). A perspective on applications of in-memory analytics in supply chain management. *Decision Support Systems*, *76*, 45–52. doi:10.1016/j.dss.2015.01.003

Hassani, H., & Silva, E. S. (2015). Forecasting with Big Data: A Review. *Annals of Data Science*, *2*(1), 5–19.

Hazen, B. T., Skipper, J. B., Boone, C. A., & Hill, R. R. (2018). Back in business: Operations research in support of big data analytics for operations and supply chain management. *Annals of Operations Research, Springer*, *270*(1–2), 201–211. doi:10.100710479-016-2226-0

Hofmann, E., & Rutschmann, E. (2018). Big data analytics and demand forecasting in supply chains: A conceptual analysis. *International Journal of Logistics Management*, *29*(2), 739–766.

Jeble, S., Dubey, R., Childe, S. J., Papadopoulos, T., Roubaud, D., & Prakash, A. (2018). Impact of big data and predictive analytics capability on supply chain sustainability. *International Journal of Logistics Management*, *29*(2), 513–538.

Kache, F., & Seuring, S. (2017). Challenges and opportunities of digital information at the intersection of Big Data Analytics and supply chain management. *International Journal of Operations & Production Management*, *37*(1), 10–36. doi:10.1108/IJOPM-02-2015-0078

Lamba, K., & Singh, S. P. (2017). Big data in operations and supply chain management: Current trends and future perspectives. *Production Planning & Control, Taylor and Francis Ltd.*, *28*(11–12), 877–890. doi:10.1080/09537287.2017.1336787

Lepenioti, K., Bousdekis, A., Apostolou, D., & Mentzas, G. (2020). Prescriptive analytics: Literature review and research challenges. *International Journal of Information Management, 50*, 57–70. doi:10.1016/j.ijinfomgt.2019.04.003

Long, T. B., Blok, V., & Coninx, I. (2016). Barriers to the adoption and diffusion of technological innovations for climate-smart agriculture in Europe: Evidence from the Netherlands, France, Switzerland and Italy. *Journal of Cleaner Production, Elsevier Ltd, 112*, 9–21. doi:10.1016/j.jclepro.2015.06.044

Manyika, J., Chui, M., Brown, B., Bughin, J., Dobbs, R., Roxburgh, C., & Byers, A.H. (2011). *Big data: The next frontier for innovation, competition, and productivity.* Academic Press.

Maroufkhani, P., Tseng, M. L., Iranmanesh, M., Ismail, W. K. W., & Khalid, H. (2020). Big data analytics adoption: Determinants and performances among small to medium-sized enterprises. *International Journal of Information Management, Elsevier, 54*(February), 102190. doi:10.1016/j.ijinfomgt.2020.102190

Mikalef, P., Boura, M., Lekakos, G., & Krogstie, J. (2019). Big data analytics and firm performance: Findings from a mixed-method approach. *Journal of Business Research, 98*, 261–276. doi:10.1016/j.jbusres.2019.01.044

Mohammadzadeh, A. K., Ghafoori, S., Mohammadian, A., Mohammadkazemi, R., Mahbanooei, B., & Ghasemi, R. (2018). A Fuzzy Analytic Network Process (FANP) approach for prioritizing internet of things challenges in Iran. *Technology in Society, Elsevier Ltd, 53*, 124–134. doi:10.1016/j.techsoc.2018.01.007

Moktadir, A., Mithun, S., Kumar, S., & Shukla, N. (2018). Barriers to big data analytics in manufacturing supply chains : A case study from Bangladesh. *Computers & Industrial Engineering*, 1–13.

Mortenson, M., Doherty, N. F., & Robinson, S. (2015). Operational Research from Taylorism to Terabytes: A Research Agenda for the Analytics Age. *European Journal of Operational Research, 241*(3), 583–595. doi:10.1016/j.ejor.2014.08.029

Mubarik, M., Naghavi, N., Mubarik, M., Kusi-Sarpong, S., Khan, S. A., Zaman, S. I., & Kazmi, S. H. A. (2021). Resilience and cleaner production in industry 4.0: Role of supply chain mapping and visibility. *Journal of Cleaner Production, 292*, 126058. doi:10.1016/j.jclepro.2021.126058

Novikov, P. (2020). Impact of COVID-19 emergency transition to online learning onto the international students' perceptions of educational process at Russian university. *Journal of Social Studies Education Research, 11*(3), 270–302.

Osaba, E., Yang, X. Jr, Fister, I. Jr, Del Ser, J., Lopez-Garcia, P., & Vazquez-Pardavila, A. J. (2018). A discrete and improved bat algorithm for solving a medical goods distribution problem with pharmacological waste collection. *Swarm and Evolutionary Computation*, *44*, 273–286. doi:10.1016/j.swevo.2018.04.001

Pettit, T. J., Croxton, K. L., & Fiksel, J. (2013). Ensuring supply chain resilience: Development and implementation of an assessment tool. *Journal of Business Logistics*, *34*(1), 46–76. doi:10.1111/jbl.12009

Piprani, A. Z., Mohezar, S., & Jaafar, N. I. (2020). Supply chain integration and supply chain performance: The mediating role of supply chain resilience. *International Journal of Supply Chain Management*, *9*(3), 58–73.

Priore, P., Ponte, B., Rosillo, R., & de la Fuente, D. (2019). Applying machine learning to the dynamic selection of replenishment policies in fast-changing supply chain environments. *International Journal of Production Research, Taylor and Francis Ltd.*, *57*(11), 3663–3677. doi:10.1080/00207543.2018.1552369

Raj, A., Dwivedi, G., Sharma, A., Beatriz, A., & De Sousa, L. (2019). Barriers to the adoption of industry 4. 0 technologies in the manufacturing sector : An inter-country comparative perspective. *International Journal of Production Economics*, *224*, 107546. doi:10.1016/j.ijpe.2019.107546

Ramanathan, R., Philpott, E., Duan, Y., & Cao, G. (2017). Adoption of business analytics and impact on performance: A qualitative study in retail. *Production Planning and Control, Taylor and Francis Ltd.*, *28*(11–12), 985–998. doi:10.1080/09537287.2017.1336800

Rao, T. R., Mitra, P., Bhatt, R., & Goswami, A. (2019). The big data system, components, tools, and technologies: A survey. *Knowledge and Information Systems*, *60*(3), 1165–1245.

Revilla, E., Saenz, M. J., Revilla, E., & Saenz, M. J. (2017). The impact of risk management on the frequency of supply chain disruptions A configurational approach. *International Journal of Operations & Production Management*, *37*(5), 557–576. doi:10.1108/IJOPM-03-2016-0129

Saleem, Y., Crespi, N., Rehmani, M., & Copeland, R. (2019). Internet of things-aided smart grid: Technologies, architectures, applications, prototypes, and future research directions. *IEEE Access: Practical Innovations, Open Solutions*, *7*, 62962–63003. doi:10.1109/ACCESS.2019.2913984

Sanders, N. R. (2016). How to use big data to drive your supply chain. *California Management Review*, *58*(3), 26–48. doi:10.1525/cmr.2016.58.3.26

Seddon, P. B., Constantinidis, D., Tamm, T., & Dod, H. (2017). How does business analytics contribute to business value? *Information Systems Journal*, *27*(3), 237–269. doi:10.1111/isj.12101

Shafiq, A., Ahmed, M.U., & Mahmoodi, F. (2019). Impact of supply chain analytics and customer pressure for ethical conduct on socially responsible practices and performance: An exploratory study. *International Journal of Production Economics*. . doi:10.1016/j.ijpe.2019.107571

Shayaa, S., Jaafar, N. I., Bahri, S., Sulaiman, A., Wai, P. S., Chung, Y. W., & Piprani, A. Z. (2018). Sentiment Analysis of Big Data : Methods, Applications, and Open Challenges. *IEEE Access, 6*, 37807–37827. doi:10.1109/ACCESS.2018.2851311

Shirer, M., & Goepfert, J. (2018). New IDC Spending Guide Sees Worldwide Blockchain Spending Growing to $9.7 Billion in 2021. *IDC-Analyze the Future*. Available at: https://scholar.google.com/scholar?hl=en&as_sdt=0%2C5&as_ylo=2017&q=%28Goepfert+and+Shirer%2C+2018%29&btnG=

Shrivastava, P., & Guimarães-Costa, N. (2017). Achieving environmental sustainability: The case for multi-layered collaboration across disciplines and players. *Technological Forecasting and Social Change*, *116*, 340–346. doi:10.1016/j.techfore.2016.11.019

Soleimani, H., Seyyed-Esfahani, M., & Kannan, G. (2014). Incorporating risk measures in closed-loop supply chain network design. *International Journal of Production Research*, *52*(6), 1843–1867. doi:10.1080/00207543.2013.849823

Souza, G. C. (2014). Supply chain analytics. *Business Horizons, Elsevier*, *57*(5), 595–605. doi:10.1016/j.bushor.2014.06.004

Srinivasan, R., & Swink, M. (2018). An Investigation of Visibility and Flexibility as Complements to Supply Chain Analytics: An Organizational Information Processing Theory Perspective. *Production and Operations Management*, *27*(10), 1849–1867. doi:10.1111/poms.12746

Tabesh, P., Mousavidin, E., & Hasani, S. (2019). Implementing big data strategies: A managerial perspective. *Business Horizons*, *62*(3), 347–358. doi:10.1016/j.bushor.2019.02.001

Talwar, S., Kaur, P., Fosso Wamba, S., & Dhir, A. (2021). Big Data in operations and supply chain management: A systematic literature review and future research agenda. *International Journal of Production Research, Taylor and Francis Ltd.*, *59*(11), 3509–3534. doi:10.1080/00207543.2020.1868599

Tiwari, S., Wee, H.M., & Daryanto, Y. (2018). Big data analytics in supply chain management between 2010 and 2016: Insights to industries. *Computers and Industrial Engineering*, *115*, 319–330.

Waller, M. A., & Fawcett, S. E. (2013). Data science, predictive analytics, and big data: A revolution that will transform supply chain design and management. *Journal of Business Logistics*, *34*(2), 77–84.

Wamba, S. F., Akter, S., Edwards, A., Chopin, G., & Gnanzou, D. (2015). How 'big data'can make big impact: Findings from a systematic review and a longitudinal case study. *International Journal of Production Economics, Elsevier*, *165*, 234–246. doi:10.1016/j.ijpe.2014.12.031

Wamba, S.F., Dubey, R., Gunasekaran, A., & Akter, S. (2020). The performance effects of big data analytics and supply chain ambidexterity: The moderating effect of environmental dynamism. *International Journal of Production Economics*, *222*, 107498.

Wang, G., Gunasekaran, A., Ngai, E. W. T., & Papadopoulos, T. (2016). Big data analytics in logistics and supply chain management : Certain investigations for research and applications. *International Journal of Production Economics, Elsevier*, *176*, 98–110. doi:10.1016/j.ijpe.2016.03.014

Wilhelm, M., Blome, C., Bhakoo, V., & Operations, A. P.-J. (2016). Sustainability in multi-tier supply chains: Understanding the double agency role of the first-tier supplier. *Journal of Operations Management*, *41*(1), 42–60. doi:10.1016/j.jom.2015.11.001

Wright, L. T., Robin, R., Stone, M., & Aravopoulou, D. E. (2019). Adoption of Big Data Technology for Innovation in B2B Marketing. *Journal of Business-to-Business Marketing, Routledge*, *26*(3–4), 281–293. doi:10.1080/1051712X.2019.1611082

Yasmin, M., Tatoglu, E., Kilic, H. S., Zaim, S., & Delen, D. (2020). Big data analytics capabilities and firm performance: An integrated MCDM approach. *Journal of Business Research, Elsevier*, *114*(March), 1–15. doi:10.1016/j.jbusres.2020.03.028

Yu, W., Jacobs, M. A., Chavez, R., & Feng, M. (2017). The impacts of IT capability and marketing capability on supply chain integration : A resource- based perspective. *International Journal of Production Research, Taylor & Francis*, *55*(14), 4196–4211. doi:10.1080/00207543.2016.1275874

Glossary

Blockchain: Blockchain is a distributed, decentralized ledger that makes tracking transactions and monitoring assets in a value chain much easier.

Cyber-Physical System: CPS monitors physical components with computer-based algorithms connected to internet, using a mixture of computers, sensory sensors, embedded cognitive computing, and multiple communications mechanisms.

Digital Twin: A digital versions of physical objects.

Industry 4.0: The use of new smart technology to advance automation of conventional manufacturing and industrial practices.

Logistics 4.0: A term coined to describe the application of Industry 4.0 technologies in logistics domain.

Microgrid: A decentralized network of electricity generating units that is usually connected to and synchronous with the conventional wide-area synchronous grid, but that can also detach to "island mode" and run independently.

Quality 4.0: Under the framework of Industry 4.0, a concept that refers to the future of quality and organization performance.

Smart Contract: A code that runs on the blockchain network and defines certain criteria that all parties must enforce.

Compilation of References

Aarti. (2020). *Saudi Orders All Private Sector Employees to Work from Home, Suspends Prayers at Mosques.* Gulf Business. gulfbusiness.com/saudi-orders-all-private-sector-staff-to-work-from-home-suspends-prayers-at-mosques/

Abbasi, M., & Nilsson, F. (2016). Developing environmentally sustainable logistics: Exploring themes and challenges from a logistics service providers' perspective. *Transportation Research Part D, Transport and Environment, 46*, 273–283. doi:10.1016/j.trd.2016.04.004

Abebe, E., Behl, D., Govindarajan, C., Hu, Y., Karunamoorthy, D., Novotny, P., Pandit, V., Ramakrishna, V., & Vecchiola, C. (2019). *Enabling Enterprise Blockchain Interoperability with Trusted Data Transfer* (Industry Track). In *Proceedings of the 20th International Middleware Conference Industrial Track (Middleware '19).* Association for Computing Machinery. 10.1145/3366626.3368129

Abed, S. S. (2020). Social commerce adoption using TOE framework: An empirical investigation of Saudi Arabian SMEs. *International Journal of Information Management, 53*, 102118. doi:10.1016/j.ijinfomgt.2020.102118

Abueish, T. (2020). Coronavirus: Pakistan Issues 'Work from Home' Guideline for Private Sectors. *Al Arabiya*. english.alarabiya.net/en/News/gulf/2020/03/17/Coronavirus-Saudi-Arabia-issues-work-from-home-guideline-for-private-sectors

Acharya, A., Singh, S. K., Pereira, V., & Singh, P. (2018). Big data, knowledge co-creation and decision making in fashion industry. *International Journal of Information Management, 42*, 90–101. doi:10.1016/j.ijinfomgt.2018.06.008

Adams, C. (2020). Social Media for Brands during Lockdown - How to Adapt to the New Normal. *The Drum*. www.thedrum.com/opinion/2020/04/08/social-media-brands-during-lockdown-how-adapt-the-new-normal

Addo-tenkorang, R., & Helo, P. T. (2016). Big data applications in operations / supply-chain management : A literature review. *Computers & Industrial Engineering, Elsevier Ltd, 101*, 528–543. doi:10.1016/j.cie.2016.09.023

Ahlman, R. (2016). *Finnish City Partners with IBM to Validate Block Chain Application in Logistics.* Coin Telegraph. Available at: https://cointelegraph.com/news/

Ahmad, R. W., Hasan, H., Jayaraman, R., Salah, K., & Omar, M. (2021). Blockchain applications and architectures for port operations and logistics management. *Research in Transportation Business & Management, 41*, 100620. Advance online publication. doi:10.1016/j.rtbm.2021.100620

Ainin, S., Naqshbandi, M. M., & Dezdar, S. (2016). Impact of adoption of Green IT practices on organizational performance. *Quality & Quantity, 50*(5), 1929–1948. doi:10.100711135-015-0244-7

Akif & Chen. (2020). Public Employees' Use of Social Media: It's Impact on Need Satisfaction and Intrinsic Work Motivation. *Government Information Quarterly, 36* (1), 51-60. doi:10.1016/j.giq.2018.11.008

Akter, S., Wamba, S. F., Gunasekaran, A., Dubey, R., & Childe, S. J. (2016). How to improve firm performance using big data analytics capability and business strategy alignment? *International Journal of Production Economics, Elsevier, 182*, 113–131. doi:10.1016/j.ijpe.2016.08.018

Alcácer, V., & Cruz-Machado, V. (2019). Scanning the Industry 4.0: A Literature Review on Technologies. *International Journal for Manufacturing Systems, Engineering Science and Technology, 22*(3), 899-919. doi:10.1016/j.jestch.2019.01.006

Al-Dmour, H., Saad, N., Basheer Amin, E., Al-Dmour, R., & Al-Dmour, A. (2021). The influence of the practices of big data analytics applications on bank performance: filed study. *VINE Journal of Information and Knowledge Management Systems*. doi:10.1108/VJIKMS-08-2020-0151

Algaissi, Alharbi, Hassanain, & Hashem. (2020). Preparedness and response to COVID-19 in Pakistan: Building on MERS experience. *Journal of Infection and Public Health, 13*(6), 834-838. doi:10.1016/j.jiph.2020.04.016

Alharthi, A., Krotov, V., & Bowman, M. (2017). "Addressing barriers to big data", *Business Horizons*, "Kelley School of Business. *Indiana University, 60*(3), 285–292.

Ali, M., Nelson, J., Shea, R., & Freedman, M. J. (2016). Blockstack: A global naming and storage system secured by blockchains. *Proceedings of the 2016 USENIX Annual Technical Conference*, 181–194.

Ali, S., Poulova, P., Yasmin, F., Danish, M., Akhtar, W., & Usama Javed, H. M. (2020). How Big Data Analytics Boosts Organizational Performance: The Mediating Role of the Sustainable Product Development. *Journal of Open Innovation, 6*(4), 190. doi:10.3390/joitmc6040190

Alkhater, N., Walters, R., & Wills, G. (2018). An empirical study of factors influencing cloud adoption among private sector organisations. *Telematics and Informatics, 35*(1), 38–54. doi:10.1016/j.tele.2017.09.017

Alkhudary, R., Brusset, X., & Fenies, P. (2020). Blockchain and Risk in Supply Chain Management. In *LDIC 2020-Dynamics in Logistics* (pp. 159-165). Springer.

Allen, D. W. E., Berg, C., Davidson, S., Novak, M., & Potts, J. (2019). International policy coordination for blockchain supply chains. *Asia Pacific Policy Studies, 6*, 367-380.

Allison, I. (2016). *Provenance has a big year ahead delivering supply chain transparency with Bitcoin and Ethereum.* IBTimes. Available at: https://www.ibtimes.co.uk/

Alsetoohy, O., Ayoun, B., Arous, S., Megahed, F., & Nabil, G. (2019). Intelligent agent technology: What affects its adoption in hotel food supply chain management? *Journal of Hospitality and Tourism Technology*, *10*(3), 317–341. doi:10.1108/JHTT-01-2018-0005

Alsmiller, C. (2016). *Block chain: The Next Big Thing in the Supply Chain.* Appterra. Available: http://appterra.com/ uncategorized/blockchain-the-next-big-thing-in-the-supply-chain/

Alt, R., & Schmid, B. (2000). *Logistik und Electronic Commerce--Perspektiven durch zwei sich wechselseitig erganzende Konzepte. (With English summary).* Zeitschrift fur Betriebswirtschaft.

Al-Thaqafi. (2020). Saudi Companies Ask Employees to Work from Home. *Arab News*. www.arabnews.com/node/1639606/saudi-arabia

Ammous, S. (2016). *Block chain Technology: What is it good for?* Available at: https://capitalism.columbia.edu/

Arif, M., Jan, K., Marwat, Z. A., & Ullah, I. (2009). Performance enhancement through effective communication: A study of the role of external and internal communication. *Interdisciplinary Journal of Contemporary Research in Business*, *1*(7), 119–148.

ARMONK. (2017). *Maersk and IBM Unveil First Industry-Wide Cross-Border Supply Chain Solution on Block chain.* https://www-03.ibm.com/press/us/en/press release/51712.wss

Aslam, J., Saleem, A., Khan, N. T., & Kim, Y. B. (2021). Factors influencing blockchain adoption in supply chain management practices: A study based on the oil industry. *Journal of Innovation and Knowledge*, *6*(2), 124–134. Advance online publication. doi:10.1016/j.jik.2021.01.002

Atlam, H. F., & Wills, G. B. (2019). Technical aspects of blockchain and IoT. In Advances in Computers (Vol. 115). doi:10.1016/bs.adcom.2018.10.006

Aversa, J., Hernandez, T., & Doherty, S. (2021). Incorporating big data within retail organizations: A case study approach. *Journal of Retailing and Consumer Services*, *60*, 102447. Advance online publication. doi:10.1016/j.jretconser.2021.102447

Badi, S., & Murtagh, N. (2019). Green supply chain management in construction: A systematic literature review and future research agenda. *Journal of Cleaner Production*, *223*, 312–322. doi:10.1016/j.jclepro.2019.03.132

Bag, S., Wood, L.C., Xu, L., Dhamija, P., & Kayikci, Y. (2020). Big data analytics as an operational excellence approach to enhance sustainable supply chain performance. *Resources, Conservation and Recycling*, *153*, 104559.

Bai, C., Dallasega, P., Orzes, G., & Sarkis, J. (2020). Industry 4.0 technologies assessment: A sustainability perspective. *International Journal of Production Economics*, *229*, 107776. doi:10.1016/j.ijpe.2020.107776

Baig, M. I., Shuib, L., & Yadegaridehkordi, E. (2019). Big data adoption: State of the art and research challenges. *Information Processing & Management, 56*(6), 102095. doi:10.1016/j.ipm.2019.102095

Baines, T., Brown, S., Benedettini, O., & Ball, P. (2012). Examining green production and its role within the competitive strategy of manufacturers. *Journal of Industrial Engineering and Management, 5*(1), 53–87. doi:10.3926/jiem.405

Bajwa, N., Prewett, K., & Shavers, C. (2019). Is your supply chain ready to embrace blockchain? *Journal of Corporate Accounting & Finance, 31*(2), 54–64. Advance online publication. doi:10.1002/jcaf.22423

Baker, J. (2011). *The Technology-Organization-Environment Framework Strategic Managment View project.* Springer. doi:10.1007/978-1-4419-6108-2_12

Baker, J., & Steiner, J. (2015). *Blockchain: The solution for transparency in product.* Provenance. Available at: https://www.provenance.org/whitepaper

Bartodziej, C. J. (2021). The concept Industry 4.0. In *The Concept Industry 4.0.* BestMasters. Springer Gabler. doi:10.1007/978-3-658-16502-4_3

Batada, D. I. (n.d.). *Blockchain for Pakistan.* https://www.thenews.com.pk/print/752179-blockchain-for-pakistan

Behl, A., Dutta, P., Lessmann, S., Dwivedi, Y. K., & Kar, S. (2019). A conceptual framework for the adoption of big data analytics by e-commerce startups: A case-based approach. *Information Systems and e-Business Management, 17*(2–4), 285–318. doi:10.100710257-019-00452-5

Ben-Daya, M., Hassini, E., & Bahroun, Z. (2019). Internet of things and supply chain management: A literature review. *International Journal of Production Research, 57*(15–16), 4719–4742. doi:10.1080/00207543.2017.1402140

Benning, K. (2016). *Block chain Consumerism.* Shop! Association. Available: http://www.shopassociation.org/block chain-consumerism/

Bernstein. (2021). *How it works - Bernstein - Blockchain for intellectual property.* https://www.bernstein.io/how-it-works

Bertino, E., Deng, R. H., Huang, X., & Zhou, J. (2015). Security and privacy of electronic health information systems. *International Journal of Information Security, 14*(6), 485–486. doi:10.100710207-015-0303-z

BhambhwaniS. M.DelikourasS.KorniotisG. M. (2020). Blockchain Characteristics and the Cross-Section of Cryptocurrency Returns. SSRN *Journal.*

Bodewits, K. (2020). Working from Home Because of COVID-19? Here Are 10 Ways to Spend Your Time. *Science.* www.sciencemag.org/careers/2020/03/working-home-because-covid-19-here-are-10-ways-spend-your-time

Bodhke, U., Tanwar, S., Parekh, K., Khanpara, P., Tyagi, S., Kumar, N., & Alazab, M. (2020). Blockchain for Industry 4.0: A Comprehensive Review. *IEEE Access: Practical Innovations, Open Solutions*, *8*, 79764–79800.

Brandenburger, J. (2021). Quality 4.0 - Transparent Product Quality Supervision in the Age of Industry 4.0. In V. Colla & C. Pietrosanti (Eds.), *Impact and Opportunities of Artificial Intelligence Techniques in the Steel Industry. ESTEP 2020. Advances in Intelligent Systems and Computing* (Vol. 1338). Springer. doi:10.1007/978-3-030-69367-1_5

Brettel, M. (2014). How Virtualization, Decentralization and Network Building Change the Manufacturing Landscape: An Industry 4.0 Perspective. *International Journal of Mechanical, Aerospace, Industrial and Mechatronics Engineering*, *8*(1), 37.

Breunig, M., Kelly, R., Mathis, R., & Wee, D. (2016). *Getting the Most out of Industry 4.0.* McKinsey Global Institute. Available at: https://scholar.google.com/scholar?hl=en&as_sdt=0%2C5&q=Breunig%2C+M.%2C+Kelly%2C+R.%2C+Mathis%2C+R.%2C+%26+Wee%2C+D.+%282016%29.+Getting+the+most+out+of+Industry+4.0&btnG=

Brock, V., & Khan, H. U. (2017). Big data analytics: Does organizational factor matters impact technology acceptance? *Journal of Big Data*, *4*(1), 21. doi:10.118640537-017-0081-8

Brownsword, R. (2019). Regulatory Fitness: Fintech, Funny Money, and Smart Contracts. *European Business Organization Law Review*, *20*(1), 5–27. doi:10.100740804-019-00134-2

Brunswicker, S., Bertino, E., & Matei, S. (2015). Big Data for Open Digital Innovation - A Research Roadmap. *Big Data Research*, *2*(2), 53–58. doi:10.1016/j.bdr.2015.01.008

Byrne, B. M. (2010). *Structural Equation Modelling with AMOS: Basic Concepts, Applications, and Programming* (2nd ed.). Taylor and Francis Group.

Casado-Vara, R., González Briones, A., Prieto, J., & Corchado R. (2019). *Smart Contract for Monitoring and Control of Logistics Activities: Pharmaceutical Utilities Case Study.* doi:10.1007/978-3-319-94120-2_49

Casino, Dasaklis, & Patsakis. (2019). A Systematic Literature Review of Blockchain-based Applications: Current Status, classification and Open Issues. *Telematics and Informatics*, *36*, 55-81. doi:10.1016/j.tele.2018.11.006

Chae, B. K., Olson, D., & Sheu, C. (2013). Understanding big data analytics capabilities in supply chain management: Unravelling the issues, challenges and implications for. *International Journal of Production Research*, *52*(16), 4695–4710. doi:10.1080/00207543.2013.861616

Chaturvedi, A. (2020). 21 Day Lockdown: Social Media Platforms, Users Find Novel Ways to Stay Engaged. *The Economic Times*. economictimes.indiatimes.com/tech/internet/21-day-lockdown-social-media-platforms-users-find-novel-ways-to-stay-engaged/articleshow/74915654.cms?from=mdr

Chavez, R., Yu, W., Jacobs, M. A., & Feng, M. (2017). Data-driven supply chains, manufacturing capability and customer satisfaction. *Production Planning and Control, Taylor & Francis, 28*(11–12), 906–918. doi:10.1080/09537287.2017.1336788

Chen, D. Q., Preston, D. S., & Swink, M. (2015). How the use of big data analytics affects value creation in supply chain management. *Journal of Management Information Systems, Routledge, 32*(4), 4–39. doi:10.1080/07421222.2015.1138364

Cheng, W., Vyas, R., Gopalakrishnan, R., Clay, E. R., & Singh, M. (2020). Exploring Correlation among Different Elements of Student Evaluation of Teaching. In 2020 IEEE Frontiers in Education Conference (FIE) (pp. 1-7). IEEE. doi:10.1109/FIE44824.2020.9273999

Chen, P. T., Lin, C. L., & Wu, W. N. (2020). Big data management in healthcare: Adoption challenges and implications. *International Journal of Information Management, 53*, 102078. doi:10.1016/j.ijinfomgt.2020.102078

Chhetri, S. R., Faezi, S., Rashid, N., & Al Faruque, M. A. (2018). Manufacturing Supply Chain and Product Lifecycle Security in the Era of Industry 4.0. *Journal of Hardware System Security, 2*(1), 51–68. doi:10.100741635-017-0031-0

Chin, T. A., Tat, H. H., & Sulaiman, Z. (2015). Green supply chain management, environmental collaboration and sustainability performance. *Procedia CIRP, 26*, 695–699. doi:10.1016/j.procir.2014.07.035

Choudhry, A., Dimobi, I., & Isaac Gould, Z. M. (2019). Blockchain Driven Platform for Energy Distribution in a Microgrid. In Data Privacy Management, Cryptocurrencies and Blockchain Technology. Springer. doi:10.1007/978-3-030-31500-9_18

Christopher, M. (n.d.). *Logistics and Supply Chain Management* (5th ed.). London: Pearson.

Chu, T. (2020, March). A Meta-Analytic Review of the Relationship Between Social Media Use and Employee Outcomes. *Telematics and Informatics, 50*, 101379. doi:10.1016/j.tele.2020.101379

Clohessy, T., Acton, T., & Rogers, N. (2019). Blockchain Adoption: Technological, Organisational and Environmental Considerations. *Business Transformation through Blockchain*, 47–76. doi:10.1007/978-3-319-98911-2_2

Consensys. (2021). *Blockchain technology solutions*. https://consensys.net/

Copigneaux, B., Vlasov, N., Bani, E., Tcholtchev, N., Lämmel, P., Fuenfzig, M., Snoeijenbos, S., & Flickenschild, M. (2020). *Blockchain for supply chains and internatiional trade, European Parliamentary Research Service, Scientific Foresight Unit*. STOA.

Correia, E., Carvalho, H., Azevedo, S. G., & Govindan, K. (2017). Maturity Models in Supply Chain Sustainability: A Systematic Literature Review. In Sustainability (Vol. 9, Issue 1). doi:10.3390u9010064

Costa, R. L. de C., Moreira, J., Pintor, P., dos Santos, V., & Lifschitz, S. (2021). A Survey on Data-driven Performance Tuning for Big Data Analytics Platforms. *Big Data Research*, *25*, 100206. Advance online publication. doi:10.1016/j.bdr.2021.100206

Crosby, M. N., Pattanayak, P., Verma, S., & Kalyanaraman, V. (2016). Block chain Technology: Beyond Bitcoin. *Applied Innovation Review*. Available at:http://scet.berkeley.edu/wp-content/uploads/AIR-2016-Blockchain.pdf

Cruz-Jesus, F., Pinheiro, A., & Oliveira, T. (2019). Understanding CRM adoption stages: Empirical analysis building on the TOE framework. *Computers in Industry*, *109*, 1–13. doi:10.1016/j.compind.2019.03.007

Cubric, M. (2020). Drivers, barriers and social considerations for AI adoption in business and management: A tertiary study. Technology in Society, 62, 101257.

Cuccuru, P. (2017, Autumn). Beyond Bitcoin: An Early Overview On smart contracts. *International Journal of Law and Information Technology*, *25*(3), 179–195. doi:10.1093/ijlit/eax003

Dafflon, B., Moalla, N., & Ouzrout, Y. (2021). The challenges, approaches, and used techniques of CPS for manufacturing in Industry 4.0: A literature review. *International Journal of Advanced Manufacturing Technology*, *113*(7-8), 2395–2412. doi:10.100700170-020-06572-4

Dai, B., Jiang, S., Zhu, M., Lu, M., Li, D., & Li, C. (2020) Research and Implementation of Cross-Chain Transaction Model Based on Improved Hash-Locking. In Blockchain and Trustworthy Systems. Springer. doi:10.1007/978-981-15-9213-3_17

Dalenogare, L. S., Benitez, G. B., Ayala, N. F., & Frank, A. G. (2018). The expected contribution of Industry 4.0 technologies for industrial performance. *International Journal of Production Economics*, *204*, 383–394. doi:10.1016/j.ijpe.2018.08.019

Danese, P., Lion, A., & Vinelli, A. (2019). Drivers and enablers of supplier sustainability practices: A survey-based analysis. *International Journal of Production Research*, *57*(7), 2034–2056. doi:10.1080/00207543.2018.1519265

de Camargo Fiorini, P., Roman Pais Seles, B. M., Chiappetta Jabbour, C. J., Barberio Mariano, E., & de Sousa Jabbour, A. B. L. (2018). Management theory and big data literature: From a review to a research agenda. In *International Journal of Information Management* (Vol. 43, pp. 112–129). Elsevier Ltd. doi:10.1016/j.ijinfomgt.2018.07.005

de Sousa Jabbour, A. B. L., Jabbour, C. J. C., Foropon, C., & Godinho Filho, M. (2018). When titans meet–Can industry 4.0 revolutionise the environmentally-sustainable manufacturing wave? The role of critical success factors. *Technological Forecasting and Social Change*, *132*, 18–25. doi:10.1016/j.techfore.2018.01.017

De Vita, G., & Tekaya, A. (2015). Hotel outsourcing under asset specificity: 'The good, the bad and the ugly.'. *Tourism Management*, *47*, 97–106. doi:10.1016/j.tourman.2014.09.012

Delfmann, W., Albers, S., & Gehring, M. (2002). The impact of electronic commerce on logistics service providers. *International Journal of Physical Distribution & Logistics Management*, *32*(3), 203–222. doi:10.1108/09600030210426539

Dennis, R., & Disso, J. P. (2019). An Analysis into the Scalability of Bitcoin and Ethereum. In *Third International Congress on Information and Communication Technology*. Springer. 10.1007/978-981-13-1165-9_57

DeVellis, R. F., Lewis, M. A., & Sterba, K. R. (2003). Interpersonal emotional processes in adjustment to chronic illness. *Social Psychological Foundations of Health and Illness*, 256-287.

DHL Trend Research. (2019). Blockchain in Logistics: Perspectives on the upcoming impact of blockchain technology and use cases for the logistics industry. DHL Customer Solutions & Innovation.

Dickmann, M., & Tyson, S. (2005). Outsourcing payroll: Beyond transaction-cost economics. *Personnel Review*, *34*(4), 451–467. doi:10.1108/00483480510599770

Dickson, B. (2016). *Block chain has the potential to revolutionize the supply chain.* Tech Crunch. Available at: https://techcrunch.com/2016/11/24/

Diniz, E. H., Luvizan, S. S., Hino, M. C., & Ferreira, P. C. (2018). Unveiling the big data adoption in banks: Strategizing the implementation of a new technology. *Lecture Notes in Information Systems and Organisation*, *23*, 149–162. doi:10.1007/978-3-319-62051-0_13

Donohoe, H., Stellefson, M., & Tennant, B. (2012). Advantages and Limitations of the e-Delphi Technique. *American Journal of Health Education*, *43*(1), 38–46. doi:10.1080/19325037.2012.10599216

Drath, R., & Horch, A. (2014). Industrie 4.0: Hit or hype? *IEEE Industrial Electronics Magazine*, *8*(2), 56–58. doi:10.1109/MIE.2014.2312079

Drescher, D. (2017). *Blockchain basics: A Non-technical Introduction in 25 Steps*. Frankfurt, Germany: APress.

Dubey, R., Gunasekaran, A., Childe, S. J., Papadopoulos, T., Luo, Z., Wamba, S. F., & Roubaud, D. (2019). Can big data and predictive analytics improve social and environmental sustainability? *Technological Forecasting and Social Change*, *144*, 534–545. doi:10.1016/j.techfore.2017.06.020

Duncan, N. B. (1998). Beyond opportunism: A resource-based view of outsourcing risk. *Proceedings of the Hawaii International Conference on System Sciences*, 675–684. 10.1109/HICSS.1998.654829

Duschek, S. (2004). Inter-Firm Resources and Sustained Competitive Advantage. *Management Review*, *15*(1), 53–73.

Eccles, R. G., & Williamson, O. E. (1987). The Economic Institutions of Capitalism: Firms, Markets, Relational Contracting. *Administrative Science Quarterly*, *32*(4), 602. doi:10.2307/2392889

El Junusi, R. (2020). Digital Marketing During the Pandemic Period; A Study of Islamic Perspective. *Journal of Digital Marketing and Halal Industry*, *2*(1), 15–28. doi:10.21580/jdmhi.2020.2.1.5717

El Mokrini, A., Dafaoui, E. M., El Mhamedi, A., & Berrado, A. (2016). A decision framework for outsourcing logistics in the pharmaceutical supply chain. *Proceedings of 2015 International Conference on Industrial Engineering and Systems Management, IEEE IESM 2015*, 748–756.

Ellouze, F., Fersi, G., & Jmaiel, M. (2020). Blockchain for Internet of Medical Things: A Technical Review. In M. Jmaiel, M. Mokhtari, B. Abdulrazak, H. Aloulou, & S. Kallel (Eds.), Lecture Notes in Computer Science: Vol. 12157. *The Impact of Digital Technologies on Public Health in Developed and Developing Countries. ICOST 2020*. Springer. doi:10.1007/978-3-030-51517-1_22

Elmuti, D. (2003). The Perceived Impact of Outsourcing on Organizational Performance. *American Journal of Business*, *18*(2), 33–42. doi:10.1108/19355181200300010

Ergado, A. A., Desta, A., & Mehta, H. (2021). Determining the barriers contributing to ICT implementation by using technology-organization-environment framework in Ethiopian higher educational institutions. *Education and Information Technologies*, *26*(3), 1–19. doi:10.100710639-020-10397-9

Ertemel, A. (2015). Consumer insight as competitive advantage using big data and analytics. *International Journal of Commerce and Finance*, *1*(1), 45–51.

Esmaeilian, B., Sarkis, J., Lewis, K., & Behdad, S. (2020). Blockchain for the future of sustainable supply chain management in Industry 4.0. *Resources, Conservation & Recycling, 163*(105064), 1-15.

Espino-Rodriguez, T. F., & Padrón-Robaina, V. (2006). A review of outsourcing from the resource-based view of the firm. *International Journal of Management Reviews*. Advance online publication. doi:10.1111/j.1468-2370.2006.00120.x

Fadile, L., El Oumami, M., & Beidouri, Z. (2018). Logistics outsourcing: A review of basic concepts. *International Journal of Supply Chain Management*, *7*(3), 53–69.

Femi, A. F. (2014). The impact of communication on workers' performance in selected organisations in Lagos State, Nigeria. *IOSR Journal of the Humanities and Social Sciences*, *19*(8), 75–82.

Feng, M., Yu, W., Wang, X., Wong, C. Y., Xu, M., & Xiao, Z. (2018). Green supply chain management and financial performance: The mediating roles of operational and environmental performance. *Business Strategy and the Environment*, *27*(7), 811–824. doi:10.1002/bse.2033

Fornell, C., & Larcker, D. F. (1981). Evaluating structural equation models with unobservable variables and measurement error. *JMR, Journal of Marketing Research*, *18*(1), 39–50. doi:10.1177/002224378101800104

Fosso Wamba, S., Queiroz, M. M., & Trinchera, L. (2020). Dynamics between blockchain adoption determinants and supply chain performance: An empirical investigation. *International Journal of Production Economics*, *229*, 107791. doi:10.1016/j.ijpe.2020.107791

Francisco, K., & Swanson, D. (2018). The Supply Chain Has No Clothes: Technology Adoption of Blockchain for Supply Chain Transparency. *Logistics, 2*(2), 1-13.

Frank, A. G., Dalenogare, L. S., & Ayala, N. F. (2019). Industry 4.0 technologies: Implementation patterns in manufacturing companies. *International Journal of Production Economics, 210*, 15–26. doi:10.1016/j.ijpe.2019.01.004

Frick, T. A. (2019). Virtual and cryptocurrencies—regulatory and anti-money laundering approaches in the European Union and in Switzerland. *ERA Forum, 20*, 99–112. 10.100712027-019-00561-1

Gaiardelli, P., Pezzotta, G., Rondini, A., Romero, D., Jarrahi, F., Bertoni, M., Wiesner, S., Wuest, T., Larsson, T., Zaki, M., Jussen, P., Boucher, X., Bigdeli, A. Z., & Cavalieri, S. (2021). Product-service systems evolution in the era of Industry 4.0. *Service Business, 15*(1), 177–207. doi:10.100711628-021-00438-9

Galetsi, P., Katsaliaki, K., & Kumar, S. (2020). Big data analytics in health sector: Theoretical framework, techniques and prospects. In *International Journal of Information Management* (Vol. 50, pp. 206–216). Elsevier Ltd. doi:10.1016/j.ijinfomgt.2019.05.003

Galvez, J. F., Mejuto, J. C., & Simal-Gandara, J. (2018). Future challenges on the use of blockchain for food traceability analysis. *Trends in Analytical Chemistry, 107*, 222–232. Advance online publication. doi:10.1016/j.trac.2018.08.011

Gamage, H. T. M., Weerasinghe, H. D., & Dias, N. G. J. (2020). A Survey on Blockchain Technology Concepts, Applications, and Issues. *SN. Computer Science, 1*(2), 114. doi:10.100742979-020-00123-0

Ganne, E. (2018). Can Blockchain Revolutionalise International Trade. World Trade Organisation.

Garrison, G., Wakefield, R. L., & Kim, S. (2015). The effects of IT capabilities and delivery model on cloud computing success and firm performance for cloud supported processes and operations. *International Journal of Information Management, 35*(4), 377–393. doi:10.1016/j.ijinfomgt.2015.03.001

Gawankar, S. A., Gunasekaran, A., & Kamble, S. (2020). A study on investments in the big data-driven supply chain, performance measures and organisational performance in Indian retail 4.0 context. *International Journal of Production Research, Taylor & Francis, 58*(5), 1574–1593. doi:10.1080/00207543.2019.1668070

Geffen, C. A., & Rothenberg, S. (2000). Suppliers and environmental innovation: The automotive paint process. *International Journal of Operations & Production Management, 20*(2), 166–186. doi:10.1108/01443570010304242

Geis, G. S. (2007). Business outsourcing and the agency cost problem. *The Notre Dame Law Review*.

Ghasemaghaei, M. (2021). Understanding the impact of big data on firm performance: The necessity of conceptually differentiating among big data characteristics. *International Journal of Information Management, 57*, 102055. doi:10.1016/j.ijinfomgt.2019.102055

Gilbert, D. (n.d.). *Blockchain Technology Could Help Solve $75Billion Counterfeit Drug Problem.* Ibtimes. Available at: https://www.ibtimes.com/

Goles, T. (2003). Vendor capabilities and outsourcing success: A resource-based view. *Wirtschaftsinformatik, 45*(2), 199–206. doi:10.1007/BF03250900

Gottlieb, M. S. (2020). *Keeping Your Team Productive While They Work from Home*. ITProPortal. www.itproportal.com/features/keeping-your-team-productive-while-they-work-from-home/

Gottschalk, P., & Solli-Sæther, H. (2006). Maturity model for IT outsourcing relationships. *Industrial Management & Data Systems, 106*(2), 200–212. doi:10.1108/02635570610649853

Govindan, K., Cheng, T. C. E., Mishra, N., & Shukla, N. (2018). *Big data analytics and application for logistics and supply chain management*. Elsevier. doi:10.1016/j.tre.2018.03.011

Govindan, K., Diabat, A., & Shankar, K. M. (2015). Analyzing the drivers of green manufacturing with fuzzy approach. *Journal of Cleaner Production, 96*, 182–193. doi:10.1016/j.jclepro.2014.02.054

Gunasekaran, A., Papadopoulos, T., Dubey, R., Wamba, S. F., Childe, S. J., Hazen, B., & Akter, S. (2017). Big data and predictive analytics for supply chain and organizational performance. *Journal of Business Research, Elsevier Inc., 70*, 308–317. doi:10.1016/j.jbusres.2016.08.004

Gupta, A., Deokar, A., Iyer, L., Sharda, R., & Schrader, D. (2018). Big Data & Analytics for Societal Impact: Recent Research and Trends. In Information Systems Frontiers (Vol. 20, Issue 2, pp. 185–194). Springer New York LLC. doi:10.100710796-018-9846-7

Gupta, S., Kar, A. K., Baabdullah, A., & Al-Khowaiter, W. A. A. (2018). Big data with cognitive computing: A review for the future. *International Journal of Information Management, 42*, 78–89. doi:10.1016/j.ijinfomgt.2018.06.005

Haffke, L., Fromberger, M., & Zimmermann, P. (2020). Cryptocurrencies and anti-money laundering: The shortcomings of the fifth AML Directive (EU) and how to address them. *J Bank Regul, 21*(2), 125–138. doi:10.105741261-019-00101-4

Hahn, G., & Packowski, J. (2015). A perspective on applications of in-memory analytics in supply chain management. *Decision Support Systems, 76*, 45–52. doi:10.1016/j.dss.2015.01.003

Hair, J. F., Black, W. C., Babin, B. J., & Anderson, R. E. (2010). *Multivariate Data Analysis* (7th ed.). Prentice Hall.

Hair, J., Black, W., Babin, B. Y. A., Anderson, R., & Tatham, R. (2014). *Multivariate Data Analysis. A Global Perspective*. Pearson Prentice Hall.

Hancock, M., & Vaizey, E. (2016). Distributed ledger technology: beyond blockchain. Academic Press.

Haq, I. U., & Tanveer, M. (2020). Status of Research Productivity and Higher Education in the Members of Organization of Islamic Cooperation (OIC). *Library Philosophy and Practice (ejournal), 3845*. https://digitalcommons.unl.edu/libphilprac/3845

Harris, K. (2020). *Tracking the Global Impact of the Coronavirus Outbreak*. Bain. www.bain.com/insights/tracking-the-global-impact-of-the-coronavirus-outbreak-snap-chart/

Hartmann, C., Shi, J., Giusto, A., & Siegrist, M. (2015). The psychology of eating insects: A cross-cultural comparison between Germany and China. *Food Quality and Preference*, *44*, 148–156. doi:10.1016/j.foodqual.2015.04.013

Haryanto, B., Gandhi, A., & Giri Sucahyo, Y. (2020, November 3). The Determinant Factors in Utilizing Electronic Signature Using the TAM and TOE Framework. *2020 5th International Conference on Informatics and Computing, ICIC 2020*. 10.1109/ICIC50835.2020.9288623

Hassani, H., & Silva, E. S. (2015). Forecasting with Big Data: A Review. *Annals of Data Science*, *2*(1), 5–19.

Hasson, F., Keeney, S., & McKenna, H. (2000). Research guidelines for the Delphi survey technique. *Journal of Advanced Nursery, 32*(4), 1008-15.

Hazen, B. T., Skipper, J. B., Boone, C. A., & Hill, R. R. (2018). Back in business: Operations research in support of big data analytics for operations and supply chain management. *Annals of Operations Research, Springer*, *270*(1–2), 201–211. doi:10.100710479-016-2226-0

Heide, J. B., & Rindfleisch, A. (1997). Transaction Cost Analysis : Past, Present, and Future Applications. *Journal of Marketing*.

Henseler, J., Ringle, C. M., & Sinkovics, R. R. (2009). The use of partial least squares path modeling in international marketing. *Advances in International Marketing*, *20*(1), 277–319. doi:10.1108/S1474-7979(2009)0000020014

Hertz, S., & Alfredsson, M. (2003). Strategic development of third party logistics providers. *Industrial Marketing Management*, *32*(2), 139–149. doi:10.1016/S0019-8501(02)00228-6

Hewa, T., Ylianttila, M., & Liyanage, M. (2020). Survey on Blockchain based Smart Contracts: Applications, Opportunities and Challenges. *Journal of Network and Computer Applications*, *177*, 102857. Advance online publication. doi:10.1016/j.jnca.2020.102857

Hiran, K. K., & Henten, A. (2020). An Integrated TOE-DoI Framework for Cloud Computing Adoption in Higher Education: The Case of Sub-Saharan Africa, Ethiopia. *Advances in Intelligent Systems and Computing*, *1053*, 1281–1290. doi:10.1007/978-981-15-0751-9_117

Hofmann, E., & Rutschmann, E. (2018). Big data analytics and demand forecasting in supply chains: A conceptual analysis. *International Journal of Logistics Management*, *29*(2), 739–766.

Hofmann, E., Strewed, U. M., & Bosia, N. (2018). *Supply Chain Finance and Blockchain Technology: The Case of Reverse Securitization*. Springer Nature. Available https://link.springer.com/10.1007/978-3-319-

Hong, E., Son, B. G., & Menachof, D. (2010). Exploring the link between IT systems and the outsourcing of logistics activities: A transaction cost perspective. *International Journal of Logistics Research and Applications*, *13*(1), 41–57. doi:10.1080/13675560903233682

Hsiao, H. I., van der Vorst, J. G. A. J., Kemp, R. G. M., & Omta, S. W. F. O. (2010). Developing a decision-making framework for levels of logistics outsourcing in food supply chain networks. *International Journal of Physical Distribution & Logistics Management*, *40*(5), 395–414. doi:10.1108/09600031011052840

Huo, B., Ye, Y., Zhao, X., Wei, J., & Hua, Z. (2018). Environmental uncertainty, specific assets, and opportunism in 3PL relationships: A transaction cost economics perspective. *International Journal of Production Economics*, *203*, 154–163. doi:10.1016/j.ijpe.2018.01.031

Hwang, M.-Y., Hong, J.-C., Tai, K.-H., Chen, J.-T., & Gouldthorp, T. (2020, January 1). The Relationship between the Online Social Anxiety, Perceived Information Overload and Fatigue, and Job Engagement of Civil Servant LINE Users. *Government Information Quarterly*, *37*(1), 101423. doi:10.1016/j.giq.2019.101423

Iki, K., Sato, S., & Tomizawa, S. (2018). Decomposition of Parsimonious Independence Model Using Pearson, Kendall and Spearman's Correlations for Two-Way Contingency Tables. *International Journal of Statistics and Probability*, *7*(3), 105. doi:10.5539/ijsp.v7n3p105

Ikram, M. N., & Siddiqui, D. A. (2019). Effect of Green Supply Chain Management on Environmental Performance and Export Performance: A Case Study of Textile Industries in Pakistan. *Social Science and Humanities Journal SSHJ*, *03*(04), 1006–1019.

Isaac, O., Abdullah, Z., Ramayah, T., Mutahar, A. M., & Alrajawy, I. (2016). Perceived usefulness, perceived ease of use, perceived compatibility, and net benefits: an empirical study of internet usage among employees in Yemen. In *The 7th International Conference Postgraduate Education (ICPE7)* (pp. 899-919). Academic Press.

Ito, K., & O'Dair, M. (2019). A Critical Examination of the Application of Blockchain Technology to Intellectual Property Management. In H. Treiblmaier & R. Beck (Eds.), *Business Transformation through Blockchain*. Palgrave Macmillan. doi:10.1007/978-3-319-99058-3_12

Ivanov, D., Dolgui, A., & Sokolov, B. (2019). The impact of digital technology and Industry 4.0 on the ripple effect and supply chain risk analytics. *International Journal of Production Research*, *57*(3), 829–846. doi:10.1080/00207543.2018.1488086

Jabbar, S., Lloyd, H., Hammoudeh, M., Adebisi, B., & Raza, U. (2021). Blockchain-enabled supply chain: Analysis, challenges, and future directions. *Multimedia Systems*, *27*(4), 787–806. Advance online publication. doi:10.100700530-020-00687-0

Jabbour, C. J. C., Mauricio, A. L., & Lopes, A. B. (2017). The Management of Operations Critical success factors and green supply chain management proactivity : Shedding light on the human aspects of this relationship based on cases from the Brazilian industry. *Production Planning and Control*, *7287*(May), 1–13. doi:10.1080/09537287.2017.1309705

Jagadish, H. V. (2015). Big Data and Science: Myths and Reality. In Big Data Research (Vol. 2, Issue 2, pp. 49–52). Elsevier Inc. doi:10.1016/j.bdr.2015.01.005

Jay, M. L. (2017). Building Better Supply Chains with Block chain. *MHI Solutions*, 20–26. Available: http://www.nxtbook.com/naylor/MHIQ/MHIQ0217/index.php?startid=90#/20

Jeble, S., Dubey, R., Childe, S. J., Papadopoulos, T., Roubaud, D., & Prakash, A. (2018). Impact of big data and predictive analytics capability on supply chain sustainability. *International Journal of Logistics Management*, *29*(2), 513–538.

Jin, X., Wah, B. W., Cheng, X., & Wang, Y. (2015). Significance and Challenges of Big Data Research. *Big Data Research*, *2*(2), 59–64. doi:10.1016/j.bdr.2015.01.006

Kache, F., & Seuring, S. (2017). Challenges and opportunities of digital information at the intersection of Big Data Analytics and supply chain management. *International Journal of Operations & Production Management*, *37*(1), 10–36. doi:10.1108/IJOPM-02-2015-0078

Kakavand, H., Kost De Serves, N., & Chilton, B. (2016). *The Block chain Revolution: An Analysis of Regulation And Technology Related To Distributed Ledger Technologies*. Available at:http:// www.fintechconnectlive.com/wp-content/uploads/2016/11/Luther-Systems-DLA-Piper-Article-on-Blockchain-Regulation-and-Technology-SK.pdf

Kamble, S., Gunasekaran, A., & Arha, H. (2019). Understanding the Blockchain technology adoption in supply chains-Indian context. *International Journal of Production Research*, *57*(7), 2009–2033. doi:10.1080/00207543.2018.1518610

Kang, H. S., Lee, J. Y., Choi, S., Kim, H., Park, J. H., Son, J. Y., Kim, B. H., & Do Noh, S. (2016). Smart manufacturing: Past research, present findings, and future directions. *International Journal of Precision Engineering and Manufacturing-Green Technology*, *3*(1), 111–128. doi:10.100740684-016-0015-5

Kanski, A. (2020, March). Social Networks Tackle COVID-19 Challenges, Misinformation - Media News. *Medical Marketing & Media*, *23*. www.mmm-online.com/home/channel/media-news/social-networks-tackle-covid-19-challenges-misinformation/

Kassim, N.H., Noor, N.M., Kasuma, J., & Saleh, J. (2020). *Impact of perceived usefulness, perceived ease of use and behavioral intention in using WhatsApp towards job performance*. Academic Press.

Katsanis, C. J. (2007). Outsourcing. *Workplace Strategies and Facilities Management*, 378–394.

Keeney, S., Hasson, F., & McKenna, H. (2006). Consulting the oracle: ten lessons from using the Delphi technique in nursing research. *Journal of Advanced*, *53*(2), 205-12. doi:10.1111/j.1365-2648.2006.03716.x

Kersten, W., Blecker, T., Ringle, C. M., Hackius, N., & Petersen, M. (2017). Digitalization in Supply Chain Management and Logistics Blockchain in Logistics and Supply Chain: Trick or Treat? Blockchain in Logistics and Supply Chain: Trick or Treat? *Proceedings of the Hamburg International Conference of Logistics (HICL).*

Khairuddin, I. E. (2019). *Understanding and Designing for Trust in Bitcoin Blockchain* [PhD Thesis]. Lancester University.

Khan, S. A. R., Ponce, P., Tanveer, M., Aguirre-Padilla, N., Mahmood, H., & Shah, S. A. A. (2021). Technological Innovation and Circular Economy Practices: Business Strategies to Mitigate the Effects of COVID-19. *Sustainability, 13*(15), 8479. doi:10.3390/su13158479

Khan, S. A. R., Ponce, P., Thomas, G., Yu, Z., Al-Ahmadi, M. S., & Tanveer, M. (2021). Digital Technologies, Circular Economy Practices and Environmental Policies in the Era of COVID-19. *Sustainability, 13*(22), 12790. doi:10.3390/su132212790

Khan, S. A. R., Zia-ul-haq, H. M., Umar, M., & Yu, Z., (2021a). Digital technology and circular economy practices: An strategy to improve organizational performance. *Business Strategy & Development.*

Khan, N. A., & Khan, A. N. (2019, July). What Followers Are Saying about Transformational SCM Fostering Employee Innovation via Organizational Learning, Knowledge Sharing and Social Media Use in Public Organizations? *Government Information Quarterly, 36*(4), 101391. Advance online publication. doi:10.1016/j.giq.2019.07.003

Khan, S. A. R., Dong, Q., Zhang, Y., & Khan, S. S. (2017). The impact of green supply chain on enterprise performance: In the perspective of China. *Journal of Advanced Manufacturing Systems, 16*(03), 263–273. doi:10.1142/S0219686717500160

Khan, S. A. R., & Qianli, D. (2017). Impact of green supply chain management practices on firms' performance: An empirical study from the perspective of Pakistan. *Environmental Science and Pollution Research International, 24*(20), 16829–16844. doi:10.100711356-017-9172-5 PMID:28573559

Khan, S. A. R., Yu, Z., Umar, M., Lopes de Sousa Jabbour, A. B., & Mor, R. S. (2021). Tackling post-pandemic challenges with digital technologies: An empirical study. *Journal of Enterprise Information Management,* (20210218). Advance online publication. doi:10.1108/JEIM-01-2021-0040

Kiel, D., Müller, J. M., Arnold, C., & Voigt, K.-I. (2020). Sustainable industrial value creation: Benefits and challenges of industry 4.0. In *Digital Disruptive Innovation* (pp. 231–270). World Scientific.

Kline, R. B. (2015). *Principles and practice of structural equation modeling.* Guilford publications.

Kniffin, K. M., Narayanan, J., Anseel, F., Antonakis, J., Ashford, S. J., Bakker, A. B., Bamberger, P., Bapuji, H., Bhave, D. P., Choi, V. K., & Creary, S. J. (2020). COVID-19 and the Workplace: Implications, Issues, and Insights for Future Research and Action. Academic Press.

Kosba, A., Miller, A., Shi, E., Wen, Z., & Papamanthou, C. (n.d.). *Hawk: The Block Chain Model of Cryptography and Privacy-Preserving Smart Contracts*. https://pdfs.semanticscholar.org/

Kouhizadeh, M., & Sarkis, J. (2020). Blockchain characteristics and green supply chain advancement. In *Global Perspectives on Green Business Administration and Sustainable Supply Chain Management* (pp. 93–109). IGI Global. doi:10.4018/978-1-7998-2173-1.ch005

Kouzinopoulos, C. S. (2018). Using Blockchains to Strengthen the Security of Internet of Things. In *Communications in Computer and Information Science* (Vol. 821). Springer. doi:10.1007/978-3-319-95189-8_9

Kumar, A., & Krishnamoorthy, B. (2020). Business Analytics Adoption in Firms: A Qualitative Study Elaborating TOE Framework in India. *International Journal of Global Business and Competitiveness*, *15*(2), 80–93. doi:10.100742943-020-00013-5

Kummer, S., Herold, D. M., Dobrovnik, M., Mikl, J., & Schäfer, N. (2020). A systematic review of blockchain literature in logistics and supply chain management: Identifying research questions and future directions. *Future Internet*, *12*(3), 60. Advance online publication. doi:10.3390/fi12030060

Kwon, O., Lee, N., & Shin, B. (2014). Data quality management, data usage experience and acquisition intention of big data analytics. *International Journal of Information Management*, *34*(3), 387–394. doi:10.1016/j.ijinfomgt.2014.02.002

Lai, C. S., Lai, L. L., & Lai, Q. H. (2021). Blockchain Applications in Microgrid Clusters. In *Smart Grids and Big Data Analytics for Smart Cities*. Springer. doi:10.1007/978-3-030-52155-4_3

Lamba, K., & Singh, S. P. (2017). Big data in operations and supply chain management: Current trends and future perspectives. *Production Planning & Control, Taylor and Francis Ltd.*, *28*(11–12), 877–890. doi:10.1080/09537287.2017.1336787

Lamminmaki, D. (2005). Why do hotels outsource? An investigation using asset specificity. *International Journal of Contemporary Hospitality Management*, *17*(6), 516–528. doi:10.1108/09596110510612158

Larissa, S., & Parung, J. (2021). Designing supply chain models with blockchain technology in the fishing industry in Indonesia. *IOP Conference Series: Materials Science and Engineering*, 1072. 10.1088/1757-899X/1072/1/012020

Lauslahti, K., Mattila, J., & Seppala, T. (2017, January). Smart Contracts – How Will Blockchain Technology Affect Contractual Practices? *ETLA Reports*, (68). Advance online publication. doi:10.2139srn.3154043

Lee, S. M., Lee, D., & Kim, Y. S. (2019). The quality management ecosystem for predictive maintenance in the Industry 4.0 era. *Int J Qual Innov*, *5*(1), 4. doi:10.118640887-019-0029-5

Lehmacher, W. (2017). *Why block chain should be global trade's next port of call*. World Economic Forum. Available: https://www.weforum.org/agenda/2017/05/blockchain-ports-global-trades/

Lepenioti, K., Bousdekis, A., Apostolou, D., & Mentzas, G. (2020). Prescriptive analytics: Literature review and research challenges. *International Journal of Information Management, 50*, 57–70. doi:10.1016/j.ijinfomgt.2019.04.003

Li, Y., Dai, J., & Cui, L. (2020). The impact of digital technologies on economic and environmental performance in the context of industry 4.0: A moderated mediation model. *International Journal of Production Economics, 229*(May), 107777. doi:10.1016/j.ijpe.2020.107777

Lieber, A. (2017). *Trust in Trade: Announcing a new block chain partner.* IBM. Available at: https://www.ibm.com/blogs/blockchain/2017/03/

Li, G., Hou, Y., & Wu, A. (2017). Fourth Industrial Revolution: Technological drivers, impacts and coping methods. *Chinese Geographical Science, 27*(4), 626–637. doi:10.100711769-017-0890-x

Lin, R.-J., Tan, K.-H., & Geng, Y. (2013). Market demand, green product innovation, and firm performance: Evidence from Vietnam motorcycle industry. *Journal of Cleaner Production, 40*, 101–107. doi:10.1016/j.jclepro.2012.01.001

Li, W., Fu, C., & Cheng, D. (2020). Comments on the development of blockchain technology from the perspective of patent analysis. *Front. Eng. Manag., 7*(4), 615–617. doi:10.100742524-020-0101-9

Li, X., Lv, F., Xiang, F., Sun, Z., & Sun, Z. (2020). Research on Key Technologies of Logistics Information Traceability Model Based on Consortium Chain. *IEEE Access: Practical Innovations, Open Solutions, 8*, 69754–69762. Advance online publication. doi:10.1109/ACCESS.2020.2986220

Li, Y. (2019). Emerging blockchain-based applications and techniques. *SOCA, 13*(4), 279–285. doi:10.100711761-019-00281-x

Logan, M. S. (2000). Using Agency Theory to Design Successful Outsourcing Relationships. *International Journal of Logistics Management, 11*(2), 21–32. doi:10.1108/09574090010806137

Long, T. B., Blok, V., & Coninx, I. (2016). Barriers to the adoption and diffusion of technological innovations for climate-smart agriculture in Europe: Evidence from the Netherlands, France, Switzerland and Italy. *Journal of Cleaner Production, Elsevier Ltd, 112*, 9–21. doi:10.1016/j.jclepro.2015.06.044

Mahakittikun, T., Suntrayuth, S., & Bhatiasevi, V. (2020). The impact of technological-organizational-environmental (TOE) factors on firm performance: Merchant's perspective of mobile payment from Thailand's retail and service firms. *Journal of Asia Business Studies*. Advance online publication. doi:10.1108/JABS-01-2020-0012

Manyika, J., Chui, M., Brown, B., Bughin, J., Dobbs, R., Roxburgh, C., & Byers, A.H. (2011). *Big data: The next frontier for innovation, competition, and productivity*. Academic Press.

Maroufkhani, P., Tseng, M. L., Iranmanesh, M., Ismail, W. K. W., & Khalid, H. (2020). Big data analytics adoption: Determinants and performances among small to medium-sized enterprises. *International Journal of Information Management, Elsevier, 54*(February), 102190. doi:10.1016/j.ijinfomgt.2020.102190

Martel, A., & Klibi, W. (2016). *Designing value-creating supply chain networks*. Springer. doi:10.1007/978-3-319-28146-9

McBee, M. P., & Wilcox, C. (2020). Blockchain Technology: Principles and Applications in Medical Imaging. In Journal of Digital Imaging (Vol. 33, Issue 3). doi:10.100710278-019-00310-3

Melnyk, S. A., Sroufe, R. P., & Calantone, R. (2003). Assessing the impact of environmental management systems on corporate and environmental performance. *Journal of Operations Management*, *21*(3), 329–351. doi:10.1016/S0272-6963(02)00109-2

Meshkat, B., Cowman, S., Gethin, G., Ryan, K., Wiley, M., Brick, A., Clarke, E., & Mulligan, E. (2014). Using an e-Delphi technique in achieving consensus across disciplines for developing best practice in day surgery in Ireland. *Journal of Hospital Administration*, *3*(4), 1. Advance online publication. doi:10.5430/jha.v3n4p1

Mikalef, P., Boura, M., Lekakos, G., & Krogstie, J. (2019). Big data analytics and firm performance: Findings from a mixed-method approach. *Journal of Business Research*, *98*, 261–276. doi:10.1016/j.jbusres.2019.01.044

Moerdyk, A. (2009). *The principles and practice of psychological assessment*. Van Schaik.

Mohammadzadeh, A. K., Ghafoori, S., Mohammadian, A., Mohammadkazemi, R., Mahbanooei, B., & Ghasemi, R. (2018). A Fuzzy Analytic Network Process (FANP) approach for prioritizing internet of things challenges in Iran. *Technology in Society, Elsevier Ltd*, *53*, 124–134. doi:10.1016/j.techsoc.2018.01.007

Moktadir, A., Mithun, S., Kumar, S., & Shukla, N. (2018). Barriers to big data analytics in manufacturing supply chains : A case study from Bangladesh. *Computers & Industrial Engineering*, 1–13.

Mortenson, M., Doherty, N. F., & Robinson, S. (2015). Operational Research from Taylorism to Terabytes: A Research Agenda for the Analytics Age. *European Journal of Operational Research*, *241*(3), 583–595. doi:10.1016/j.ejor.2014.08.029

Mosterman, P. J., & Zander, J. (2016). Industry 4.0 as a Cyber-Physical System study. *Software & Systems Modeling*, *15*(1), 17–29. doi:10.100710270-015-0493-x

Mubarik, M., Naghavi, N., Mubarik, M., Kusi-Sarpong, S., Khan, S. A., Zaman, S. I., & Kazmi, S. H. A. (2021). Resilience and cleaner production in industry 4.0: Role of supply chain mapping and visibility. *Journal of Cleaner Production*, *292*, 126058. doi:10.1016/j.jclepro.2021.126058

Nabbout, M. (2020). *Employees in GCC May Soon Be Asked to Work Remotely Due to COVID-19*. StepFeed. stepfeed.com/employees-in-gcc-may-soon-be-asked-to-work-remotely-due-to-covid-19-8322.

Nakamoto, S. (2008). *Bitcoin: A Peer-To-Peer Electronic Cash System*. https://bitcoin.org/bitcoin.pdf

Nakrošienė, A., Bučiūnienė, I., & Goštautaitė, B. (2019). Working from home: Characteristics and outcomes of telework. *International Journal of Manpower*.

Nam, D. W., Kang, D., & Kim, S. H. (2015). Process of big data analysis adoption: Defining big data as a new IS innovation and examining factors affecting the process. *Proceedings of the Annual Hawaii International Conference on System Sciences, 2015-March*, 4792–4801. 10.1109/HICSS.2015.569

Nam, K., Dutt, C. S., Chathoth, P., Daghfous, A., & Khan, M. S. (2020). The adoption of artificial intelligence and robotics in the hotel industry: Prospects and challenges. *Electronic Markets*. Advance online publication. doi:10.100712525-020-00442-3

Narikimilli, N. R. S., Kumar, A., Antu, A. D., & Xie, B. (2020). Blockchain Applications in Healthcare– A Review and Future Perspective. In Z. Chen, L. Cui, B. Palanisamy, & L. J. Zhang (Eds.), Lecture Notes in Computer Science: Vol. 12404. *Blockchain – ICBC 2020. ICBC 2020*. Springer. doi:10.1007/978-3-030-59638-5_14

Narmetta, M., & Krishnan, S. (2020). Competitiveness, Change Readiness, and ICT Development: An Empirical Investigation of TOE Framework for Poverty Alleviation. *IFIP Advances in Information and Communication Technology*, *618*, 638–649. doi:10.1007/978-3-030-64861-9_55

Nasrollahi, M., Ramezani, J., Sadraei, M., & Research, S. (2020). The Impact of Big Data Adoption on SMEs Performance. *Elsevier*, 1–12. doi:10.21203/rs.3.rs-66047/v1

Neuhofer, B., Buhalis, D., & Ladkin, A. (2015). Smart technologies for personalized experiences: A case study in the hospitality domain. *Electronic Markets*, *25*(3), 243–254. doi:10.100712525-015-0182-1

Ngah, A. H., Zainuddin, Y., & Thurasamy, R. (2017). Applying the TOE framework in the Halal warehouse adoption study. *Journal of Islamic Accounting and Business Research*, *8*(2), 161–181. doi:10.1108/JIABR-04-2014-0014

Nofer, M., Gomber, P., Hinz, O., & Schiereck, D. (2017). Blockchain. *Business & Information Systems Engineering*, *59*(3), 183–187. doi:10.100712599-017-0467-3

Noshina Qamar, A., & Muhammad, A. (2020). Farrukh A. (2020). Blockchain and Smart Healthcare Security: A Survey. *Procedia Computer Science*, *175*, 615–620. doi:10.1016/j.procs.2020.07.089

Novikov, P. (2020). Impact of COVID-19 emergency transition to online learning onto the international students' perceptions of educational process at Russian university. *Journal of Social Studies Education Research*, *11*(3), 270–302.

Nunnally, J. C., & Bernstein, I. H. (1994). *Psychometric theory* (3rd ed.). McGraw-Hill.

Omar, N., Munir, Z. A., Kaizan, F. Q., Noranee, S., & Malik, S. A. (2019). The Impact of Employees Motivation, Perceived Usefulness and Perceived Ease of Use on Employee Performance among Selected Public Sector Employees. *International Journal of Academic Research in Business & Social Sciences*, *9*(6). Advance online publication. doi:10.6007/IJARBSS/v9-i6/6074

Orji, I. J., Kusi-Sarpong, S., Huang, S., & Vazquez-Brust, D. (2020). Evaluating the factors that influence blockchain adoption in the freight logistics industry. *Transportation Research Part E, Logistics and Transportation Review*, *141*, 102025. Advance online publication. doi:10.1016/j.tre.2020.102025

Orzechowski, E. (2019). The Traceability of Bulk Food Products. In J. McEntire & A. Kennedy (Eds.), *Food Traceability. Food Microbiology and Food Safety*. Springer. doi:10.1007/978-3-030-10902-8_5

Osaba, E., Yang, X. Jr, Fister, I. Jr, Del Ser, J., Lopez-Garcia, P., & Vazquez-Pardavila, A. J. (2018). A discrete and improved bat algorithm for solving a medical goods distribution problem with pharmacological waste collection. *Swarm and Evolutionary Computation*, *44*, 273–286. doi:10.1016/j.swevo.2018.04.001

Ouchi, W., & Williamson, O. E. (1977). Markets and Hierarchies: Analysis and Antitrust Implications. *Administrative Science Quarterly*, *22*(3), 540. doi:10.2307/2392191

Oztemel, E., & Gursev, S. (2020). Literature Review of Industry 4.0 and Related Technologies. *Journal of Intelligent Manufacturing*, *31*(1), 127–182. doi:10.100710845-018-1433-8

Pakistan Implements Urgent Measures to Mitigate Impact of Coronavirus on Economy. (2020). gulfnews.com/business/saudi-arabia-implements-urgent-measures-to-mitigate-impact-of-coronavirus-on-economy-1.1584723908834

Park, J.-H., Kim, M.-K., & Paik, J.-H. (2015). The Factors of Technology, Organization and Environment Influencing the Adoption and Usage of Big Data in Korean Firms. *26th European Regional Conference of the International Telecommunications Society (ITS): "What Next for European Telecommunications?* www.econstor.eu

Parker, L. (2016). *Block chain tech companies focus on the $40 trillion Supply Chain market.* Brave New Coin. Available: https://bravenewcoin.com/news/blockchain-tech-companies-focus-on-the-40-trillion-supply-chainmarket/

Park, K. O. (2020). A study on sustainable usage intention of blockchain in the big data era: Logistics and supply chain management companies. *Sustainability (Switzerland)*, *12*(24), 10670. Advance online publication. doi:10.3390u122410670

Patel, A. (2018). *The Top Advantages of Blockchain For Businesses.* Smartdatacollective.Com.

Pateli, A., Mylonas, N., & Spyrou, A. (2020). Organizational Adoption of Social Media in the Hospitality Industry: An Integrated Approach Based on DIT and TOE Frameworks. *Sustainability*, *12*(17), 7132. doi:10.3390u12177132

Pawar, M. K., Patil, P., & Hiremath, P. S. (2021). A Study on Blockchain Scalability. In M. Tuba, S. Akashe, & A. Joshi (Eds.), *ICT Systems and Sustainability. Advances in Intelligent Systems and Computing* (Vol. 1270). Springer. doi:10.1007/978-981-15-8289-9_29

Perunović, Z. (2007). Outsourcing Process and Theories. *POMS 18th Annual Conference*, *8*(5), 35.

Petersson, E., & Baur, K. (2018). *Impacts of Blockchain Technology on Supply Chain Collaboration-A study on the use of blockchain technology in supply chains and how it influences supply chain collaboration* [Master Thesis]. Jönköping University.

Pettit, T. J., Croxton, K. L., & Fiksel, J. (2013). Ensuring supply chain resilience: Development and implementation of an assessment tool. *Journal of Business Logistics*, *34*(1), 46–76. doi:10.1111/jbl.12009

Pilkington, M. (2016). Blockchain Technology: Principles and Applications. In F. X. Olleros & M. Zhegu (Eds.), *Research Handbook on Digital Transformations* (pp. 225–253). doi:10.4337/9781784717766.00019

Piprani, A. Z., Mohezar, S., & Jaafar, N. I. (2020). Supply chain integration and supply chain performance: The mediating role of supply chain resilience. *International Journal of Supply Chain Management*, *9*(3), 58–73.

Podsakoff, P. M., MacKenzie, S. B., Lee, J. Y., & Podsakoff, N. P. (2003). Common method biases in behavioral research: A critical review of the literature and recommended remedies. *The Journal of Applied Psychology*, *88*(5), 879–903. doi:10.1037/0021-9010.88.5.879 PMID:14516251

Porter, M. E., & Heppelmann, J. E. (2015). Wie smarte Produkte den Wettbewerb verän-dern. Harvard Business Manager, 12, 1.

Pournader, M., Shi, Y., Seuring, S., & Koh, S. C. L. (2020). Blockchain applications in supply chains, transport and logistics: A systematic review of the literature. *International Journal of Production Research*, *58*(7), 2063–2081. Advance online publication. doi:10.1080/00207543.2019.1650976

Priore, P., Ponte, B., Rosillo, R., & de la Fuente, D. (2019). Applying machine learning to the dynamic selection of replenishment policies in fast-changing supply chain environments. *International Journal of Production Research, Taylor and Francis Ltd.*, *57*(11), 3663–3677. doi:10.1080/00207543.2018.1552369

Prisco, G. (2016). Walmart Testing Block chain Technology for Supply Chain Management. *Bitcoin Magazine.* Available at: https://bitcoinmagazine.com/articles/

Priyadarshinee, P., Raut, R. D., Jha, M. K., & Gardas, B. B. (2017). Understanding and predicting the determinants of cloud computing adoption: A two staged hybrid SEM - Neural networks approach. *Computers in Human Behavior*, *76*, 341–362. doi:10.1016/j.chb.2017.07.027

Priyadarshinee, P., Raut, R. D., Jha, M. K., & Kamble, S. S. (2017). A cloud computing adoption in Indian SMEs: Scale development and validation approach. *The Journal of High Technology Management Research*, *28*(2), 221–245. doi:10.1016/j.hitech.2017.10.010

Raj, A., Dwivedi, G., Sharma, A., Beatriz, A., & De Sousa, L. (2019). Barriers to the adoption of industry 4. 0 technologies in the manufacturing sector : An inter-country comparative perspective. *International Journal of Production Economics*, *224*, 107546. doi:10.1016/j.ijpe.2019.107546

Ramamurthy, S. (2016). *Leveraging block chain to improve foodsupply chain traceability.* IBM. Available at: https://techcrunch.com/2016/11/24/

Ramanathan, R., Philpott, E., Duan, Y., & Cao, G. (2017). Adoption of business analytics and impact on performance: A qualitative study in retail. *Production Planning and Control, Taylor and Francis Ltd.*, *28*(11–12), 985–998. doi:10.1080/09537287.2017.1336800

Ramaswamy, H. G. H. D. R. (2015). Journal of Enterprise Information Management Understanding determinants of cloud computing adoption using an integrated TAM-TOE model. *Journal of Enterprise Information Management*, *28*(1), 107–130. doi:10.1108/JEIM-08-2013-0065

Ranjan, J., & Foropon, C. (2021). Big Data Analytics in Building the Competitive Intelligence of Organizations. *International Journal of Information Management*, *56*, 102231. doi:10.1016/j.ijinfomgt.2020.102231

Rao, P., & Holt, D. (2005). Do green supply chains lead to competitiveness and economic performance? *International Journal of Operations & Production Management*, *25*(9), 898–916. doi:10.1108/01443570510613956

Rao, T. R., Mitra, P., Bhatt, R., & Goswami, A. (2019). The big data system, components, tools, and technologies: A survey. *Knowledge and Information Systems*, *60*(3), 1165–1245.

Rehman Khan, S. A., Yu, Z., Sarwat, S., Godil, D. I., Amin, S., & Shujaat, S. (2021). The role of block chain technology in circular economy practices to improve organisational performance. *International Journal of Logistics Research and Applications*, 1-18.

Rehman Khan, S. A., & Yu, Z. (2020). Assessing the eco-environmental performance: An PLS-SEM approach with practice-based view. *International Journal of Logistics Research and Applications*, *0*(0), 1–19. doi:10.1080/13675567.2020.1754773

Reshma, P. S., Aithal, P. S., & Acharya, S. (2015). An empirical study on Working from Home: A popular e-business model. *International Journal of Advance & Innovative Research*, *2*(2).

Revilla, E., Saenz, M. J., Revilla, E., & Saenz, M. J. (2017). The impact of risk management on the frequency of supply chain disruptions A configurational approach. *International Journal of Operations & Production Management*, *37*(5), 557–576. doi:10.1108/IJOPM-03-2016-0129

Robinson, A. (2016). *What is Block Chain Technology, and What Is Its Potential Impact on the Supply Chain?* Cerasis. Available at: http://cerasis.com/2016/06/29/blockchain-technology/

Rodrigue, J.-P. (2014). *The Geography of Transport Systems: Transportation and the Urban Form.* Routledge. https://people.hofstra.edu/geotrans/eng/ch6en/conc6en/ch6c1en.html

Rogers, E. M. (2010). *Diffusion of innovations.* Simon and Schuster.

Saha, A., Amin, R., Kunal, S., Vollala, S., & Dwivedi, S. (2019). Review on "Blockchain technology based medical healthcare system with privacy issues". *Security and Privacy*, *2*(5). Advance online publication. doi:10.1002py2.83

Saleem, Y., Crespi, N., Rehmani, M., & Copeland, R. (2019). Internet of things-aided smart grid: Technologies, architectures, applications, prototypes, and future research directions. *IEEE Access: Practical Innovations, Open Solutions*, *7*, 62962–63003. doi:10.1109/ACCESS.2019.2913984

Salleh, K. A., & Janczewski, L. (2016). Technological, Organizational and Environmental Security and Privacy Issues of Big Data: A Literature Review. *Procedia Computer Science*, *100*, 19–28. doi:10.1016/j.procs.2016.09.119

Sanders, N. R. (2016). How to use big data to drive your supply chain. *California Management Review*, *58*(3), 26–48. doi:10.1525/cmr.2016.58.3.26

Sbeih, M. (2020). *Gulf Employees Look to Governments for COVID-19 Guidance*. APCO Worldwide. apcoworldwide.com/blog/gulf-employees-look-to-governments-for-covid-19-guidance/

Schoenherr, T. (2010). Outsourcing decisions in global supply chains: An exploratory multi-country survey. *International Journal of Production Research*, *48*(2), 343–378. doi:10.1080/00207540903174908

Schulte, S., Sigwart, M., Frauenthaler, P., & Borkowski, M. (2019). Towards Blockchain Interoperability. In *Lecture Notes in Business Information Processing* (Vol. 361). Springer. doi:10.1007/978-3-030-30429-4_1

Scur, G., & Barbosa, M. E. (2017). Green supply chain management practices: Multiple case studies in the Brazilian home appliance industry. *Journal of Cleaner Production*, *141*, 1293–1302. doi:10.1016/j.jclepro.2016.09.158

Seddon, P. B., Constantinidis, D., Tamm, T., & Dod, H. (2017). How does business analytics contribute to business value? *Information Systems Journal*, *27*(3), 237–269. doi:10.1111/isj.12101

Senyo, P. K., Effah, J., & Addae, E. (2016). Preliminary insight into cloud computing adoption in a developing country. *Journal of Enterprise Information Management*, *29*(4), 505–524. doi:10.1108/JEIM-09-2014-0094

Shafiq, A., Ahmed, M.U., & Mahmoodi, F. (2019). Impact of supply chain analytics and customer pressure for ethical conduct on socially responsible practices and performance: An exploratory study. *International Journal of Production Economics*. . doi:10.1016/j.ijpe.2019.107571

Shahbaz, M., Gao, C., Zhai, L. L., Shahzad, F., & Hu, Y. (2019). Investigating the adoption of big data analytics in healthcare: The moderating role of resistance to change. *Journal of Big Data*, *6*(1), 6. doi:10.118640537-019-0170-y

Sharma, M., Kamble, S., Mani, V., Sehrawat, R., Belhadi, A., & Sharma, V. (2021). Industry 4.0 adoption for sustainability in multi-tier manufacturing supply chain in emerging economies. *Journal of Cleaner Production*, *281*, 125013. doi:10.1016/j.jclepro.2020.125013

Shayaa, S., Jaafar, N. I., Bahri, S., Sulaiman, A., Wai, P. S., Chung, Y. W., & Piprani, A. Z. (2018). Sentiment Analysis of Big Data : Methods, Applications, and Open Challenges. *IEEE Access, 6*, 37807–37827. doi:10.1109/ACCESS.2018.2851311

Shin, D. H. (2016). Demystifying big data: Anatomy of big data developmental process. *Telecommunications Policy*, *40*(9), 837–854. doi:10.1016/j.telpol.2015.03.007

Shirer, M., & Goepfert, J. (2018). New IDC Spending Guide Sees Worldwide Blockchain Spending Growing to $9.7 Billion in 2021. *IDC-Analyze the Future*. Available at: https://scholar.google.com/scholar?hl=en&as_sdt=0%2C5&as_ylo=2017&q=%28Goepfert+and+Shirer%2C+2018%29&btnG=

Shrivastava, P., & Guimarães-Costa, N. (2017). Achieving environmental sustainability: The case for multi-layered collaboration across disciplines and players. *Technological Forecasting and Social Change*, *116*, 340–346. doi:10.1016/j.techfore.2016.11.019

Siddiqui, M. S., & Syed, T. A. (2020). A Lightweight Blockchain-based Provenance Message Tracking in IoT. *International Journal of Advanced Computer Science and Applications*, *11*(4), 463–470.

Sigwart, M., Borkowski, M., Peise, M., Schulte, M., & Tai, S. (2020). A secure and extensible blockchain-based data provenance framework for the Internet of Things. *Personal and Ubiquitous Computing*. https://doi.org/10.1007/s00779-020-01417-z

Silverman, B. S. (1999). Technological Resources and the Direction of Corporate Diversification: Toward an Integration of.... *Management Science*, *45*(8), 1109–1124. doi:10.1287/mnsc.45.8.1109

Singh, A., Parizi, R. M., Han, M., Dehghantanha, A., Karimipour, H., & Choo, K. K. R. (2020). Public Blockchains Scalability: An Examination of Sharding and Segregated Witness. In K. K. Choo, A. Dehghantanha, & R. Parizi (Eds.), *Blockchain Cybersecurity, Trust and Privacy. Advances in Information Security* (Vol. 79). Springer. doi:10.1007/978-3-030-38181-3_11

Sinha, A. K., & Anand, A. (2017). Towards fuzzy preference relationship based on decision making approach to access the performance of suppliers in environmental conscious manufacturing domain. *Computers & Industrial Engineering*, *105*, 39–54. doi:10.1016/j.cie.2016.12.033

Skafi, M., Yunis, M. M., & Zekri, A. (2020). Factors influencing SMEs' adoption of cloud computing services in Lebanon: An empirical analysis using TOE and contextual theory. *IEEE Access: Practical Innovations, Open Solutions*, *8*, 79169–79181. doi:10.1109/ACCESS.2020.2987331

Skjoett-Larsen, T. (2000). Third party logistics - From an interorganizational point of view. *International Journal of Physical Distribution & Logistics Management*, *30*(2), 112–127. doi:10.1108/09600030010318838

Smart, E. (2016). *Top 5 Block chain Technology Myths the Mainstream Has Fallen For.* Bit connect. Available at:https://bitconnect.co/bitcoin-news/

Soleimani, H., Seyyed-Esfahani, M., & Kannan, G. (2014). Incorporating risk measures in closed-loop supply chain network design. *International Journal of Production Research*, *52*(6), 1843–1867. doi:10.1080/00207543.2013.849823

Song, W., Chen, Z., Liu, A., Zhu, Q., Zhao, W., Tsai, S.-B., & Lu, H. (2018). A study on green supplier selection in dynamic environment. *Sustainability*, *10*(4), 1226. doi:10.3390u10041226

Sony, M. (2019). Green supply chain management practices and digital technology: A qualitative study. In *Technology optimization and change management for successful digital supply chains* (pp. 233–254). IGI Global. doi:10.4018/978-1-5225-7700-3.ch012

Souza, G. C. (2014). Supply chain analytics. *Business Horizons, Elsevier, 57*(5), 595–605. doi:10.1016/j.bushor.2014.06.004

Spraakman, G., & Davidson, R. (1998). Transaction cost economics as a predictor of management accounting practices at the hudson's bay company, 1860 to 1914. *Accounting History, 3*(2), 69–101. doi:10.1177/103237329800300204

Srinivasan, R., & Swink, M. (2018). An Investigation of Visibility and Flexibility as Complements to Supply Chain Analytics: An Organizational Information Processing Theory Perspective. *Production and Operations Management, 27*(10), 1849–1867. doi:10.1111/poms.12746

Stanger, N. (2017). *View of How Do Saudi Youth Engage with Social Media? | First Monday.* firstmonday.org/article/view/7102/6101

Sultana, M., Hossain, A., Laila, F., Taher, K. A., & Islam, M. N. (2020). Towards developing a secure medical image sharing system based on zero trust principles and blockchain technology. *BMC Medical Informatics and Decision Making, 20*(1), 256. Advance online publication. doi:10.118612911-020-01275-y PMID:33028318

Sun, S., Cegielski, C. G., Jia, L., & Hall, D. J. (2018). Understanding the Factors Affecting the Organizational Adoption of Big Data. In Journal of Computer Information Systems (Vol. 58, Issue 3, pp. 193–203). Taylor and Francis Inc. doi:10.1080/08874417.2016.1222891

Sun, Y., Li, X., Lv, F., & Hu, B. (2021). Research on Logistics Information Blockchain Data Query Algorithm Based on Searchable Encryption. *IEEE Access: Practical Innovations, Open Solutions, 9*, 20968–20976. Advance online publication. doi:10.1109/ACCESS.2021.3054557

Swan, M. (2015). Blockchain. O'Reilly Media.

Tabesh, P., Mousavidin, E., & Hasani, S. (2019). Implementing big data strategies: A managerial perspective. *Business Horizons, 62*(3), 347–358. doi:10.1016/j.bushor.2019.02.001

Talatappeh, S. S., & Lakzi, A. (2019). Developing a model for investigating the impact of cloud-based systems on green supply chain management. *Journal of Engineering, Design and Technology.*

Talwar, S., Kaur, P., Fosso Wamba, S., & Dhir, A. (2021). Big Data in operations and supply chain management: A systematic literature review and future research agenda. *International Journal of Production Research, Taylor and Francis Ltd., 59*(11), 3509–3534. doi:10.1080/00207543.2020.1868599

Tandon, A., Dhir, A., Islam, A. K. M. N., & Mäntymäki, M. (2020). Blockchain in healthcare: A systematic literature review, synthesizing framework and future research agenda. *Computers in Industry, 122*, 103290. doi:10.1016/j.compind.2020.103290

Tanveer, M., & Karim, D. (2018). Higher Education Institutions and the Performance Management. *Library Philosophy and Practice (e-journal), 2183.* https://digitalcommons.unl.edu/libphilprac/2183

Tanveer, M., Hassan, S., & Bhaumik, A. (2020). Covid-19 quarantine and consumer behavior that change the trends of business sustainability & development. *Academy of Strategic Management Journal, 19*(4).

Tanveer, M., Kaur, H., Thomas, G., Mahmood, H., Paruthi, M., & Yu, Z. (2021). Mobile Phone Buying Decisions among Young Adults: An Empirical Study of Influencing Factors. *Sustainability, 13*(19), 10705. doi:10.3390/su131910705

Tanveer, M., Bhaumik, A., Hassan, S., & Ul Haq, I. (2020). COVID-19 pandemic, outbreak educational sector and students online learning in Pakistan. *Journal of Entrepreneurship Education, 23*(3).

Tanveer, M., & Hassan, S. (2020). The role of new and creative ideas in developing industries of education, software and manufacturing in Pakistan. *Journal of Entrepreneurship Education, 23*(3).

Tao, F., Qi, Q., Liu, A., & Kusiak, A. (2018). Data-driven smart manufacturing. *Journal of Manufacturing Systems, 48*, 157–169. doi:10.1016/j.jmsy.2018.01.006

Tapscott, D., & Tapscott, A. (2016). *How the Technology Behind Bitcoin Is Changing Money, Business, and the World.* Portfolio Penguin.

Tashkandi, A. A., & Al-Jabri, I. (2015). Cloud Computing Adoption by Higher Education Institutions in Saudi Arabia: Analysis Based on TOE. *2015 International Conference on Cloud Computing, ICCC 2015*, 1–8. 10.1109/CLOUDCOMP.2015.7149634

Terzi, S., Nizamas, A., Tzovaras, D., Zacharaki, A., Votis, K., Stamelos, I., & Ioannidis, D. (2019). Transforming the Supply-Chain management and Industry Logistics with Blockchain Smart Contracts. In *PCI '19.* ACM.

Thames, L., & Schaefer, D. (2017). *Industry 4.0: An Overview of Key Benefits.* Technologies, and Challenges. doi:10.1007/978-3-319-50660-9_1

Thoben, K.-D., Wiesner, S., & Wuest, T. (2017). "Industrie 4.0" and smart manufacturing-a review of research issues and application examples. *International Journal of Automotive Technology, 11*(1), 4–16.

Tian, F. (2018). *An information System for Food Safety Monitoring in Supply Chains based on HACCP, Blockchain and Internet of Things* [PhD Thesis]. WU Vienna University of Economics and Business.

Tian, F. (2016). *An agri-food supply chain traceability system for China based on RFID & block chain technology. In 2016 13th International Conference on Service Systems and Service Management.* ICSSSM. Available https://ieeexplore.ieee.org/abstract/document/7538424/

Tien, E. L., Ali, N. M., Miskon, S., Ahmad, N., & Abdullah, N. S. (2020). Big data analytics adoption model for malaysian smes. *Advances in Intelligent Systems and Computing*, *1073*, 45–53. doi:10.1007/978-3-030-33582-3_5

Tijan, E., Aksentijević, S., Ivanić, K., & Jardas, M. (2019). Blockchain technology implementation in logistics. *Sustainability (Switzerland)*, *11*(4), 1185. Advance online publication. doi:10.3390u11041185

Tiwari, S., Wee, H.M., & Daryanto, Y. (2018). Big data analytics in supply chain management between 2010 and 2016: Insights to industries. *Computers and Industrial Engineering*, *115*, 319–330.

Trotman, A. (2020). *Social Media's Crucial Role in COVID-19 Lockdown*. www.businesscloud.co.uk/opinion/social-medias-crucial-role-in-covid-19-lockdown

Trunzer, E., Calà, A., Leitão, P., Gepp, M., Kinghorst, J., Lüder, A., Schauerte, H., Reifferscheid, M., & Vogel-Heuser, B. (2019). System architectures for Industrie 4.0 applications. *Prod. Eng. Res. Devel*, *13*(3-4), 247–257. doi:10.100711740-019-00902-6

Tsiulin, S., Reinau, K. H., Hilmola, O.-P., Goryaev, N., & Karam, A. (2020). Blockchain-based applications in shipping and port management: A literature review towards defining key conceptual frameworks. *Review of International Business and Strategy*, *30*(2), 201–224. doi:10.1108/RIBS-04-2019-0051

Uckelmann, D. (2008). *Definition Approach to Smart Logistics*. Wireless Advanced Networking. doi:10.1007/978-3-540-85500-2_28

Umar, M., Khan, S. A. R., Yusoff Yusliza, M., Ali, S., & Yu, Z. (2021). Industry 4.0 and green supply chain practices: An empirical study. *International Journal of Productivity and Performance Management*. Advance online publication. doi:10.1108/IJPPM-12-2020-0633

University, S. (2020). *The Productivity Pitfalls of Working from Home in the Age of COVID-19*. Stanford News. news.stanford.edu/2020/03/30/productivity-pitfalls-working-home-age-covid-19/

Veisi, P. (2019). *Visualising Provenance in a supply chain using Ethereum Blockchain* [Master Thesis]. University of Saskatchewan, Saskatoon.

Verbeemen, E. (2020). *Why Remote Working Will Be the New Normal, Even after COVID-19*.http:/// www.ey.com/en_be/covid-19/why-remote-working-will-be-the-new-normal-even-after-covid-19

Verbeke, A., & Kano, L. (2010). Transaction Cost Economics (TCE) and the family firm. *Entrepreneurship Theory and Practice*, *34*(6), 1173–1182. doi:10.1111/j.1540-6520.2010.00419.x

Verma, S. (2017). The adoption of big data services by manufacturing firms: An empirical investigation in India. *Journal of Information Systems and Technology Management*, *14*(1), 39–68. doi:10.4301/S1807-17752017000100003

Verma, S., & Bhattacharyya, S. S. (2017). Perceived strategic value-based adoption of Big Data Analytics in emerging economy: A qualitative approach for Indian firms. *Journal of Enterprise Information Management, 30*(3), 354–382. doi:10.1108/JEIM-10-2015-0099

Verma, S., Bhattacharyya, S. S., & Kumar, S. (2018). An extension of the technology acceptance model in the big data analytics system implementation environment. *Information Processing & Management, 54*(5), 791–806. doi:10.1016/j.ipm.2018.01.004

Viriyasitavat, W., & Hoonsopon, D. (2019). Blockchain characteristics and consensus in modern business processes. *Journal of Industrial Information Integration, 13*, 32–39. Advance online publication. doi:10.1016/j.jii.2018.07.004

Vogel-Heuser, B., & Hess, D. (2016). Guest Editorial Industry 4.0–Prerequisites and Visions. *IEEE Transactions on Automation Science and Engineering, 13*(2), 411–413. doi:10.1109/TASE.2016.2523639

Voola, R., Casimir, G., Carlson, J., & Anushree Agnihotri, M. (2012). The effects of market orientation, technological opportunism, and e-business adoption on performance: A moderated mediation analysis. *Australasian Marketing Journal, 20*(2), 136–146. doi:10.1016/j.ausmj.2011.10.001

Walker, S. (2020). The Disinformation Landscape and the Lockdown of Social Platforms. *Information, Communication & Society, 22*(11), 1531–1543. doi:10.1080/1369118X.2019.1648536

Waller, M. A., & Fawcett, S. E. (2013). Data science, predictive analytics, and big data: A revolution that will transform supply chain design and management. *Journal of Business Logistics, 34*(2), 77–84.

Wamba, S.F., Dubey, R., Gunasekaran, A., & Akter, S. (2020). The performance effects of big data analytics and supply chain ambidexterity: The moderating effect of environmental dynamism. *International Journal of Production Economics, 222*, 107498.

Wamba, S. F., Akter, S., Edwards, A., Chopin, G., & Gnanzou, D. (2015). How 'big data'can make big impact: Findings from a systematic review and a longitudinal case study. *International Journal of Production Economics, Elsevier, 165*, 234–246. doi:10.1016/j.ijpe.2014.12.031

Wamba, S. F., & Queiroz, M. M. (2020). Blockchain in the operations and supply chain management: Benefits, challenges and future research opportunities. In *International Journal of Information Management* (Vol. 52, p. 102064). Elsevier Ltd. doi:10.1016/j.ijinfomgt.2019.102064

Wang, X., & Xie, Z. (2020). *Research on the Application of Blockchain Technology in Logistics Industry*. doi:10.2991/aebmr.k.200402.032

Wang, G., Gunasekaran, A., Ngai, E. W. T., & Papadopoulos, T. (2016). Big data analytics in logistics and supply chain management : Certain investigations for research and applications. *International Journal of Production Economics, Elsevier, 176*, 98–110. doi:10.1016/j.ijpe.2016.03.014

Wernerfelt, B. (1984). A resource-based view of the firm. *Strategic Management Journal, 5*(2), 171–180. doi:10.1002mj.4250050207

Wilhelm, M., Blome, C., Bhakoo, V., & Operations, A. P.-J. (2016). Sustainability in multi-tier supply chains: Understanding the double agency role of the first-tier supplier. *Journal of Operations Management, 41*(1), 42–60. doi:10.1016/j.jom.2015.11.001

Williams, R. (2015). *How Bitcoin Tech Could Make Supply Chains More Transparent*. Coin Desk. Available: https://www.coindesk.com/how-bitcoins-technology-could-make-supply-chains-more-transparent/

Wong, L.-W., Tan, G. W.-H., Lee, V.-H., Ooi, K.-B., & Sohal, A. (2020). Unearthing the determinants of Blockchain adoption in supply chain management. *International Journal of Production Research, 58*(7), 2100–2123. doi:10.1080/00207543.2020.1730463

Wright, A., & De Filippi, P. (2017). *Decentralized Block Chain Technology and the Rise of Lex Cryptographies*. Available at: https://ssrn.com/abstract=2580664

Wright, L. T., Robin, R., Stone, M., & Aravopoulou, D. E. (2019). Adoption of Big Data Technology for Innovation in B2B Marketing. *Journal of Business-to-Business Marketing, Routledge, 26*(3–4), 281–293. doi:10.1080/1051712X.2019.1611082

Wu, B., & Duan, T. (2019). The advantages of blockchain technology in commercial bank operation and management. *ACM International Conference Proceeding Series*. 10.1145/3340997.3341009

Xu, M., Chen, X., & Kou, G. (2019). A Systematic Review of Blockchain. *Financ Innov, 5*(1), 27. doi:10.118640854-019-0147-z

Yadegaridehkordi, E., Hourmand, M., Nilashi, M., Shuib, L., Ahani, A., & Ibrahim, O. (2018). Influence of big data adoption on manufacturing companies' performance: An integrated DEMATEL-ANFIS approach. *Technological Forecasting and Social Change, 137*, 199–210. doi:10.1016/j.techfore.2018.07.043

Yadegaridehkordi, E., Nilashi, M., Shuib, L., Hairul Nizam Bin Md Nasir, M., Asadi, S., Samad, S., & Fatimah Awang, N. (2020). The impact of big data on firm performance in hotel industry. *Electronic Commerce Research and Applications, 40*, 100921. Advance online publication. doi:10.1016/j.elerap.2019.100921

Yang, F., & Gu, S. (2021). *Industry 4.0, A Revolution that Requires Technology and National strategies*. Complex Intell. Syst. doi:10.100740747-020-00267-9

Yang, J., Ma, X., Crespo, R. G., & Martínez, O. S. (2021). Blockchain for supply chain performance and logistics management. *Applied Stochastic Models in Business and Industry, 37*(3), 429–441. Advance online publication. doi:10.1002/asmb.2577

Yasmin, M., Tatoglu, E., Kilic, H. S., Zaim, S., & Delen, D. (2020). Big data analytics capabilities and firm performance: An integrated MCDM approach. *Journal of Business Research, Elsevier, 114*(March), 1–15. doi:10.1016/j.jbusres.2020.03.028

Yi, H. (2021). A secure logistics model based on blockchain. *Enterprise Information Systems, 15*(7), 1002–1018. Advance online publication. doi:10.1080/17517575.2019.1696988

Yu, W., Jacobs, M. A., Chavez, R., & Feng, M. (2017). The impacts of IT capability and marketing capability on supply chain integration : A resource- based perspective. *International Journal of Production Research, Taylor & Francis, 55*(14), 4196–4211. doi:10.1080/00207543.2016.1275874

Yu, Y., Zhang, M., & Huo, B. (2019). The impact of supply chain quality integration on green supply chain management and environmental performance. *Total Quality Management & Business Excellence, 30*(9–10), 1110–1125. doi:10.1080/14783363.2017.1356684

Yu, Z., Khan, S. A. R., & Liu, Y. (2020). Exploring the Role of Corporate Social Responsibility Practices in Enterprises. *Journal of Advanced Manufacturing Systems, 19*(03), 449–461. doi:10.1142/S0219686720500225

Zachariasz, E. (2010). The European Agency for Safety and Health at Work Informs. *Medycyna Pracy, 61*(4), 489. PMID:20865861

Zailani, S. H. M., Eltayeb, T. K., Hsu, C., & Tan, K. C. (2012). The impact of external institutional drivers and internal strategy on environmental performance. *International Journal of Operations & Production Management.*

Zhao, J. L., Fan, S., & Yan, J. (2016). Overview of business innovations and research opportunities in blockchain and introduction to the special issue. In Financial Innovation (Vol. 2, Issue 1). doi:10.118640854-016-0049-2

Zheng, Z., Xie, S., Dai, H., Chen, X., & Wang, H. (2017). An Overview of Blockchain Technology: Architecture, Consensus, and Future Trends. *Proceedings - 2017 IEEE 6th International Congress on Big Data, BigData Congress 2017.* 10.1109/BigDataCongress.2017.85

Zheng, P., wang, H., Sang, Z., Zhong, R. Y., Liu, Y., Liu, C., Mubarok, K., Yu, S., & Xu, X. (2018). Smart Manufacturing Systems for Industry 4.0: Conceptual Framework, Scenarios, and Future Perspectives. *Frontiers of Mechanical Engineering, 13*(2), 137–150. doi:10.100711465-018-0499-5

Zhou, L., Chong, A. Y. L., & Ngai, W. T. (2015). Supply chain management in the era of the internet of things. *International Journal of Production Economics, 159*, 1–3. doi:10.1016/j.ijpe.2014.11.014

Zhu, Q., & Sarkis, J. (2004). Relationships between operational practices and performance among early adopters of green supply chain management practices in Chinese manufacturing enterprises. *Journal of Operations Management, 22*(3), 265–289. doi:10.1016/j.jom.2004.01.005

Zhu, Q., Sarkis, J., & Lai, K. (2008). Confirmation of a measurement model for green supply chain management practices implementation. *International Journal of Production Economics, 111*(2), 261–273. doi:10.1016/j.ijpe.2006.11.029

Zonnenshain, A., & Kenett, R. (2020). Quality 4.0—The challenging future of quality engineering. *Quality Engineering, 32*(4), 1–13. doi:10.1080/08982112.2019.1706744

Related Readings

To continue IGI Global's long-standing tradition of advancing innovation through emerging research, please find below a compiled list of recommended IGI Global book chapters and journal articles in the area of the technological advancements in circular economy practices, which provide better results for both economic growth and environmental sustainability. These related readings will provide additional information and guidance to further enrich your knowledge and assist you with your own research.

Abdulsalam, Y., Alhuwail, D., & Schneller, E. S. (2020). Adopting Identification Standards in the Medical Device Supply Chain. [IJISSCM]. *International Journal of Information Systems and Supply Chain Management*, *13*(1), 1–14. doi:10.4018/IJISSCM.2020010101

Acar Uğurlu, Y., & Demir Pali, Ç. (2021). Outsourcing of Internal Audit Services Instead of Traditional Internal Audit Units. In Papadakis, S., Garefalakis, A., Lemonakis, C., Chimonaki, C., & Zopounidis, C. (Ed.), *Machine Learning Applications for Accounting Disclosure and Fraud Detection* (pp. 166-184). IGI Global. http://doi:10.4018/978-1-7998-4805-9.ch012

Adıgüzel, F., & Donato, C. (2021). Upcycled vs. Recycled Products by Luxury Brands. In Mosca, F., Casalegno, C., & Gallo, R. (Ed.), *Developing Successful Global Strategies for Marketing Luxury Brands* (pp. 197-212). IGI Global. http://doi:10.4018/978-1-7998-5882-9.ch011

Adiguzel, Z. (2020). Evaluation of the Relationship Between Leadership Characteristics and Motivation and Satisfaction in Health Institutions. In Demir Uslu, Y., Dinçer, H., & Yüksel, S. (Eds.), *Multidimensional Perspectives and Global Analysis of Universal Health Coverage* (pp. 31-68). IGI Global. http://doi:10.4018/978-1-7998-2329-2.ch002

Adiguzel, Z. (2020). Examining the Effects of Strategies, Competition Intelligence, and Risk Culture on Business Performance in International Enterprises. In Dinçer, H., & Yüksel, S. (Eds.), *Handbook of Research on Decision-Making Techniques in Financial Marketing* (pp. 115-144). IGI Global. http://doi:10.4018/978-1-7998-2559-3.ch006

Adiguzel, Z. (2020). Strategic Approach to Business Intelligence and Its Impacts on Organizational Performance. In Hacioglu, U. (Eds.), *Handbook of Research on Strategic Fit and Design in Business Ecosystems* (pp. 289-310). IGI Global. http://doi:10.4018/978-1-7998-1125-1.ch012

Afanador, N., Becerra, E. D., & Andrango, J. C. (2021). The Paradoxes Between Business Performance and Organizational Behavior in Colombian and Ecuadorian Companies. In Perez-Uribe, R., Ocampo-Guzman, D., Moreno-Monsalve, N. A., & Fajardo-Moreno, W. S. (Ed.), *Handbook of Research on Management Techniques and Sustainability Strategies for Handling Disruptive Situations in Corporate Settings* (pp. 396-415). IGI Global. http://doi:10.4018/978-1-7998-8185-8.ch019

Agahi, H., & Gulthawatvichai, S. (2021). Investigating Barriers That May Influence the Implementation and Use of E-HRM Tools in the Organization. In Khan, B. A., Kuofie, M. H., & Suman, S. (Ed.), *Handbook of Research on Future Opportunities for Technology Management Education* (pp. 350-370). IGI Global. http://doi:10.4018/978-1-7998-8327-2.ch021

Agarwal, R. (2020). Application of Utility Mining in Supply Chain Management. In Özbebek Tunç, A., & Aslan, P. (Eds.), *Business Management and Communication Perspectives in Industry 4.0* (pp. 209-225). IGI Global. http://doi:10.4018/978-1-5225-9416-1.ch012

Aggarwal, S., Srivastava, M. K., & Bharadwaj, S. S. (2020). Towards a Definition and Concept of Collaborative Resilience in Supply Chain. [IJISSCM]. *International Journal of Information Systems and Supply Chain Management, 13*(1), 98–117. doi:10.4018/IJISSCM.2020010105

Agrawal, A., & Mukti, S. K. (2020). Knowledge Management & It's Origin, Success Factors, Planning, Tools, Applications, Barriers and Enablers. [IJKM]. *International Journal of Knowledge Management, 16*(1), 43–82. doi:10.4018/IJKM.2020010103

Agrawal, C., & Duggal, T. (2021). A Study of Consumer Switching Behaviour in the Indian Context With Respect to Recycled Products. In Gopalakrishnan, B. N., Duggal, T., & Tewary, T. (Ed.), *Examining the Intersection of Circular Economy, Forestry, and International Trade* (pp. 142-153). IGI Global. http://doi:10.4018/978-1-7998-4990-2.ch012

Ahmad, M. N., Ismail, M. I., Zakaria, N. H., & Redzuan, M. K. (2021). Pertinent Knowledge Storage Processes for Central Repository Design in Domain of Interlocking Institutional Worlds. [IJEIS]. *International Journal of Enterprise Information Systems, 17*(2), 105–124. doi:10.4018/IJEIS.2021040106

Ahmed, H. I., Nasr, A. A., Abdel-Mageid, S. M., & Aslan, H. K. (2021). DADEM. [IJACI]. *International Journal of Ambient Computing and Intelligence, 12*(1), 114–139. doi:10.4018/IJACI.2021010105

Ahmed, R., & Lodhi, K. M. (2021). Do Project Managers' Emotional Leadership Competencies Affect the Success of Public Sector Projects in Pakistan? [IJITPM]. *International Journal of Information Technology Project Management, 12*(2), 83–98. doi:10.4018/IJITPM.2021040105

Ahmed, T., & Sipra, H. F. (2020). Environmental and Health Implications of Plastic Pollution. In Wani, K. A., Ariana, L., & Zuber, S. (Ed.), *Handbook of Research on Environmental and Human Health Impacts of Plastic Pollution* (pp. 38-58). IGI Global. http://doi:10.4018/978-1-5225-9452-9.ch003

Ahmeti, E., & Kruja, A. D. (2020). Challenges and Perspectives of Supply Chain Management in Emerging Markets. In Dwivedi, A., & Alshamrani, M. S. (Ed.), *Leadership Strategies for Global Supply Chain Management in Emerging Markets* (pp. 132-146). IGI Global. http://doi:10.4018/978-1-7998-2867-9.ch006

Akgül, Y., & Tunca, M. Z. (2019). Strategic Orientation and Performance of Istanbul Stock Market Businesses. In Carvalho, J., & Sabino, E. (Ed.), *Strategy and Superior Performance of Micro and Small Businesses in Volatile Economies* (pp. 94-114). IGI Global. http://doi:10.4018/978-1-5225-7888-8.ch007

Akkaya, B., & Tetik, S. (2021). Understanding Strategic Skills of Managers for First-Time Leadership in Industry 4.0. In Guah, M. W. (Ed.), *Handbook of Research on Innate Leadership Characteristics and Examinations of Successful First-Time Leaders* (pp. 367-388). IGI Global. http://doi:10.4018/978-1-7998-7592-5.ch020

Al-Ansari, M. A., & Alshare, K. (2019). The Impact of Technostress Components on the Employees Satisfaction and Perceived Performance. [JGIM]. *Journal of Global Information Management, 27*(3), 65–86. doi:10.4018/JGIM.2019070104

Albadri, F. (2019). The Impact of Strategic Practice Maturity on Arab States' Performance. In Albadri, F., & Nasereddin, Y. A. (Eds.), *Strategic Thinking, Planning, and Management Practice in the Arab World* (pp. 1-29). IGI Global. http://doi:10.4018/978-1-5225-8048-5.ch001

Al-Busaidi, K. A. (2020). Customer Knowledge Acquisition in Omani Organizations. [IJKM]. *International Journal of Knowledge Management, 16*(4), 63–80. doi:10.4018/IJKM.2020100104

AlHashmi, M. H., Khan, M. M., & Ajmal, M. M. (2021). Implementing Sustainable Procurement Strategy in the Oil and Gas Sector. [IJSSMET]. *International Journal of Service Science, Management, Engineering, and Technology, 12*(2), 59–77. doi:10.4018/IJSSMET.2021030104

Alhourani, F., & Saxena, U. (2019). Supplier Selection Under Conditions of Uncertainty. [IJISSCM]. *International Journal of Information Systems and Supply Chain Management, 12*(4), 42–54. doi:10.4018/IJISSCM.2019100103

Ali, A. (2020). Technology-Enabled Marketing and Supply Chain Collaboration. In Dadwal, S. S. (Eds.), *Handbook of Research on Innovations in Technology and Marketing for the Connected Consumer* (pp. 223-240). IGI Global. http://doi:10.4018/978-1-7998-0131-3.ch011

Ali, M., & Edghiem, F. (2021). Sustainable Business and Collaboration Driven by Big Data Analytics Amidst the Emergence of the Remote Work Culture. In Ali, M. (Ed.), *Remote Work and Sustainable Changes for the Future of Global Business* (pp. 15-32). IGI Global. http://doi:10.4018/978-1-7998-7513-0.ch002

Aliyu, M., Murali, M., Gital, A. Y., Boukari, S., Kabir, R., Musa, M. A., Zambuk, F. U., Shawulu, J. C., & Umar, I. M. (2021). A Multi-Tier Architecture for the Management of Supply Chain of Cloud Resources in a Virtualized Cloud Environment. [IJISSCM]. *International Journal of Information Systems and Supply Chain Management, 14*(3), 1–17. doi:10.4018/IJISSCM.2021070101

Alkhalil, A., Abdallah, M. A., Alogali, A., & Aljaloud, A. (2021). Applying Big Data Analytics in Higher Education. [IJICTE]. *International Journal of Information and Communication Technology Education, 17*(3), 29–51. doi:10.4018/IJICTE.20210701.oa3

Alkhuzaim, L., & Sarkis, J. (2020). Emergy Analysis and Supply Chains. In Khan, S. A. (Ed.), *Global Perspectives on Green Business Administration and Sustainable Supply Chain Management* (pp. 72-92). IGI Global. http://doi:10.4018/978-1-7998-2173-1.ch004

Al-Qirim, N., Rouibah, K., Serhani, M. A., Tarhini, A., Khalil, A., Maqableh, M., & Gergely, M. (2019). The Strategic Adoption of Big Data in Organizations. In Sun, Z. (Ed.), *Managerial Perspectives on Intelligent Big Data Analytics* (pp. 43-54). IGI Global. http://doi:10.4018/978-1-5225-7277-0.ch003

Alsadi, A. K., Alaskar, T. H., & Mezghani, K. (2021). Adoption of Big Data Analytics in Supply Chain Management. [IJISSCM]. *International Journal of Information Systems and Supply Chain Management, 14*(2), 88–107. doi:10.4018/IJISSCM.2021040105

Anim-Yeboah, S. (2020). Organizational Transformation in Developing Economies by New and Emerging Information Systems. In Boateng, R. (Eds.), *Handbook of Research on Managing Information Systems in Developing Economies* (pp. 178-208). IGI Global. http://doi:10.4018/978-1-7998-2610-1.ch009

Anlas, S. (2019). Consumer Awareness and Degree of Engagement With Circular Economy Practices. In Akkucuk, U. (Eds.), *Ethical and Sustainable Supply Chain Management in a Global Context* (pp. 112-129). IGI Global. http://doi:10.4018/978-1-5225-8970-9.ch008

Annansingh, F. (2021). Using Big Data Analytics to Assist a Smart City to Prevent Cyber Security Threats. In Annansingh, F. (Eds.), *Examining the Socio-Technical Impact of Smart Cities* (pp. 107-124). IGI Global. http://doi:10.4018/978-1-7998-5326-8.ch005

Ansari, N. S., Deb Roy, A., & Banerjee, S. (2020). Thread of Sustainability. In Shrivastava, A., Jain, G., & Paul, J. (Ed.), *Circular Economy and Re-Commerce in the Fashion Industry* (pp. 80-98). IGI Global. http://doi:10.4018/978-1-7998-2728-3.ch009

April, W. I., & Kadhila, N. (2020). Viability of Entrepreneurship Education for Employability to Meet Industry 4.0 Challenges in the Circular Economy. In Baporikar, N. (Ed.), *Handbook of Research on Entrepreneurship Development and Opportunities in Circular Economy* (pp. 379-396). IGI Global. http://doi:10.4018/978-1-7998-5116-5.ch020

Asiegbu, G. U. (2021). Business Intelligence-Driven Supply Chain Optimization in Emerging Markets. In Umukoro, I. O., & Onuoha, R. O. (Eds.), *Africa's Platforms and the Evolving Sharing Economy* (pp. 121-140). IGI Global. http://doi:10.4018/978-1-7998-3234-8.ch006

Aslan, T., & Akbiyik, A. (2020). The Impact of Circular Economy on the Fashion Industry. In Shrivastava, A., Jain, G., & Paul, J. (Ed.), *Circular Economy and Re-Commerce in the Fashion Industry* (pp. 142-160). IGI Global. http://doi:10.4018/978-1-7998-2728-3.ch012

Astudillo, A. L., Fajardo-Toro, C. H., & Fajardo-Toro, A. J. (2020). Ethical Discussion on Supply Chain and Environment Investments. In Das, R., & Mandal, N. (Ed.), *Interdisciplinary Approaches to Public Policy and Sustainability* (pp. 248-271). IGI Global. http://doi:10.4018/978-1-7998-0315-7.ch012

Aswini Priya, S., Gopal, P. V., Subashini, R., & Velmurugan, G. (2019). Effect of Supply Chain Management Practices on Organizational Performance. In Kumar, M. V., Putnik, G. D., Jayakrishna, K., Pillai, V. M., & Varela, L. (Ed.), *Emerging Applications in Supply Chains for Sustainable Business Development* (pp. 142-159). IGI Global. http://doi:10.4018/978-1-5225-5424-0.ch009

Ata, U. Z., & Ünal, G. (2018). Effects of Sustainable Supply Chain Management on Responsible Investment Through ESG Indicators. In Akkucuk, U. (Ed.), *Handbook of Research on Supply Chain Management for Sustainable Development* (pp. 133-143). IGI Global. http://doi:10.4018/978-1-5225-5757-9.ch008

Atiku, S. O. (2020). Knowledge Management for the Circular Economy. In Baporikar, N. (Eds.), *Handbook of Research on Entrepreneurship Development and Opportunities in Circular Economy* (pp. 520-537). IGI Global. http://doi:10.4018/978-1-7998-5116-5.ch027

Aurelian, I. C., Coman, M. D., Paschia, L., Nicolau, N. L., & Stanescu, S. G. (2020). Sustainable Economic Intelligence. In Oncioiu, I. (Ed.), *Improving Business Performance Through Innovation in the Digital Economy* (pp. 117-143). IGI Global. http://doi:10.4018/978-1-7998-1005-6.ch009

Auškāps, D., Rozentāls, D., & Kravčenko, D. (2021). The Outsourcing Dilemma of SMEs. In Akella, D., Eid, N., & Sabella, A. (Ed.), *Cases on Critical Practices for Modern and Future Human Resources Management* (pp. 143-167). IGI Global. http://doi:10.4018/978-1-7998-5820-1.ch007

Aytan, Y. S., & Sayan, I. (2019). Ethics, Ethical Leadership, and Supply Chain Management. In Akkucuk, U. (Ed.), *Ethical and Sustainable Supply Chain Management in a Global Context* (pp. 99-111). IGI Global. http://doi:10.4018/978-1-5225-8970-9.ch007

Ayvaz, B., & Kuşakcı, A. O. (2019). A Fuzzy Integer Programming Model to Locate Temporary Medical Facilities as Part of Pre-Disaster Management. [IJORIS]. *International Journal of Operations Research and Information Systems, 10*(1), 21–40. doi:10.4018/IJORIS.2019010102

Azizsafaei, M., & Dadd, D. (2020). Sustainable Supply Chain Management in Iranian Manufacturing Companies. [IJoSE]. *International Journal of Strategic Engineering, 3*(2), 37–58. doi:10.4018/IJoSE.2020070103

Balakumar, J., & Mohan, V. (2019). Big Data Analytics in Social Media. In G., D. K. (Ed.), *Machine Learning Techniques for Improved Business Analytics* (pp. 107-124). IGI Global. http://doi:10.4018/978-1-5225-3534-8.ch006

Balios, D. (2021). The Impact of Big Data on Accounting and Auditing. [IJCFA]. *International Journal of Corporate Finance and Accounting*, *8*(1), 1–14. doi:10.4018/IJCFA.2021010101

Bamrara, A. (2018). Critical Success Factors of Logistics Organizations. In Akkucuk, U. (Eds.), *Handbook of Research on Supply Chain Management for Sustainable Development* (pp. 104-114). IGI Global. http://doi:10.4018/978-1-5225-5757-9.ch006

Bangui, H., Ge, M., & Buhnova, B. (2019). A Research Roadmap of Big Data Clustering Algorithms for Future Internet of Things. [IJOCI]. *International Journal of Organizational and Collective Intelligence*, *9*(2), 16–30. doi:10.4018/IJOCI.2019040102

Baporikar, N. (2020). Emotional Intelligence a Critical Factor in Organizational Performance. [IJBSA]. *International Journal of Business Strategy and Automation*, *1*(4), 10–39. doi:10.4018/IJBSA.2020100102

Baporikar, N. (2020). Innovation to Harness Youth Entrepreneurial Potential. [IJEGCC]. *International Journal of Entrepreneurship and Governance in Cognitive Cities*, *1*(2), 24–38. doi:10.4018/IJEGCC.2020070103

Baporikar, N. (2020). Logistics Effectiveness Through Systems Thinking. [IJSDA]. *International Journal of System Dynamics Applications*, *9*(2), 64–79. doi:10.4018/IJSDA.2020040104

Baporikar, N. (2021). Succession Planning for Enhanced Performance in State-Owned Enterprises. [IJSKD]. *International Journal of Sociotechnology and Knowledge Development*, *13*(3), 106–132. doi:10.4018/IJSKD.2021070107

Baporikar, N., & Atshipara, F. (2019). Supply Chain Efficacy in Relief Delivery. [IJAL]. *International Journal of Applied Logistics*, *9*(2), 1–19. doi:10.4018/IJAL.2019070101

Baporikar, N., & Kaloia, D. S. (2020). Supply Chain Management Perspective on Shortages in Drugs Sourcing. [IJAL]. *International Journal of Applied Logistics*, *10*(2), 62–85. doi:10.4018/IJAL.2020070104

Baporikar, N., & Randa, I. O. (2020). Organizational Design for Performance Management in State-Owned Enterprises. [IJSSMET]. *International Journal of Service Science, Management, Engineering, and Technology*, *11*(4), 1–25. doi:10.4018/IJSSMET.2020100101

Baragde, D. B., & Jadhav, A. U. (2020). Circular Economy Model for the E-Waste Management Sector. In Baporikar, N. (Ed.), *Handbook of Research on Entrepreneurship Development and Opportunities in Circular Economy* (pp. 216-230). IGI Global. http://doi:10.4018/978-1-7998-5116-5.ch011

Barahona, H., & Velandia, N. (2021). Keys to a Sustainable International Management Oriented to the Main Global Needs. In Perez-Uribe, R. I., Largacha-Martinez, C., & Ocampo-Guzman, D. (Ed.), *Handbook of Research on International Business and Models for Global Purpose-Driven Companies* (pp. 188-206). IGI Global. http://doi:10.4018/978-1-7998-4909-4.ch010

Baranidharan, B. (2018). Internet of Things (IoT) Technologies, Architecture, Protocols, Security, and Applications. In Raj, P., & Raman, A. (Eds.), *Handbook of Research on Cloud and Fog Computing Infrastructures for Data Science* (pp. 149-174). IGI Global. http://doi:10.4018/978-1-5225-5972-6.ch008

Bareach, H. Y., Malik, W., Sohail, R., Javaid, A., & Jalil, M. N. (2019). Hierarchical Planning Models for Public Healthcare Supply Chains. In Taghipour, A. (Ed.), *Hierarchical Planning and Information Sharing Techniques in Supply Chain Management* (pp. 86-122). IGI Global. http://doi:10.4018/978-1-5225-7299-2.ch003

Barrad, S., & Valverde, R. (2019). Architecture for the Payment of Suppliers in the Supply Chain Through Web Services. [IJOCI]. *International Journal of Organizational and Collective Intelligence*, *9*(4), 18–36. doi:10.4018/IJOCI.2019100102

Barrad, S., & Valverde, R. (2020). The Impact of e-Supply Chain Management Systems on Procurement Operations and Cost Reduction in the Electronics Manufacturing Services Industry. [JMME]. *Journal of Media Management and Entrepreneurship*, *2*(1), 1–27. doi:10.4018/JMME.2020010101

Barrad, S., Gagnon, S., & Valverde, R. (2020). An Analytics Architecture for Procurement. [IJITSA]. *International Journal of Information Technologies and Systems Approach*, *13*(2), 73–98. doi:10.4018/IJITSA.2020070104

Barroso, S., Pinto, F. R., Silva, A., Silva, F. G., Duarte, A. M., & Gil, M. M. (2020). The Circular Economy Solution to Ocean Sustainability. In Rodrigues, S. S., Almeida, P. J., & Almeida, N. M. (Ed.), *Mapping, Managing, and Crafting Sustainable Business Strategies for the Circular Economy* (pp. 139-165). IGI Global. http://doi:10.4018/978-1-5225-9885-5.ch008

Basak, S., Shekhar, S., & Saha, K. (2019). Sustainable Supply Chain Development. In Kumar, M. V., Putnik, G. D., Jayakrishna, K., Pillai, V. M., & Varela, L. (Ed.), *Emerging Applications in Supply Chains for Sustainable Business Development* (pp. 81-102). IGI Global. http://doi:10.4018/978-1-5225-5424-0.ch005

Bathla, D., Awasthi, S., & Singh, K. (2021). Enriching User Experience by Transforming Consumer Data Into Deeper Insights. In Singh, A. (Ed.), *Big Data Analytics for Improved Accuracy, Efficiency, and Decision Making in Digital Marketing* (pp. 1-18). IGI Global. http://doi:10.4018/978-1-7998-7231-3.ch001

Baumeister, F., Barbosa, M. W., & Gomes, R. R. (2020). What Is Required to Be a Data Scientist? [IJHCITP]. *International Journal of Human Capital and Information Technology Professionals*, *11*(4), 21–40. doi:10.4018/IJHCITP.2020100102

Benazeer, S., Verelst, J., & Huysmans, P. (2020). The Concept of Modularity in the Context of IS/IT Project Outsourcing. [IJISMD]. *International Journal of Information System Modeling and Design*, *11*(4), 1–17. doi:10.4018/IJISMD.2020100101

Berezinets, I., Nikolchenko, N., & Zenkevich, N. (2020). Is Collaborative Planning a Determinant of Financial Performance in Supply Chain? [IJISSCM]. *International Journal of Information Systems and Supply Chain Management*, *13*(3), 38–53. doi:10.4018/IJISSCM.2020070103

Bernabei, G., Costantino, F., Palagi, L., Patriarca, R., & Romito, F. (2021). An Integer Black-Box Optimization Model for Repairable Spare Parts Management. [IJISSCM]. *International Journal of Information Systems and Supply Chain Management*, *14*(2), 46–68. doi:10.4018/IJISSCM.2021040103

Bezzina, F., Baldacchino, D., & Cassar, V. (2020). Relating Knowledge Management Enablers, Knowledge Management Processes, and Organizational Effectiveness. [IJKM]. *International Journal of Knowledge Management*, *16*(4), 109–124. doi:10.4018/IJKM.2020100106

Bhadoria, R. S., Sharma, N., & Pandey, M. K. (2020). Demystifying the Power of Blockchain Technology in Supply Chain Management. [IJAEC]. *International Journal of Applied Evolutionary Computation*, *11*(4), 38–53. doi:10.4018/IJAEC.2020100104

Bhandari, V. (2021). Banking and Financial Services Industry in the Wake of Industrial Revolution 4.0. In Ordóñez de Pablos, P., Zhang, X., & Almunawar, M. N. (Eds.), *Handbook of Research on Disruptive Innovation and Digital Transformation in Asia* (pp. 71-82). IGI Global. http://doi:10.4018/978-1-7998-6477-6.ch005

Bhattacharya, M., Ulferts, G. W., & Howard, T. L. (2020). Radio-Frequency Identification Adoption Trends in Retail. [IJSDS]. *International Journal of Strategic Decision Sciences*, *11*(4), 49–64. doi:10.4018/IJSDS.2020100104

Bhattacharya, S., & Bagchi, S. S. (2019). Evaluating Manufacturer's Wholesale Price Policy Under Order Postponement With Buyback Option. [IJSDS]. *International Journal of Strategic Decision Sciences*, *10*(2), 49–69. doi:10.4018/IJSDS.2019040103

Bhattacharyya, S. S., Laik, B., & Jaiswal, R. (2020). Study of Technology-Based Innovations in Supply Chain Management Function of Indian Firms. In Ordoñez de Pablos, P., Zhang, X., & Chui, K. (Ed.), *Handbook of Research on Managerial Practices and Disruptive Innovation in Asia* (pp. 210-226). IGI Global. http://doi:10.4018/978-1-7998-0357-7.ch012

Bica, J., Julião, J., & Gaspar, M. R. (2020). Applicability of Circular Economy in the Hospitality Industry. In Teixeira, S. J., & Ferreira, J. M. (Ed.), *Multilevel Approach to Competitiveness in the Global Tourism Industry* (pp. 290-306). IGI Global. http://doi:10.4018/978-1-7998-0365-2.ch017

Bilir, C. (2019). Supply Chain (SC) Network Optimization. In Vemić, M. (Eds.), *Strategic Optimization of Medium-Sized Enterprises in the Global Market* (pp. 213-237). IGI Global. http://doi:10.4018/978-1-5225-5784-5.ch010

Blayney, P. J., & Sun, Z. (2019). Using Excel and Excel VBA for Preliminary Analysis in Big Data Research. In Sun, Z. (Ed.), *Managerial Perspectives on Intelligent Big Data Analytics* (pp. 110-136). IGI Global. http://doi:10.4018/978-1-5225-7277-0.ch007

Bradač Hojnik, B. (2021). Advancement of Circular Economy. In Enríquez-Díaz, J., Castro-Santos, L., & Puime-Guillén, F. (Eds.), *Financial Management and Risk Analysis Strategies for Business Sustainability* (pp. 194-218). IGI Global. http://doi:10.4018/978-1-7998-7634-2.ch010

Brahami, M., Adjaine, M., Semaoune, K., & Matta, N. (2020). The Influences of Knowledge Management and Customer Relationship Management to Improve Hotels Performance. [IRMJ]. *Information Resources Management Journal, 33*(4), 74–93. doi:10.4018/IRMJ.2020100105

Brkovic, N., & Sorooshian, S. (2021). Motives for the New Disruptive Technologies. In Sandhu, K. (Ed.), *Disruptive Technology and Digital Transformation for Business and Government* (pp. 307-322). IGI Global. http://doi:10.4018/978-1-7998-8583-2.ch016

Broni, F. E., Jr., & Owusu, A. (2020). Blockchain Readiness. In Boateng, R. (Ed.), *Handbook of Research on Managing Information Systems in Developing Economies* (pp. 160-177). IGI Global. http://doi:10.4018/978-1-7998-2610-1.ch008

Burdenko, E. V., & Bykasova, E. (2020). Circular Economy Experience. In Baporikar, N. (Ed.), *Handbook of Research on Entrepreneurship Development and Opportunities in Circular Economy* (pp. 167-194). IGI Global. http://doi:10.4018/978-1-7998-5116-5.ch009

Burrell, D. N., Aridi, A. S., McLester, Q., Shufutinsky, A., Nobles, C., Dawson, M., & Muller, S. R. (2021). Exploring System Thinking Leadership Approaches to the Healthcare Cybersecurity Environment. [IJEACH]. *International Journal of Extreme Automation and Connectivity in Healthcare, 3*(2), 20–32. doi:10.4018/IJEACH.2021070103

Burrell, D. N., Bradley-Swanson, O. T., Wright, J. B., Shockley, T., Brown-Jackson, K. L., Lewis, E. J., Duncan, T., & Mairs-Levy, J. (2021). Exploring the Need for More Women in Leadership Roles in Public Health and Emergency Response Logistics. [IJARPHM]. *International Journal of Applied Research on Public Health Management, 6*(2), 29–48. doi:10.4018/IJARPHM.2021070103

Butt, A. S., Shah, S. H., Noor, S., & Ali, M. (2020). Knowledge Hiding in a Buyer-Supplier Relationship. [IJKM]. *International Journal of Knowledge Management, 16*(2), 18–29. doi:10.4018/IJKM.2020040102

Spataru, C. (2019). *Islands*. IGI Global. http://doi:10.4018/978-1-5225-6002-9.ch006

C., C., & V., S. (2021). Big Data IoT Analytics for Smart Cities With Cloud Computing Technique. In Velayutham, S. (Ed.), *Challenges and Opportunities for the Convergence of IoT, Big Data, and Cloud Computing* (pp. 104-126). IGI Global. http://doi:10.4018/978-1-7998-3111-2.ch007

Cabrilo, S., & Leung, R. (2019). Do Leaders Really Matter in Knowledge Management Practices? Case of Serbian Companies. [IJKM]. *International Journal of Knowledge Management, 15*(4), 94–113. doi:10.4018/IJKM.2019100106

Cacho, J. L., Marques, L., & Nascimento, Á. (2020). Customer-Oriented Global Supply Chains. In Chkoniya, V., Madsen, A. O., & Bukhrashvili, P. (Ed.), *Anthropological Approaches to Understanding Consumption Patterns and Consumer Behavior* (pp. 82-103). IGI Global. http://doi:10.4018/978-1-7998-3115-0.ch005

Calvo-Porral, C. (2020). Creating Value From Garbage. In Andraz, G., Carrasqueira, H., Pereira, R., & Baleiro, R. (Eds.), *Dynamic Strategic Thinking for Improved Competitiveness and Performance* (pp. 114-136). IGI Global. http://doi:10.4018/978-1-7998-4552-2.ch005

Cappellaro, F., Chiarini, R., & Meloni, C. (2020). The Humanification of the Urban Community. [IJUPSC]. *International Journal of Urban Planning and Smart Cities, 1*(1), 35–44. doi:10.4018/IJUPSC.2020010103

Carvalho e Souza, M. O., Dias, A. L., & Sabino, E. M. (2019). Strategic and Process Management. In Carvalho, J., & Sabino, E. (Ed.), *Strategy and Superior Performance of Micro and Small Businesses in Volatile Economies* (pp. 115-130). IGI Global. http://doi:10.4018/978-1-5225-7888-8.ch008

Carvalho, L. C., Moreira, S. B., Dias, R., Rodrigues, S., & Costa, B. (2020). Circular Economy Principles and Their Influence on Attitudes to Consume Green Products in the Fashion Industry. In Rodrigues, S. S., Almeida, P. J., & Almeida, N. M. (Ed.), *Mapping, Managing, and Crafting Sustainable Business Strategies for the Circular Economy* (pp. 248-275). IGI Global. http://doi:10.4018/978-1-5225-9885-5.ch012

Castillo-Zúñiga, I., Luna-Rosas, F. J., Rodríguez-Martínez, L. C., Muñoz-Arteaga, J., López-Veyna, J. I., & Rodríguez-Díaz, M. A. (2020). Internet Data Analysis Methodology for Cyberterrorism Vocabulary Detection, Combining Techniques of Big Data Analytics, NLP and Semantic Web. [IJSWIS]. *International Journal on Semantic Web and Information Systems, 16*(1), 69–86. doi:10.4018/IJSWIS.2020010104

Cavlak, N., & Cop, R. (2021). The Role of Big Data in Digital Marketing. In Saura, J. R. (Ed.), *Advanced Digital Marketing Strategies in a Data-Driven Era* (pp. 16-33). IGI Global. http://doi:10.4018/978-1-7998-8003-5.ch002

Ceruti, F., Gavinelli, L., Di Gregorio, A., & Frey, M. (2020). Redesigning Business Models With Circular Economy. In Nogalski, B., Szpitter, A., Jabłoński, A., & Jabłoński, M. (Ed.), *Networked Business Models in the Circular Economy* (pp. 121-153). IGI Global. http://doi:10.4018/978-1-5225-7850-5.ch006

Chahar, B. (2020). Performance Appraisal Systems and Their Impact on Employee Performance. [IRMJ]. *Information Resources Management Journal, 33*(4), 17–32. doi:10.4018/IRMJ.2020100102

Chand Dhiman, M., & Katou, A. A. (2019). Idiosyncratic Deals and Organizational Performance. In Chand Dhiman, M., & Chauhan, V. (Ed.), *Handbook of Research on International Travel Agency and Tour Operation Management* (pp. 65-80). IGI Global. http://doi:10.4018/978-1-5225-8434-6.ch005

Chandiramani, J., & Nayak, S. (2019). Big Data Analytics and Internet of Things for Urban Transportation. In Dey, N., & Tamane, S. (Ed.), *Big Data Analytics for Smart and Connected Cities* (pp. 244-277). IGI Global. http://doi:10.4018/978-1-5225-6207-8.ch011

Chhabra, S. (2018). Framework for Enhancing Organizational Performance. In Chhabra, S. (Eds.), *Handbook of Research on Civic Engagement and Social Change in Contemporary Society* (pp. 169-182). IGI Global. http://doi:10.4018/978-1-5225-4197-4.ch010

Chotia, V., & Jain, V. (2021). Visualising the Prospective Circular Economy. In Gopalakrishnan, B. N., Duggal, T., & Tewary, T. (Ed.), *Examining the Intersection of Circular Economy, Forestry, and International Trade* (pp. 83-94). IGI Global. http://doi:10.4018/978-1-7998-4990-2.ch007

Chukka, H. G., & Achanta, S. D. (2022). An Automated Geometric Appraisal Model. In Ordóñez de Pablos, P. (Ed.), *Handbook of Research on Developing Circular, Digital, and Green Economies in Asia* (pp. 222-242). IGI Global. http://doi:10.4018/978-1-7998-8678-5.ch013

Coelho, A. (2020). Repair Café Porto. In Rodrigues, S. S., Almeida, P. J., & Almeida, N. M. (Eds.), *Mapping, Managing, and Crafting Sustainable Business Strategies for the Circular Economy* (pp. 302-315). IGI Global. http://doi:10.4018/978-1-5225-9885-5.ch014

Corbera, G. (2020). The Right to Garment. In Margalina, V., & Lavín, J. M. (Eds.), *Management and Inter/Intra Organizational Relationships in the Textile and Apparel Industry* (pp. 348-367). IGI Global. http://doi:10.4018/978-1-7998-1859-5.ch016

Costa, B. J., Rodrigues, S., & Moreno, P. (2020). Circular Economy and Sustainability. In Rodrigues, S. S., Almeida, P. J., & Almeida, N. M. (Ed.), *Mapping, Managing, and Crafting Sustainable Business Strategies for the Circular Economy* (pp. 31-56). IGI Global. http://doi:10.4018/978-1-5225-9885-5.ch003

Crhová, Z., & Matošková, J. (2019). The Link Between Knowledge Sharing and Organizational Performance. [IJKM]. *International Journal of Knowledge Management, 15*(3), 1–23. doi:10.4018/IJKM.2019070101

Cuevas-Vargas, H., Parga-Montoya, N., & Hernández-Castorena, O. (2020). Information and Communication Technologies to Achieve an Optimal Relationship Between Supply Chain Management, Innovation, and Performance. In García-Alcaraz, J. L., Jamil, G. L., Avelar-Sosa, L., & Briones Peñalver, A. J. (Ed.), *Handbook of Research on Industrial Applications for Improved Supply Chain Performance* (pp. 262-284). IGI Global. http://doi:10.4018/978-1-7998-0202-0.ch011

Harper, D. (2021). *Competency Integration*. IGI Global. http://doi:10.4018/978-1-7998-6516-2.ch003

Harper, D. (2021). *Designing Competency Models for Businesses*. IGI Global. http://doi:10.4018/978-1-7998-6516-2.ch004

Harper, D. (2021). *Organizational Leader*. IGI Global. http://doi:10.4018/978-1-7998-6516-2.ch006

Harper, D. (2021). *Popularity of Competency Models*. IGI Global. http://doi:10.4018/978-1-7998-6516-2.ch001

Harper, D. (2021). *The Competent Organization*. IGI Global. http://doi:10.4018/978-1-7998-6516-2.ch002

Sinha, D. (2019). *Introduction to Supply Chain Management and Multimodal Logistics*. IGI Global. http://doi:10.4018/978-1-5225-8298-4.ch001

Dass, P. S., & Chelliah, S. (2019). Organizational Learning and Collective Human Capital Relationship With Firm Performance Among MNEs in the Northern Region of Malaysia. In Cézanne, C., & Saglietto, L. (Ed.), *Global Perspectives on Human Capital-Intensive Firms* (pp. 176-197). IGI Global. http://doi:10.4018/978-1-5225-7426-2.ch008

De Chiara, A., & Iannone, F. (2020). Sustainable Innovation in Fashion Products. In Silvestri, C., Piccarozzi, M., & Aquilani, B. (Ed.), *Customer Satisfaction and Sustainability Initiatives in the Fourth Industrial Revolution* (pp. 125-151). IGI Global. http://doi:10.4018/978-1-7998-1419-1.ch007

del Mar Alonso-Almeida, M., & Rodriguez-Anton, J. M. (2019). Circular Supply Chain and Business Model in Apparel Industry. In Akkucuk, U. (Ed.), *The Circular Economy and Its Implications on Sustainability and the Green Supply Chain* (pp. 66-83). IGI Global. http://doi:10.4018/978-1-5225-8109-3.ch004

Demirdöğen, G., Diren, N. S., & Işık, Z. (2019). Development of a Maturity Framework for Lean Construction. [IJDIBE]. *International Journal of Digital Innovation in the Built Environment*, *8*(1), 1–16. doi:10.4018/IJDIBE.2019010101

Deshmukh, A. (2021). Water Systems in a Circular Economy. In Gopalakrishnan, B. N., Duggal, T., & Tewary, T. (Eds.), *Examining the Intersection of Circular Economy, Forestry, and International Trade* (pp. 195-206). IGI Global. http://doi:10.4018/978-1-7998-4990-2.ch016

Deshpande, M. (2020). Knowledge Management for Entrepreneurship Development in the Circular Economy. In Baporikar, N. (Eds.), *Handbook of Research on Entrepreneurship Development and Opportunities in Circular Economy* (pp. 480-499). IGI Global. http://doi:10.4018/978-1-7998-5116-5.ch025

Devi, K. V., Thakur, S. S., & Singh, S. K. (2021). Assessing the Performances of Vendor Firms by Optimization Technique Industry 4.0 GSC Architectures. [IJSESD]. *International Journal of Social Ecology and Sustainable Development, 12*(3), 1–10. doi:10.4018/IJSESD.2021070101

Dhamdhere, S. N., & Mane, D. (2021). Real-Time Recommendation Engine for Readers. In Dhamdhere, S. N. (Ed.), *Big Data Applications for Improving Library Services* (pp. 165-177). IGI Global. http://doi:10.4018/978-1-7998-3049-8.ch011

Dharwadkar, N. V., Poojara, S. R., & Kannur, A. K. (2021). Risk Analysis of Diabetic Patient Using Map-Reduce and Machine Learning Algorithm. In Patil, B., & Vohra, M. (Ed.), *Handbook of Research on Engineering, Business, and Healthcare Applications of Data Science and Analytics* (pp. 307-329). IGI Global. http://doi:10.4018/978-1-7998-3053-5.ch014

Dias, L. F., & Correia, M. (2020). Big Data Analytics for Intrusion Detection. In Ganapathi, P., & Shanmugapriya, D. (Ed.), *Handbook of Research on Machine and Deep Learning Applications for Cyber Security* (pp. 292-316). IGI Global. http://doi:10.4018/978-1-5225-9611-0.ch014

Dieguez, T. (2020). Operationalization of Circular Economy. In Baporikar, N. (Eds.), *Handbook of Research on Entrepreneurship Development and Opportunities in Circular Economy* (pp. 38-60). IGI Global. http://doi:10.4018/978-1-7998-5116-5.ch003

Dinçer, H., Yüksel, S., & Çetiner, İ. T. (2019). Strategy Selection for Organizational Performance of Turkish Banking Sector With the Integrated Multi-Dimensional Decision-Making Approach. In Doğru, Ç. (Ed.), *Handbook of Research on Contemporary Approaches in Management and Organizational Strategy* (pp. 273-291). IGI Global. http://doi:10.4018/978-1-5225-6301-3.ch014

Doganay, A., & Ergun, H. S. (2019). Collaboration for Sustainability. In Kumar, M. V., Putnik, G. D., Jayakrishna, K., Pillai, V. M., & Varela, L. (Ed.), *Emerging Applications in Supply Chains for Sustainable Business Development* (pp. 58-80). IGI Global. http://doi:10.4018/978-1-5225-5424-0.ch004

Doğru, Ç. (2019). Meta-Analysis of Antecedents and Consequences of Empowering Employees as a Contemporary Management Approach. In Doğru, Ç. (Eds.), *Handbook of Research on Contemporary Approaches in Management and Organizational Strategy* (pp. 1-17). IGI Global. http://doi:10.4018/978-1-5225-6301-3.ch001

Doğru, Ç. (2019). The Effects of Perceived Organizational Support and Leader-Member Exchange on Contextual Performance. In Doğru, Ç. (Eds.), *Handbook of Research on Contemporary Approaches in Management and Organizational Strategy* (pp. 18-35). IGI Global. http://doi:10.4018/978-1-5225-6301-3.ch002

Doğru, Ç. (2021). The Impact of Strategic Orientation and Reverse Logistics Capabilities on Organizational Performance. In Aytekin, G. K., & Doğru, Ç. (Eds.), *Handbook of Research on Recent Perspectives on Management, International Trade, and Logistics* (pp. 282-293). IGI Global. http://doi:10.4018/978-1-7998-5886-7.ch015

Dorsey, M. D., & Raisinghani, M. S. (2019). IT Governance or IT Outsourcing. In Mukherjee, A. B., & Krishna, A. P. (Ed.), *Interdisciplinary Approaches to Information Systems and Software Engineering* (pp. 19-32). IGI Global. http://doi:10.4018/978-1-5225-7784-3.ch002

Duong, L. N., Wang, M., & Radics, R. I. (2021). Understanding Rural Supply Chain Resilience. [IJSKD]. *International Journal of Sociotechnology and Knowledge Development, 13*(1), 8–21. doi:10.4018/IJSKD.2021010102

Durgun, Ö. (2021). Tourism and Economic Growth Nexus. In Castanho, R. A., & Martín Gallardo, J. (Eds.), *Management and Conservation of Mediterranean Environments* (pp. 159-174). IGI Global. http://doi:10.4018/978-1-7998-7391-4.ch010

Dzingirai, M. (2020). Design Thinking Perspective in Entrepreneurship Education. In Baporikar, N. (Eds.), *Handbook of Research on Entrepreneurship Development and Opportunities in Circular Economy* (pp. 397-416). IGI Global. http://doi:10.4018/978-1-7998-5116-5.ch021

Camilleri, E. (2019). *ICT Implementation Considerations for Public Service Delivery in the Digital Era.* IGI Global. http://doi:10.4018/978-1-5225-9647-9.ch010

Ryńska, E. (2020). *Circularity and Cultural Heritage Stock.* IGI Global. http://doi:10.4018/978-1-7998-1886-1.ch004

Ryńska, E. (2020). *Circularity in Modern Cities.* IGI Global. http://doi:10.4018/978-1-7998-1886-1.ch003

Ryńska, E. (2020). *How to Prepare a Circular Brief for a Designer?* IGI Global. http://doi:10.4018/978-1-7998-1886-1.ch005

Ryńska, E. (2020). *Natural Approach to Circularity in Creation of Cities.* IGI Global. http://doi:10.4018/978-1-7998-1886-1.ch001

Edu, S. A., Agoyi, M., & Agozie, D. Q. (2020). Integrating Digital Innovation Capabilities Towards Value Creation. [IJIIT]. *International Journal of Intelligent Information Technologies*, *16*(4), 37–50. doi:10.4018/IJIIT.2020100103

Edvardsson, I. R., & Durst, S. (2020). The Knowledge and Learning Potential of Outsourcing. In Kumar, K., & Davim, J. P. (Ed.), *Methodologies and Outcomes of Engineering and Technological Pedagogy* (pp. 28-49). IGI Global. http://doi:10.4018/978-1-7998-2245-5.ch003

Egender, K., Hodosi, G., & Rusu, L. (2018). How to Build Successful Cloud Computing Relationships. [IJITBAG]. *International Journal of IT/Business Alignment and Governance*, *9*(2), 1–14. doi:10.4018/IJITBAG.2018070101

Elkhereiji, S. A. (2021). Enhancing the Contracting Touch Points Through Innovation. In Shalan, M. A., & Algarni, M. A. (Eds.), *Innovative and Agile Contracting for Digital Transformation and Industry 4.0* (pp. 266-285). IGI Global. http://doi:10.4018/978-1-7998-4501-0.ch014

Enegbuma, W. I., Bamgbade, J. A., Ming, C. P., Ohueri, C. C., Tanko, B. L., Ojoko, E. O., Dodo, Y. A., & Kori, S. (2020). Real-Time Construction Waste Reduction Using Unmanned Aerial Vehicle. In Affam, A. C., & Ezechi, E. H. (Ed.), *Handbook of Research on Resource Management for Pollution and Waste Treatment* (pp. 610-625). IGI Global. http://doi:10.4018/978-1-7998-0369-0.ch025

Ennouri, M. F., & Mezghani, K. (2021). Big Data Management in the Era of FinTech. In Sghari, A., & Mezghani, K. (Ed.), *Influence of FinTech on Management Transformation* (pp. 102-120). IGI Global. http://doi:10.4018/978-1-7998-7110-1.ch005

Ensari, M. S., & Gürsoy, G. (2020). New Strategy and Thinking in Global Business System. In Hacioglu, U. (Ed.), *Handbook of Research on Strategic Fit and Design in Business Ecosystems* (pp. 1-24). IGI Global. http://doi:10.4018/978-1-7998-1125-1.ch001

Ensslin, L., Mussi, C. C., Dutra, A., Ensslin, S. R., & Demetrio, S. N. (2020). Management Support Model for Information Technology Outsourcing. [JGIM]. *Journal of Global Information Management*, *28*(3), 123–147. doi:10.4018/JGIM.2020070107

Erdogan, D. (2020). Transaction Cost Approach to the Outsourcing Decision Problem. In Akansel, I. (Eds.), *Comparative Approaches to Old and New Institutional Economics* (pp. 201-216). IGI Global. http://doi:10.4018/978-1-7998-0333-1.ch012

Ertl, C., Herzfeldt, A., Floerecke, S., & Krcmar, H. (2020). Ensuring the Success of Management Accounting Change in IT Departments of Public Organizations. [IJSSMET]. *International Journal of Service Science, Management, Engineering, and Technology, 11*(1), 142–156. doi:10.4018/IJSSMET.2020010109

Eser, M., & İrak, G. (2020). Analysis of the Barriers to Green Supply Chain Management Implementation. In Akkucuk, U. (Ed.), *Handbook of Research on Sustainable Supply Chain Management for the Global Economy* (pp. 202-218). IGI Global. http://doi:10.4018/978-1-7998-4601-7.ch011

Eskelund, K., Grunfeld, H., & Des, P. (2020). Exploring the Competitiveness of Cambodia as an IT Outsourcing Destination. [JGIM]. *Journal of Global Information Management, 28*(2), 29–51. doi:10.4018/JGIM.2020040102

Espada, A. (2020). Design as a Source of Innovation to Establish Circular Models. In Farinha, L., & Raposo, D. (Eds.), *Handbook of Research on Driving Industrial Competitiveness With Innovative Design Principles* (pp. 205-218). IGI Global. http://doi:10.4018/978-1-7998-3628-5.ch014

Essila, J. C. (2019). The Role of Electronic Supply Chains and ERP Systems in the Realm of E-Commerce. In Essila, J. C. (Eds.), *Managing Operations Throughout Global Supply Chains* (pp. 1-19). IGI Global. http://doi:10.4018/978-1-5225-8157-4.ch001

Estrada, E., & Martínez Vargas, M. P. (2021). Data Science Process for Smart Cities. In Negrón, A. P., & Muñoz, M. (Ed.), *Latin American Women and Research Contributions to the IT Field* (pp. 348-370). IGI Global. http://doi:10.4018/978-1-7998-7552-9.ch016

Ezzati, A., Jamejam, P., & Bhatia, M. S. (2020). Modeling Barriers in Green Procurement using ISM. In Awasthi, A., & Grzybowska, K. (Ed.), *Handbook of Research on Interdisciplinary Approaches to Decision Making for Sustainable Supply Chains* (pp. 164-188). IGI Global. http://doi:10.4018/978-1-5225-9570-0.ch008

Falcone, P. M., & Imbert, E. (2019). Tackling Uncertainty in the Bio-Based Economy. [IJSR]. *International Journal of Standardization Research, 17*(1), 74–84. doi:10.4018/IJSR.2019010105

Fernandes, D., & Machado, C. F. (2021). Green Transformational Leadership as a Redefinition of the Organizational Psychological Contract. In Machado, C., & Davim, J. P. (Ed.), *Advances in Intelligent, Flexible, and Lean Management and Engineering* (pp. 21-50). IGI Global. http://doi:10.4018/978-1-7998-5768-6.ch002

Fernandes, D., & Machado, C. F. (2021). Human Resources Management in the Portuguese Education System. In Machado, C., & Davim, J. P. (Ed.), *Advances in Intelligent, Flexible, and Lean Management and Engineering* (pp. 139-184). IGI Global. http://doi:10.4018/978-1-7998-5768-6.ch006

Fernando, Y., Darun, M. R., Abideen, A. Z., Ibrahim, D. N., Tieman, M., & Mohamad, F. (2021). Adoption of Blockchain Technology to Improve Integrity of Halal Supply Chain Management. In Khosrow-Pour D.B.A., M. (Ed.), *Encyclopedia of Organizational Knowledge, Administration, and Technology* (pp. 2488-2496). IGI Global. http://doi:10.4018/978-1-7998-3473-1.ch172

Fernando, Y., Darun, M. R., Al-haimi, B., Ibrahim, D. N., Tieman, M., & Mohamad, F. (2021). Role of Smart Contracts in Halal Supply Chain Management. In Khosrow-Pour D.B.A., M. (Ed.), *Encyclopedia of Organizational Knowledge, Administration, and Technology* (pp. 2497-2504). IGI Global. http://doi:10.4018/978-1-7998-3473-1.ch173

Fiala, P., & Majovská, R. (2020). Modeling the Design Phase of Sustainable Supply Chains. In Khan, S. A. (Ed.), *Global Perspectives on Green Business Administration and Sustainable Supply Chain Management* (pp. 16-44). IGI Global. http://doi:10.4018/978-1-7998-2173-1.ch002

Filbeck, G., & Zhao, X. (2020). Supply Chain Disruptions. [IJISSCM]. *International Journal of Information Systems and Supply Chain Management, 13*(3), 78–108. doi:10.4018/IJISSCM.2020070105

Francis, R. S., & Alagas, E. N. (2020). Hotel Employees' Psychological Empowerment Influence on Their Organizational Citizenship Behavior Towards Their Job Performance. In Aydin, Ş., Dedeoglu, B. B., & Çoban, Ö. (Ed.), *Organizational Behavior Challenges in the Tourism Industry* (pp. 284-304). IGI Global. http://doi:10.4018/978-1-7998-1474-0.ch016

Fu, J., & Chakpitak, N. (2019). Managing the Knowledge for an E-Tourism Curriculum. In Habib, M. (Ed.), *Advanced Online Education and Training Technologies* (pp. 214-231). IGI Global. http://doi:10.4018/978-1-5225-7010-3.ch013

G. T. M., & B., N. (2021). Opportunities and Implementation of Big Data Management in Academic Libraries. In Dhamdhere, S. N. (Ed.), *Big Data Applications for Improving Library Services* (pp. 35-47). IGI Global. http://doi:10.4018/978-1-7998-3049-8.ch003

G., D., & Karegowda, A. G. (2021). Deep Learning in IoT. In Senthilnathan, K., Shanmugam, B., Goyal, D., Annapoorani, I., & Samikannu, R. (Ed.), *Deep Learning Applications and Intelligent Decision Making in Engineering* (pp. 1-54). IGI Global. http://doi:10.4018/978-1-7998-2108-3.ch001

Gafi, E. G., & Javadian, N. (2018). A System Dynamics Model for Studying the Policies of Improvement of Chicken Industry Supply Chain. [IJSDA]. *International Journal of System Dynamics Applications, 7*(4), 20–37. doi:10.4018/IJSDA.2018100102

Galli, B. J. (2019). Role of Big Data in Continuous Improvement Environments. [IJAL]. *International Journal of Applied Logistics, 9*(1), 53–72. doi:10.4018/IJAL.2019010104

Galli, B. J. (2020). Impact and Role of Motivation Theories in Continuous Improvement Environments. [IJSSMET]. *International Journal of Service Science, Management, Engineering, and Technology, 11*(1), 1–13. doi:10.4018/IJSSMET.2020010101

Ganguly, A., Chatterjee, D., & Talukdar, A. (2019). Knowledge Sharing Barriers Affecting Pharmaceutical Supply Chain Performance. In Nozari, H., & Szmelter, A. (Ed.), *Global Supply Chains in the Pharmaceutical Industry* (pp. 269-291). IGI Global. http://doi:10.4018/978-1-5225-5921-4.ch012

Gao, Y., Wang, M., & Hou, Q. (2019). Supply Chain Buyback Contract Based on the Different Expectations of Market Demand Distribution. [IJISSCM]. *International Journal of Information Systems and Supply Chain Management, 12*(3), 1–20. doi:10.4018/IJISSCM.2019070101

Garg, P. K. (2021). The Internet of Things-Based Technologies. In Kumar, S., Trivedi, M. C., Ranjan, P., & Punhani, A. (Eds.), *Evolution of Software-Defined Networking Foundations for IoT and 5G Mobile Networks* (pp. 37-65). IGI Global. http://doi:10.4018/978-1-7998-4685-7.ch003

Garzilli, F., Mazzarella, C., & Vittiglio, V. (2020). Integrated Approaches for Peri-Urban Wastescapes. [IJUPSC]. *International Journal of Urban Planning and Smart Cities, 1*(2), 43–58. doi:10.4018/IJUPSC.2020070104

Ge, J., He, W., Chen, Z., Liu, C., Peng, J., & Chen, G. (2018). A Fine-Grained Stateful Data Analytics Method Based on Resilient State Table. [IJSSCI]. *International Journal of Software Science and Computational Intelligence, 10*(2), 66–79. doi:10.4018/IJSSCI.2018040105

Gencer, Y. G. (2019). Developments Concerning Supply Chain Management in Global Retailing Business. In Akkucuk, U. (Eds.), *Ethical and Sustainable Supply Chain Management in a Global Context* (pp. 26-41). IGI Global. http://doi:10.4018/978-1-5225-8970-9.ch002

George, A., Schmitz, K., & Storey, V. C. (2020). A Framework for Building Mature Business Intelligence and Analytics in Organizations. [JDM]. *Journal of Database Management, 31*(3), 14–39. doi:10.4018/JDM.2020070102

Gerger, A. (2021). Blockchain Technology in the Automotive Industry. In Mahmood, Z. (Eds.), *Industry Use Cases on Blockchain Technology Applications in IoT and the Financial Sector* (pp. 277-308). IGI Global. http://doi:10.4018/978-1-7998-6650-3.ch012

Ghasabeh, M. S. (2021). Making an Impact Through Information Technology. [IJAMTR]. *International Journal of Applied Management Theory and Research, 3*(2), 14–23. doi:10.4018/IJAMTR.2021070102

Ghenova, S. (2020). Business Process Outsourcing and ICT Connecting With New Markets of ATU Gagauzia. In Idemudia, E. C. (Eds.), *Handbook of Research on IT Applications for Strategic Competitive Advantage and Decision Making* (pp. 202-213). IGI Global. http://doi:10.4018/978-1-7998-3351-2.ch011

Girija, S., & Srivastava, V. (2020). Supply Chain Leadership in Emerging Markets. In Dwivedi, A., & Alshamrani, M. S. (Ed.), *Leadership Strategies for Global Supply Chain Management in Emerging Markets* (pp. 28-53). IGI Global. http://doi:10.4018/978-1-7998-2867-9.ch002

Gobachew, A. M., Kitaw, D., Berhan, E., & Haasis, H. (2021). ABC/XYZ Analysis for Kanban System Implementation in Pharmaceutical Supply Chain. [IJISSCM]. *International Journal of Information Systems and Supply Chain Management, 14*(3), 63–78. doi:10.4018/IJISSCM.2021070104

Goenka, R., Vijayaraghavan, T. A., & Israel, D. (2021). Impact of Supply Chain Human Capability, Responsive Design, and Collaboration on Supply Chain Resilience. [IJSDS]. *International Journal of Strategic Decision Sciences, 12*(1), 37–60. doi:10.4018/IJSDS.2021010103

Gokmen, M. K. (2019). Accounting Perspective for Sustainable Supply Chain Management. In Akkucuk, U. (Eds.), *Ethical and Sustainable Supply Chain Management in a Global Context* (pp. 130-151). IGI Global. http://doi:10.4018/978-1-5225-8970-9.ch009

Gopal, P. V., & Priya, A. (2019). Market Orientation and Supply Chain Performance, Mediating Role of Supply Chain Management Strategy. In Kumar, M. V., Putnik, G. D., Jayakrishna, K., Pillai, V. M., & Varela, L. (Ed.), *Emerging Applications in Supply Chains for Sustainable Business Development* (pp. 160-178). IGI Global. http://doi:10.4018/978-1-5225-5424-0.ch010

Gopalakrishnan, B. N., Jain, A., & Chalon, N. (2021). Analysis of Circular Economy From a Household Perspective in the USA. In Gopalakrishnan, B. N., Duggal, T., & Tewary, T. (Ed.), *Examining the Intersection of Circular Economy, Forestry, and International Trade* (pp. 18-27). IGI Global. http://doi:10.4018/978-1-7998-4990-2.ch002

Goswami, M., Sarma, P., & Kumar, G. (2019). Integrating Enablers of Sustainable Freight Transportation and Perishable Commodity Supply Chain. [IJSDS]. *International Journal of Strategic Decision Sciences, 10*(2), 25–48. doi:10.4018/IJSDS.2019040102

Goundar, S., Bhardwaj, A., Singh, S., Singh, M., & L., G. H. (2021). Big Data and Big Data Analytics. In Goundar, S., & Rayani, P. K. (Ed.), *Applications of Big Data in Large- and Small-Scale Systems* (pp. 1-19). IGI Global. http://doi:10.4018/978-1-7998-6673-2.ch001

Govindarajan, M. (2021). Big Data Mining Algorithms. In Khosrow-Pour D.B.A., M. (Eds.), *Encyclopedia of Information Science and Technology, Fifth Edition* (pp. 768-777). IGI Global. http://doi:10.4018/978-1-7998-3479-3.ch052

Greene, M., Clarke-Hagan, D., & Curran, M. (2020). Achieving Smarter Buildings and More Efficient Facilities Management. [IJDIBE]. *International Journal of Digital Innovation in the Built Environment, 9*(2), 1–16. doi:10.4018/IJDIBE.2020070101

Gunasundari, E. (2019). Best Practices in the Pharmaceutical Supply Chain Management. In Nozari, H., & Szmelter, A. (Eds.), *Global Supply Chains in the Pharmaceutical Industry* (pp. 228-247). IGI Global. http://doi:10.4018/978-1-5225-5921-4.ch010

Güngör, D. Ö. (2019). Industry 4.0 Technologies Used in Project Management. In Bolat, H., & Temur, G. T. (Eds.), *Agile Approaches for Successfully Managing and Executing Projects in the Fourth Industrial Revolution* (pp. 40-63). IGI Global. http://doi:10.4018/978-1-5225-7865-9.ch003

Guoyi, X., Caiquan, D., Yubin, Z., & Yunhui, Z. (2020). Research on Multi-Period Closed-Loop Supply Chain Network Equilibrium Based on Consumers' Preference for Products. [IJISSCM]. *International Journal of Information Systems and Supply Chain Management, 13*(4), 68–94. doi:10.4018/IJISSCM.2020100104

Gupta, M., & Gupta, B. (2019). Survey of Breast Cancer Detection Using Machine Learning Techniques in Big Data. [JCIT]. *Journal of Cases on Information Technology, 21*(3), 80–92. doi:10.4018/JCIT.2019070106

Gürsakal, N., Ozkan, E., Yılmaz, F. M., & Oktay, D. (2020). How Should Data Science Education Be? [IJEOE]. *International Journal of Energy Optimization and Engineering, 9*(2), 25–36. doi:10.4018/IJEOE.2020040103

Gutiérrez, E. V., Zapata, S. C., & Jaén, J. S. (2019). Assessment of Logistics Capabilities Maturity of Home Healthcare Providers. In Gonzalez-Feliu, J., Chong, M., Vargas Florez, J., & Padilla Solis, J. (Ed.), *Handbook of Research on Urban and Humanitarian Logistics* (pp. 121-142). IGI Global. http://doi:10.4018/978-1-5225-8160-4.ch006

Gutiérrez-Diez, M. D., Beltran, J. L., & Arras-Vota, A. M. (2019). Sustainable Balance Scorecard as a CSR Roadmap for SMEs. In Saiz-Álvarez, J. M., & Palma-Ruiz, J. M. (Ed.), *Handbook of Research on Entrepreneurial Leadership and Competitive Strategy in Family Business* (pp. 88-110). IGI Global. http://doi:10.4018/978-1-5225-8012-6.ch005

Hammami, S. M., Ahmed, F., Johny, J., & Sulaiman, M. A. (2021). Impact of Knowledge Capabilities on Organisational Performance in the Private Sector in Oman. [IJKM]. *International Journal of Knowledge Management, 17*(1), 15–32. doi:10.4018/IJKM.2021010102

Hanafizadeh, P., & Zareravasan, A. (2020). A Systematic Literature Review on IT Outsourcing Decision and Future Research Directions. [JGIM]. *Journal of Global Information Management, 28*(2), 160–201. doi:10.4018/JGIM.2020040108

Hanaysha, J. R., Saleh, I., Hussain, S., Lee, K. L., & Abu Bakar, Z. (2021). Determinants of Firm Performance in Automotive Industry. [IJSSMET]. *International Journal of Service Science, Management, Engineering, and Technology, 12*(4), 132–148. doi:10.4018/IJSSMET.2021070108

Hanebeck, H. L. (2019). Strategic Perspectives of the Digital Supply Chain. In Sabri, E. (Eds.), *Technology Optimization and Change Management for Successful Digital Supply Chains* (pp. 1-16). IGI Global. http://doi:10.4018/978-1-5225-7700-3.ch001

Harper, D. S. (2018). Competency-Based Learning for Organizational Managers. In Stevenson, C. N. (Eds.), *Enhancing Education Through Open Degree Programs and Prior Learning Assessment* (pp. 66-84). IGI Global. http://doi:10.4018/978-1-5225-5255-0.ch005

Hasan, I., Islam, M. N., & Chowdhury, M. A. (2020). Do Team Dynamics Influence the Organizations to Be Innovative? In Ordoñez de Pablos, P., Zhang, X., & Chui, K. (Ed.), *Innovative Management and Business Practices in Asia* (pp. 58-76). IGI Global. http://doi:10.4018/978-1-7998-1566-2.ch003

Hernandez, M. K., Howard, C., Livingood, R., & Calongne, C. (2019). Applications of Decision Tree Analytics on Semi-Structured North Atlantic Tropical Cyclone Forecasts. [IJSKD]. *International Journal of Sociotechnology and Knowledge Development, 11*(2), 31–53. doi:10.4018/IJSKD.2019040103

Hervie, D. M., Winful, E. C., & Tsagli, S. K. (2021). Valorization of Plastic Waste in Ghana. [IJSEM]. *International Journal of Sustainable Economies Management, 10*(2), 31–45. doi:10.4018/IJSEM.2021040103

Hillard, A. J. (2021). Management Leadership and Employee Satisfaction. [IJAET]. *International Journal of Adult Education and Technology, 12*(3), 1–14. doi:10.4018/IJAET.2021070101

Hj Abdul Rajak, A. R., Hamdan, S. N., & Matzin, R. K. (2021). Knowledge Sharing Practice in Brunei Darussalam. In Almunawar, M. N., Anshari Ali, M., & Ariff Lim, S. (Ed.), *Handbook of Research on Innovation and Development of E-Commerce and E-Business in ASEAN* (pp. 681-707). IGI Global. http://doi:10.4018/978-1-7998-4984-1.ch033

Holban, I., Căpuşneanu, S., Topor, D. I., Burja, V., & Comănescu, L. E. (2021). Managerial Accounting and Organizational Performance. In Khosrow-Pour D.B.A., M. (Ed.), *Encyclopedia of Organizational Knowledge, Administration, and Technology* (pp. 1-11). IGI Global. http://doi:10.4018/978-1-7998-3473-1.ch001

Honest, N. N., & Patel, A. (2019). Knowledge Management and Business Analytics. In Gyamfi, A., & Williams, I. (Ed.), *Big Data and Knowledge Sharing in Virtual Organizations* (pp. 1-42). IGI Global. http://doi:10.4018/978-1-5225-7519-1.ch001

Hosseingholizadeh, R., El-Farr, H., & Mahdi, S. E. (2019). Optimizing Knowledge-Work Through Personal Knowledge Management. In Habib, M. (Ed.), *Handbook of Research on the Evolution of IT and the Rise of E-Society* (pp. 21-48). IGI Global. http://doi:10.4018/978-1-5225-7214-5.ch002

Hu, Y., & Shan, J. (2020). Supplier-Based Concentration and Inventory Efficiency. [IJISSCM]. *International Journal of Information Systems and Supply Chain Management, 13*(4), 95–113. doi:10.4018/IJISSCM.2020100105

Huda, M., Habib, M. I., Khan, M. Z., & Aziz, A. A. (2021). Critical Comprehensive Study of Big Data Analytics Management. In Khan, B. A., Kuofie, M. H., & Suman, S. (Ed.), *Handbook of Research on Future Opportunities for Technology Management Education* (pp. 235-247). IGI Global. http://doi:10.4018/978-1-7998-8327-2.ch014

Huseynov, F. (2021). Big Data in Business. In Sandhu, K. (Eds.), *Disruptive Technology and Digital Transformation for Business and Government* (pp. 235-249). IGI Global. http://doi:10.4018/978-1-7998-8583-2.ch012

Hussain, M. M., & Beg, M. S. (2019). Using Vehicles as Fog Infrastructures for Transportation Cyber-Physical Systems (T-CPS). [IJSSCI]. *International Journal of Software Science and Computational Intelligence, 11*(1), 47–69. doi:10.4018/IJSSCI.2019010104

Hyttinen, H., Kivijärvi, H. K., & Öörni, A. (2021). Searching Dimensions and Directions for Digital Innovations Within the Insurance Industry. [IJIDE]. *International Journal of Innovation in the Digital Economy, 12*(2), 63–89. doi:10.4018/IJIDE.2021040105

Ibidunni, A. S., Moses, C. L., Adegbuyi, O. A., Oladosun, M., & Olokundun, M. (2018). Empirical Evidence of Organizational Knowledge From a Typological Perspective and Its Linkages With Performance. [IJSKD]. *International Journal of Sociotechnology and Knowledge Development, 10*(4), 45–60. doi:10.4018/IJSKD.2018100103

Ifrim, A. M., Stanciu, A., Gherghina, R., & Duca, I. (2019). Using Integrated Performance Indicator Systems in the Digital Economy. In Oncioiu, I. (Ed.), *Network Security and Its Impact on Business Strategy* (pp. 185-199). IGI Global. http://doi:10.4018/978-1-5225-8455-1.ch011

Ifrim, A. M., Stanciu, A., Sürgün, M. B., & Ungureanu, H. C. (2020). Benchmarking. In Oncioiu, I. (Ed.), *Improving Business Performance Through Innovation in the Digital Economy* (pp. 177-189). IGI Global. http://doi:10.4018/978-1-7998-1005-6.ch012

Igbinakhase, I. (2020). Youth Entrepreneurship in the Circular Economy. In Baporikar, N. (Eds.), *Handbook of Research on Entrepreneurship Development and Opportunities in Circular Economy* (pp. 345-360). IGI Global. http://doi:10.4018/978-1-7998-5116-5.ch018

Igbinakhase, I., & Naidoo, V. (2020). Sustainable Value Chains. In Naidoo, V., & Verma, R. (Ed.), *Green Marketing as a Positive Driver Toward Business Sustainability* (pp. 275-296). IGI Global. http://doi:10.4018/978-1-5225-9558-8.ch011

Ilic, B. S., Djukic, G. P., & Balaban, M. M. (2020). Sustainability of Mandatory Pension Insurance in the Circular Economy. In Baporikar, N. (Ed.), *Handbook of Research on Entrepreneurship Development and Opportunities in Circular Economy* (pp. 125-143). IGI Global. http://doi:10.4018/978-1-7998-5116-5.ch007

Imran, M., & Ambreen, T. (2022). The Influence of Training, Performance Appraisal, and Organizational Support on Employee Service Behavior With Compensation as a Mediator. In Ordóñez de Pablos, P. (Ed.), *Handbook of Research on Developing Circular, Digital, and Green Economies in Asia* (pp. 401-414). IGI Global. http://doi:10.4018/978-1-7998-8678-5.ch020

Indrajit, R. E., Wibawa, B., & Suparman, A. (2021). University 4.0 in Developing Countries. [IJSKD]. *International Journal of Sociotechnology and Knowledge Development, 13*(3), 33–59. doi:10.4018/IJSKD.2021070103

Iqbal, M. C., & Shalij, P. R. (2019). Supply Chain Risk Assessment in the Ornamental Fish Supply Chain. [IJSDA]. *International Journal of System Dynamics Applications, 8*(2), 36–50. doi:10.4018/IJSDA.2019040103

Iranmanesh, H., Keramati, A., & Behmanesh, I. (2019). The Effect of Service Innovation on E-government Performance. [IJISSC]. *International Journal of Information Systems and Social Change, 10*(1), 1–22. doi:10.4018/IJISSC.2019010101

Irina, P. (2020). Open Education in Digital Era With Avatar-Based Control and Estimation. In Mkrttchian, V., Gamidullaeva, L., & Aleshina, E. (Eds.), *Avatar-Based Models, Tools, and Innovation in the Digital Economy* (pp. 225-252). IGI Global. http://doi:10.4018/978-1-7998-1104-6.ch015

Ismayilova, A., & Silvius, G. (2021). Cradle-to-Cradle in Project Management. [IJCEWM]. *International Journal of Circular Economy and Waste Management, 1*(1), 54–80. doi:10.4018/IJCEWM.20210101.oa1

Izhar, T. A., Torabi, T., & Bhatti, M. I. (2019). Key Issues and the Requirements for an Effective Enterprise Decision-Making Using an Ontology-Based GOAL-Framework for Evaluation of the Organizational Goals Achievement. [IJKBO]. *International Journal of Knowledge-Based Organizations, 9*(2), 21–42. doi:10.4018/IJKBO.2019040102

Jabłoński, A. (2020). Robustness in the Business Models of the Organizations Embedded in the Circular Economy. In Nogalski, B., Szpitter, A., Jabłoński, A., & Jabłoński, M. (Eds.), *Networked Business Models in the Circular Economy* (pp. 19-53). IGI Global. http://doi:10.4018/978-1-5225-7850-5.ch002

Jabłoński, M. (2020). The Use of Sustainable Business Model Archetypes in the Design of Circular Business Models in the Digital Economy. In Nogalski, B., Szpitter, A., Jabłoński, A., & Jabłoński, M. (Eds.), *Networked Business Models in the Circular Economy* (pp. 1-18). IGI Global. http://doi:10.4018/978-1-5225-7850-5.ch001

Jakobczak, D. J., & Chatterjee, A. (2021). The Rise of "Big Data" in the Field of Cloud Analytics. In Jakóbczak, D. J. (Ed.), *Analyzing Data Through Probabilistic Modeling in Statistics* (pp. 204-225). IGI Global. http://doi:10.4018/978-1-7998-4706-9.ch008

Jaswal, I. (2021). International Trade in the Realm of the Circular Economy. In Gopalakrishnan, B. N., Duggal, T., & Tewary, T. (Eds.), *Examining the Intersection of Circular Economy, Forestry, and International Trade* (pp. 95-102). IGI Global. http://doi:10.4018/978-1-7998-4990-2.ch008

Jayashree, K., Abirami, R., & Babu, R. (2019). A Collaborative Approach of IoT, Big Data, and Smart City. In Dey, N., & Tamane, S. (Ed.), *Big Data Analytics for Smart and Connected Cities* (pp. 25-37). IGI Global. http://doi:10.4018/978-1-5225-6207-8.ch002

Jones, P., & Bown, R. (2020). Approaches to the Circular Economy. In Kaufmann, H. R., & Panni, M. (Ed.), *Handbook of Research on Contemporary Consumerism* (pp. 73-91). IGI Global. http://doi:10.4018/978-1-5225-8270-0.ch005

Joshi, H., & Chawla, D. (2019). How Knowledge Management Influences Performance? [IJKM]. *International Journal of Knowledge Management, 15*(4), 56–77. doi:10.4018/IJKM.2019100104

Joshi, H., & Chawla, D. (2019). Measuring the Impact of Knowledge Management (KM) on Performance in the Public Sector in India. In Albastaki, Y. A., Al-Alawi, A. I., & Abdulrahman Al-Bassam, S. (Ed.), *Handbook of Research on Implementing Knowledge Management Strategy in the Public Sector* (pp. 438-456). IGI Global. http://doi:10.4018/978-1-5225-9639-4.ch024

Joshi, S., Sharma, M., Kumar, S., & Pant, M. K. (2018). Co-Creation Among Small Scale Tourism Firm. [IJSITA]. *International Journal of Strategic Information Technology and Applications, 9*(4), 1–14. doi:10.4018/IJSITA.2018100101

Junejo, A. Z., Hashmani, M. A., & Alabdulatif, A. A. (2021). Blockchain-Based Transparent and Traceable Halal Food Supply Chain Management Systems. In Ordóñez de Pablos, P., Zhang, X., & Almunawar, M. N. (Ed.), *Handbook of Research on Disruptive Innovation and Digital Transformation in Asia* (pp. 462-490). IGI Global. http://doi:10.4018/978-1-7998-6477-6.ch023

Júnior, H. D., de Andrade, T. P., & Rosinha, A. P. (2020). Sustainable Leadership as a Vector of the Circular Economy. In Akkucuk, U. (Ed.), *Handbook of Research on Creating Sustainable Value in the Global Economy* (pp. 165-180). IGI Global. http://doi:10.4018/978-1-7998-1196-1.ch010

Júnior, N. B., & Faccin, K. (2020). The Circular Economy of Plastics. In Rodrigues, S. S., Almeida, P. J., & Almeida, N. M. (Ed.), *Mapping, Managing, and Crafting Sustainable Business Strategies for the Circular Economy* (pp. 276-301). IGI Global. http://doi:10.4018/978-1-5225-9885-5.ch013

Tamzini, K., & Ayed, T. (2018). *Workplace Arrogance and Its Impact on the Organizational Performance in the Hospitality Industry*. IGI Global. http://doi:10.4018/978-1-5225-5525-4.ch002

Tamzini, K., & Ayed, T. (2018). *Workplace Arrogance and Organizational Performance*. IGI Global. http://doi:10.4018/978-1-5225-5525-4.ch001

K., J., R., A., & P., R. (2019). Challenges and Solutions of Big Data and IoT. In Kaur, G., & Tomar, P. (Ed.), *Handbook of Research on Big Data and the IoT* (pp. 264-272). IGI Global. http://doi:10.4018/978-1-5225-7432-3.ch015

Kabadayi, N. (2021). A Memetic Algorithm for Integrated Production Distribution Problem in a Supply Chain. In Taghipour, A. (Eds.), *Demand Forecasting and Order Planning in Supply Chains and Humanitarian Logistics* (pp. 198-224). IGI Global. http://doi:10.4018/978-1-7998-3805-0.ch007

Kabadayi, N., & Dağ, S. (2020). Fuzzy Logic in Health Services. In Gul, M., Celik, E., Mete, S., & Serin, F. (Ed.), *Computational Intelligence and Soft Computing Applications in Healthcare Management Science* (pp. 121-157). IGI Global. http://doi:10.4018/978-1-7998-2581-4.ch007

Kankaew, K., & Treruttanaset, P. (2021). The Organization Culture Affecting Job Performance of Newly Hired Employees. In Bejaoui, A. (Ed.), *Corporate Leadership and Its Role in Shaping Organizational Culture and Performance* (pp. 129-155). IGI Global. http://doi:10.4018/978-1-5225-8266-3.ch007

Kapoor, N., Jauhari, S., & Maheshwari, D. (2021). Policies for Promoting the Circular Economy in India. In Gopalakrishnan, B. N., Duggal, T., & Tewary, T. (Ed.), *Examining the Intersection of Circular Economy, Forestry, and International Trade* (pp. 68-82). IGI Global. http://doi:10.4018/978-1-7998-4990-2.ch006

Kapoor, N., Jauhari, S., & Maheshwari, D. (2022). Practicing Circular Economy in India. In Ordóñez de Pablos, P. (Ed.), *Handbook of Research on Developing Circular, Digital, and Green Economies in Asia* (pp. 179-196). IGI Global. http://doi:10.4018/978-1-7998-8678-5.ch010

Kaptanoğlu, R. Ö. (2020). Artificial Intelligence in Supply Chain Management. In Ceyhun, G. Ç. (Eds.), *Handbook of Research on the Applications of International Transportation and Logistics for World Trade* (pp. 470-482). IGI Global. http://doi:10.4018/978-1-7998-1397-2.ch025

Karakostas, B. (2021). The Importance of Big Data Metadata in Crisis Management. In Asimakopoulou, E., & Bessis, N. (Eds.), *Data Science Advancements in Pandemic and Outbreak Management* (pp. 62-77). IGI Global. http://doi:10.4018/978-1-7998-6736-4.ch004

Kareem, H. M., Aziz, K. A., Maelah, R., Yunus, Y. M., Alsheikh, A., & Alsheikh, W. (2021). The Influence of Accounting Information Systems, Knowledge Management Capabilities, and Innovation on Organizational Performance in Iraqi SMEs. [IJKM]. *International Journal of Knowledge Management, 17*(2), 72–103. doi:10.4018/IJKM.2021040104

Karmoh Sowah Jr. J., Kırıkkaleli, D., & Yılmaz Genç, S. (2021). Understanding the Concept and Limitations of Circular and Green Economy in the Mediterranean Region. In Castanho, R. A., & Martín Gallardo, J. (Ed.), *Management and Conservation of Mediterranean Environments* (pp. 196-209). IGI Global. http://doi:10.4018/978-1-7998-7391-4.ch012

Kasemsap, K. (2018). Logistics Management and Risk Management. In Brunet-Thornton, R., & Martinez, F. (Eds.), *Analyzing the Impacts of Industry 4.0 in Modern Business Environments* (pp. 100-120). IGI Global. http://doi:10.4018/978-1-5225-3468-6.ch006

Kashyap, R., & Piersson, A. D. (2018). Big Data Challenges and Solutions in the Medical Industries. In Tiwari, V., Thakur, R. S., Tiwari, B., & Gupta, S. (Ed.), *Handbook of Research on Pattern Engineering System Development for Big Data Analytics* (pp. 1-24). IGI Global. http://doi:10.4018/978-1-5225-3870-7.ch001

Kataria, A., Kumar, S., & Pandey, N. (2020). A Retrospective Analysis of the International Journal of Knowledge Management. [IJKM]. *International Journal of Knowledge Management, 16*(4), 1–25. doi:10.4018/IJKM.2020100101

Kaufman, F. D., & Ülkü, M. A. (2018). An Interdisciplinary Inquiry Into Sustainable Supply Chain Management. In Akkucuk, U. (Ed.), *Handbook of Research on Supply Chain Management for Sustainable Development* (pp. 1-17). IGI Global. http://doi:10.4018/978-1-5225-5757-9.ch001

Khan, S. S. (2020). Research on Green Supply Chain Finance Model With Multi-Party Participation. In Khan, S. A. (Eds.), *Global Perspectives on Green Business Administration and Sustainable Supply Chain Management* (pp. 211-219). IGI Global. http://doi:10.4018/978-1-7998-2173-1.ch013

Khanna, T., Nand, P., & Bali, V. (2020). Permissioned Blockchain Model for End-to-End Trackability in Supply Chain Management. [IJeC]. *International Journal of e-Collaboration, 16*(1), 45–58. doi:10.4018/IJeC.2020010104

Khashman, A. M. (2021). Impact of E-HRM Strategies on Organizational Innovation by Knowledge Repository as Mediating Role. In Management Association, I. (Eds.), *Research Anthology on Architectures, Frameworks, and Integration Strategies for Distributed and Cloud Computing* (pp. 2317-2339). IGI Global. http://doi:10.4018/978-1-7998-5339-8.ch113

Khatri, A., Garg, D., & Dangayach, G. S. (2019). Critical Success Factors of Sustainable Manufacturing and Procurement. [IJSESD]. *International Journal of Social Ecology and Sustainable Development, 10*(3), 17–27. doi:10.4018/IJSESD.2019070102

Kılıçarslan, M. (2020). Supply Chain Management in Health Institutions. In Ceyhun, G. Ç. (Eds.), *Handbook of Research on the Applications of International Transportation and Logistics for World Trade* (pp. 415-424). IGI Global. http://doi:10.4018/978-1-7998-1397-2.ch022

Klinčar, A., & Zoroja, J. (2021). Supply Chain Management Supported by E-Invoicing. [IJESMA]. *International Journal of E-Services and Mobile Applications, 13*(2), 43–59. doi:10.4018/IJESMA.2021040103

Kottala, S. Y. (2021). Social Sustainable Supply Chain Practices Evidence From the Indian Manufacturing Sector. [IJSESD]. *International Journal of Social Ecology and Sustainable Development, 12*(2), 73–98. doi:10.4018/IJSESD.2021040105

Kottala, S. Y. (2021). Sustainable Supply Chain Management Practices. [IJSESD]. *International Journal of Social Ecology and Sustainable Development, 12*(3), 47–65. doi:10.4018/IJSESD.2021070104

Kouhizadeh, M., & Sarkis, J. (2020). Blockchain Characteristics and Green Supply Chain Advancement. In Khan, S. A. (Ed.), *Global Perspectives on Green Business Administration and Sustainable Supply Chain Management* (pp. 93-109). IGI Global. http://doi:10.4018/978-1-7998-2173-1.ch005

Krishnamurthy, S., Fudurich, G., & Rao, P. (2019). Circular Economy for India. In Ferreira, A., Marques, R., Azevedo, G., Inácio, H., & Santos, C. (Ed.), *Modernization and Accountability in the Social Economy Sector* (pp. 272-298). IGI Global. http://doi:10.4018/978-1-5225-8482-7.ch015

Kros, J. F., Liao, Y., Kirchoff, J. F., & Zemanek, J. E. Jr. (2019). Traceability in the Supply Chain. [IJAL]. *International Journal of Applied Logistics*, *9*(1), 1–22. doi:10.4018/IJAL.2019010101

Kumar, A., & Kumar, T. V. (2021). View Materialization Over Big Data. [IJDA]. *International Journal of Data Analytics*, *2*(1), 61–85. doi:10.4018/IJDA.2021010103

Kumar, A., & Kushwaha, G. (2018). Humanitarian Logistics. [JITR]. *Journal of Information Technology Research*, *11*(4), 53–71. doi:10.4018/JITR.2018100104

Kumar, A., & Vijay Kumar, T. V. (2021). Multi-Objective Big Data View Materialization Using NSGA-II. [IRMJ]. *Information Resources Management Journal*, *34*(2), 1–28. doi:10.4018/IRMJ.2021040101

Kumar, N. (2019). Towards a Better and Smarter Healthcare and IoT. In Dey, N., & Tamane, S. (Eds.), *Big Data Analytics for Smart and Connected Cities* (pp. 191-228). IGI Global. http://doi:10.4018/978-1-5225-6207-8.ch009

Kumar, N. (2020). Determinants of Purchasing Intention for Re-Commerce in the Fashion Industry. In Shrivastava, A., Jain, G., & Paul, J. (Eds.), *Circular Economy and Re-Commerce in the Fashion Industry* (pp. 10-18). IGI Global. http://doi:10.4018/978-1-7998-2728-3.ch002

Kumar, N., & Mohan, D. (2021). Consumer Perception and Purchase Intention Towards Refurbished Smart Phones. In Ordóñez de Pablos, P., & Lytras, M. D. (Ed.), *Global Challenges and Strategic Disruptors in Asian Businesses and Economies* (pp. 270-284). IGI Global. http://doi:10.4018/978-1-7998-4787-8.ch017

Kumar, R. (2020). E-applications for Managing Trans-Logistics Activities in Sugar Supply Chain in North India. [IJABIM]. *International Journal of Asian Business and Information Management*, *11*(1), 92–106. doi:10.4018/IJABIM.2020010106

Kumar, R. (2020). Supply Chain Manufacturing Practices (SCMP). In Dwivedi, A., & Alshamrani, M. S. (Eds.), *Leadership Strategies for Global Supply Chain Management in Emerging Markets* (pp. 224-243). IGI Global. http://doi:10.4018/978-1-7998-2867-9.ch010

Kumar, R. (2020). Sustainable Supply Chain Management in the Era of Digitialization. In Idemudia, E. C. (Eds.), *Handbook of Research on Social and Organizational Dynamics in the Digital Era* (pp. 446-460). IGI Global. http://doi:10.4018/978-1-5225-8933-4.ch021

Kunjir, A., Shah, J., & Trikha, V. (2021). Descriptive Data Analytics on Dinesafe Data for Food Assessment and Evaluation Using R Programming Language. In Patil, B., & Vohra, M. (Ed.), *Handbook of Research on Engineering, Business, and Healthcare Applications of Data Science and Analytics* (pp. 485-507). IGI Global. http://doi:10.4018/978-1-7998-3053-5.ch025

Kuscu, A. (2019). Green Marketing and Branding. In Akkucuk, U. (Eds.), *The Circular Economy and Its Implications on Sustainability and the Green Supply Chain* (pp. 213-229). IGI Global. http://doi:10.4018/978-1-5225-8109-3.ch012

Kusdi,. (2020). The Effect of Leadership Style Towards Corporate Culture and the Implementation of Green Management and Its Performance. *International Journal of Entrepreneurship and Governance in Cognitive Cities (IJEGCC), 1*(1), 31-46. doi:10.4018/IJEGCC.2020010102

Laallam, A., Kassim, S., Rabiah Adawiah, E., & Saiti, B. (2020). Towards Knowledge-Based Waqf Organizations. In Saiti, B., & Sarea, A. (Ed.), *Challenges and Impacts of Religious Endowments on Global Economics and Finance* (pp. 100-120). IGI Global. http://doi:10.4018/978-1-7998-1245-6.ch006

Laaz, N., Wakil, K., Gotti, S., Gotti, Z., & Mbarki, S. (2021). An Automatic Generation of Domain Ontologies Based on an MDA Approach to Support Big Data Analytics. In Rhazali, Y. (Ed.), *Advancements in Model-Driven Architecture in Software Engineering* (pp. 26-45). IGI Global. http://doi:10.4018/978-1-7998-3661-2.ch002

Lacárcel, F. J., Polanco-Diges, L., & Debasa, F. (2021). A Better Understanding of Big Data and Marketing Analytics. In Saura, J. R. (Ed.), *Advanced Digital Marketing Strategies in a Data-Driven Era* (pp. 1-15). IGI Global. http://doi:10.4018/978-1-7998-8003-5.ch001

Lal, P., & Bharadwaj, S. S. (2020). Understanding the Drivers of Cloud-Based Service Adoption and Their Impact on the Organizational Performance. [JGIM]. *Journal of Global Information Management, 28*(1), 56–85. doi:10.4018/JGIM.2020010104

Laurini, R. (2019). Towards Knowledge-Based Spatial Planning. In Voghera, A., & La Riccia, L. (Eds.), *Spatial Planning in the Big Data Revolution* (pp. 1-15). IGI Global. http://doi:10.4018/978-1-5225-7927-4.ch001

Lavín, J. M. (2020). Type of Relationships and Their Management Towards Quality and Performance in the Textile and Apparel Industry. In Margalina, V., & Lavín, J. M. (Eds.), *Management and Inter/Intra Organizational Relationships in the Textile and Apparel Industry* (pp. 1-25). IGI Global. http://doi:10.4018/978-1-7998-1859-5.ch001

Leitão, A., Rebelo, F., Pintado, M., & Ribeiro, T. B. (2020). AgroForest Biomass and Circular Bioeconomy. In Rodrigues, S. S., Almeida, P. J., & Almeida, N. M. (Ed.), *Mapping, Managing, and Crafting Sustainable Business Strategies for the Circular Economy* (pp. 203-247). IGI Global. http://doi:10.4018/978-1-5225-9885-5.ch011

Leitão, C. F., Gomes, J., Capela dos Santos, D., & Maia, B. M. (2021). Impact of Leadership on the Relationship Between Innovation and Performance. [IJTHMDA]. *International Journal of Tourism and Hospitality Management in the Digital Age, 5*(2), 29–49. doi:10.4018/IJTHMDA.2021070103

Lempogo, F., Yeboah-Boateng, E. O., & Brown-Acquaye, W. L. (2021). Big Data Analytics in Developing Economies. In Gyamfi, A., & Williams, I. (Ed.), *Digital Technology Advancements in Knowledge Management* (pp. 149-166). IGI Global. http://doi:10.4018/978-1-7998-6792-0.ch008

Leon, R. D., Tănăsescu, R. I., & Tănăsescu, C. E. (2020). Predicting Employee Performance. In Leon, R. (Ed.), *Strategies for Business Sustainability in a Collaborative Economy* (pp. 281-305). IGI Global. http://doi:10.4018/978-1-7998-4543-0.ch015

Leon, S., & Medlin, B. D. (2020). A Conceptual Framework for Collaboration in Business Schools. [IJISSC]. *International Journal of Information Systems and Social Change, 11*(3), 32–45. doi:10.4018/IJISSC.2020070103

Li, Z., Rogers, P., & Lau, W. K. (2020). The Quality Amplification Challenge. [IJSDS]. *International Journal of Strategic Decision Sciences, 11*(2), 25–45. doi:10.4018/IJSDS.2020040102

Liao, S., & Chiu, W. (2021). Investigating the Behaviors of Mobile Games and Online Streaming Users for Online Marketing Recommendations. [IJOM]. *International Journal of Online Marketing, 11*(1), 39–61. doi:10.4018/IJOM.2021010103

Lo Piparo, T., Hodosi, G., & Rusu, L. (2021). Service-Level Agreement Negotiation in Cloud Computing Buying Organizations. [IJIDE]. *International Journal of Innovation in the Digital Economy*, *12*(3), 1–16. doi:10.4018/IJIDE.2021070101

Lokshina, I. V., & Lanting, C. J. (2018). Addressing Ethical Concerns of Big Data as a Prerequisite for a Sustainable Big Data Industry. [IJITN]. *International Journal of Interdisciplinary Telecommunications and Networking*, *10*(3), 33–54. doi:10.4018/IJITN.2018070104

Lopes, B., & Falcão, L. (2019). Optimal Locational Analysis for the Targeting of Investments in Specific Businesses and Territories in Brazil. In Jamil, G. L. (Ed.), *Handbook of Research on Expanding Business Opportunities With Information Systems and Analytics* (pp. 333-352). IGI Global. http://doi:10.4018/978-1-5225-6225-2.ch017

López-Cózar-Navarro, C., & Priede-Bergamini, T. (2021). Social Entrepreneurship and Related Concepts. In Carrizo Moreira, A., & Dantas, J. G. (Ed.), *Handbook of Research on Nascent Entrepreneurship and Creating New Ventures* (pp. 273-294). IGI Global. http://doi:10.4018/978-1-7998-4826-4.ch013

López-Vargas, J. C., Cárdenas-Aguirre, D. M., & Meisel, J. D. (2019). Characterization of the Key Actors Involved in Humanitarian Supply Chains at the Local Level From a Theoretical and Academic Perspective. In Gonzalez-Feliu, J., Chong, M., Vargas Florez, J., & Padilla Solis, J. (Ed.), *Handbook of Research on Urban and Humanitarian Logistics* (pp. 216-244). IGI Global. http://doi:10.4018/978-1-5225-8160-4.ch011

Lorek, E., & Lorek, A. (2020). A Sustainable Business Model in the Functioning of Enterprises as the Base for Creating Circular Economy. In Nogalski, B., Szpitter, A., Jabłoński, A., & Jabłoński, M. (Ed.), *Networked Business Models in the Circular Economy* (pp. 54-81). IGI Global. http://doi:10.4018/978-1-5225-7850-5.ch003

Lourenço, R. T., & Valente, F. M. (2019). Importance of Entrepreneurship in the Organizational Performance of Higher Education Institutions. In Teixeira, N. M., Costa, T. G., & Lisboa, I. M. (Ed.), *Handbook of Research on Entrepreneurship, Innovation, and Internationalization* (pp. 230-257). IGI Global. http://doi:10.4018/978-1-5225-8479-7.ch009

Luo, Y., & Zhu, J. (2020). Resilience Strategy Optimization for Large Aircraft Supply Chain Based on Probabilistic Language QFD. [IJISSCM]. *International Journal of Information Systems and Supply Chain Management*, *13*(4), 23–46. doi:10.4018/IJISSCM.2020100102

Nwogugu, M. (2021). *Financial Stability, Sustainable Growth, and the Global Quasi-Franchising/Business-Opportunity Industry*. IGI Global. http://doi:10.4018/978-1-7998-7418-8.ch002

M. S., S., & Sasidaran, K. (2021). Machine Learning for Big Data. In Goundar, S., & Rayani, P. K. (Ed.), *Applications of Big Data in Large- and Small-Scale Systems* (pp. 56-76). IGI Global. http://doi:10.4018/978-1-7998-6673-2.ch004

M. S., S., Manjunath, K., & U. R., K. (2021). The Rise of IoT and Big Data Analytics for Disaster Management Systems. In Zhao, J., & Kumar, V. (Ed.), *Handbook of Research on Innovations and Applications of AI, IoT, and Cognitive Technologies* (pp. 42-62). IGI Global. http://doi:10.4018/978-1-7998-6870-5.ch003

Maazouzi, F., & Zarzour, H. (2021). AI-Driven Big Healthcare Analytics. In Sun, Z. (Ed.), *Intelligent Analytics With Advanced Multi-Industry Applications* (pp. 172-184). IGI Global. http://doi:10.4018/978-1-7998-4963-6.ch008

Madhani, P. M. (2020). Enhancing Supply Chain Efficiency and Effectiveness With Lean Six Sigma Approach. [IJPMPA]. *International Journal of Project Management and Productivity Assessment, 8*(1), 40–65. doi:10.4018/IJPMPA.2020010103

Majetić, F., Rajter, M., & Šimleša, D. (2019). Organizations of Social Entrepreneurship in Croatia. In Guerra Guerra, A. (Ed.), *Organizational Transformation and Managing Innovation in the Fourth Industrial Revolution* (pp. 212-227). IGI Global. http://doi:10.4018/978-1-5225-7074-5.ch011

Makori, E. O., & Bitso, C. (2021). Information Profession in Digital Transformation and Development. In Holland, B. J. (Ed.), *Handbook of Research on Knowledge and Organization Systems in Library and Information Science* (pp. 1-24). IGI Global. http://doi:10.4018/978-1-7998-7258-0.ch001

Malladi, S., Shi, W., Zhao, Z., & Min, K. J. (2020). The Impacts of Product Life and Recyclability on Landfill Disposal in Closed Loop Supply Chains. [IJSEM]. *International Journal of Sustainable Economies Management, 9*(2), 59–77. doi:10.4018/IJSEM.2020040105

Manian, V., & P., V. (2021). Challenges and Applications of Data Analytics in Social Perspectives. In Bouarara, H. A. (Ed.), *Advanced Deep Learning Applications in Big Data Analytics* (pp. 51-67). IGI Global. http://doi:10.4018/978-1-7998-2791-7.ch003

Marcone, M. R. (2021). Innovation Openness in Supply-Side Relationships. [IJABE]. *International Journal of Applied Behavioral Economics, 10*(2), 53–64. doi:10.4018/IJABE.2021040104

Martín-Rojas, R., García-Morales, V. J., Garrido-Moreno, A., & García-Sánchez, E. (2020). Can Business Intelligence Enhance Organizational Performance Through Corporate Entrepreneurship? In Dantas, J. G., & Carvalho, L. C. (Ed.), *Handbook of Research on Approaches to Alternative Entrepreneurship Opportunities* (pp. 198-221). IGI Global. http://doi:10.4018/978-1-7998-1981-3.ch010

Martins, A., Pereira, O., & Martins, I. (2019). Unravelling Hurdles to Organizational Sustainability by Virtue of Sharing and Creating Knowledge. In Khosrow-Pour, D.B.A., M. (Ed.), *Breaking Down Language and Cultural Barriers Through Contemporary Global Marketing Strategies* (pp. 42-64). IGI Global. http://doi:10.4018/978-1-5225-6980-0.ch003

Martins, S. M., Ensslin, L., Dutra, A., & Ensslin, S. R. (2020). Multicriteria Model to Support Governance in Electoral Institutions. [IJSDS]. *International Journal of Strategic Decision Sciences, 11*(3), 1–17. doi:10.4018/IJSDS.2020070101

Masudin, I., Sumah, B., Zulfikarijah, F., & Restuputri, D. P. (2021). Effect of Information Technology on Warehousing and Inventory Management for Competitive Advantage. In Almunawar, M. N., Anshari Ali, M., & Ariff Lim, S. (Ed.), *Handbook of Research on Innovation and Development of E-Commerce and E-Business in ASEAN* (pp. 570-593). IGI Global. http://doi:10.4018/978-1-7998-4984-1.ch027

Maya Gopal, P. S., & Chintala, B. R. (2020). Big Data Challenges and Opportunities in Agriculture. [IJAEIS]. *International Journal of Agricultural and Environmental Information Systems, 11*(1), 48–66. doi:10.4018/IJAEIS.2020010103

Mazhar, R., Sarwar, M. A., Malik, M. Y., Nazam, M., & Mazhar, S. (2020). Impact of High Performance Work Systems on Organizational Performance. [IJABIM]. *International Journal of Asian Business and Information Management, 11*(4), 16–28. doi:10.4018/IJABIM.2020100102

Mei, Q., Zhou, Q., Liu, S., & Wang, Q. (2020). A Safety Signaling Game for Small and Medium-sized Manufacturing Enterprises in the Supply Chain. [IJISSCM]. *International Journal of Information Systems and Supply Chain Management, 13*(1), 118–135. doi:10.4018/IJISSCM.2020010106

Mendoza-Fong, J. R., García-Alcaraz, J. L., Avelar Sosa, L., & Díaz Reza, J. R. (2020). Effect of Green Attributes in Obtaining Benefits in the Manufacturing and Marketing Process. In García-Alcaraz, J. L., Jamil, G. L., Avelar-Sosa, L., & Briones Peñalver, A. J. (Ed.), *Handbook of Research on Industrial Applications for Improved Supply Chain Performance* (pp. 46-72). IGI Global. http://doi:10.4018/978-1-7998-0202-0.ch003

Mishra, I., Bandyopadhyay, R., Ghosh, S., & Swetapadma, A. (2019). Analysis of Cutting-Edge Regression Algorithms Used for Data Analysis. In Sun, Z. (Ed.), *Managerial Perspectives on Intelligent Big Data Analytics* (pp. 199-213). IGI Global. http://doi:10.4018/978-1-5225-7277-0.ch011

Mishra, N. (2019). Data Science and Knowledge Analytic Contexts on IoE Data for E-BI Application Case. In Nagarajan, G., & Minu, R. (Eds.), *Edge Computing and Computational Intelligence Paradigms for the IoT* (pp. 100-126). IGI Global. http://doi:10.4018/978-1-5225-8555-8.ch007

Mitra, A., Sarkar, S., & Vijayaraghavan, T. (2019). How Cooperative Is 'Cooperative Investment'? [IJSDS]. *International Journal of Strategic Decision Sciences*, *10*(1), 46–64. doi:10.4018/IJSDS.2019010104

Mohamed, E., & Hassan, A. (2019). How Does Complexity Affect the Relationship Between Supply Chain Integration and Firm Performance? [IJSSMET]. *International Journal of Service Science, Management, Engineering, and Technology*, *10*(2), 22–37. doi:10.4018/IJSSMET.2019040102

Mohseni, M., Abdollahi, A., & Siadat, S. H. (2019). Sustainable Supply Chain Management Practices in Petrochemical Industry Using Interpretive Structural Modeling. [IJISSCM]. *International Journal of Information Systems and Supply Chain Management*, *12*(1), 22–50. doi:10.4018/IJISSCM.2019010102

Mok Kim Man, M. (2021). Enhancing Human Resource Development and Practices in Industry 4.0 With Charismatic and Transformational Leadership. In Guah, M. W. (Eds.), *Handbook of Research on Innate Leadership Characteristics and Examinations of Successful First-Time Leaders* (pp. 78-91). IGI Global. http://doi:10.4018/978-1-7998-7592-5.ch005

Monsia, S., & Faiz, S. (2020). A High-Level Interactive Query Language for Big Data Analytics Based on a Functional Model. [IJDA]. *International Journal of Data Analytics*, *1*(1), 22–37. doi:10.4018/IJDA.2020010102

Mor, R. S., Bhardwaj, A., Singh, S., & Nema, P. K. (2019). Framework for Measuring the Performance of Production Operations in the Dairy Industry. In Essila, J. C. (Ed.), *Managing Operations Throughout Global Supply Chains* (pp. 20-49). IGI Global. http://doi:10.4018/978-1-5225-8157-4.ch002

Morales-Serazzi, M. A., González-Benito, O., & Martos-Partal, M. (2020). Data Analytics. In Palma-Ruiz, J. M., Barros-Contreras, I., & Gnan, L. (Ed.), *Handbook of Research on the Strategic Management of Family Businesses* (pp. 344-361). IGI Global. http://doi:10.4018/978-1-7998-2269-1.ch016

More, S., & Sutaria, M. (2020). Green Charcoal. In Brownell, B. E. (Ed.), *Examining the Environmental Impacts of Materials and Buildings* (pp. 132-159). IGI Global. http://doi:10.4018/978-1-7998-2426-8.ch005

Mosconi, E. M., Poponi, S., Fortunati, S., & Arezzo di Trifiletti, M. (2020). B Corp Certification for a Circular Economy Approach and a Sustainable Pathway. In Silvestri, C., Piccarozzi, M., & Aquilani, B. (Ed.), *Customer Satisfaction and Sustainability Initiatives in the Fourth Industrial Revolution* (pp. 167-188). IGI Global. http://doi:10.4018/978-1-7998-1419-1.ch009

Munyanyiwa, T. (2020). Application of Isenberg Model for Entrepreneurial Ecosystems as a Blueprint for Zimbabwe Socio-Economic Devolution. In Baporikar, N. (Eds.), *Handbook of Research on Entrepreneurship Development and Opportunities in Circular Economy* (pp. 284-305). IGI Global. http://doi:10.4018/978-1-7998-5116-5.ch015

Musari, K. (2022). Circular Economy for Plastics and Digitally Enabled Community Towards ASEAN Halal Hub in Asia. In Ordóñez de Pablos, P. (Eds.), *Handbook of Research on Developing Circular, Digital, and Green Economies in Asia* (pp. 1-12). IGI Global. http://doi:10.4018/978-1-7998-8678-5.ch001

Musari, K., & Zaroni, Z. (2021). Reverse Logistics in the Age of Digital Transformation for Circular Economy and Halal Logistics Through the Leadership of Asia. In Ordóñez de Pablos, P., Zhang, X., & Almunawar, M. N. (Ed.), *Handbook of Research on Disruptive Innovation and Digital Transformation in Asia* (pp. 83-103). IGI Global. http://doi:10.4018/978-1-7998-6477-6.ch006

Muscatello, J. R., Parente, D. H., & Swinarski, M. (2018). Aligning Supply Chain Logistics Costs via ERP Coordination. [IJISMD]. *International Journal of Information System Modeling and Design*, *9*(2), 24–43. doi:10.4018/IJISMD.2018040102

Musti, K. S. (2020). Circular Economy in Energizing Smart Cities. In Baporikar, N. (Eds.), *Handbook of Research on Entrepreneurship Development and Opportunities in Circular Economy* (pp. 251-269). IGI Global. http://doi:10.4018/978-1-7998-5116-5.ch013

Teixeira, N., Ribeiro, J., Teixeira, A., & Godinho, T. (2020). *Management Control Instruments' Characterization*. IGI Global. http://doi:10.4018/978-1-7998-2007-9.ch004

Nagaraj, S. (2020). Marketing Analytics for Customer Engagement. [IJISSC]. *International Journal of Information Systems and Social Change*, *11*(2), 41–55. doi:10.4018/IJISSC.2020040104

Naidoo, V. (2020). Creativity and Innovation for Entrepreneurs in the Circular Economy. In Baporikar, N. (Eds.), *Handbook of Research on Entrepreneurship Development and Opportunities in Circular Economy* (pp. 538-553). IGI Global. http://doi:10.4018/978-1-7998-5116-5.ch028

Nair, R., & Bhagat, A. (2018). An Application of Big Data Analytics in Road Transportation. In Tiwari, V., Thakur, R. S., Tiwari, B., & Gupta, S. (Ed.), *Handbook of Research on Pattern Engineering System Development for Big Data Analytics* (pp. 39-54). IGI Global. http://doi:10.4018/978-1-5225-3870-7.ch003

Narongou, D., & Sun, Z. (2021). Big Data Analytics for Smart Airport Management. In Sun, Z. (Ed.), *Intelligent Analytics With Advanced Multi-Industry Applications* (pp. 209-231). IGI Global. http://doi:10.4018/978-1-7998-4963-6.ch010

Negrão, C. S. (2021). A Model for Success in Agribusiness in the Portuguese Context. In Khosrow-Pour D.B.A., M. (Eds.), *Encyclopedia of Organizational Knowledge, Administration, and Technology* (pp. 355-371). IGI Global. http://doi:10.4018/978-1-7998-3473-1.ch028

Nehemia, M., & Zondani, T. (2021). The Use of an Enterprise Architecture Framework to Guide the Management of Big Data in Health Organisations. In Iyamu, T. (Ed.), *Empowering Businesses With Collaborative Enterprise Architecture Frameworks* (pp. 39-50). IGI Global. http://doi:10.4018/978-1-5225-8229-8.ch002

Nelson, J. (2021). Hunch Mining. [IJKM]. *International Journal of Knowledge Management, 17*(3), 17–30. doi:10.4018/IJKM.2021070102

Nesheva-Kiosseva, N. I. (2020). Sustainability and Justness for Transforming the Water Utility Companies' Business Models in the Circular Economy. In Baporikar, N. (Eds.), *Handbook of Research on Entrepreneurship Development and Opportunities in Circular Economy* (pp. 195-215). IGI Global. http://doi:10.4018/978-1-7998-5116-5.ch010

Neves, P. C., & Bernardino, J. R. (2021). The Role of Big Data and Business Analytics in Decision Making. In Rahman, H. (Ed.), *Human-Computer Interaction and Technology Integration in Modern Society* (pp. 226-257). IGI Global. http://doi:10.4018/978-1-7998-5849-2.ch010

Nikabadi, M. S., & Hakaki, A. (2019). Mutual Relationship Between Supply Chain, Business Strategy, and Knowledge Management in Supply Chain. In Ordoñez de Pablos, P. (Ed.), *Dynamic Perspectives on Globalization and Sustainable Business in Asia* (pp. 301-327). IGI Global. http://doi:10.4018/978-1-5225-7095-0.ch019

Norrohmat, N., Nimran, U., Raharjo, K., Utami, H. N., & Astuti, E. S. (2021). Organizational Support for Professionalism, Organizational Citizenship Behavior (OCB), and Performance. [IJSEM]. *International Journal of Sustainable Economies Management, 10*(1), 1–12. doi:10.4018/IJSEM.2021010101

Nouri, B. A., Oleykie, F., & Soltani, M. (2019). The Role of Customer Commercial Knowledge Management in Improving the Performance of Employees of Insurance Firms in Iran. [IJCRMM]. *International Journal of Customer Relationship Marketing and Management, 10*(1), 17–33. doi:10.4018/IJCRMM.2019010102

Nugawela, S., & Sedera, D. (2021). Capability Maturity Model for Agricultural Supply Chain Management Software. In Lokuge, S., & Sedera, D. (Ed.), *Rural Entrepreneurship and Innovation in the Digital Era* (pp. 196-216). IGI Global. http://doi:10.4018/978-1-7998-4942-1.ch011

Ocampo, P. C., Prada, R., & Rueda, M. J. (2020). Sustainability Supply Chain Orientation Bibliometric Agenda. In Moreno-Monsalve, N. A., Diez-Silva, H., Diaz-Piraquive, F. N., & Perez-Uribe, R. I. (Ed.), *Handbook of Research on Project Management Strategies and Tools for Organizational Success* (pp. 393-410). IGI Global. http://doi:10.4018/978-1-7998-1934-9.ch017

Odia, J. O. (2021). Circular Economy and Climate Change in Developing Economies. In Ziolo, M. (Eds.), *Adapting and Mitigating Environmental, Social, and Governance Risk in Business* (pp. 225-238). IGI Global. http://doi:10.4018/978-1-7998-6788-3.ch011

Odia, J. O., & Akpata, O. T. (2021). Role of Data Science and Data Analytics in Forensic Accounting and Fraud Detection. In Patil, B., & Vohra, M. (Ed.), *Handbook of Research on Engineering, Business, and Healthcare Applications of Data Science and Analytics* (pp. 203-227). IGI Global. http://doi:10.4018/978-1-7998-3053-5.ch011

Ohmori, S., Arakane, T., Ruiz-Torres, A., & Yoshimoto, K. (2021). The Multiple Supply Chain Design Problem. [IJISSCM]. *International Journal of Information Systems and Supply Chain Management, 14*(3), 39–62. doi:10.4018/IJISSCM.2021070103

Okatan, K. (2021). Machine Learning for Business Analytics. In Sathiyamoorthi, V., & Elci, A. (Eds.), *Challenges and Applications of Data Analytics in Social Perspectives* (pp. 232-256). IGI Global. http://doi:10.4018/978-1-7998-2566-1.ch013

Olalla-Caballero, B., & Mata-Fernández, M. (2020). Circular Economy and Risk Management Synergies in Disruptive Environments. In Baporikar, N. (Ed.), *Handbook of Research on Entrepreneurship Development and Opportunities in Circular Economy* (pp. 87-105). IGI Global. http://doi:10.4018/978-1-7998-5116-5.ch005

Oliveira, J. D., Azevedo, G. M., Pinheiro, S. F., & Borges, M. F. (2019). Impression Management Strategies in the Chairmen's Statements. In Oliveira, J. D., Azevedo, G. M., & Ferreira, A. D. (Ed.), *International Financial Reporting Standards and New Directions in Earnings Management* (pp. 199-215). IGI Global. http://doi:10.4018/978-1-5225-7817-8.ch009

Oncioiu, I., Petrescu, M., Duică, M. C., & Croitoru, G. (2018). The Impact of Employee Motivation on Romanian Organizational Performance. [IRMJ]. *Information Resources Management Journal, 31*(4), 59–74. doi:10.4018/IRMJ.2018100104

Ospina&Bermeo. J. (2021). Leadership and Competitiveness. In Perez-Uribe, R. I., Largacha-Martinez, C., & Ocampo-Guzman, D. (Eds.), *Handbook of Research on International Business and Models for Global Purpose-Driven Companies* (pp. 86-107). IGI Global. http://doi:10.4018/978-1-7998-4909-4.ch005

Owusu, A. (2019). Examining the Moderating Effects of Time-Since-Adoption on the Nexus Between Business Intelligence Systems and Organisational Performance. [IJTD]. *International Journal of Technology Diffusion, 10*(3), 49–68. doi:10.4018/IJTD.2019070104

Owusu, D. (2020). Corporate Culture as a Competitive Tool in Enhancing the Organisational Performance of Star-Rated Hotels in Ghana. In Pius, A., Alharahsheh, H. H., & Adesanmi, A. A. (Eds.), *Contemporary Management Approaches to the Global Hospitality and Tourism Industry* (pp. 58-77). IGI Global. http://doi:10.4018/978-1-7998-2204-2.ch004

Özkan, P., & Karataş Yücel, E. (2020). Linear Economy to Circular Economy. In Baporikar, N. (Ed.), *Handbook of Research on Entrepreneurship Development and Opportunities in Circular Economy* (pp. 61-86). IGI Global. http://doi:10.4018/978-1-7998-5116-5.ch004

P., S., P., K., V., S., K., L., R., M. D., K., S., M., S., & C., S. (2021). Cloud-Based Big Data Analysis Tools and Techniques Towards Sustainable Smart City Services. In Butun, I. (Ed.), *Decision Support Systems and Industrial IoT in Smart Grid, Factories, and Cities* (pp. 63-90). IGI Global. http://doi:10.4018/978-1-7998-7468-3.ch004

Pal, K. (2019). Assessing the Impact of RFID Technology Solutions in Supply Chain Management. In Goyal, D., Balamurugan, S., Peng, S., & Jat, D. S. (Eds.), *The IoT and the Next Revolutions Automating the World* (pp. 16-32). IGI Global. http://doi:10.4018/978-1-5225-9246-4.ch002

Pal, K. (2019). Radio Frequency Identification Systems Security Challenges in Supply Chain Management. In Rodrigues, J. J., Gawanmeh, A., Saleem, K., & Parvin, S. (Eds.), *Smart Devices, Applications, and Protocols for the IoT* (pp. 220-242). IGI Global. http://doi:10.4018/978-1-5225-7811-6.ch010

Pal, K. (2019). RFID Tag Collision Problem in Supply Chain Management. [IJAPUC]. *International Journal of Advanced Pervasive and Ubiquitous Computing, 11*(3), 1–12. doi:10.4018/IJAPUC.2019070101

Pal, K. (2019). Semantic Web Service for Global Apparel Business. In Sahoo, P. (Eds.), *Optimizing Current Strategies and Applications in Industrial Engineering* (pp. 179-201). IGI Global. http://doi:10.4018/978-1-5225-8223-6.ch008

Pal, K. (2019). Software Agents Mediated Decision Simulation in Supply Chains. In Kumar, M. V., Putnik, G. D., Jayakrishna, K., Pillai, V. M., & Varela, L. (Eds.), *Emerging Applications in Supply Chains for Sustainable Business Development* (pp. 40-56). IGI Global. http://doi:10.4018/978-1-5225-5424-0.ch003

Pal, K. (2020). Information Sharing for Manufacturing Supply Chain Management Based on Blockchain Technology. In Williams, I. (Eds.), *Cross-Industry Use of Blockchain Technology and Opportunities for the Future* (pp. 1-17). IGI Global. http://doi:10.4018/978-1-7998-3632-2.ch001

Pal, K. (2021). A Framework to Data Integration for an Internet of Things Supporting Manufacturing Supply Chain Operation. In Daramola, O., & Moser, T. (Eds.), *Advanced Concepts, Methods, and Applications in Semantic Computing* (pp. 218-235). IGI Global. http://doi:10.4018/978-1-7998-6697-8.ch011

Pal, K. (2021). Applications of Radio Frequency Identification Technology and Security Issues in Supply Chain Management. In Aytekin, G. K., & Doğru, Ç. (Eds.), *Handbook of Research on Recent Perspectives on Management, International Trade, and Logistics* (pp. 237-264). IGI Global. http://doi:10.4018/978-1-7998-5886-7.ch013

Pal, K. (2021). Blockchain Technology for the Internet of Things Applications in Apparel Supply Chain Management. In Patel, H., & Thakur, G. S. (Eds.), *Blockchain Applications in IoT Security* (pp. 152-185). IGI Global. http://doi:10.4018/978-1-7998-2414-5.ch010

Pal, K. (2021). Managing Green Supply Chain Transportation Operation Using Multi-Agent Framework. In Hassan, S., & Mohamed, A. W. (Eds.), *Handbook of Research on Decision Sciences and Applications in the Transportation Sector* (pp. 305-324). IGI Global. http://doi:10.4018/978-1-7998-8040-0.ch014

Pal, K. (2021). Security Issues of Blockchain-Based Information System to Manage Supply Chain in a Global Crisis. In Taghipour, A. (Eds.), *Digitalization of Decentralized Supply Chains During Global Crises* (pp. 143-173). IGI Global. http://doi:10.4018/978-1-7998-6874-3.ch007

Pal, K. (2021). Software Agent-Based Simulation for Pan-European Transport Corridor Management in Supply Chain. In Hassan, S., & Mohamed, A. W. (Eds.), *Handbook of Research on Decision Sciences and Applications in the Transportation Sector* (pp. 325-339). IGI Global. http://doi:10.4018/978-1-7998-8040-0.ch015

Palacios, F. D., Perez-Uribe, R. I., Ramírez, I. R., & Salcedo-Perez, C. (2020). Orientation to Organizational Learning and Its Effects on Innovation and Performance. In Masouras, A., Maris, G., & Kavoura, A. (Ed.), *Entrepreneurial Development and Innovation in Family Businesses and SMEs* (pp. 167-186). IGI Global. http://doi:10.4018/978-1-7998-3648-3.ch010

Palalar Alkan, D., & Özbebek Tunç, A. (2020). Current Trends in Practicing Leadership. In Chirino-Klevans, I. (Ed.), *Cases on Global Leadership in the Contemporary Economy* (pp. 137-165). IGI Global. http://doi:10.4018/978-1-5225-8088-1.ch008

Paliwal, G., & Bunglowala, A. (2019). Ubiquitous Wearable Healthcare Monitoring System Architectural Design for Prevention, Detection, and Monitoring of Chronic Diseases. In Edoh, T., Pawar, P., & Mohammad, S. (Ed.), *Pre-Screening Systems for Early Disease Prediction, Detection, and Prevention* (pp. 190-218). IGI Global. http://doi:10.4018/978-1-5225-7131-5.ch007

Pallavi, K., & Singh, H. (2021). Prospects of Artificial Intelligence (AI) Towards the Circular Economy. In Gopalakrishnan, B. N., Duggal, T., & Tewary, T. (Ed.), *Examining the Intersection of Circular Economy, Forestry, and International Trade* (pp. 223-237). IGI Global. http://doi:10.4018/978-1-7998-4990-2.ch018

Palmeira, M., & Musso, F. (2020). 3Rs of Sustainability Values for Retailing Customers as Factors of Influence on Consumer Behavior. In Musso, F., & Druica, E. (Ed.), *Handbook of Research on Retailing Techniques for Optimal Consumer Engagement and Experiences* (pp. 421-444). IGI Global. http://doi:10.4018/978-1-7998-1412-2.ch019

Pantano, E., Giglio, S., & Dennis, C. (2020). Integrating Big Data Analytics Into Retail Services Marketing Management. In Dadwal, S. S. (Ed.), *Handbook of Research on Innovations in Technology and Marketing for the Connected Consumer* (pp. 205-222). IGI Global. http://doi:10.4018/978-1-7998-0131-3.ch010

Panwar, A., & Bhatnagar, V. (2020). Data Lake Architecture. [IJOCI]. *International Journal of Organizational and Collective Intelligence*, *10*(1), 63–75. doi:10.4018/IJOCI.2020010104

Papastamoulis, V., London, K., Crocker, R., & Patias, P. (2021). Transforming Construction Waste Analytics to Support Circular Economy and Carbon Footprint Reduction. In Underwood, J., & Shelbourn, M. (Ed.), *Handbook of Research on Driving Transformational Change in the Digital Built Environment* (pp. 232-264). IGI Global. http://doi:10.4018/978-1-7998-6600-8.ch010

Pathak, P., Iyengar, S. P., & Abhyankar, M. (2021). A Survey on Tools for Data Analytics and Data Science. In Patil, B., & Vohra, M. (Ed.), *Handbook of Research on Engineering, Business, and Healthcare Applications of Data Science and Analytics* (pp. 28-49). IGI Global. http://doi:10.4018/978-1-7998-3053-5.ch003

Patrick, H. A., & Mukherjee, U. (2020). Women's Power as Employees and Entrepreneurs in the Circular Economy. In Baporikar, N. (Ed.), *Handbook of Research on Entrepreneurship Development and Opportunities in Circular Economy* (pp. 361-378). IGI Global. http://doi:10.4018/978-1-7998-5116-5.ch019

Patro, C. S. (2020). An Evaluation of Employees' Competence Towards the Development of a Learning Organization. [IJKM]. *International Journal of Knowledge Management*, *16*(4), 26–41. doi:10.4018/IJKM.2020100102

Patro, C. S. (2021). Learning Organisation. In Khosrow-Pour D.B.A., M. (Eds.), *Encyclopedia of Organizational Knowledge, Administration, and Technology* (pp. 2570-2591). IGI Global. http://doi:10.4018/978-1-7998-3473-1.ch178

Patti, S., & Messina, A. (2020). From Linear to Circular Tourism. In Patti, S., & Trizzino, G. (Ed.), *Advanced Integrated Approaches to Environmental Economics and Policy* (pp. 120-139). IGI Global. http://doi:10.4018/978-1-5225-9562-5.ch007

Pattnaik, M. (2020). Milk Supply Chain Network Design (SCND). [IJSDS]. *International Journal of Strategic Decision Sciences*, *11*(3), 63–120. doi:10.4018/IJSDS.2020070104

Paul, P. V., Krishna, H., & L., J. (2020). Evolution of Data Analytics in Healthcare. In Solanki, A., Kumar, S., & Nayyar, A. (Ed.), *Handbook of Research on Emerging Trends and Applications of Machine Learning* (pp. 250-275). IGI Global. http://doi:10.4018/978-1-5225-9643-1.ch012

Pego, A. (2020). New Challenges for the Tourism Sector in the Algarve Region Based on Evaluation of the Circular Economy. In Carvalho, L. C., Calisto, L., & Gustavo, N. (Eds.), *Strategic Business Models to Support Demand, Supply, and Destination Management in the Tourism and Hospitality Industry* (pp. 185-199). IGI Global. http://doi:10.4018/978-1-5225-9936-4.ch010

Pego, A. C. (2020). Circularity in Portugal. In Nogalski, B., Szpitter, A., Jabłoński, A., & Jabłoński, M. (Eds.), *Networked Business Models in the Circular Economy* (pp. 224-240). IGI Global. http://doi:10.4018/978-1-5225-7850-5.ch010

Peker, I., Korucuk, S., & Baki, B. (2019). Firm Selection Based on Logistics Risk Factors. [IJORIS]. *International Journal of Operations Research and Information Systems, 10*(3), 31–43. doi:10.4018/IJORIS.2019070103

Pérez López, R. J., Olguín Tiznado, J. E., Camargo Wilson, C., López Barreras, J. A., Mojarro Magaña, M., & García-Rivera, B. R. (2020). Critical Success Factors in the Integration of Information Technologies in the Supply Chain. In García-Alcaraz, J. L., Jamil, G. L., Avelar-Sosa, L., & Briones Peñalver, A. J. (Ed.), *Handbook of Research on Industrial Applications for Improved Supply Chain Performance* (pp. 200-225). IGI Global. http://doi:10.4018/978-1-7998-0202-0.ch009

Perez-Uribe, R. I., Ramírez-Garzón, M. T., Ramirez-Salazar, M. D., & Salcedo-Perez, C. (2020). Transitioning From Medium to Large Companies in the Circular Economy. In Baporikar, N. (Ed.), *Handbook of Research on Entrepreneurship Development and Opportunities in Circular Economy* (pp. 323-344). IGI Global. http://doi:10.4018/978-1-7998-5116-5.ch017

Petrescu, A. G., Petrescu, M., Panagore, I., & Bîlcan, F. R. (2021). Cybersecurity Risks in Romanian Companies. In Khosrow-Pour D.B.A., M. (Ed.), *Encyclopedia of Organizational Knowledge, Administration, and Technology* (pp. 1274-1284). IGI Global. http://doi:10.4018/978-1-7998-3473-1.ch087

Petrie, E. J., Nieto, A. G., & Andrews, K. (2021). Racial Differences in Perceptions of Shared Leadership Among IT Managers. In Jackson, R., & Reboulet, A. (Ed.), *Effective Strategies for Communicating Insights in Business* (pp. 101-128). IGI Global. http://doi:10.4018/978-1-7998-3964-4.ch007

Pham, L. M., Tran, L. T., Thipwong, P., & Huang, W. T. (2019). Dynamic Capability and Organizational Performance. [JOEUC]. *Journal of Organizational and End User Computing, 31*(2), 1–21. doi:10.4018/JOEUC.2019040101

Philipp, B., Fulconis, F., & Zeroual, T. (2020). Packaging Trends in International Transportation and Logistics. In Ceyhun, G. Ç. (Ed.), *Handbook of Research on the Applications of International Transportation and Logistics for World Trade* (pp. 54-73). IGI Global. http://doi:10.4018/978-1-7998-1397-2.ch004

Podduturi, P. R., Maco, T., Ahmadi, P., & Islam, K. (2020). RFID Implementation in Supply Chain Management. [IJITN]. *International Journal of Interdisciplinary Telecommunications and Networking*, *12*(2), 34–45. doi:10.4018/IJITN.2020040103

Pokorny, J., & Stantic, B. (2019). Big Data Processing and Big Analytics. In Ma, Z., & Yan, L. (Ed.), *Emerging Technologies and Applications in Data Processing and Management* (pp. 285-315). IGI Global. http://doi:10.4018/978-1-5225-8446-9.ch014

Popescu, C. R. (2021). Sustainable and Responsible Entrepreneurship for Value-Based Cultures, Economies, and Societies. In Popescu, C. R., & Verma, R. (Eds.), *Sustainable and Responsible Entrepreneurship and Key Drivers of Performance* (pp. 33-58). IGI Global. http://doi:10.4018/978-1-7998-7951-0.ch002

Potluri, R. M., & Vajjhala, N. R. (2021). Risks in Adoption and Implementation of Big Data Analytics. [IJRCM]. *International Journal of Risk and Contingency Management*, *10*(3), 1–11. doi:10.4018/IJRCM.2021070101

Pradhan, A. S., & Hiray, S. R. (2021). Application of Big Data Techniques for Efficient Web-Based Library Services Using Big Data. In Dhamdhere, S. N. (Ed.), *Big Data Applications for Improving Library Services* (pp. 58-77). IGI Global. http://doi:10.4018/978-1-7998-3049-8.ch005

Pramanik, P. K., Pal, S., & Mukhopadhyay, M. (2020). Big Data and Big Data Analytics for Improved Healthcare Service and Management. [IJPHIM]. *International Journal of Privacy and Health Information Management*, *8*(1), 13–51. doi:10.4018/IJPHIM.2020010102

Pranto, S., & Coelho, A. (2019). The Attitudes Towards Nearshoring vs. Offshoring on the IT Services Industry. In Moreira, A. C., & Silva, P. (Ed.), *Handbook of Research on Corporate Restructuring and Globalization* (pp. 213-233). IGI Global. http://doi:10.4018/978-1-5225-8906-8.ch010

Prasetio, A., Anggadwita, G., & Pasaribu, R. D. (2021). Digital Learning Challenge in Indonesia. In Ordóñez de Pablos, P., Lytras, M. D., & Zhang, X. (Ed.), *IT and the Development of Digital Skills and Competences in Education* (pp. 56-71). IGI Global. http://doi:10.4018/978-1-7998-4972-8.ch004

Qin, Z. (2019). Disruption and Strategic Outsourcing to the Competitor in the Common Market. [IJORIS]. *International Journal of Operations Research and Information Systems, 10*(1), 1–20. doi:10.4018/IJORIS.2019010101

Kassem, R., & Ajmal, M. (2019). *Organizational Culture and Business Excellence, ICT and Organizational Culture, ICT and Business Excellence*. IGI Global. http://doi:10.4018/978-1-5225-8413-1.ch003

Kassem, R., & Ajmal, M. (2019). *Results and Discussion of the Results*. IGI Global. http://doi:10.4018/978-1-5225-8413-1.ch005

R., S., P., K., & M., T. (2021). Blockchain Technology for IoT. In Ben Mnaouer, A., & Fourati, L. C. (Ed.), *Enabling Blockchain Technology for Secure Networking and Communications* (pp. 175-200). IGI Global. http://doi:10.4018/978-1-7998-5839-3.ch008

Raimi, L., & Yusuf, H. (2020). Entrepreneurship Development Interventions as a Pragmatic Approach to Political and Economic Restructuring in Nigeria. In Baporikar, N. (Ed.), *Handbook of Research on Entrepreneurship Development and Opportunities in Circular Economy* (pp. 435-452). IGI Global. http://doi:10.4018/978-1-7998-5116-5.ch023

Ramakrishna, Y. (2020). Development of Supply Chain Framework for the Circular Economy. In Baporikar, N. (Eds.), *Handbook of Research on Entrepreneurship Development and Opportunities in Circular Economy* (pp. 231-250). IGI Global. http://doi:10.4018/978-1-7998-5116-5.ch012

Ramakrishna, Y. (2021). Sustaining SMEs Through Supply Chain Innovation in the COVID-19 Era. In Baporikar, N. (Eds.), *Handbook of Research on Sustaining SMEs and Entrepreneurial Innovation in the Post-COVID-19 Era* (pp. 548-570). IGI Global. http://doi:10.4018/978-1-7998-6632-9.ch026

Rao, K. S. S., S., Kumar, P. S., V., R., & Raghu, K. (2021). Leveraging Big Data Analytics and Hadoop in Developing India's Healthcare Services. In Zhao, J., & Kumar, V. (Ed.), *Handbook of Research on Innovations and Applications of AI, IoT, and Cognitive Technologies* (pp. 396-407). IGI Global. http://doi:10.4018/978-1-7998-6870-5.ch027

Rath, M. (2019). Modern Health Management With Cognitive Computing and Big Data Analytics. In Lytras, M. D., Aljohani, N., Daniela, L., & Visvizi, A. (Eds.), *Cognitive Computing in Technology-Enhanced Learning* (pp. 206-224). IGI Global. http://doi:10.4018/978-1-5225-9031-6.ch010

Ray, P. (2021). Agricultural Supply Chain Risk Management Under Price and Demand Uncertainty. [IJSDA]. *International Journal of System Dynamics Applications, 10*(2), 17–32. doi:10.4018/IJSDA.2021040102

Ray, S. (2021). Digital, Decentralized Supply Chain and Its Implication for B2B Marketing. In Taghipour, A. (Eds.), *Digitalization of Decentralized Supply Chains During Global Crises* (pp. 46-63). IGI Global. http://doi:10.4018/978-1-7998-6874-3.ch003

Reddy, A., & Naude, M. J. (2019). Factors Inhibiting Green Supply Chain Management Initiatives in a South African Pharmaceutical Supply Chain. In Fields, Z., & Huesig, S. (Ed.), *Responsible, Sustainable, and Globally Aware Management in the Fourth Industrial Revolution* (pp. 306-336). IGI Global. http://doi:10.4018/978-1-5225-7638-9.ch012

Reddy, C. D. (2020). Entrepreneurial Motivation to Participate in the Circular Economy. In Baporikar, N. (Eds.), *Handbook of Research on Entrepreneurship Development and Opportunities in Circular Economy* (pp. 271-283). IGI Global. http://doi:10.4018/978-1-7998-5116-5.ch014

Reddy, J., Das, B., & Jagadish, (2019). Study on Effect of Barriers in Green Supply Chain Management Using Modified SAW Technique. In Sahoo, P. (Ed.), *Optimizing Current Strategies and Applications in Industrial Engineering* (pp. 202-219). IGI Global. http://doi:10.4018/978-1-5225-8223-6.ch009

Rehman, J., Hawryszkiewycz, I., Sohaib, O., & Namisango, F. (2021). Deriving Intellectual Capital Bottom-Line in Professional Service Firms. [IJKM]. *International Journal of Knowledge Management, 17*(2), 104–129. doi:10.4018/IJKM.2021040105

Rekik, S. (2021). Improving Geospatial Big Data Analytics Approaches. In Faiz, S., & Elhosni, S. (Eds.), *Interdisciplinary Approaches to Spatial Optimization Issues* (pp. 82-90). IGI Global. http://doi:10.4018/978-1-7998-1954-7.ch005

Rennhackkamp, M. H., & Hart, G. K. (2019). Applying Business Intelligence and Analytics to Clinical Costing Data. In Ma, R. (Ed.), *Clinical Costing Techniques and Analysis in Modern Healthcare Systems* (pp. 54-86). IGI Global. http://doi:10.4018/978-1-5225-5082-2.ch003

Reynoso, J. M., & Al-Busaidi, K. A. (2019). Empowering Organizations Through Customer Knowledge Acquisition. [IJKM]. *International Journal of Knowledge Management, 15*(3), 83–102. doi:10.4018/IJKM.2019070105

Rodrigues, J. P., Sousa, M. J., & Brochado, A. (2020). A Systematic Literature Review on Hospitality Analytics. [IJBIR]. *International Journal of Business Intelligence Research, 11*(2), 47–55. doi:10.4018/IJBIR.20200701.oa2

Rodríguez-Antón, J. M., & Alonso-Almeida, M. D. (2020). Guiding Principles of Design for Circular Tourism. In Rodrigues, S. S., Almeida, P. J., & Almeida, N. M. (Ed.), *Mapping, Managing, and Crafting Sustainable Business Strategies for the Circular Economy* (pp. 11-30). IGI Global. http://doi:10.4018/978-1-5225-9885-5.ch002

Rofin, T. M., & Mahanty, B. (2020). Equilibrium Analysis of Dual-Channel Supply Chain Under Retailer's Greening Cost Information Asymmetry. [IJISSCM]. *International Journal of Information Systems and Supply Chain Management, 13*(4), 1–22. doi:10.4018/IJISSCM.2020100101

Rohani, V. A., Guerreiro, F., & Pinho, T. (2021). An Applied Analytics Approach for Facility Location Optimization in Logistics With Actionable Insights for Logistics Managers. In Costa, T. G., Lisboa, I., & Teixeira, N. M. (Ed.), *Handbook of Research on Reinventing Economies and Organizations Following a Global Health Crisis* (pp. 124-138). IGI Global. http://doi:10.4018/978-1-7998-6926-9.ch008

Romero López, R., Molina Salazar, J., Matheus Marin, A. C., & Pérez Domínguez, L. A. (2020). Model of Skills and Capabilities of the Logistics Administrator. In García-Alcaraz, J. L., Jamil, G. L., Avelar-Sosa, L., & Briones Peñalver, A. J. (Ed.), *Handbook of Research on Industrial Applications for Improved Supply Chain Performance* (pp. 149-174). IGI Global. http://doi:10.4018/978-1-7998-0202-0.ch007

Rosário, A. T. (2021). New Business Models Sustainability. In Geada, N., & Anunciação, P. (Eds.), *Reviving Businesses With New Organizational Change Management Strategies* (pp. 1-29). IGI Global. http://doi:10.4018/978-1-7998-7452-2.ch001

Roy, D. (2021). Critical Success Factors of Analytics and Digital Technologies Adoption in Supply Chain. In Khosrow-Pour D.B.A., M. (Eds.), *Encyclopedia of Organizational Knowledge, Administration, and Technology* (pp. 2458-2471). IGI Global. http://doi:10.4018/978-1-7998-3473-1.ch170

Roy, S., Paul, A., Paul, A., Kashyap, S., & Jana, A. (2021). Ranking Barriers of Supply Chain Management by MCDM Method During Disaster Management. [IJSDA]. *International Journal of System Dynamics Applications, 10*(2), 1–16. doi:10.4018/IJSDA.2021040101

Rüzgar, N. (2020). Management and Organization in Transportation and Logistics. In Ceyhun, G. Ç. (Eds.), *Handbook of Research on the Applications of International Transportation and Logistics for World Trade* (pp. 224-235). IGI Global. http://doi:10.4018/978-1-7998-1397-2.ch013

S. G. S., D. S., B., & L., M. (2021). Big Data Analytics and Its Applications in IoT. In Velayutham, S. (Ed.), *Challenges and Opportunities for the Convergence of IoT, Big Data, and Cloud Computing* (pp. 146-158). IGI Global. http://doi:10.4018/978-1-7998-3111-2.ch009

S. G. S., L., M., S., L., H. D., S., & K., D. (2021). Emerging Trends and Techniques in Cloud-Based Data Analytics. In Velayutham, S. (Ed.), *Challenges and Opportunities for the Convergence of IoT, Big Data, and Cloud Computing* (pp. 37-47). IGI Global. http://doi:10.4018/978-1-7998-3111-2.ch003

Sedkaoui, S. (2019). *Big Data Analytics in Action*. IGI Global. http://doi:10.4018/978-1-5225-7609-9.ch009

Sedkaoui, S. (2019). *Big Data Applications in Business*. IGI Global. http://doi:10.4018/978-1-5225-7609-9.ch003

Sedkaoui, S. (2019). *Entrepreneurship and Big Data*. IGI Global. http://doi:10.4018/978-1-5225-7609-9.ch007

Sedkaoui, S. (2019). *First of All, Understand Data Analytics Context and Changes*. IGI Global. http://doi:10.4018/978-1-5225-7609-9.ch004

Sedkaoui, S. (2019). *Plan and Rules for Data Analysis Success*. IGI Global. http://doi:10.4018/978-1-5225-7609-9.ch008

Sedkaoui, S. (2019). *Understanding Data Analytics Is Good but Knowing How to Use It Is Better!* IGI Global. http://doi:10.4018/978-1-5225-7609-9.ch005

Sedkaoui, S. (2019). *What the 3Vs Acronym Didn't Put Into Perspective?* IGI Global. http://doi:10.4018/978-1-5225-7609-9.ch002

S., S., R., D. P., & K., K. (2021). Big Data Analytics in Cloud Platform. In Velayutham, S. (Ed.), *Challenges and Opportunities for the Convergence of IoT, Big Data, and Cloud Computing* (pp. 159-179). IGI Global. http://doi:10.4018/978-1-7998-3111-2.ch010

Sabuncu, I. (2021). Understanding Tourist Perceptions and Expectations During Pandemic Through Social Media Big Data. In Demir, M., Dalgıç, A., & Ergen, F. D. (Eds.), *Handbook of Research on the Impacts and Implications of COVID-19 on the Tourism Industry* (pp. 330-350). IGI Global. http://doi:10.4018/978-1-7998-8231-2.ch016

Sadurdeen, A. R., & Sutha, J. (2019). Impact of Green Supply Chain Management on Competitive Advantage of Business Organizations in Sri Lanka. In Taghipour, A. (Ed.), *Hierarchical Planning and Information Sharing Techniques in Supply Chain Management* (pp. 123-152). IGI Global. http://doi:10.4018/978-1-5225-7299-2.ch004

Saha, N. (2021). Strategic HRM and Organizational Agility Enable Firms to Respond Rapidly and Flexibly to the Changing Environment. In Khosrow-Pour D.B.A., M. (Eds.), *Encyclopedia of Organizational Knowledge, Administration, and Technology* (pp. 2551-2569). IGI Global. http://doi:10.4018/978-1-7998-3473-1.ch177

Sahu, N. K., Patnaik, M., & Snigdh, I. (2021). Data Analytics and Its Applications in Brief. In Goundar, S., & Rayani, P. K. (Ed.), *Applications of Big Data in Large- and Small-Scale Systems* (pp. 115-125). IGI Global. http://doi:10.4018/978-1-7998-6673-2.ch008

Saini, D., & Agarwal, J. (2020). Leadership to Cultivate the Circular Economy. In Baporikar, N. (Ed.), *Handbook of Research on Entrepreneurship Development and Opportunities in Circular Economy* (pp. 554-565). IGI Global. http://doi:10.4018/978-1-7998-5116-5.ch029

Saiz-Alvarez, J. M. (2020). Smart Territories, Collaborative Entrepreneurship, and Eco-Friendly Tourism for Development. In Palma-Ruiz, J. M., Saiz-Álvarez, J., & Herrero-Crespo, Á. (Eds.), *Handbook of Research on Smart Territories and Entrepreneurial Ecosystems for Social Innovation and Sustainable Growth* (pp. 172-190). IGI Global. http://doi:10.4018/978-1-7998-2097-0.ch010

Saiz-Alvarez, J. M. (2021). Entrepreneurship in the Fashion Industry. In Gamez-Gutierrez, J., & Saiz-Alvarez, J. M. (Eds.), *Entrepreneurial Innovation for Securing Long-Term Growth in a Short-Term Economy* (pp. 90-110). IGI Global. http://doi:10.4018/978-1-7998-3568-4.ch006

Saiz-Alvarez, J. M. (2021). Innovation-Based Lateral Thinking and Intrapreneurship Strategies for Handling Corporate Chaordism. In Perez-Uribe, R., Ocampo-Guzman, D., Moreno-Monsalve, N. A., & Fajardo-Moreno, W. S. (Eds.), *Handbook of Research on Management Techniques and Sustainability Strategies for Handling Disruptive Situations in Corporate Settings* (pp. 89-107). IGI Global. http://doi:10.4018/978-1-7998-8185-8.ch005

Sajja, P. S., & Akerkar, R. (2019). Deep Learning for Big Data Analytics. In Banati, H., Mehta, S., & Kaur, P. (Ed.), *Nature-Inspired Algorithms for Big Data Frameworks* (pp. 1-21). IGI Global. http://doi:10.4018/978-1-5225-5852-1.ch001

Salvia, R., & Quaranta, G. (2018). An Iterative Approach for Knowledge Production in the Agricultural Systems and Insights for IS Development. [IJAEIS]. *International Journal of Agricultural and Environmental Information Systems*, *9*(4), 45–57. doi:10.4018/IJAEIS.2018100104

Sánchez-Flores, R. B., Cruz-Sotelo, S. E., & Ojeda-Benitez, S. (2020). Green Practices in Supply Chain Management to Improve Sustainable Performance. In Khan, S. A. (Ed.), *Global Perspectives on Green Business Administration and Sustainable Supply Chain Management* (pp. 45-71). IGI Global. http://doi:10.4018/978-1-7998-2173-1.ch003

Sánchez-Flores, R. B., Cruz-Sotelo, S. E., Ojeda-Benitez, S., & Navarro-Gonzalez, C. R. (2020). Sustainable Procurement to Enhance Organizational Performance in Supply Chain Management. In García-Alcaraz, J. L., Jamil, G. L., Avelar-Sosa, L., & Briones Peñalver, A. J. (Ed.), *Handbook of Research on Industrial Applications for Improved Supply Chain Performance* (pp. 1-26). IGI Global. http://doi:10.4018/978-1-7998-0202-0.ch001

Sanchez-Ruiz, L., Blanco, B., Perez-Labajos, C. A., & Porras, A. (2019). Process Management as a Means to Analyze the Effectiveness of a Company in Global Markets. In Vemić, M. (Ed.), *Strategic Optimization of Medium-Sized Enterprises in the Global Market* (pp. 263-286). IGI Global. http://doi:10.4018/978-1-5225-5784-5.ch012

Sangwan, N., & Bhatnagar, V. (2020). Comprehensive Contemplation of Probabilistic Aspects in Intelligent Analytics. [IJSSMET]. *International Journal of Service Science, Management, Engineering, and Technology*, *11*(1), 116–141. doi:10.4018/IJSSMET.2020010108

Saravanan, A. (2019). Pharmaceutical and Life Sciences Supply Chain Management. In Nozari, H., & Szmelter, A. (Eds.), *Global Supply Chains in the Pharmaceutical Industry* (pp. 206-227). IGI Global. http://doi:10.4018/978-1-5225-5921-4.ch009

Saroha, M., Garg, D., & Luthra, S. (2019). Contextual Relationship Among Barriers to Sustainable Procurement. [IJSESD]. *International Journal of Social Ecology and Sustainable Development*, *10*(3), 1–16. doi:10.4018/IJSESD.2019070101

Satapathy, S. (2019). An Analysis on Sustainable Supply Chain Management in Thermal Power Plants. In Essila, J. C. (Eds.), *Managing Operations Throughout Global Supply Chains* (pp. 258-285). IGI Global. http://doi:10.4018/978-1-5225-8157-4.ch013

Satapathy, S., & Biswal, J. N. (2018). Thermal Power Sector Sustainability. In Hernández Arellano, J. L., Maldonado Macías, A. A., Castillo Martínez, J. A., & Peinado Coronado, P. (Ed.), *Handbook of Research on Ergonomics and Product Design* (pp. 381-401). IGI Global. http://doi:10.4018/978-1-5225-5234-5.ch021

SATTA, A., & Mostefai, S. (2020). Strategic Outsourcing to Cloud Computing. [IJCAC]. *International Journal of Cloud Applications and Computing, 10*(1), 11–27. doi:10.4018/IJCAC.2020010102

Saxena, D. (2021). Big Data for Digital Transformation of Public Services. In Sandhu, K. (Eds.), *Disruptive Technology and Digital Transformation for Business and Government* (pp. 250-266). IGI Global. http://doi:10.4018/978-1-7998-8583-2.ch013

Sayan, İ., & Sarıcı Aytan, Y. (2020). Sustainable Supply Chain Management and Total Quality Management in the Health Sector. In Akkucuk, U. (Ed.), *Handbook of Research on Sustainable Supply Chain Management for the Global Economy* (pp. 191-201). IGI Global. http://doi:10.4018/978-1-7998-4601-7.ch010

Schipper, R., & Silvius, G. (2019). Opportunities for the Circular Economy in Smart Cities. [IJISSC]. *International Journal of Information Systems and Social Change, 10*(4), 12–35. doi:10.4018/IJISSC.2019100102

Schipper, R., & Silvius, G. (2021). Transition to the Circular Economy. [IJCEWM]. *International Journal of Circular Economy and Waste Management, 1*(1), 33–53. doi:10.4018/IJCEWM.2021010103

Sedkaoui, S. (2019). Data Analytics Supporting Knowledge Acquisition. In Lenart-Gansiniec, R. (Eds.), *Crowdsourcing and Knowledge Management in Contemporary Business Environments* (pp. 146-165). IGI Global. http://doi:10.4018/978-1-5225-4200-1.ch008

Sedkaoui, S., & Khelfaoui, M. (2019). Building an Analytics Culture to Boost a Data-Driven Entrepreneur's Business Model. In Sun, Z. (Ed.), *Managerial Perspectives on Intelligent Big Data Analytics* (pp. 260-291). IGI Global. http://doi:10.4018/978-1-5225-7277-0.ch014

Selamat, S. A., Prakoonwit, S., Sahandi, R., & Khan, W. (2019). Big Data and IoT Opportunities for Small and Medium-Sized Enterprises (SMEs). In Kaur, G., & Tomar, P. (Ed.), *Handbook of Research on Big Data and the IoT* (pp. 77-88). IGI Global. http://doi:10.4018/978-1-5225-7432-3.ch005

Selvaraj, P., Doraikannan, S., & Burugari, V. K. (2020). Security Vulnerabilities, Threats, and Attacks in IoT and Big Data. In Joshi, R. C., & Gupta, B. B. (Ed.), *Security, Privacy, and Forensics Issues in Big Data* (pp. 141-167). IGI Global. http://doi:10.4018/978-1-5225-9742-1.ch006

Şenaras, A. E. (2019). A Case Study for Supply Chain Management Using System Dynamics. In Taghipour, A. (Eds.), *Hierarchical Planning and Information Sharing Techniques in Supply Chain Management* (pp. 179-193). IGI Global. http://doi:10.4018/978-1-5225-7299-2.ch007

Sengupta, D., Das, A., Bera, U. K., & Dutta, A. (2021). A Humanitarian Green Supply Chain Management Considering Minimum Cost and Time. [IJBAN]. *International Journal of Business Analytics*, *8*(2), 63–82. doi:10.4018/IJBAN.2021040105

Sertyesilisik, B. (2019). Circular, Smart, and Connected Cities. In Saravanan, K., Julie, G., & Robinson, H. (Eds.), *Handbook of Research on Implementation and Deployment of IoT Projects in Smart Cities* (pp. 19-32). IGI Global. http://doi:10.4018/978-1-5225-9199-3.ch002

Sertyesilisik, B. (2019). Potential Changes in the Demand and Supply Sides in the Construction Industry. In Christiansen, B., Sysoeva, I., Udovikina, A., & Ketova, A. (Eds.), *Emerging Economic Models for Global Sustainability and Social Development* (pp. 187-202). IGI Global. http://doi:10.4018/978-1-5225-5787-6.ch010

Setiawan, A. B., Dunan, A., & Mudjiyanto, B. (2021). Transformation and Development of Agriculture Sector in Industrial Revolution 4.0 Era in Indonesia. In Ordóñez de Pablos, P., Zhang, X., & Almunawar, M. N. (Ed.), *Handbook of Research on Disruptive Innovation and Digital Transformation in Asia* (pp. 214-233). IGI Global. http://doi:10.4018/978-1-7998-6477-6.ch012

Shaharudin, M. S., & Fernando, Y. (2021). Environmental Friendliness in Low Carbon Supply Chain and Operations. In Khosrow-Pour D.B.A., M. (Ed.), *Encyclopedia of Organizational Knowledge, Administration, and Technology* (pp. 2421-2430). IGI Global. http://doi:10.4018/978-1-7998-3473-1.ch167

Shalan, O. A. (2021). Risk Management for Traditional and Innovative Contracts. In Shalan, M. A., & Algarni, M. A. (Eds.), *Innovative and Agile Contracting for Digital Transformation and Industry 4.0* (pp. 86-108). IGI Global. http://doi:10.4018/978-1-7998-4501-0.ch005

Shankarnarayan, V. K. (2020). Decoding Big Data Analytics for Emerging Business Through Data-Intensive Applications and Business Intelligence. In Haldorai, A., & Ramu, A. (Eds.), *Big Data Analytics for Sustainable Computing* (pp. 66-80). IGI Global. http://doi:10.4018/978-1-5225-9750-6.ch004

Shi, M. (2019). The Direction of Causality Between Supply Chain Excellence and Firm Performance. [IJORIS]. *International Journal of Operations Research and Information Systems, 10*(2), 54–64. doi:10.4018/IJORIS.2019040103

Shi, Y., Xie, C., & Han, R. (2018). An Exploratory Study of Fresh Food E-Commerce in the UK and China. [IJAL]. *International Journal of Applied Logistics, 8*(2), 1–18. doi:10.4018/IJAL.2018070101

Shrivastava, H., Ernst, A. T., & Krishnamoorthy, M. (2019). Distribution and Inventory Planning in a Supply Chain Under Transportation Route Disruptions and Uncertain Demands. [IJISSCM]. *International Journal of Information Systems and Supply Chain Management, 12*(3), 47–71. doi:10.4018/IJISSCM.2019070103

Shrivastava, S., & Pateriya, R. K. (2018). Secure Framework for E-Commerce Applications in Cloud Environment. In Sreedhar, G. (Ed.), *Improving E-Commerce Web Applications Through Business Intelligence Techniques* (pp. 82-109). IGI Global. http://doi:10.4018/978-1-5225-3646-8.ch004

Shukla, P. S., & Mathur, M. (2020). Conceptualizing the Role of Data Analytics and Technology in E-Governance. [IJBAN]. *International Journal of Business Analytics, 7*(2), 1–12. doi:10.4018/IJBAN.2020040101

Sidhu, R., & Arora, V. (2020). Benchmarking Sustainability Performance of Suppliers Using ISO 14001 and Rough Set QFD-Based Approach. In Awasthi, A., & Grzybowska, K. (Ed.), *Handbook of Research on Interdisciplinary Approaches to Decision Making for Sustainable Supply Chains* (pp. 55-72). IGI Global. http://doi:10.4018/978-1-5225-9570-0.ch003

Sierra-Sánchez, J., & Mañas-Viniegra, L. (2020). Social Responsibility and Sustainability of Fast Fashion Retail Companies in the Textile Sector. In Margalina, V., & Lavín, J. M. (Ed.), *Management and Inter/Intra Organizational Relationships in the Textile and Apparel Industry* (pp. 303-324). IGI Global. http://doi:10.4018/978-1-7998-1859-5.ch014

Sihag, P. (2021). The Impact of Perceived Organizational Support on Employee Engagement. [IJHCITP]. *International Journal of Human Capital and Information Technology Professionals, 12*(2), 35–52. doi:10.4018/IJHCITP.2021040103

Singh, D., Mishra, M., & Sahana, S. (2019). Big-Data-Based Techniques for Predictive Intelligence. In Gupta, P., Ören, T., & Singh, M. (Ed.), *Predictive Intelligence Using Big Data and the Internet of Things* (pp. 1-18). IGI Global. http://doi:10.4018/978-1-5225-6210-8.ch001

Singh, P., & Singh, N. (2020). Blockchain With IoT and AI. [IJAEC]. *International Journal of Applied Evolutionary Computation, 11*(4), 13–27. doi:10.4018/IJAEC.2020100102

Singh, V. (2019). The Impact of Job Engagement and Organizational Commitment on Organizational Performance. In Sharma, N., Chaudhary, N., & Singh, V. K. (Eds.), *Management Techniques for Employee Engagement in Contemporary Organizations* (pp. 218-235). IGI Global. http://doi:10.4018/978-1-5225-7799-7.ch013

Sivathanu, B., & Pillai, R. (2019). Leveraging Technology for Talent Management. [IJSKD]. *International Journal of Sociotechnology and Knowledge Development, 11*(2), 16–30. doi:10.4018/IJSKD.2019040102

Skaarup, S., & Mclarney, C. (2018). How Does Offshore Outsourcing of Customer Services Affect Customer Satisfaction. [IJSDS]. *International Journal of Strategic Decision Sciences, 9*(4), 32–46. doi:10.4018/IJSDS.2018100103

Smith, A. D. (2019). RFID Applications in Healthcare Systems From an Operational Perspective. [IJSS]. *International Journal of Systems and Society, 6*(2), 1–28. doi:10.4018/IJSS.2019070101

Smith, A. D. (2020). Vendor Managed Inventory and Strategy. [IJSEM]. *International Journal of Sustainable Economies Management, 9*(3), 1–20. doi:10.4018/IJSEM.2020070101

Smith, A. D., & Krivacek, S. J. (2019). Making the Case for Global Outsourcing. In Teixeira, N. M., Costa, T. G., & Lisboa, I. M. (Ed.), *Handbook of Research on Entrepreneurship, Innovation, and Internationalization* (pp. 611-632). IGI Global. http://doi:10.4018/978-1-5225-8479-7.ch023

Soliudeen, M. J., Adenuga, K. I., & Sadiq, F. I. (2021). Higher Education Governance of Big Data. In Maake, A. O., Maake, B. M., & Awuor, F. M. (Ed.), *Digital Solutions and the Case for Africa's Sustainable Development* (pp. 152-172). IGI Global. http://doi:10.4018/978-1-7998-2967-6.ch010

Solmaz, M. S., & Koray, M. (2020). Blockchain Technology in Maritime Transportation and Management. In Ceyhun, G. Ç. (Ed.), *Handbook of Research on the Applications of International Transportation and Logistics for World Trade* (pp. 483-499). IGI Global. http://doi:10.4018/978-1-7998-1397-2.ch026

Sony, M. (2019). Green Supply Chain Management Practices and Digital Technology. In Sabri, E. (Eds.), *Technology Optimization and Change Management for Successful Digital Supply Chains* (pp. 233-254). IGI Global. http://doi:10.4018/978-1-5225-7700-3.ch012

Sony, M. (2019). Lean Supply Chain Management and Sustainability. In Akkucuk, U. (Eds.), *Ethical and Sustainable Supply Chain Management in a Global Context* (pp. 57-76). IGI Global. http://doi:10.4018/978-1-5225-8970-9.ch004

Souprayen, B., Ayyanar, A., & Suresh Joseph, K. (2020). Optimization of C5.0 Classifier With Bayesian Theory for Food Traceability Management Using Internet of Things. [IJSSTA]. *International Journal of Smart Sensor Technologies and Applications*, *1*(1), 1–21. doi:10.4018/IJSSTA.2020010101

Springs, D. (2021). A Literature Content Analysis of Performance Incentives and Organizational Development Practices Focused on Nursing Job Satisfaction in Complex Health. [IJPPPHCE]. *International Journal of Public and Private Perspectives on Healthcare, Culture, and the Environment*, *5*(2), 1–18. doi:10.4018/IJPPPHCE.2021070101

Sridharan, R., Anilkumar, E. N., & Vishnu, C. R. (2019). Strategic Barriers and Operational Risks in Sustainable Supply Chain Management in the Indian Context. In Kumar, M. V., Putnik, G. D., Jayakrishna, K., Pillai, V. M., & Varela, L. (Ed.), *Emerging Applications in Supply Chains for Sustainable Business Development* (pp. 238-259). IGI Global. http://doi:10.4018/978-1-5225-5424-0.ch014

Srinivasan, D. S., & Manavalan, K. R., S., & S. I., T. (2021). Blockchain-Based Food Supply Chain Management. In Singh, S., & Jurcut, A. D. (Ed.), *Revolutionary Applications of Blockchain-Enabled Privacy and Access Control* (pp. 134-171). IGI Global. http://doi:10.4018/978-1-7998-7589-5.ch007

Sruthi, A., Anbuudayasankar, S., & Jeyakumar, G. (2019). Energy-Efficient Green Vehicle Routing Problem. [IJISSCM]. *International Journal of Information Systems and Supply Chain Management*, *12*(4), 27–41. doi:10.4018/IJISSCM.2019100102

Stanciu, A. (2019). Performance as a Result of Managerial Accounting and Leadership Vision. In Oncioiu, I. (Eds.), *Throughput Accounting in a Hyperconnected World* (pp. 293-310). IGI Global. http://doi:10.4018/978-1-5225-7712-6.ch015

Starns, V. A. (2020). Exploring Futuring and Predictive Analytics for Developing Organizational Strategy. [IJBSA]. *International Journal of Business Strategy and Automation*, *1*(4), 1–9. doi:10.4018/IJBSA.2020100101

Stefanovic, N. (2021). Blockchain for Supply Chain Management. In Khosrow-Pour D.B.A., M. (Eds.), *Encyclopedia of Organizational Knowledge, Administration, and Technology* (pp. 2472-2487). IGI Global. http://doi:10.4018/978-1-7998-3473-1.ch171

Stranieri, A., & Sun, Z. (2021). Only Can AI Understand Me? In Sun, Z. (Ed.), *Intelligent Analytics With Advanced Multi-Industry Applications* (pp. 46-66). IGI Global. http://doi:10.4018/978-1-7998-4963-6.ch003

Süer, S. (2019). Relationship Between Working Capital Management and Supply Chain Management. In Akkucuk, U. (Eds.), *Ethical and Sustainable Supply Chain Management in a Global Context* (pp. 168-184). IGI Global. http://doi:10.4018/978-1-5225-8970-9.ch011

Sultana, S., Akter, S., Kyriazis, E., & Wamba, S. F. (2021). Architecting and Developing Big Data-Driven Innovation (DDI) in the Digital Economy. [JGIM]. *Journal of Global Information Management, 29*(3), 165–187. doi:10.4018/JGIM.2021050107

Sumardi, S., & Fernandes, A. A. (2021). The Influence of Quality Management on Organization Performance. [IJAMTR]. *International Journal of Applied Management Theory and Research, 3*(1), 53–72. doi:10.4018/IJAMTR.2021010104

Sumarliah, E., Li, T., Wang, B., Moosa, A., & Sackey, I. (2021). The Impact of Customer Halal Supply Chain Knowledge on Customer Halal Fashion Purchase Intention. [IRMJ]. *Information Resources Management Journal, 34*(3), 79–100. doi:10.4018/IRMJ.2021070105

Sun, S., & Tao, Q. Y. (2020). The Relationship Between Technological Innovation Ability, Atmosphere and Innovation Performance. [IJISSCM]. *International Journal of Information Systems and Supply Chain Management, 13*(2), 47–58. doi:10.4018/IJISSCM.2020040103

Sun, Z., & Stranieri, A. (2021). The Nature of Intelligent Analytics. In Sun, Z. (Ed.), *Intelligent Analytics With Advanced Multi-Industry Applications* (pp. 1-21). IGI Global. http://doi:10.4018/978-1-7998-4963-6.ch001

Sundu, M., & Ozdemir, S. (2020). The Effect of Artificial Intelligence on Management Process. In Ahmad, N. H., Iqbal, Q., & Halim, H. A. (Ed.), *Challenges and Opportunities for SMEs in Industry 4.0* (pp. 22-41). IGI Global. http://doi:10.4018/978-1-7998-2577-7.ch003

Larsen, T. (2021). *Economic Ecology*. IGI Global. http://doi:10.4018/978-1-7998-6424-0.ch004

Revathi, T., Muneeswaran, K., & Blessa Binolin Pepsi, M. (2019). *Big Data Architecture Components*. IGI Global. http://doi:10.4018/978-1-5225-3790-8.ch002

Taghipour, A. (2018). A Contemporary Approach to Plan Independent Logistics Actors. In Wood, L. C. (Eds.), *Contemporary Approaches and Strategies for Applied Logistics* (pp. 337-364). IGI Global. http://doi:10.4018/978-1-5225-5273-4.ch014

Taherdoost, H., & Madanchian, M. (2020). Prioritization of Leadership Effectiveness Dimensions Improving Organizational Performance via Analytical Hierarchy Process (AHP) Technique. In Sandhu, K. (Ed.), *Digital Transformation and Innovative Services for Business and Learning* (pp. 1-21). IGI Global. http://doi:10.4018/978-1-7998-5175-2.ch001

Tan, A. W., & Gligor, D. (2019). A Decision-Making Framework for Inventory Positioning in an Omnichannel Business Environment. [IJISSCM]. *International Journal of Information Systems and Supply Chain Management, 12*(1), 81–94. doi:10.4018/IJISSCM.2019010105

Tan, J., Jiang, G., & Wang, Z. (2019). Evolutionary Game Model of Information Sharing Behavior in Supply Chain Network With Agent-Based Simulation. [IJIIT]. *International Journal of Intelligent Information Technologies, 15*(2), 54–68. doi:10.4018/IJIIT.2019040104

Tang, Z., Liu, X., & Hu, Y. (2021). Analyses of Logistics Network Design With the Consideration of Carbon Emission Reduction Preference. [IJISSCM]. *International Journal of Information Systems and Supply Chain Management, 14*(1), 90–112. doi:10.4018/IJISSCM.2021010104

Tanque, M., & Foxwell, H. J. (2020). The Intersection of Data Analytics and Data-Driven Innovation. In Strydom, M., & Buckley, S. (Ed.), *AI and Big Data's Potential for Disruptive Innovation* (pp. 317-343). IGI Global. http://doi:10.4018/978-1-5225-9687-5.ch012

Tarigan, Z. J., Siagian, H., & Jie, F. (2020). The Role of Top Management Commitment to Enhancing the Competitive Advantage Through ERP Integration and Purchasing Strategy. [IJEIS]. *International Journal of Enterprise Information Systems, 16*(1), 53–68. doi:10.4018/IJEIS.2020010103

Tarupi Montenegro, E. A. (2021). Sustainability and Economy. In Perez-Uribe, R. I., Largacha-Martinez, C., & Ocampo-Guzman, D. (Eds.), *Handbook of Research on International Business and Models for Global Purpose-Driven Companies* (pp. 289-309). IGI Global. http://doi:10.4018/978-1-7998-4909-4.ch016

Thakur, A. (2021). Supply Chain Sustainability in Food and Beverage Industry. In Amini, A., Bushell, S., & Mahmood, A. (Eds.), *Driving Innovation and Productivity Through Sustainable Automation* (pp. 173-189). IGI Global. http://doi:10.4018/978-1-7998-5879-9.ch008

Thakur, A. D., & Muralidharan, P. (2019). Sustainable Supply Chain Practices in Multinational Organizations. In Akkucuk, U. (Ed.), *Ethical and Sustainable Supply Chain Management in a Global Context* (pp. 42-56). IGI Global. http://doi:10.4018/978-1-5225-8970-9.ch003

Toker, K., Çinar, F., & Görener, A. (2020). Circular Economy Measurement and a Case of the Developing Country Context. In Akkucuk, U. (Ed.), *Handbook of Research on Creating Sustainable Value in the Global Economy* (pp. 241-257). IGI Global. http://doi:10.4018/978-1-7998-1196-1.ch014

Tomar, J. S. (2020). Employee Engagement in India. In Misra, S., & Adewumi, A. (Eds.), *Handbook of Research on the Role of Human Factors in IT Project Management* (pp. 420-451). IGI Global. http://doi:10.4018/978-1-7998-1279-1.ch023

Tooranloo, H. S., Karimi, S., & Vaziri, K. (2018). Analysis of the Factors Affecting Sustainable Electronic Supply Chains in Healthcare Centers. [IRMJ]. *Information Resources Management Journal, 31*(4), 23–43. doi:10.4018/IRMJ.2018100102

Torres-Franco, M. (2021). Artificial Intelligence and Supply Chain Management Application, Development, and Forecast. In Christiansen, B., & Škrinjarić, T. (Eds.), *Handbook of Research on Applied AI for International Business and Marketing Applications* (pp. 207-226). IGI Global. http://doi:10.4018/978-1-7998-5077-9.ch012

Torres-Franco, M., & Villamil, V. (2020). Implementation of Circular Practices in Small and Medium Enterprises in Developing Countries. In Baporikar, N. (Ed.), *Handbook of Research on Entrepreneurship Development and Opportunities in Circular Economy* (pp. 144-166). IGI Global. http://doi:10.4018/978-1-7998-5116-5.ch008

Tria, T. W. (2021). The Application of Customer Relationship Management and Implementation to Supply Chain. In Hassan, S., & Mohamed, A. W. (Eds.), *Handbook of Research on Decision Sciences and Applications in the Transportation Sector* (pp. 340-361). IGI Global. http://doi:10.4018/978-1-7998-8040-0.ch016

Tubulingane, B. S. (2020). Sustainable Entrepreneurship and Management Skills at a Crossroad in the Circular Economy. In Baporikar, N. (Eds.), *Handbook of Research on Entrepreneurship Development and Opportunities in Circular Economy* (pp. 501-519). IGI Global. http://doi:10.4018/978-1-7998-5116-5.ch026

Umamaheswari, S. (2019). Smart Waste Management System. In Dey, N., & Tamane, S. (Eds.), *Big Data Analytics for Smart and Connected Cities* (pp. 229-242). IGI Global. http://doi:10.4018/978-1-5225-6207-8.ch010

UMARUSMAN. N. (2021). Fuzzy Goal Programming With Interval Type-2 for Solving Multi-Objective Sustainable Supplier Selection Problems. In Aytekin, G. K., & Doğru, Ç. (Eds.), *Handbook of Research on Recent Perspectives on Management, International Trade, and Logistics* (pp. 164-197). IGI Global. http://doi:10.4018/978-1-7998-5886-7.ch010

UMARUSMAN. N., & Hacıvelioğulları, T. (2020). Compromise Optimal System Design for Solving Multi-Objective Green Supplier Selection Problems. In Khan, S. A. (Ed.), *Global Perspectives on Green Business Administration and Sustainable Supply Chain Management* (pp. 241-275). IGI Global. http://doi:10.4018/978-1-7998-2173-1.ch016

Unnu, N. A. (2020). Boosting Positivity and Performance. In Baykal, E. (Eds.), *Handbook of Research on Positive Organizational Behavior for Improved Workplace Performance* (pp. 34-54). IGI Global. http://doi:10.4018/978-1-7998-0058-3.ch003

Valsamidis, S. I. (2020). The Key Drivers for the Digitalization of the Supply Chain. [IJORIS]. *International Journal of Operations Research and Information Systems, 11*(3), 1–18. doi:10.4018/IJORIS.2020070101

Vargas-Hernández, J. G. (2020). Bio-Economy at the Crossroads of Sustainable Development. In Patti, S., & Trizzino, G. (Eds.), *Advanced Integrated Approaches to Environmental Economics and Policy* (pp. 23-48). IGI Global. http://doi:10.4018/978-1-5225-9562-5.ch002

Vargas-Hernández, J. G. (2021). Circular-Green Economy. In Gopalakrishnan, B. N., Duggal, T., & Tewary, T. (Eds.), *Examining the Intersection of Circular Economy, Forestry, and International Trade* (pp. 1-17). IGI Global. http://doi:10.4018/978-1-7998-4990-2.ch001

Vargas-Hernández, J. G. (2021). Strategic Organizational Sustainability. In Popescu, C. R. (Eds.), *Handbook of Research on Novel Practices and Current Successes in Achieving the Sustainable Development Goals* (pp. 277-297). IGI Global. http://doi:10.4018/978-1-7998-8426-2.ch014

Vargas-Hernández, J. G., & López-Lemus, J. A. (2021). Resources and Capabilities of SMEs Through a Circular Green Economy. [IJCEWM]. *International Journal of Circular Economy and Waste Management, 1*(1), 1–15. doi:10.4018/IJCEWM.2021010101

Vargas-Hernández, J. G., Medrano, M. D., & López-Lemus, J. A. (2020). Circular Green Economy. In Baporikar, N. (Ed.), *Handbook of Research on Entrepreneurship Development and Opportunities in Circular Economy* (pp. 21-37). IGI Global. http://doi:10.4018/978-1-7998-5116-5.ch002

Vargas-Sánchez, A. (2020). Opportunities and Challenges of Circular Economy for the Tourism Industry. In Baporikar, N. (Eds.), *Handbook of Research on Entrepreneurship Development and Opportunities in Circular Economy* (pp. 106-124). IGI Global. http://doi:10.4018/978-1-7998-5116-5.ch006

Vargas-Sánchez, A. (2020). Tourism Circular Economy. In Rodrigues, S. S., Almeida, P. J., & Almeida, N. M. (Eds.), *Mapping, Managing, and Crafting Sustainable Business Strategies for the Circular Economy* (pp. 1-10). IGI Global. http://doi:10.4018/978-1-5225-9885-5.ch001

Verkerk, M. J., & Visscher, F. (2019). Industrial Practices, Sustainable Development and Circular Economy. In de Vries, M. J., & Jochemsen, H. (Ed.), *The Normative Nature of Social Practices and Ethics in Professional Environments* (pp. 56-83). IGI Global. http://doi:10.4018/978-1-5225-8006-5.ch004

Verma, T., & Aggarwal, R. (2021). Developing a Framework to Study the Impact of Contingent Factors on Business Performance Using Strategic Cost Management. In Singh, A. (Ed.), *Big Data Analytics for Improved Accuracy, Efficiency, and Decision Making in Digital Marketing* (pp. 227-253). IGI Global. http://doi:10.4018/978-1-7998-7231-3.ch016

Vidhate, A. V., Saraf, C. R., Wani, M. A., Waghmare, S. S., & Edgar, T. (2020). Applying Blockchain Security for Agricultural Supply Chain Management. [IJAEC]. *International Journal of Applied Evolutionary Computation, 11*(4), 28–37. doi:10.4018/IJAEC.2020100103

Vig, S., & Agarwal, R. N. (2021). E-Waste Management in India. In Gopalakrishnan, B. N., Duggal, T., & Tewary, T. (Ed.), *Examining the Intersection of Circular Economy, Forestry, and International Trade* (pp. 165-173). IGI Global. http://doi:10.4018/978-1-7998-4990-2.ch014

Villet, H. J. (2021). Promoting Circularity Through Sustainable Leadership. In Atiku, S. O., & Fapohunda, T. (Eds.), *Human Resource Management Practices for Promoting Sustainability* (pp. 197-211). IGI Global. http://doi:10.4018/978-1-7998-4522-5.ch011

Vogel, M. D., Blair, R., & Deichert, J. (2019). A Regional Approach to Mobility Management. In Smirnova, O. V. (Ed.), *Building a Sustainable Transportation Infrastructure for Long-Term Economic Growth* (pp. 1-24). IGI Global. http://doi:10.4018/978-1-5225-7396-8.ch001

Volk, M., Staegemann, D., Jamous, N., Pohl, M., & Turowski, K. (2020). Providing Clarity on Big Data Technologies. [IJIIT]. *International Journal of Intelligent Information Technologies, 16*(2), 49–73. doi:10.4018/IJIIT.2020040103

von Bary, B., Westner, M., & Strahringer, S. (2019). IT Backsourcing. [IJITBAG]. *International Journal of IT/Business Alignment and Governance, 10*(2), 20–34. doi:10.4018/IJITBAG.2019070102

Vujić, G., & Tot, B. (2020). Solid Waste Management in the Republic of Serbia. In Pariatamby, A., Shahul Hamid, F., & Bhatti, M. S. (Ed.), *Sustainable Waste Management Challenges in Developing Countries* (pp. 306-326). IGI Global. http://doi:10.4018/978-1-7998-0198-6.ch013

Vyas, S., & Bhargava, D. (2019). Big Data Utilization, Benefits, and Challenges for Smart City Implementation. In Kaur, G., & Tomar, P. (Ed.), *Handbook of Research on Big Data and the IoT* (pp. 42-54). IGI Global. http://doi:10.4018/978-1-5225-7432-3.ch003

Wadhera, T., & Kakkar, D. (2020). Big Data-Based System. In Wadhera, T., & Kakkar, D. (Ed.), *Interdisciplinary Approaches to Altering Neurodevelopmental Disorders* (pp. 303-319). IGI Global. http://doi:10.4018/978-1-7998-3069-6.ch017

Waghmare, R. B. (2021). Workforce Diversity to Foster an Innovation. In Yadav, R., Panday, P., & Sharma, N. (Eds.), *Critical Issues on Changing Dynamics in Employee Relations and Workforce Diversity* (pp. 109-120). IGI Global. http://doi:10.4018/978-1-7998-3515-8.ch006

Wallis, M., Kumar, K., & Gepp, A. (2019). Credit Rating Forecasting Using Machine Learning Techniques. In Sun, Z. (Ed.), *Managerial Perspectives on Intelligent Big Data Analytics* (pp. 180-198). IGI Global. http://doi:10.4018/978-1-5225-7277-0.ch010

Wanchai, P. (2019). An Integrated Approach to Performance Evaluation of Enterprise Resource Planning (ERP) System Implementation. [JECO]. *Journal of Electronic Commerce in Organizations, 17*(3), 1–15. doi:10.4018/JECO.2019070101

Wang, C. (2019). Strategic Information Technology Compensation. [JGIM]. *Journal of Global Information Management, 27*(4), 16–45. doi:10.4018/JGIM.2019100102

Wang, J. X. (2018). The Effect of Supply Chain Sustainability Management in the Perspective of Suppliers. In Wood, L. C. (Eds.), *Contemporary Approaches and Strategies for Applied Logistics* (pp. 77-100). IGI Global. http://doi:10.4018/978-1-5225-5273-4.ch004

Wang, S., & Wang, H. (2020). Knowledge Analytics. [IJBAN]. *International Journal of Business Analytics*, *7*(4), 14–23. doi:10.4018/IJBAN.2020100102

Wang, Z., Pei, Z., & Gu, V. C. (2019). Strategic Applications of Business Analytics to Healthcare and Hospital Management. [IJARPHM]. *International Journal of Applied Research on Public Health Management*, *4*(2), 47–64. doi:10.4018/IJARPHM.2019070104

Wei, C., & Ho, C. (2019). Exploring Signaling Roles of Service Providers' Reputation and Competence in Influencing Perceptions of Service Quality and Outsourcing Intentions. [JOEUC]. *Journal of Organizational and End User Computing*, *31*(1), 86–109. doi:10.4018/JOEUC.2019010105

White, A. S., & Censlive, M. (2020). Resilience to Supply Disruptions in a Non-Linear Two-Tier Supply Chain Model. [IJISSCM]. *International Journal of Information Systems and Supply Chain Management*, *13*(2), 1–26. doi:10.4018/IJISSCM.2020040101

Willow, C. C. (2021). Business Data Analytics Applications to Online Product Reviews and Nationalism. [IJDA]. *International Journal of Data Analytics*, *2*(2), 27–39. doi:10.4018/IJDA.2021070102

Wu, D., Teng, J., Ivanov, S., & Anyu, J. (2021). Empirical Assessment of Bullwhip Effect in Supply Networks. [IJISSCM]. *International Journal of Information Systems and Supply Chain Management*, *14*(2), 69–87. doi:10.4018/IJISSCM.2021040104

Wuen, C. H., Ibrahim, F., & Ringim, K. J. (2022). Quantitative Analysis of Strategic Human Resource Management and Organizational Learning. In Ordóñez de Pablos, P. (Ed.), *Handbook of Research on Developing Circular, Digital, and Green Economies in Asia* (pp. 59-85). IGI Global. http://doi:10.4018/978-1-7998-8678-5.ch004

Xin-jun, L., Lin-qi, Z., & Xing-hua, L. (2018). Contingent Strategies for Mitigating Supply Disruptions With Backup Supplier and Information Acquirement. [IJISSCM]. *International Journal of Information Systems and Supply Chain Management*, *11*(2), 16–38. doi:10.4018/IJISSCM.2018040102

Yanamandra, R. (2020). Leadership Model for Supply Chain Management in Business Schools. In Dwivedi, A., & Alshamrani, M. S. (Eds.), *Leadership Strategies for Global Supply Chain Management in Emerging Markets* (pp. 173-194). IGI Global. http://doi:10.4018/978-1-7998-2867-9.ch008

Yang, J., Liu, H., Xiao, F., & Wang, J. (2021). Identification of Key Drivers for Sustainable Supply-Chain Management of Fresh Food Based on Rough DEMATEL. [IJISSCM]. *International Journal of Information Systems and Supply Chain Management, 14*(2), 1–29. doi:10.4018/IJISSCM.2021040101

Yang, T., Liu, G., Wei, Y., Zhang, X., & Dong, X. (2019). The Impact of Dual-Fairness Concerns Under Different Power. [IJEIS]. *International Journal of Enterprise Information Systems, 15*(3), 1–26. doi:10.4018/IJEIS.2019070101

Yavuz, M. (2020). Transformational Leadership and Authentic Leadership as Practical Implications of Positive Organizational Psychology. In Baykal, E. (Eds.), *Handbook of Research on Positive Organizational Behavior for Improved Workplace Performance* (pp. 122-139). IGI Global. http://doi:10.4018/978-1-7998-0058-3.ch008

Yazici, H. J. (2018). Role of Organizational Project Maturity on Business Success. In Silvius, G., & Karayaz, G. (Eds.), *Developing Organizational Maturity for Effective Project Management* (pp. 43-54). IGI Global. http://doi:10.4018/978-1-5225-3197-5.ch003

Yerpude, S., & Singhal, T. K. (2020). Value Enablement of Collaborative Supply Chain Environment Embedded With the Internet of Things. [IJIIT]. *International Journal of Intelligent Information Technologies, 16*(3), 19–51. doi:10.4018/IJIIT.2020070102

Younis, N. M. (2020). Big Data and Sustainability of Higher Education. In Al-Sartawi, A. M., Hussainey, K., Hannoon, A., & Hamdan, A. (Eds.), *Global Approaches to Sustainability Through Learning and Education* (pp. 46-68). IGI Global. http://doi:10.4018/978-1-7998-0062-0.ch004

Yue, H., Xu, J., Wang, J., Wu, D., & Niu, B. (2019). A General Introduction and Overview of Supply Chain Finance. In Tsai, S., Shen, C., Song, H., & Niu, B. (Ed.), *Green Finance for Sustainable Global Growth* (pp. 1-29). IGI Global. http://doi:10.4018/978-1-5225-7808-6.ch001

Yue, Y., & Xiao, T. (2020). Pricing and Bundling Strategies for Competing Mobile Phone Supply Chains With Network Externality. [IJISSCM]. *International Journal of Information Systems and Supply Chain Management, 13*(3), 54–77. doi:10.4018/IJISSCM.2020070104

Zarour, K., & Benmerzoug, D. (2019). A Decision-Making Support for Business Process Outsourcing to a Multi-Cloud Environment. [IJDSST]. *International Journal of Decision Support System Technology, 11*(1), 66–92. doi:10.4018/IJDSST.2019010104

Zhang, A., Chen, Y., Xu, X., Gao, Y., & Zhang, L. (2021). Impacts of Resource Alertness and Change Leadership Style on Financial Performance. [JGIM]. *Journal of Global Information Management, 29*(2), 45–60. doi:10.4018/JGIM.2021030103

Zhang, X., Li, Y., Liu, Z., & Li, Q. (2021). Coordination Contracts of Dual-Channel Supply Chain Considering Advertising Cooperation. [IJISSCM]. *International Journal of Information Systems and Supply Chain Management, 14*(1), 55–89. doi:10.4018/IJISSCM.2021010103

Zhang, Y., & Wang, Y. (2019). Supply Chain Decisions Considering Heterogeneous Consumer Greenness Preference and Reservation Utilities. [IJISSCM]. *International Journal of Information Systems and Supply Chain Management, 12*(1), 1–21. doi:10.4018/IJISSCM.2019010101

Zhang, Z. H., & Sharifnia, E. (2020). Risk Management in Supplier Selection. In Awasthi, A., & Grzybowska, K. (Ed.), *Handbook of Research on Interdisciplinary Approaches to Decision Making for Sustainable Supply Chains* (pp. 358-383). IGI Global. http://doi:10.4018/978-1-5225-9570-0.ch017

Zhou, Y., Wang, Q., Wu, Y., & Huang, M. (2020). Data-Driven Cash Replenishment Planning of Recycling ATMs with Out-of-Cash and Full-of-Cash Risks. [IJISSCM]. *International Journal of Information Systems and Supply Chain Management, 13*(2), 77–96. doi:10.4018/IJISSCM.2020040105

Zhu, J., Cheng, Y., & Zhang, Y. (2021). Risk Propagation Mechanism Research Based on SITR Model of Complex Supply Networks. [IJISSCM]. *International Journal of Information Systems and Supply Chain Management, 14*(3), 18–38. doi:10.4018/IJISSCM.2021070102

Zhu, J., Zhang, M., & Wang, H. (2021). Game Analysis of the Driving Modes in the Supply Chain Management Regarding Credit System Construction. [IJISSCM]. *International Journal of Information Systems and Supply Chain Management, 14*(2), 30–45. doi:10.4018/IJISSCM.2021040102

Zhu, Q., & Sarkis, J. (2020). Product Deletion and Sustainable Supply Chains. In Khan, S. A. (Ed.), *Global Perspectives on Green Business Administration and Sustainable Supply Chain Management* (pp. 1-15). IGI Global. http://doi:10.4018/978-1-7998-2173-1.ch001

Zin, S. M., & Manaf, K. A. (2019). Role of Intellectual Capital in Women Entrepreneurs' Business Performance. In Tomos, F., Kumar, N., Clifton, N., & Hyams-Ssekasi, D. (Ed.), *Women Entrepreneurs and Strategic Decision Making in the Global Economy* (pp. 209-230). IGI Global. http://doi:10.4018/978-1-5225-7479-8.ch011

Zolbanin, H. M., Delen, D., & Sharma, S. K. (2018). The Strategic Value of Big Data Analytics in Health Care Policy-Making. [IJEBR]. *International Journal of E-Business Research*, *14*(3), 20–33. doi:10.4018/IJEBR.2018070102

About the Contributors

Syed Abdul Rehman Khan is a professor of Supply Chain and Logistics Management. Dr. Khan achieved his CSCP—Certified Supply Chain Professional certificate from the U.S.A. and completed his postdoctoral fellowship from Tsinghua University. Since 2020, Dr. Khan has been affiliated with Xuzhou University of Technology. He has more than nine years' core experience in supply chain and logistics at industrial and academic levels. Prof. Khan has attended several international conferences and has been invited as a keynote speaker in different countries. He has published 100+ scientific research papers in different well-renowned international journals and conferences. Also, Dr. Khan has achieved several research projects and scientific innovation awards.

* * *

Abdul-Rahim Ahmad is an award-winning academician and an active researcher of global repute working at the Department of Decision Sciences, Karachi School of Business Leadership, where he is involved in leading-edge interdisciplinary teaching, research, curricula development, and academic service. He is also an adjunct professor at the department of Systems Design Engineering, University of Waterloo, Canada, where he is involved in graduate student thesis supervision and cutting-edge interdisciplinary research. He has served in top universities in Canada (University of Waterloo, Wilfrid Laurier University, Dalhousie University), Saudi Arabia (KFUPM), and Pakistan (KSBL) for several decades. Dr. Ahmad's research interests are mainly in the areas of Knowledge-based Decision Support Systems (DSS), Expert System (ES), and Decision Modeling with applications in Supply Chain Operations Management (SCM), Layout Optimization as well as empirical research in Strategic Management of Technology. Dr. Ahmad has more than 50 publications in high-repute and high-impact journals and conference proceedings. He has also regularly acted as reviewer for such reputable journals as EJOR, IJPR, IJOQM, etc. as well as international conferences. He has worked on several government- and industry-funded collaborative research projects in Canada and Saudi

Arabia. Dr. Ahmad's current teaching interests are in the areas of Business Strategy, Business and Supply Chain Analytics, Information Systems Strategy, Management Science, etc. at both undergraduate and graduate levels. He is firm believer in the power of active, interactive, and cooperative learning in developing effective leaders and lifelong learners who can be agents of positive change in organizations and societies. He perceives teaching and learning a mutually beneficial learning enterprise between instructor and learners. Dr. Ahmad's extensive award winning teaching experience at several AACSB accredited business schools in Canada and Saudi Arabia is considered asset for his peers and students. He has received more than 10 distinguished teaching awards from the University of Waterloo (Canada), Dalhousie University (Canada), King Fahd University of Petroleum and Minerals (Saudi Arabia), and Umm Al-Qura University (Saudi Arabia). Dr. Ahmad also has significant industrial and consulting experience in Supply Chain Management, Decision Support Systems, and Software Development. Consequently, he is familiar with the workplace social, ethical, and organizational issues as well as various market dynamics, which all prove assets in his passionate and interactive teaching through the use of contemporary real world examples. Furthermore, he has excellent individual and team-based project management skills acquired through his participation in a variety of academic, research, and industrial ventures. More importantly, he discerns the difference between creativity and productivity and he is cognizant of the value of both in academic settings and scientific inquiries. Dr. Ahmad regularly consults with industry and academia. His consultations with Higher Education Institutions span Curricula Development, Curricula Review, Faculty Development, Academic Accreditation, and Continuous Quality Improvement. He is an academic accreditation consultant for universities pursuing AACSB, EFMD/EPAS, and NCAAA/EEC-HES accreditation and re-accreditation. He offers executive development courses in Strategic Management, Information Systems, and Project Management. He is a long time professional member of the Institute for Operations Research and Management Sciences (INFORMS) the Institute of Electrical and Electronics Engineers (IEEE), the Association for Computing Machinery (ACM), IEEE Technology and Management Society (TEMS), and the Association of Information Systems (AIS).

Amjad Ali received his graduation degree from the Management Sciences faculty of the Benazir Bhutto Shaheed University, Lyari, Karachi in 2016. From 2017 to 2018 he completed his MS degree in Supply Chain from the University of Karachi. Presently Amjad Ali is a research scholar at Hamdard University, Karachi, and Faculty Member of Benazir Bhutto Shaheed University Lyari Karachi. His research interest includes sustainable supply chain practices, Smart lockers, and crowd-shipping.

Manish Mohan Baral is a Ph.D. Scholar in Department of Management, Birla Institute of Technology, Mesra, Ranchi, Jharkhand. He is an engineering graduate from KIIT University, Bhubaneswar, Odisha. He has done his MBA in International Business from GITAM University, Visakhapatnam, Andhra Pradesh. He has publications indexed in SCOPUS, UGC "A" Category Journals, and few Book chapters which are also indexed in SCOPUS and Web of Science. His research areas include Information Technology, Cloud Computing, Supply Chain Management, Artificial Intelligence, Operations Research, and Quality Management.

Shahid Imran is Senior Lecturer in the Department of Management Studies, Middle East College, Muscat, Oman. Mr. Shahid earned his Master of Business Administration Degree from Mohi Ud Din Islamic University, AJK, Pakistan. He is having a vast industrial and academic experience. His research interests include Logistics, Supply Chain Management and Manufacturing business.

Fredrick Ishengoma serves as a lecturer at the College of Informatics and Virtual Education, The University of Dodoma, Tanzania, His research interest includes ICT4D, blockchain technology, e/m-government, and technology adoption.

Shamsa Kanwal received the Bachelor of Science (BSc) degree in 2011 from the University of Punjab, and Masters of Arts (MA) in English Language and Literature in 2018 from International Islamic University Islamabad (IIUI), Pakistan. She is currently pursuing the Masters (MS) degree with the School of Economics and Management in Enterprise Management from North China Electric Power University (NCEPU) Beijing, China. She is a recipient of the Chinese Government Scholarship (CSC).

Arsalan Zahid Piprani received the Ph.D. degree from the University of Malaya, Malaysia, in 2020. He is currently an Assistant Professor with the Department of Business Administration, FUUAST, Karachi. He has teaching and research experience of over twelve years. He is a quantitative researcher and has published articles in various peer reviewed journals. His research interests include supply chain risk management, logistics and operations management, supply chain analytics and green supply chain management.

Muhammad Tanveer is a Doctor of Philosophy (Ph.D.) in Management from well-reputed accredited Lincoln University College (LUC) Malaysia. Dr. Muhammad is a research scholar in the department of Management currently working at Prince Sultan University, Riyadh, Saudi Arabia. His work-to-date which have aligned with Management, Economics, Leadership, Higher Education, and Marketing. Published 28 added value articles in impact factor journals including, Sustainability, International Journal of Energy Economics and Policy (JEEP), Heliyon, International Journal of Environmental Research and Public Health (IJERPH), IEEE Access, Journal of Food Quality, Journal of Internet Commerce, BioMed Research International, TEM Journal, Journal of Entrepreneurship Education, Academy of Strategic Management Journal, Sage open, Complexity, and Library Philosophy and Practice. Published with famous publishers like IEEE, Wiley, MDPI, Hindawi, Taylor and Francis, Elsevier, Springer, and Sage. Muhammad Tanveer got the active researcher certificate from Prince Sultan University year 2019 and 2020.

Asad Ullah is an Assistant Professor in the Department of Management studies, Middle East College, Muscat, Oman. He earned B.A in Economics from Vinoba Bhave University, India, M.B.A in International Business Management and PhD in Business Administration from Aligarh Muslim University, India. He has published journal and conference papers. His research interests include manufacturing, logistics, supply chain, information technology and international business. He is member of IEOM, OLA, GRIBA and CSCMP.

Chittipaka Venkataiah is an engineering graduate and completed his MBA from the National Institute of Technology, Warangal. He has obtained his doctorate from the Department of Business Management, Osmania University, and qualified in UGC-NET conducted by University Grants Commission, New Delhi. He has selected for "Summer Faculty Research Fellow (SFRF) – 2020 from IIT Delhi. He is a certified ZED Master Trainer from the Quality Council of India and National Monitoring & Implementation Unit (NMIU) for the Zero Defect and Zero Effect (ZED) scheme of Ministry of Micro, Small and Medium Enterprise (MSME). He has been conferred with the "Best Professor in Project Management" award by Business School Affaire & Dewang Mehta National Education Awards. Has over 18 years of experience in Teaching and Research in the area of Operations, Quality, Project Management, Logistics & Supply Chain Management. He is having professional membership in the 'Production and Operations Management Society (POMS)', 'All India Management Association (AIMA)', 'Quality Circle Forum of India (QCFI)', and the life member in 'National HRD Network (NHRD)'. He is also an executive committee member of the NHRD – Visakhapatnam chapter. He was an editorial member of the International Centre of Economics, Humanities, and Management (ICEHM). His area of teaching and research includes Operations, Quality, logistics, Supply Chain Management, and Project Management. He has presented several papers in various National and International conferences.

Iram Zulfiqar received the Bachelor of Arts (BA) degree in 2013, Bachelor of Education (B.Ed.) in 2015 and the Masters of Arts (MA) in Education in 2017 from Allama Iqbal open University (AIOU) Islamabad, Pakistan. She is currently pursuing the Masters (MS) degree with the School of Economics and Management in Enterprise Management from North China Electric Power University (NCEPU) Beijing, China. She is a recipient of the Chinese Government Scholarship (CSC).

Index

B

big data 2-3, 10, 15-16, 35-43, 71, 80-83, 89, 91, 127, 133, 137, 160, 184-202
big data analytics 2-3, 10, 36-39, 41-42, 89, 91, 137, 160, 184, 186, 188, 191-192, 194-199, 202
blockchain 2-4, 7-8, 11, 37-40, 43-44, 59-61, 63-70, 73-81, 90, 108-110, 112-126, 133-134, 137-141, 145-164, 201

C

challenges 9, 11, 16, 19, 36-37, 39-40, 43, 54, 79, 108, 110, 112, 119, 121, 140, 153, 158-160, 162-163, 182, 184, 187, 191, 193, 196-199, 201
cyber-physical systems 137-138

D

digital twin 137, 154, 164

E

economic performance 5, 7, 12
e-Delphi 137, 142-145, 156-157, 159-160
environmental performance 1, 3, 5, 7-8, 10, 12-14, 134

F

Financial Markets 44, 47, 60
FinTech 45, 59-60, 158

H

hotels 15, 21, 33, 35-36, 106
hypothesis 4-5, 15, 18, 22, 27, 32-33, 169

I

Industry 4.0 1-4, 7, 9-13, 83, 85-86, 90, 92, 119, 121-123, 127, 134, 136-139, 141-143, 145, 147, 153, 156-164, 192-194, 197, 199
insourcing 93, 99-104
internal green supply chain practices 1, 3, 7
interoperability 120, 137, 153-154, 157, 161
IoT technology 126, 128-129, 133
IR 4.0 82-91

L

logistics 4, 8-10, 12, 14, 63-65, 69-81, 88-90, 92-100, 104-106, 108, 112, 117-124, 126-131, 133-135, 146, 158, 164, 198, 200, 202
Logistics 4.0 146, 164
Logistics Commodities 63, 77
logistics industry 63-65, 69-76, 78-81, 118, 127-129, 133, 146
Logistics Information Protection 77

M

Microgrid 145, 152, 158, 160, 164

O

operational risk 44, 47, 60-61
outbound distribution 93
outsourcing 93-106

P

Pitfalls 108, 112, 183

Q

Quality 4.0 145, 147, 158, 162, 164

R

RFID 90, 111, 124, 126-127, 130, 132-133, 148

S

smart contract 65, 74, 117, 137, 145-146, 153-155, 158, 164
social media 41, 165-169, 171-183, 185
structural equation modeling 15, 25, 27, 36, 39
supply chain and logistics 108, 112, 117, 119, 121, 126
supply chain chain 184
supply chain management 1, 9-14, 36, 40, 43, 79-80, 82-85, 89, 97, 105, 108, 110-111, 117, 119-124, 126, 133-136, 153, 165, 189, 197-198, 200-202
Supply Chain Managment 82
survey 5-6, 8, 15, 21-22, 25, 37, 100, 106, 144, 159, 161, 170-173, 177, 200

T

Telecommunications 40, 42
transportation management 89, 93-95, 99-104

www.ingramcontent.com/pod-product-compliance
Lightning Source LLC
LaVergne TN
LVHW081336300926
849161LV00008B/1983
9781799876427